Early Chinese Civilization Series

Foal-shaped *tsun* from Mei-hsien (from *WWTKTL*, 1957:4)

CHO-YUN HSU and
KATHERYN M. LINDUFF

Western Chou
Civilization

YALE UNIVERSITY PRESS
NEW HAVEN AND LONDON

Set in Meridian type.
Printed in the United States of America by
Vail-Ballou Press, Binghamton, New York.

Library of Congress Cataloging-in-Publication Data
Hsu, Cho-yun.
    Western Chou civilization.
    (Early Chinese civilization series)
    Includes bibliographies and index.
    1. China—History—Chou dynasty, 1122–221 B.C.
I. Linduff, Katheryn M.   II. Title.   III. Series.
DS747.H79   1988   931'.03   87–6178
ISBN 0–300–03772–4 (alk. paper)

The paper in this book meets the guidelines for
permanence and durability of the Committee
on Production Guidelines for Book Longevity
of the Council on Library Resources.

10   9   8   7   6   5   4   3   2   1

To our parents

Contents

Illustrations

Foal-shaped *Tsun* from Mei-hsien   Frontispiece

Tables

Acknowledgments

This book was written with support from a Basic Research Grant from the National Endowment for the Humanities, research grants from the University of Pittsburgh Center for International Studies, and sabbatical leaves. For the help extended by these institutions, we are grateful.

This is an opportunity to remember the great masters in the field of ancient history who are no longer with us but who had so much to teach us. To them we are indebted for leading us into this fascinating world of ancient China. They are Li Chi, Li Tsung-t'ung, Ling Hsün-sheng, and Tung Tso-pin. Likewise, John Wilson and Shen Kang-po presented a broadened view and suggested that we reach beyond China.

Among our teachers, friends, students, and colleagues who have inspired, guided, and helped us in the process of writing this book, we especially thank Chang Kwang-chih, Ch'en P'an, Ch'ien Mu, Chu Wen-djang, H. G. Creel, Wolfram Eberhard, S. N. Eisenstadt, J. F. Haskins, David Keightley, Kao Chu-hsün, Lao Kan, Evelyn Rawski, Ruey Yih-fu, Shih Chang-ju, Edward Shaughnessy, Shirakawa Shizuka, Tu Cheng-sheng, Y. T. Wang, M. C. Wiens, Eugene Wu, Yang Hsi-mei, Yeh Ta-hsiung, Anthony Yü, and Yü Ying-shih. In the process of researching and writing this book we have learned from each other, much more than will appear on the pages of this manuscript. The process has allowed both of us to grow and learn. Our colleagues and the members of the staffs of the departments of History and Fine Arts, the University Center for International Studies, and the Program of Asian Studies at Pitt provided valued encouragement and indispensable services. We are grateful to all of them. The librarians at Pitt, especially those of its East Asian collections, and friends at Harvard-Yenching Library, the Library of Congress, the Fu Ssu-nien Library at Academia Sinica, and the East Asian Library at the University of California at Berkeley generously helped us in different stages of research; to them we owe thanks as well. The preparation of the illustrations was patiently done by Matthew Roper, and Kathleen Hower carefully typed the manuscript. Lisa Wu edited the Chinese romanization. Sally Serafim patiently and thoughtfully prepared the copyedited text. Their assistance was invaluable.

The encouragement and affection of our families have sustained our efforts for many years. To our parents we owe a very special debt, and to them, with respect and love, we dedicate this volume.

Cho-yun Hsu
Katheryn M. Linduff

Introduction

STATE OF THE FIELD

The Western Chou 西周 period is often regarded as the fountainhead of Chinese civilization. This period was one in which a small but vigorous group of people gained power, developed a massive feudal network, and proclaimed themselves the rightful directors of a grand cultural and political program. That they acted out this drama can be documented through an accumulation of evidence from varied sources. Many of China's significant institutions, including the traditional aristocratic kinship structure, and ideologies such as the notion of the Mandate of Heaven are thought to have originated in this period. Most revealing, however, was the establishment of *Chung-kuo* 中國 (the Central Kingdom), or Hua-Hsia 華夏, as it was called by the Chou people in the eleventh century B.C. The concept of *Chung-kuo* simultaneously defined "China" as a state, a nation, and a civilization qualifying it as a "universal state." By the eighth century B.C., the political dominance of the Chou royal house had waned. Nevertheless, the Chou culture survived the political downfall and remained the foundation of Chinese civilization. Strangely, however, the Western Chou period has not attracted as much scholarly attention as the preceding period, the Shang, or the Eastern Chou, which followed it.

In the case of Shang studies, the large number of inscriptions on oracle bones as well as archaeological findings excavated at major sites provide a rich reservoir of historical information. A solid scholarship has been built by many, especially by Tung Tso-pin 董作賓 and Li Chi 李濟, and recently by K. C. Chang 張光直 and David Keightley.[1] Constructions of the history of the Eastern Chou have been aided for generations by the rich details available in the ancient annals.

Due to the recent accumulation of both archaeological and scholarly materials the time is ripe for a thorough examination of the vast and mounting body of information and analyses pertinent to the Western Chou. We have made an effort to describe and interpret the ideological,

1. Their works are cited in the bibliography.

institutional, and cultural content of the period. Archaeological material, examined from historical, sociological, anthropological, and cultural perspectives, both informs the analysis of the characteristic features of the Central Kingdom and reveals the processes by which civilizational change was brought about.

PREVIOUS CONTRIBUTIONS

Traditionally, research on the Western Chou consisted of studies of classical literary sources, epigraphic analyses of bronze inscriptions, and archaeological and art historical studies of artifacts. Important contributions on specific subjects ranging from chronology to metallurgical technology have been made by scholars in China, Japan, and the West. These scholars include especially Noel Barnard, Derk Bodde, Ch'en Meng-chia 陳夢家, Chou Fa-kao 周法高, H. G. Creel, Fu Ssu-nien 傅斯年, Hsia Nai 夏鼐, Kao Ch'ü-hsün 高去尋, Itō Michiharu 伊藤道治, Kaizuka Shigeki 貝塚茂樹, Kuo Mo-jo 郭沫若, Li Hsüeh-ch'in 李學勤, Li Ya-nung 李亞農, Max Loehr, Miyazaki Ichisada 宮崎市定, David Nivison, Edwin G. Pulleyblank, and Shirakawa Shizuka 白川靜.[2]

Past efforts to present a comprehensive historical synthesis of the period based on broad, developmental themes, however, are relatively rare. In Chinese, Kuo Mo-jo and Li Ya-nung[3] prepared Marxist interpretations, studies handicapped by an inflexible, predominantly economic approach. In Japanese, Itō and Kaizuka[4] analyzed the structure of the Chou state. Though their work is structurally complete, its political and social focus relegated the historical and cultural dimensions to a supporting role. In English, Creel's pathfinding contribution is, perhaps, the only major work in a Western language focused on a broad theme in which the corpus of bronze inscriptions of that time was extensively used as a primary source. However, fifteen years have passed since the publication of Creel's *Origins of Statecraft in China*,[5] and the amount of archaeological data has trebled.

RECENT ARCHAEOLOGICAL DATA AND CLASSICAL LITERATURE

In recent years, archaeological reports from China have provided a tremendous amount of new information on Chou sites and their contents. Most important are the recently discovered sites (1976) located

2. Their works are cited in the bibliography.
3. Kuo Mo-jo, 1957, 1961; Li Ya-nung, 1962.
4. Itō Michiharu, 1975; Kaizuka Shigeki, 1962.
5. Creel, 1970.

in the district of the early Chou capital. Excavations in this Ch'i-shan 岐山 area have yielded clusters of sites that reveal settlement patterns and burial customs suggesting the structure of Chou social stratification. The material content of these sites includes bronzes, oracle bones, and other artifacts that can be studied in order to reconstruct the earliest stage of Chou civilization.

Scores of other sites illustrate the complexity and extent of early Chou culture in many other regions of China. Moreover, more than five hundred inscribed bronzes have been found in recent decades; this triples the sum of epigraphic materials known previously. Several of these bronze inscriptions bear significant information on early Chou history; they record battles, ceremonies of investiture, royal inspection trips, and "king-lists," to name but a few. These precious new documents allow for a reassessment of classical literary sources as well as for new insight into the process of formation of Chou cultural institutions. From the several available studies of epigraphic materials, we have selected the series of bronze inscriptions collected by Shirakawa Shizuka as the standard reference. It includes the most up-to-date data as well as the most extensive coverage of current scholarship on epigraphic materials.[6]

Our proposed reconstruction of Chou institutions includes the kinship structure, the feudal system, the rudimentary bureaucracy, the nature of the bronze industry, and aesthetic symbolism, for instance. All discussions are based on newly discovered materials. In addition, these sources were used to verify or supplement the remarkably reliable ancient literary records. These sources will also be used to evaluate issues that might not have concerned the ancients, such as the dynamic growth and spread of Chou culture.

The classical sources consulted in this volume are limited to a few that are regarded as contemporary with the period or are confirmed by Chou sources. From the *Shu-ching* 書經 (*Book of Documents*), we rely only on the chapters that scholars have generally accepted as reliable Chou source materials. H. G. Creel's summary of the scholarship on the authenticity of the chapters was useful as a guide.[7] The *Shih-ching* 詩經 (*Book of Poetry*) is commonly taken as an anthology of Chou verses. We realize that most of the "Kuo-feng" 國風 pieces were regional lyrics, some of which definitely were later works. From this work, we selected the verses in the "Ta-ya" 大雅, the "Hsiao-ya" 小雅 and the "Sung" 頌 because they are contemporary with the Western Chou.[8] Both the

---

6. Shirakawa Shizuka, *KBTS*, 1962–75 and *KBHS*, 1978–79.
7. Creel, 1970:448–63.
8. Creel, 1970: 463; Hsu, 1965:165.

Tso-chuan 左傳 and the *Ch'un-ch'iu Chronicles* 春秋 are of a later date but were used here with caution. The *Tso-chuan* contains a rich reservoir of information on the Western Chou period presented as a background for Ch'un-ch'iu events. Scholars of the 1930s had doubts about the authenticity of the *Tso-chuan*, but now it is generally accepted as a worthy source on ancient China.[9] The *Kuo-yü* 國語 (*The Discourses of the States*) is not used much here as a source because it contains little material that can be surely attributed to the Western Chou. These materials, however, seem to be compatible with data included in other more reliable sources.[10] The *I-Chou-shu* 逸周書 may not be an original form of the text. The content of a few chapter is, however, consistent with the information found in newly discovered bronze inscriptions. Such new material greatly enhances the validity of those chapters of the *I-Chou-shu.*[11] The *Chu-shu-chi-nien* 竹書紀年 (*The Bamboo Chronicles*) is also an excavated book, found at the same time as the *I-Chou-shu.* The presently available version is, however, suspected as a forgery. We have used only the fragments of the original that are cited in early works, such as those cited in the early commentaries of the *Han-shu* 漢書.[12]

RECENT STUDIES

In the past decade, critical literature on particular aspects of the Chou period has increased considerably, and with the reopening of China we have gained access to a large number of Chinese publications. The new sites and their contents have stimulated research in both Japan and the United States. In Japanese alone, more than three hundred titles on the Chou period have been published in books or articles in scholarly journals. Over five hundred titles in English have appeared in juried journals in this decade. Notwithstanding their usually high quality, these studies are most often confined to analysis of specific, highly technical problems.

The body of detailed research projects on Western Chou civilization has reached such a magnitude that a comprehensive synthesis is needed to merge and integrate the contours of the Chou developmental pattern with the wealth of detailed, technical, and essentially disparate research that had already been generated. To overcome the discipline-specific interpretations of this wealth of archaeological and literary source material, an interdisciplinary approach was developed. We hope that the

9. Karlgren, 1926, 1931; Creel, 1970:475–77; Hsu, 1965:184–86.
10. Karlgren, 1926:58–59; Hsu, 1965:186.
11. Ch'ü Wan-li, 1965; Ku Chieh-kang, 1963; Ch'en Meng-chia, 1954.
12. Creel, 1970:483–85.

approach outlined below has allowed a meaningful interpretation of this important ancient civilization.

METHOD OF ANALYSIS

Our aim here is to present an integrated study of the development of Chou civilization and to locate its position in the history of Chinese culture and in that of the ancient world in general. Guiding our work is the view that ancient cultures were systems and that change in culture was a regular process. We view Chinese culture, like all others, therefore, as a system that was open, dynamic, and tended toward growth and differentiation. As with all studies of the past, we have been unable to control quantity or even identify many of the variables in the system. The choice of chapter headings reflects, however, those parts of the Chou civilization that we felt able to analyze. Further, our assumption is that the parts cohere with one another and affect each other reciprocally. For example, we assume material culture to be an important part of a multifaceted culture; change in structure or appearance in the artifact would be explained, therefore, through search for causes of that change, ones often found outside the industry in which the object was produced. Such is the case as well with the study of political, social, and economic structures. The goal is, then, to describe what changes occurred during the period from the beginning of the dynasty to the move of the capital in 771 B.C. We have respected chronology in the organization of chapters and sought to explain how and why Chinese culture changed during that time. Each chapter is devoted to a particular aspect of the Chou culture, and each change is discussed with respect to an evolutionary course. Both the historical background and the result of those changes are included in the discussions.

Our method was informed by many other scholars who have addressed the same question: How can we interpret the past? V. Gordon Childe, the champion of evolutionary and materialist modes of interpretation, thought of stages of history according to social and economic patterns. He called the stage that began with the urban revolution "civilization." These first literate communities were dense settlements with complex bureaucracies indicative of a state political organization. These features were apparent in China in ancient times but did not develop either in one place or at one time. Many of the features of "civilization," in Childe's parlance, can be found in the Western Chou period. Such a milestone was reached when the Chou conceived of themselves as the "Central Kingdom." This kingdom, its outline, and the principles that governed the formation and functioning of its institutions are addressed in chapters 4, 5, and 7. Preceding, however, are several chapters that examine the principles which provoked and directed the evolution and transformation of Chou life. Chapter 6 assumes an established state organization and focuses on analysis of the process of expansion, incorporation, and eventual loss of potency. Chapter 8 notes conditions that caused the Western Chou's disintegration and final collapse, and draws parallels between the fall of the Western Chou and that of other ancient cultures. We looked at the positing and legacy of Chou ideas in cultural life, noticing that culture change was a regular process. Chapters 9 and 10 are devoted to discussions of Chou material culture and everyday life developed through review of available archaeological materials. Views of others, particularly Steward,[13] White,[14] and Binford,[15] also informed and guided our work, especially with regard to formulating the kinds of questions to be asked.

Historians, archaeologists, and classical scholars of many disciplines have argued about the reasons for the rise of complex societies. Many factors have been singled out for special attention, and each scholar has argued why a certain factor was a prime mover in the rise of civilization. Ruth Whitehouse,[16] for instance, has emphasized environment and subsistence economy, population, technology, trade, and social organization. Causative factors examined by others have included irrigation, warfare,[17] population growth and social conscription,[18] trade and symbiosis, cooperation and competition, and the integrative power of great religions and art styles.[19] Some combination of these factors often contributed to cementing a number of groups into a permanent coalition called a state.[20] We examine analyses of a number of these features in our discussions of the dynamic nature of the Western Chou civilization.

The Chou period saw the proliferation of city-states through colonization and feudalism beginning in the twelfth century B.C. Before this time, however, there were centers that were capitals of territorial states. The only clearly documented one is the Great City Shang, the namesake of the Shang kingdom.[21] Certainly the Shang culture, with its

13. Steward, 1955.
14. White, 1975.
15. Binford, 1972.
16. Whitehouse, 1977.
17. Carneiro, 1979:733–738.
18. Webster, 1975.
19. Flannery, 1972.
20. Cohen and Service, 1978.
21. Chang, 1980:69–73.

writing system, religious and ritual practices, sophisticated organization, and bronze production, should be regarded as an advanced civilization, and we discuss the formation of Chou traditions in the light of the legacy and the distinctive character of the Shang.

The Chinese conception of "civilization" suggests another guiding principle for our discussions. The Chinese term for civilization, *wen-ming* 文明, consists of *wen*, meaning (simultaneously) decoration, written script, and peaceful manner, and *ming*, translated as brilliance, clarity, enlightenment. The combination of *wen* and *ming* connotes a type of human activity organized on the principle of rationality (versus impulse) and, peace (versus coercion)—or, simply, the civilized manner. Although complete fulfillment of such expectations must be envisioned as utopian, the aspirations, no matter how vague or implicit, probably marked the line between pre-civilization and civilization. The effort to cross that threshold must be regarded as a criterion of civilization that is of paramount significance in human history. Entrance into civilization marked a difference in content, for the main concerns of people prior to this stage were to secure resources. During the Chou period the concerns were dealing with fellow human beings, with problems of conflict between groups and cooperation within the larger group, and with distribution of resources. The broader such a circle of communication was, the more momentum was gathered for cultural achievement—and the more pertinent the orderly sharing and distribution of resources became. We view civilization here, then, as a basic unit of history because of the distinctive way it orders economic, sociopolitical, and ideological life. How the Chou organized and expressed that order is the focus of our attention. In doing such work we hope to expose the values of Chou civilization—how the Chou saw themselves and their charge in the Central Kingdom and how they incorporated their values into Chinese life for the many centuries that followed.

Note on Editorial Method
and Illustrations

A full bibliography, arranged alphabetically according to the names of the authors and divided among Western, Chinese, and Japanese languages, is given at the end of the book. In the footnotes only the names of the authors and the dates of the works are given. For works in Western languages, only the surname of the author is given; the full name is given for works in Chinese and Japanese.

All works are listed under the name of the author or authors when the name is given in the publications. The following abbreviations are used in the notes and figure captions:

KBHS	*Kinbun hoshaku*
KBTS	*Kinbun tsūshaku*
KK	*K'ao-ku*
KKHP	*K'ao-ku hsüeh-pao*
WW	*Wen-wu*
WWTKTL	*Wen-wu ts'an-k'ao tzu-liao*

Periodicals are listed according to standard Western practice by volume number, except for certain Chinese periodicals that use citation by year rather than by volume number.

We have endeavored to use illustrations of high quality. In some cases, however, the only extant photograph or diagram of an important object or site is a poor one; with reluctance, we have included these illustrations.

Western Chou

Civilization

1 The Neolithic and
Shang Background

The Chou nation of the late second millennium B.C. became the most powerful one in north China and overtook its neighbors, including the Shang. The Chou view of themselves was as the inheritors of an already defined Hua-Hsia 華夏, or Chinese culture. They defined their group to include the Chinese of north China. They borrowed from and absorbed from the non-China groups there as well.

It is vital to understand the conditions during the neolithic and early dynastic periods preceding the Chou takeover in order to understand its outcome. Interaction patterns among neolithic groups, for instance, made fusion necessary and inevitable. Competition for various commodities caused interaction during the early historic period and forced organization of a political entity that could maintain stability. The groups who possessed that organizational ability were potentially powerful in north China. The political succession from the Hsia to the Shang carried with it an increase in breadth of power and control. Even stronger controls buttressed the Shang state.

The study of archaeological materials from the known northern neolithic traditions and from the Hsia and the Shang has allowed us to trace various patterns as well as the substance of the interaction among these groups and the conditions and models that formed the Chou state.

NEOLITHIC LIFE IN CHINA

The Three Dynasties (Hsia 夏, Shang 商, and Chou 周) rose from a broad and varied culture base in north China during the second and first millennia B.C. They were the primary contributors to the social, political, economic, and cultural life of subsequent dynastic systems. In order to understand the development of dynastic China, however, we need to discern fully the neolithic background that preceded the Three

Dynasties. Fortunately, the archaeological context of the Chinese neolithic is rich. Published analyses of the excavation record stress horizontal dimensions of society and have provided a normative view of the cultures. As we present and investigate that information here, we will attempt to make fresh observations about the processes that allowed for the formation of the Chou civilization. Mortuary practices, settlement patterns, aspects of material culture, and so on, will be viewed as examples of human behavior—as actions taken by ancient peoples that reveal their relationships with each other, whether as individuals or groups, and thereby reveal the values that formed their identity. The goal is first to identify the groups, then to examine the processes through which they interacted, and finally to explore and interpret the external forms (governmental and social structure, music, literature, philosophy, et cetera) in which Chou civilization was manifest.

We will begin by surveying the geography. The majority of neolithic sites that have been discovered and excavated are in the area that we call China proper. More precisely, the main stage of cultural activities in ancient China was the area dominated by the Yellow River in the north, the Yangtze River 揚子 in the south and the coastal regions stretching from the Shantung 山東 Peninsula south to the lakes and rivers in present-day Kiangsu 江蘇 and Chekiang 浙江 provinces (map 1)—an area of truly remarkable geographic variation. As the Yellow River turns south, then east, the terrain gradually changes from mountainous, yellow-earth plateau to a vast plain in which the great Yellow River and its tributaries deposit increasingly large amounts of sediment. The eastern end of this vast plain meets a rather stony and hilly peninsula that is part of the mountain range extending from Manchuria to Shantung Province 山東. This Yellow River region is separated from the Yangtze Valley in the south by a cluster of hills spreading from the rim of the Szechwan 四川 basin to the east coast. Immediately to the south of these intermediate zones is an area of lakes and rivers, which is actually the remnant of an inland sea. The mighty Yangtze River flows eastward across this area, and at its delta a large alluvial plain is formed. In this land that was occupied by neolithic communities, five major geographic divisions may be designated that are appropriate to our study: the Yellow River (Northern Region, Region I), the Shantung Peninsula (Eastern Region, Region II), the Eastern Coast (Region III), the Yangtze Valley (Southern Region, Region IV) and the Wei River 渭水 Highland (Western Region, Region V), a small and somewhat peripheral area adjacent to the Northern Region (map 1). Not long ago, the Northern Region was regarded as the nuclear area from which the Yangshao 仰韶 and Lungshan 龍山 cultures developed and radiated outward during the

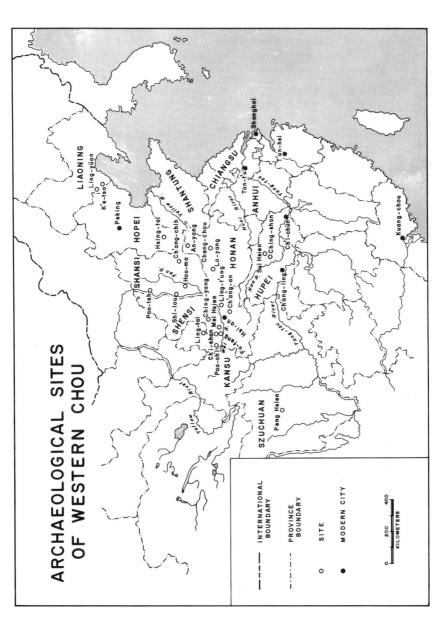

1. Archaeological sites of Western Chou

late phase of the third millennium B.C. The Yellow River Plain was known as the "Cradle of East."[1] Recent discoveries, however, have favored the hypothesis of a multitradition base for the neolithic in China.

The Yangshao culture is no longer considered the earliest stage of northern neolithic development, since an earlier phase, the P'ei-li-kang 裴李崗 culture, is C-14-dated around seven thousand years ago. It is characterized by a rather crude, hand-formed earthenware pottery, of loose texture and low firing temperature (700–960°C), decorated with pressed and scratched marks on uneven black-, red-, or orange-colored clay. The stone implements bear some neolithic characteristics. Settlement sizes are not as extensive as at Yangshao, although dwellings are primarily semi-subterranean. Agriculture was developed by these people, and surplus grain, probably millet, has been found in storage pits in excavation. Stone querns and pestles are typical items in the P'ei-li-kang sites, suggesting that the cereal grain was milled. P'ei-li-kang type sites have been found near the foothills of the T'ai-hang 太行 Mountains near the Yellow River Plain. The sites are often located on terraces twenty-five to forty meters above, and a few hundred meters away from, the river. The latitude of the areas where the P'ei-li-kang sites are located is almost parallel to that of the West Asian crescent of ancient cultures, suggesting that comparable conditions supported development of early farming communities in each place. The climate at that period in China is believed to have been warmer than today, by an average of two to three degrees Centigrade, or five degrees in January, an atmosphere clearly favorable to agriculture.[2]

Above the P'ei-li-kang remains is the very rich cultural tradition known as the Yangshao (*ca.* 5150–2960 B.C.). The Yangshao sites can be identified in an extensive region throughout the Northern and Western regions outlined on map 1. The settlement sizes are often very large and agriculture is well developed, especially the cultivation of millet and vegetables. The red-based pottery is polished, and the best-known style, painted with geometric designs and an occasional representational image, has given Yangshao the name "Painted Pottery" culture.[3] The security provided by a developed agriculture resulted in an increase in population.[4] Not only are the Yangshao sites much larger than those of P'ei-li-kang, but the splitting of a village into satellites can also be found. In one of the late-phase Yangshao sites, a cemetery was shared by

1. Ho, 1975:48–56, 342–43.
2. An Chih-min, 1979B:394–95; Yen Wen-ming, 1979:45–50; Kao T'ien-lin, 1979:51–55, 81; An Chih-min, 1979A:335–46; Li Yu-mou et al., 1979:347–51.
3. An Chih-min, 1979B:396; Chang, 1977:91–114.
4. Boulding, 1969:25–27.

several neighboring villages. It seems very likely that fission of old settlements into new ones gradually filled the vacant spaces between sites.[5] The expansion of the Yangshao culture itself could well have been the consequence of population growth, as the steady fission of settlements eventually pushed the culture communities across a broader area.

When neolithic agriculture dispersed to places even farther away, "local" cultures were formed.[6] The last phase of neolithic development in north China has been termed "Lungshanoid" by Chang Kwang-chih 張光直, who stated in 1977 that virtually all contemporary local cultures across north China were offspring of the Yangshao.[7] Recent discoveries of early cultural remains in the Yangtze Valley and on the Shantung Peninsula, however, have altered the picture. It now seems that the Honan Lungshan 河南龍山 culture was a direct descendant of the Yangshao, but the Shensi Lungshan 陝西龍山, although very closely related to the Honan Lungshan, was affected by its western neighbors in Kansu 甘肅. The Honan Lungshan was directly above the Yangshao material at Miao-ti-kou 廟底溝, dated 2780–2145 B.C.; this culture lasted until the end of the third millennium B.C.[8]

The Lungshan culture, in contrast to Yangshao, maintained permanent villages and possibly even farmed fields continuously, instead of developing fields through slash-and-burn methods. The growth of population must have restricted land use so that extensive slash-and-burn farming was not possible. Among the stone tools found in Lungshan sites, there are more carpentry tools (adzes, chisels, antler wedges, etc.) than tree-felling tools (such as axes). This particular phenomenon demonstrates that less clearing of·fields was done in the Lungshan period than in the Yangshao phase.[9] As the land-to-man ratio declined, population pressure stimulated changes in farming techniques that could have raised per-area yields.[10] Harvest implements are common in the Lungshan finds, evidence that swelling agricultural harvests must have increased their use.

Warfare, or the threat of it, associated with the phenomenon of population pressure must explain the Lungshan habit of protecting villages with earthen walls and long, deep ditches.[11] The fissioning process reached its peak in the Yellow River region during the Lungshan period, the last phase of the neolithic in north China. The circumscription of

5. Chang, 1977:106.
6. Ibid., 144ff.
7. Ibid., 151–53.
8. An Chih-min, 1979B:398.
9. Chang, 1977:152–53.
10. Boserup, 1965.
11. Chang, 1977:152, 178.

communities by geographic limits and population increases initiated interaction among these groups, which eventually transformed their form of interchange. The increased need for foodstuffs and the necessity to cooperate for exchange of goods eventually required a social and political structure sufficient to allow cross-"nation" interaction. The most ambitious of these groups devised the earliest state structures.

In Region II, the Eastern Region, undecorated, thin-walled black pottery was found at a site called Lungshan in the Shantung Peninsula. This discovery brought to Chinese archaeology the appellation "Black Pottery" culture, regarded as synonymous with the Lungshan.[12] The Black Pottery culture was contrasted to the Yangshao, the Painted Pottery culture, and they were considered as separately generated traditions. A study of legends and myths in early literature suggested a contrast between two clusters of ancient peoples, one in the eastern plains along the Yellow River extending to the coast and one in the west in the hilly loess areas.[13] These two groups were thought to correspond to the Yangshao and Lungshan and to two distinct life-styles. Such a theory was widely accepted by Chinese archaeologists and historians until the stratigraphy at Miao-ti-kou II 廟底溝二期 confirmed a sequence from Yangshao to Lungshan.[14] The Yangshao was thereby considered the forerunner of all the local Lungshan cultures radiating from the central plain or the nuclear area. Recently, however, the discoveries at Ta-wen-k'ou 大汶口 on the Shantung Peninsula stimulated yet another revision of the nuclear-area theory.

The Ta-wen-k'ou culture is now identified as an old and long neolithic tradition (*ca.* 4300–*ca.* 1900 B.C.)[15] which can be located in a broad area from Po-hai 渤海 (or Chihli 直隸) Bay on the Shantung Peninsula, west into the eastern parts of the loess plain, and south to the periphery of the Yangtze delta. The Ta-wen-k'ou culture spanned two and one-half millennia until the Shantung Lungshan superseded it around 2000 B.C. Although Ta-wen-k'ou pottery is distinctive, Yangshao morphological and decorative features are apparent in it even in the early stages. In addition, Ta-wen-k'ou influence was evident in some of the Yangshao sites as far west as central Honan. The wide spread of Ta-wen-k'ou influence to the north and south testifies to its dynamic nature. The groups cultivated millet and supplemented farming with fishing and hunting.[16] A remarkable discovery in Ta-wen-k'ou excavations are the

---

12. Ibid., 145–48.
13. Fu Ssu-nien, 1952, vol. 4:31–96.
14. Chang, 1977:157.
15. Hsia Nai, 1977:225. An Chih-min, 1979B:396–97.
16. Shan-tung ta-hsüeh, Department of History, 1979:1–12, 13–28.

graphs etched onto the sides of some of the black pots. These are the earliest known script in China. Although potters' marks were found on Yangshao vessels, they were relatively simple scratches and may or may not have been part of a true writing system of symbols used for the purpose of communication.[17] The Ta-wen-k'ou scripts, by contrast, are identifiable and decipherable according to the etymological principles of Chinese writing in Shang and later days. Moreover, at least one character was found that was identical to another on a pot excavated at a considerable distance away. The date of the Ta-wen-k'ou scripts is now thought to be late in the period, or during the second half of the third millennium B.C.[18] The transition from Ta-wen-k'ou to Lungshan lifestyle is such a smooth process that in excavated levels it is difficult to mark where one begins and the other ends. The transition from east to west, from Shantung to Honan Lungshan, is so gradual that it is equally difficult to locate a strict border. The influence of the Shantung Lungshan on the local cultures in southern Manchuria across Po-hai Bay, however, is definable.[19] In other words, the interaction between the descendants of the Ta-wen-k'ou and their counterparts in Honan in the heartland of Region I was an uninhibited process of exchange of ideas and technology, facilitated by the pressure of densely distributed settlements that proliferated due to population growth.

Region III in the south has often been regarded as nothing but cultural overflow from north China. The discovery of rice cultivation at Ho-mu-tu 河姆渡, however, required archaeologists to reconsider the possibility of a separate southern tradition. Ho-mu-tu is located on Hang-chou Bay, near the Ch'ien-t'ang 錢塘 River and it is considered the oldest site extant in the southeastern coastal region. It is dated about five thousand years B.C., contemporary with the Yangshao of north China. The pottery is hand-made, low-fired, and of loose texture.[20] The Ho-mu-tu culture sites yielded rice remains in abundance. They have been identified as *Oryza sativa L. subsp.*, or *Hsien Ting* 丁氏秈, a species very closely related to the rice cultivated there now. A special kind of bone spade was used to adapt the field conditions to the requirements of rice paddies.[21]

Another discovery of great significance at Ho-mu-tu was a large group of wooden dwellings constructed on posts situated in the soft soil. These wooden structures were fastened with various kinds of mortices and

17. Li Hsiao-ting, 1979:431−83; Ho, 1975:223−32.
18. Shan-tung ta-hsüeh, Department of History, 1979:79−95; 120−46; Li Hsiao-ting, 1979:431−43.
19. An Chih-min, 1979B:398.
20. Ibid., 400; Che-chiang sheng wen-kuan-hui, 1978:92−93.
21. Yu Hsiu-ling, 1976:20−23; Che-chiang sheng po-wu-kuan, 1978:103.

tenons.[22] Since the northern Lungshan sites included dwellings made of stamped-earth platforms and thatched roofs, the wooden structures found in Ho-mu-tu shed new light on the origins of wooden architecture in China.

The later phases of southeastern coast neolithic suggest interaction with both the northern Yangshao and the coastal Lungshan peoples. The Ma-chia-pang 馬家浜 people, located in the Yangtze delta, followed the Ho-mu-tu in producing earthenware pots fired at low temperatures. Their choices of clays were different, however, and the shapes of vessels often repeated those common in north China. Rice remains were also found.[23] The Liang-chu 良渚 culture represents the last stage of the neolithic in southeast China. It continued the Ma-chia-pang tradition and is dated from about 3310 to 2250 B.C., or roughly contemporary with the Lungshan in north China. A relationship with the Shantung Lungshan can be deduced because of the black-based and black-burnished pottery in Liangchu sites. In all three periods from the Ho-mu-tu to the Liangchu, rice remains have been excavated. In the Liangchu sites *Keng* 粳 rice, a subspecies, was discovered. Melon seeds, fava beans, peanuts, and sesame seeds, as well as silk and hemp, were found. These products, especially silk, which was responsible for sericulture, were extremely important contributions to Chinese civilization.[24]

Identification of the neolithic cultures in the intermediate zone between the Yellow River and the Yangtze River is still difficult. Some scholars suggest that the groups clustered in the Huai River Valley should be identified with the Ch'ing-lien-kang 青蓮崗 culture, including a northern spur reaching to Shantung and Ta-wen-k'ou and a southern division including Ma-chia-pang and others.[25] Several scholars, however, prefer to identify one tradition in the north and one in the south.[26] This particular problem in scholarship reflects the very nature of transition between traditions. The shift from the eastern (Shantung) local culture to a culture with features of the central plain (Honan) traditions appears to have been very gradual. Likewise, the Ch'ü-chia-ling 屈家嶺 culture in the Han 漢 River Valley shared features with the Lungshan to the north, yet its agriculture was based on rice cultivation, borrowed from its neighbors to the southwest.[27]

The gradual exchange and acquisition of local features of one culture

22. Che-chiang-sheng wen-kuan-hui, 1978:42–54.

23. An Chih-min, 1979B:400; Mou Yung-k'ang et al., 1978:67–68.

24. An Chih-min, 1979B:400; Mou Yung-k'ang and Wei Cheng-chin, 1978:70–71.

25. Nan-ching po-wu-kuan, 1978:46–57.

26. Shan-tung ta-hsüeh, Department of History, 1979:13–28; the same article also appears in *Wen-wu*, 1978 (5):58–66; Mou Yung-k'ang et al., 1978:71–72.

27. An Chih-min, 1979A:399.

with those of another, both along an east-west and a south-north course, reflects the process of convergence that took place in the later phases of the neolithic. The interaction was probably the consequence of across-the-board population growth and the subsequent fission of settlements. Although there is some homogeneity in late neolithic cultures in north China and a single name to designate all cultures as local variations has been suggested recently,[28] local variations were so strong that the cultural fusions initiated in the neolithic seem not to have achieved unification at all. In fact, several local variations, such as the Shantung Lungshan, remained isolated and distinctive for long periods of time. Even the newly formed fusions were apparently localized. Each might in itself create a local "nation," with its own special features adapted to its specific surroundings. The memory of those "nations" and their respective cultures must be the basis of the existence of claims of many "peoples" in ancient literature and for the political entities called "states".

The late neolithic in China, as we know it from archaeology, reflects the conditions for the development of the state posited by D. Webster— namely, that several juxtaposed entities within reach of one another and population pressure stimulated agricultural production in order to create the surplus necessary to sustain the political units.[29] If these neolithic clusters were circumscribed by competing "nations," both a political order and a social order able to distribute, organize, and utilize resources would be stimulated. In other words, the conditions that provoked the establishment of a state were already manifest in north China in the late neolithic, by the second millennium B.C.

Indeed, one of the late neolithic states in north China, discovered at Erh-li-t'ou 二里頭, is now dated from about 1900 to 1600 B.C.[30] Coincidentally, it is comparable in date to the Hsia dynasty, conventionally dated from 2005 to 1784 B.C. Four cultural levels were excavated at Erh-li-t'ou, and evidence for bronze making in an early stage was found in the third. Molds for casting were located there, as were bronze tools and weapons, workshops for pottery making, bone artifacts, and jade and stone ritual objects and musical instruments. The foundation of a large house called a "palace" by the archaeologists was discovered; it is the oldest such building yet excavated[31] (figs. 1.1, 1.2). The remains of this structure include a rectangular, stamped-earth platform measuring 30.4 by 11.4 meters square and 0.8 meter high. The total amount of earth necessary to form the platform amounted to about twenty

28. Ibid., 403.
29. Webster, 1975:464–72.
30. Hsia Nai, 1977:222.
31. Yin Wei-chang, 1978:1–4.

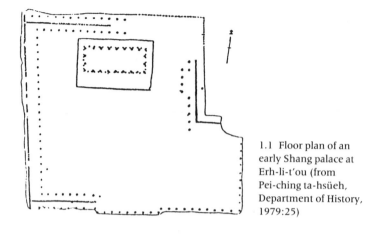

1.1 Floor plan of an
early Shang palace at
Erh-li-t'ou (from
Pei-ching ta-hsüeh,
Department of History,
1979:25)

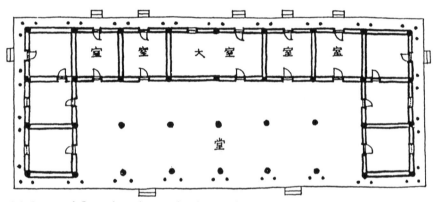

1.2 Suggested floor plan of an early Shang palace at Erh-li-t'ou (from Yang
Hung-hsün, 1981:18)

thousand cubic meters, and the job has been estimated to have taken
more than one hundred thousand working days to complete. The building itself had a wooden superstructure with eight bays across and three
deep. Rows of post holes with stones at the base must have supported a
large thatched roof. The area of the front courtyard is estimated at about
five to six thousand square meters, large enough to hold more than ten
thousand persons. The complex was surrounded by side buildings connected by hallways. Situated in the front of the courtyard is a gate with
eight rooms across the façade. The fact that the building of the entire
complex must have required hundreds of thousands of work days makes
clear the magnitude of the authority available to the builders. Evidence
of such control implies the existence of a fairly complex political organization. Moreover, features of this early city were the guiding principles

for the Chou when they build their new capital. Symmetry, axiality, orientation to the south, horizontality across an east-west axis, and the use of a large front courtyard, connecting buildings, and elaborate gates were essential to the Chou capital.

By contrast, the ordinary residences at Erh-li-t'ou were small, shallow semi-subterranean pits.[32] The variation in house types confirms social differentiation in the community. The bronze weapons found at the site included large axes and halberds as well as arrowheads; the bronze tools found were small. All bronze objects imitated their counterparts in stone or bone, suggesting that bronze use was at a beginning stage. Nevertheless, production of bronze required job differentiation. On some pottery belonging to the same phase, incised graphs that approximate known Shang models were used.[33] Large palace buildings and the use of bronze require strong political authority, including forced labor and production by specialized labor. The existence of written graphs speaks for the possibility of a written system as such. The presence of all these features at Erh-li-t'ou clearly points to the dawning of the centralized political authority and stratified social order that characterize the rise of a state. Moreover, a drastic change recently noticed in Level 3 of the excavation has been attributed to a shift in power, from the Hsia to the Shang, and Erh-li-t'ou is thought to be the first capital of the new dynasty.[34]

If these speculations are correct, the Erh-li-t'ou site may very likely be the point of juncture between field archaeology and literary history. The Hsia was regarded as the very first of the "Three Dynasties" and, according to legend, was attributed with a unique feature; it was the first dynasty with a father-to-son succession of rulers. Earlier leaders were selected by their predecessors from a number of worthy candidates, regardless of family ties. Those dynasties (or polities) excluded from the "Three" sanctioned by early literature were ones that did not follow the tradition of succession of rulers. Thus, the Hsia must have established a state with some degree of stability and institutionalized political authority. On the other hand, the title given to Hsia rulers was Lord (*hou* 侯), rather than King (*wang* 王). The first ruler of the Hsia, legend tells us, convened chiefs of numerous states before him.[35] Hsia authority, therefore, does seem to be less than that of a monarchy, resembling that of a confederacy of states. Very possibly, the Hsia was a political entity that was evolving from a confederacy to a monarchy.

The appearance of the state, features of which are confirmed in the

---

32. Erh-li-t'ou kung-tso-tui, 1974; Lo-yang fa-chüeh-tui, 1965:215.

33. Tsou Heng, 1980:135–44.

34. Wu Ju-tso, 1978:70–73; Sun Fei, 1980:79–84. Currently the Erh-li-t'ou phase is being reexamined with a view to identifying it with the Hsia civilization.

35. *Shih-chi hui-chu k'ao-cheng*, hereafter *Shih-chi*, 1/33, 43, 52; 2/41, 51.

Erh-li-t'ou remains, verifies the emergence of civilization, for community concerns were focused on human relationships rather than merely on obtaining food. The likelihood that the Erh-li-t'ou culture represents the remains of the Hsia state leads us to conclude that civilization had already begun, then and there.[36] What actually did happen at the time of Erh-li-t'ou in north China appears to be the consequence of local conditions rather than outside stimulation.[37]

The proximity of at least three separate neolithic traditions suggests that these traditions could not have avoided contact and mutual stimulation. Such unusual conditions are not readily reproduced in the history of other civilizations. Mesopotamia and Egypt were separated by a formidable desert and considerable distance. Mutual interaction enriched the content of each Chinese tradition and probably initiated, through a chain reaction, changes across a broad geographic area. Because of the geographic conditions and the proximity of villages, this process and the changes thus begun were widely felt. The course of that development was continued by means of open and continued contact and mutual incorporation. Some groups, under certain conditions, intensified the process and eventually managed to acquire ways to organize their own lives with order and meaning, ways that would become widely accepted political, social, and intellectual systems. The appearance and character of those forms will be our focus throughout this study.

THE HSIA STATE AND ANCIENT NATIONS

Whether Erh-li-t'ou was the locus of the Hsia power or not, the evidence there should not be interpreted as the beginning of a unified China. Even the various neolithic cultures described above should not be viewed as a single neolithic culture system. The area under control of the Hsia would have been very limited, probably not extending much beyond the middle reaches of the lower Yellow River Valley. Fragments of information about other tribes, or "nations", are found in ancient literary sources, and modern scholars have worked out classifications of them. The reports differ in detail. The most noteworthy systems are those proposed by Meng Wen-t'ung 蒙文通, Hsü Hsü-sheng 徐旭生, and Fu Ssu-nien 傅斯年. Meng suggested that there were three clusters of nations: the Chiang-Han 江漢 group (those who inhabited the valleys of

---

36. Wilson, 1951:36–42. Stimulus from Mesopotamia to Egypt is a well-established theory.

37. For instance, Ho, 1975. Cause for change is disputed there.

the Yangtze and Han 漢 rivers), the Ho-Lo 河洛 group (those in the middle reaches of the lower Yellow River) and the Hai-Tai 海岱 group (those in the coastal areas of north China). Hsü also suggested a three-part system: the Hua-Hsia 華夏 of the western yellow-earth plain, the Eastern I 夷 on the east coast, and the Miao-Man 苗蠻 of south China in the Yangtze Valley and further south. Fu viewed the struggles between the Eastern I bloc and the Western Hsia bloc as a main theme of this early history. Meng and Hsü derived their classification by analyzing ancient texts, but Fu took into consideration archaeological materials available in the 1930s, that is, material from the Yangshao in the west and the Lungshan in the east,[38] and saw these as contending cultures of the Eastern and Western blocs.

Evidence from physical anthropology underscores the value of those traditional classifications. Human remains from the neolithic sites do show some physical differences among the ancient peoples of China. The people of Yangshao in the Wei River Valley from about 5000 to 4000 B.C. had moderate-to-high foreheads, somewhat broad faces, low eyes, and broad noses; they were of medium height. They were probably closely related to the people of the Hua-Hsia nations. In the lower Yellow River, including the present areas of southern Shantung and northern Kiangsu 江蘇, the neolithic people had higher foreheads and broader faces and were taller than the Wei Valley inhabitants. Human remains in Ta-wen-k'ou often bore evidence of artificially deformed skulls and extraction of teeth. Geography suggests that these people probably were related to the traditional Eastern I 夷. Nevertheless, the people of the Miao-ti-kou II culture, although slightly more recent than the Yangshao and the Ta-wen-k'ou, were closely related to both groups. In southeast China, the Ho-mu-tu people had long heads, low faces, and flat, broad noses. They were a local group living on the lower Yangtze and were distinctive in type from the people on the northern plains. Further to the south, along the coast of Fukien 福建 and Kwangtung 廣東 and the Kwangsi 廣西 backland, the neolithic remains were of a later date. The long heads and low faces of these people were features closer to the Ho-mu-tu than to the northern neolithic groups, even though they were descendants of the ancient Miao-Man group. On the whole, of course, these neolithic peoples were local variants of the Mongoloid,[39] but variants with widely divergent cultural expression, life-style, and physical type.

Archaeological evidence of the neolithic cannot simply be reduced neatly into two or three cohesive divisions. In the central plain, the

38. Meng Wen-t'ung, 1933; Hsü Hsü-sheng, 1960; Fu Ssu-nien, 1935.
39. P'an Ch'i-feng et al., 1980.

Hua-Hsia (or the western Hsia, or the Ho-Lo) was the dominant type. The Lungshan groups in Honan and Shensi, as well as the Kuang-she 光社 in Hopei, are difficult to distinguish. The eight nations of the Chu-jung 祝融, an important cluster, were orginally located in the Yellow River Valley, except for one, which was located in the Han Valley (map 2). Although the Chu-jung were traditionally thought to be a southern group, their survivors did not move to the Yangtze-Han valleys until the mighty Shang gradually extinguished the major body of the Chu-jung.[40]

The combined evidence from archaeological and literary sources points to the identification of the Eastern I as a composite of the Ta-wen-k'ou and the Lungshan peoples. Archaeologically, their remains occupied the entire Shantung Peninsula and extended west into eastern Honan and north into the Liao-tung 遼東 region of southern Manchuria and south to Anhui 安徽 and Kiangsu. A legend recited by a duke of the Ch'un-ch'iu period asserted that ancient people with bird totems claimed their ancestry from Shao-hao, a legendary king from remote antiquity. Fu Ssu-nien has convincingly argued that the descendants of Shao-hao 少皥 were the Eastern I and that the Shang kingdom was established by them.[41] In a recent examination of the origin of the Shang, Tsou Heng noticed that the proto-Shang sites were distributed along the eastern slopes of the T'ai-hang 太行 Mountains, north and west of the lower Yellow River. There was only one site on the south side of the river.[42] The proto-Shang people, neighbors of the Shao-hao people, were so closely related to each other that Fu Ssu-nien was led to identify them as members of the same Eastern I group. Nevertheless, the Shang constantly fought in the eastern region, and the war against the Eastern I (called Jen-fang 人方) in the reign of the last Shang king exhausted the strength of the dynasty. The Eastern I were not under the control of the Shang, but evidently were nearly equal competitors.

The area occupied by the proto-Shang lay outside the purview of the Hsia at Erh-li-t'ou, but Shang was probably a nation contemporary with and comparable to the Hsia culture. The Hsia was a direct descendant of the Honan Lungshan culture, and the Shang was founded on the Hopei Lungshan. When the Shang people displaced the Hsia as the dominant political entity on the central plain they were both a rival and successor. Furthermore, the development of the proto-Shang nation was coeval with that of its neighbor, the Shantung Lungshan, from whom the

40. Li Tsung-t'ung 1954, vol. 1:16–25.
41. Fu Ssu-nien, 1935.
42. Tsou Heng, 1980:118, 139.

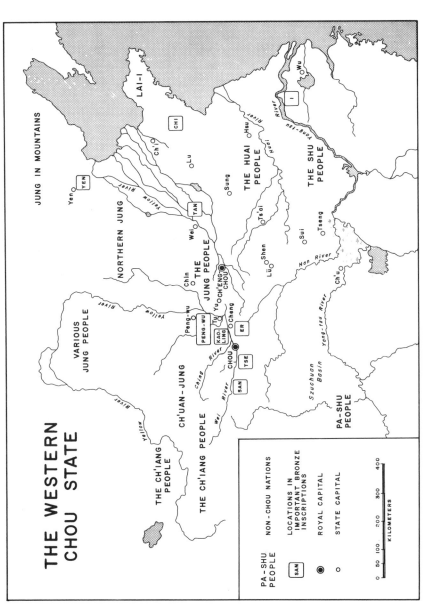

2. The Western Chou state

Shang also absorbed important cultural elements.[43] The sites with remains of the Ta-hsi 大溪 and the Ch'ü-chia-ling cultures are in the Yangtze-Han valleys, where the Chu-jung groups were known to have lived in the second millennium B.C. But since the Chu-jung originally lived in Honan, far to the north, there may have been other neolithic peoples in the Yangtze-Han valleys before their arrival. Although known today as inhabitants of the mountains of the southwest of China, the Miao-Man group was likely the group living in the Yangtze Valley in that period. The literary record suggests that the Miao-Man lived in what is present-day Hupei 湖北 Province, in an area between the ancient Yün-meng 雲夢 and P'eng-li 彭蠡 lakes.[44] These lakeside dwellers were pushed further to the south by the Chu-jung, who in turn were elbowed out of the central plain by the Shang.

The Yangtze delta was the home of the ancient Yüeh 越. Archaeologically, the succession of neolithic cultures from the Ho-mu-tu to the Liangchu are represented in the delta and in sites where a characteristic imprinted hard pottery is found. The Yüeh occupied the entire southeast region contemporary with the northern bronze age.[45] In the Yangtze delta, the active, dynamic local Yüeh culture produced hard-paste pottery and glazed ceramics fired at high temperatures. They eventually were influenced in life-style by the bronze-producing culture of the Shang.

These archaeological data have confirmed the notion in ancient literary sources that the world of the Hsia and the Shang was multicultural. Many local cultures developed as nations or as groups of people with a defined identity. Interaction among them allowed the transfer of bronze technology and signaled a change that finally pulled these local cultures into a common arena dominated by a single political entity. One such group was the Hsia nation, presumably the first supravillage powerful enough to mobilize tens of thousands of laborers to build structures such as the palaces at Erh-li-t'ou. They were simply the strongest among many tribes. The title Overlord of Hsia and the legend that the Great Yü (the first lord of the Hsia) was able to convene an assembly of state-chiefs were the necessary ingredients needed to legitimate a succession of Hsia leaders. After the death of Yü 禹, both his son and a lieutenant already designated as a successor contended for the position as the leader. According to legend, the Hsia people chose to support the legitimate son of Yü as their leader, thus creating a

43. Chang Kwang-chih, 1978; Tsou Heng, 1980:139, 157–59, 257–73; Chang Kwang-chih, 1976:151–69; 1980:344–48.
44. Hsü Hsü-sheng 1960:57–59; Wang Yü-che, 1950.
45. Su Ping-ch'i, 1978.

precedent. By taking this step, the Hsia created a more developed state and decisively moved toward becoming a dynasty.

SHANG MATERIAL CULTURE

Prior to the time of Shang political dominance, the Shang culture was far less advanced than the Hsia. The stamped-earth constructions at Erh-li-t'ou and the ritual weapons and tools found there have no counterpart in the proto-Shang sites. Only small bronze knives and arrowheads have been excavated at the pre-dynastic Shang sites. Stone implements excavated at Erh-li-t'ou included harvest tools such as elongated, flat knives and horn-shaped scythes. By contrast, proto-Shang stone tools were not differentiated. Hsia pottery was dominated by the shape *hu* 壺, a round-bottomed urn decorated with a variety of imprinted designs. The typical Shang three-legged pots named *li* 鬲 were often embellished only with simple chisel-like triangles. White clay and hard-paste potteries were made by the Hsia but were absent from proto-Shang sites. Both types of pottery bore graphs which belonged to the writing tradition that was known in the Ta-wen-k'ou culture.[46]

When the Shang began to dominate north China in the second millennium B.C., they adopted many features of the Hsia and other cultures. During the Shang period, much of the ancient Chinese world began to produce bronze.[47] A brief discussion of that accomplishment is germane to understanding the social and political organization formulated by the Shang and inherited and modified by the Chou. Achievements of broadest significance include those from material culture—bronze, pottery, architecture—as well as institutional and ideological aspects—state organization, agriculture, divination, and the writing system.

SHANG BRONZE INDUSTRY

The origin of the Chinese metal industry has been debated frequently in the past. Because bronze abruptly appeared in general use during the Shang at a sophisticated technological and design level, scholars questioned whether the earliest Chinese metallurgists had learned the technique from outsiders, or if the local beginnings of the industry were simply undiscovered. Only recently have new archaeological finds located an incipient stage of bronze making in north China. Advocates

46. Tsou Heng, 1980:140–44.
47. Chang 1980, discusses that development in full.

for the indigenous origin of bronze metallurgy now have convincing evidence for their argument. Copper knives and awls have been discovered in Shensi, Kansu, and Shantung and have been dated 3000 B.C., or earlier. This confirms that some Chinese artisans were experimenting with metal working prior to their use of metal-casting techniques.[48] This line of development has a precedent in the Near East, where copper working was superseded by use of *cire-perdue* (lost-wax) casting in the fourth millennium B.C. Proto-Shang sites have yielded bronze artifacts not more complex than small knives and arrowheads that could be made in simple direct-cast molds. Erh-li-t'ou and middle Shang sites such as Cheng-chou 鄭州, on the other hand, yielded bronze containers of complicated design that were cast in sets and preserved in tombs. The appearance of these complex casts clearly marks an advance in technology accompanied by an elaboration in ritual and a monopoly of bronze production and use by aristocrats. After King P'an Keng 盤庚 moved the capital to An-yang 安陽, Shang artisans created all sorts of bronze objects—ritual vessels, weapons, and tools—which have been discovered by the thousands.

Throughout the Shang, bronze foundries were located near city centers. The casting methods included both direct and piece-mold methods. In the early stages, bivalvular molds were used for small items, which could be produced repeatedly from the single mold. In the later phase, direct casting was continued, but section-mold assemblages developed to accommodate the complex shapes of ritual materials as well as their exterior ornamentation. Surface decorations were first painted on the clay mold and then were carved out of the surface of the clay. The cast designs were reproduced in positive relief on the bronze object. This casting method was in use at Cheng-chou, thus no later than about 1350 B.C. The use of piece-mold casting is unusual and early by comparison with sister bronze-using cultures in the ancient world, where the lost-wax process evolved directly from metal-working methods. Presumably the piece-mold method developed early in China because of the unusually sophisticated knowledge of clays there.

The degree of social and political organization necessary to operate the bronze industry may be understood from the following example. After preparation of the model-mold assemblage, the molten alloy was poured into it from a tip-bottomed crucible nicknamed "the general's helmet" by Chinese archaeologists. The capacity of each "helmet" was limited, because it was hand-carried while filled with molten metal. Although a few cruciblesful would be sufficient to cast a small item, the production of large pieces required hundreds of loads. For example, the Ssu-mu-wu

48. Chang, 1977A:274–79; Fong, 1980:36; Ho, 1975:177–221.

司母戊 *fang-ting* 方鼎, which is 133 centimeters high, 110 centimeters long and 78 centimeters wide and weighs 87 kilograms, required at least 3 or 4 persons to lift each of 70 crucibles, in order to pour enough molten metal to cast the vessel. The total labor force engaged in the production of one such large piece had to include at least three hundred persons working almost simultaneously. Moreover, even though the natural resources—clay, copper, tin, fuel for furnaces, et cetera—were all within easy reach of the Shang foundries, all the extraction and preparation activities had to be accomplished and coordinated.[49] Mobilization of manpower sufficient to carry on that industry alone required centralized authority; in this case, royalty. Both political and social hierarchies had to have been well established by the late Shang and each member's role in that society was well known.

The capacity for bronze production itself is indicative of the ordered political and social structure already in place in the middle Shang, or by the time of the Cheng-chou phase of the dynasty. The bronze objects and their decoration, along with chariots, flags, jades, feathered bows, bronze bells, and drums, were symbols of authority of the kings of Shang, and subsequently of the Chou. The ultimate symbols of the Shang were those venerable sets of ritual bronzes used for the ancestral rites of the upper class. All bronzes were indicative of high status, and most were covered with a special style of ornament. Shang decoration consisted of animal designs featuring faces and body parts of animals of various sorts, principal among them tigers, cattle, and birds. All those animals figured importantly in Shang myths as messengers of communication with the ancestors.[50] The most common design, the *t'ao-t'ieh* 饕餮, was a composite of many parts of such animals. It dominated the program of decor on Shang and early Chou ritual materials, and as a single motif it must have carried special significance. The design and its underlying religious, social, and political associations were perhaps signs or emblems of Shang authority. When the *t'ao-t'ieh*, which appeared on most ritual materials used during the late Shang, came into view, it may have notified observers of the presence of authority and disclosed the rules that would govern their position in the society.[51]

Although elsewhere the development of monumental art forms often accompanied the rise of state, examples of this conjunction are missing from China. The most conspicuous candidates as an art form in early historic China were the bronzes. They were a specialized production,

49. Pei-ching ta-hsüeh, Department of History, 1979:32−36, 44−47; Barnard, 1961.
50. Chang, 1980:204−09.
51. This case will be further argued in chapter 9.

one put to ritual use. They were not conceived of as art for art's sake. As examples of "working art," their significance and the symbolic meaning of their decor must be as an aristocratic message. And although their use changed in the Western Chou, the bronzes were retained as political and social markers of status and position. The specific emblem of power was, however, adjusted to meet the desires and needs of the Western Chou patrons.

SHANG POTTERY

The Shang potting industry grew out of the late neolithic in north China. Shang potters produced new hard-paste and glazed pottery, which was fired at very high temperatures, and set up trade networks to import the special white clay, kaolin, preferred for these high-fired wares. This clay was obtained only in the south, although only the kilns in the north were capable of firing at high temperatures.

In the late Shang, the so-called white pottery was made of kaolin clay and was fired at about 1000°C. White pottery pieces bore refined and regular carved designs on the surface and were probably used and owned by the wealthiest nobles, including the royalty.

Throughout the Shang period, pottery workshops occupied a sizable area in habitation sites. Often, several kilns were clustered together and adjoining buildings were pottery workshops. At Cheng-chou, excavated clay fragments suggest that a limited range of vessels were made. Such a concentration of types can only be interpreted as a consequence of professional specialization. It is still to be determined, however, if distribution was governed by a marketing mechanism.[52]

SHANG ARCHITECTURE AND CITIES

Shang architecture may be studied in the few Shang cities that have been excavated. Cheng-chou flourished about thirty-five centuries ago, and, after several seasons of excavation, we know that the center was surrounded by a wall of pounded earth, which measured about seven kilometers on each of four sides. This wall was built in courses, in the same manner used today in China. In ancient times, however, high, upright walls could not be constructed without sloping sides to provide support. It is estimated that these walls at Cheng-chou consisted of 870,000 cubic meters of stamped earth, a capacity forty times that used in the Erh-li-t'ou palace construction. The job would have required thirteen million working days to complete. With ten thousand laborers

52. Pei-ching ta-hsüeh, Department of History, 1979:48–50.

working in the field, it would have taken four years to complete the city wall! Organization of supplies and workers was complex and must have tested the rulers' ability to control resources. Inside the walls of the city were numerous other ruins, including stamped-earth platforms and foundations of other buildings. In the northeast section, platforms, presumably of palaces, were densely distributed, and massive quantities of jade fragments were found. Near the walled cities were sites of bronze, pottery, and bone workshops; farther away were agricultural settlements. The presence of industries and agriculture in the vicinity of the royal capital attests to its self-sufficiency as well as to job differentiation closely related to the phenomenon of urbanization.[53]

The P'an-lung-ch'eng 盤龍城 site in Hupei represents another type of early Shang city. The ruins of this southern city still stand above ground —a rough square of 290 meters along the north-south axis and 260 meters along the east-west. The walls were of stamped earth comparable in construction to those at Cheng-chou. Ruins of large palaces (fig. 1.3) were found there on the northeast highland, again similar in location and construction to those in the northern site. Outside the walls of the city were foundations of smaller houses. P'an-lung was only one-twenty-fifth the size of Cheng-chou, but the physical layout and the structure of the city walls were virtually identical. These Shang cities were primarily political and military centers, a character that Chinese cities maintained throughout history.[54]

An-yang, the first of the Shang cities to be excavated, covered an area of more than twenty-four square kilometers. The Huan River 洹水 cut through the site separating the palace area in the south (Hsiao-t'un 小屯) and the mortuary section (Hsi-pei-kang 西北崗) to the north. The remains at Hsiao-t'un were densest at the center, and the amount of occupation debris decreased farther from there. Settlements of common people as well as burial grounds dot the space between Hsiao-t'un and Hsi-pei-kang. Workshops, although numerous, do not form an area that can be called the "industrial zone." The most modest settlements probably were residences of workers.[55]

The Hsiao-t'un district can be divided into three sections. In the north (known as Assembly A) there are fifteen large stamped-earth platforms that were the foundations of large buildings. In the center (Assembly B), there are twenty-one large houses forming rows oriented north-south. Under each structure were several, ancient drainage ditches. Between Assemblies A and B, one square foundation seemed to form some kind

53. Ho-nan sheng po-wu-kuan et al., 1977.
54. Hu-pei sheng po-wu-kuan, 1976.
55. K'ao-ku yen-chiu-so, An-yang fa-chüeh-tui, 1961.

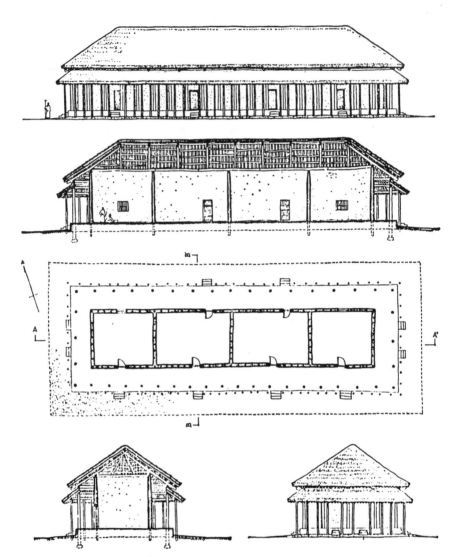

1.3 Restoration of Shang palace at P'an-lung-ch'eng (from Hu-pei sheng po-wu-kuan, 1976:23)

of altar. In the southwest (Assembly C) there are seventeen neatly aligned stamped-earth foundations. Most experts surmise that the platforms in Assembly A were royal palaces, those in B were ancestral temples, and in C they were ceremonial centers. Ordinary people resided either in semi-subterranean pit dwellings or in houses at ground level.[56] Strangely, no city wall has been discovered at An-yang, but a large trench, seven to twenty-one meters in width and five to ten meters in depth, ran from the southwest to the northeast. This trench must have been a defense structure substituting for a city wall.[57]

In the Hsi-pei-kang mortuary areas, there are eleven mausolea and 1,232 small tombs. Settlements and workshops were dotted here and there among the grave sites. It would probably have taken more than seven thousand working days to dig and remove the earth for each large mausoleum, since each consists of four long ramps leading into a chamber ten meters deep. Bodies of sacrificed victims, both those forced to death and others who chose to accompany their leaders, were scattered inside and outside the graves. Rows of pits set in neat order are graves of the royal armed guards, placed in squad formation.[58] The concentration of mausolea and the spectacular scale of these burial grounds have led some to speculate that this Shang city was primarily a mortuary center.[59] Although this is an interesting suggestion, no proof has confirmed it. The features of these Shang cities foretell the disposition of Chinese cities in later centuries, with political, military, and ceremonial functions emphasized over commercial activities.

The Shang palace and temple buildings were constructed symmetrically along a north-south axis. They were covered with double, thatched roofs, which in turn were supported by rows of pillars standing on a large pounded-earth platform raised several steps above the courtyard.[60] In the middle Shang site at Cheng-chou, rows of pillars stood on stone bases. The palace at P'an-lung included four rooms surrounded by hallways and covered by a double roof. Although one-tenth the size of the Cheng-chou palace, this house and its attendant buildings filled only the northeastern section of the city. Three platforms were perfectly aligned along the direction of the city wall. These basic patterns are similar to those governing the layout at An-yang. The construction of the cities followed requisite steps. First the platforms were formed and then the pillar bases were set to mark the center columns and the side supports for the eaves. Such procedures were

56. Shih Chang-ju, 1959; Chang, 1976:50.
57. K'ao-ku yen-chiu-so, An-yang fa-chüeh-tui, 1961.
58. Li, 1976:82−94.
59. Miyazaki Ichisada, 1970.
60. Shih Chang-ju, 1970, 1976.

followed in palace construction during the Western Chou. The symmetrical layout of the Erh-li-t'ou courtyard more closely resembles the Western Chou type than that of the Shang. Shang technology was learned by the Chou, whereas the Chou preferred a Hsia style of layout.[61]

SHANG STATE ORGANIZATION

Rudiments of the political organization in the early dynastic period may be deduced from the archaeological data at the Erh-li-t'ou site and from other sources. As reported in the literature, Hsia kingship had evolved into a father-to-son succession to the throne. Other than this meager bit of related evidence, little can be speculated about the political institutions of the early Shang period except what can be reconstructed from information contained on oracle bones and from scattered references in classical literature. It is conventionally believed that the succession of kings in the Shang was patrilineal as well as fraternal. Chang Kwang-chih proposed that there was a rotation system in which kingship passed among members of ten segments of the Shang ruling class, of which three dominated the majority of shares of the throne. These segments also figured importantly in marriage alliances. If Chang's proposition is true, Shang state institutions were also heavily reliant on the kinship system.[62] If the kinship groups other than the kings were more powerful and more visible than the political authority of the state, such a phenomenon has not been verified by inscriptional evidence.

The location of the Shang capital shifted frequently during the early dynasty. After P'an Keng moved the location to An-yang (*ca.* 1300 B.C.), the Shang kings ruled from there to the very end of the dynasty, thus providing physical stability for the state. Although no definitive conclusion can be reached yet about the rule of succession of Shang kings, evidence that there were cycles of services for the spirits of deceased kings and queens does confirm the existence of a concept of main-stem lineage. There is little evidence to suggest a system of primogeniture comparable to the *tsung-fa* 宗法 system of the Chou, but the notion of inherited succession to the throne belongs to both the Shang and the Chou, even if the specifics of the lineal rotation varied.[63]

The center of late Shang activity was at the "Great City Shang," but how this "great city" functioned is much disputed.[64] "Shang" simply

61. Pei-ching ta-hsüeh, Department of History, 1979:64–69.
62. Chang, 1980:175–78. Chang Kwang-chih, 1963.
63. Wang Kuo-wei, 1959:451–59.
64. Chang, 1980:211–14.

referred to the homeland of the Shang people, for the capital moved frequently with changes in kingship until it was finally settled at An-yang. The area around the capital was called the *nei-fu* 內服, or inner territory. Li Hsüeh-ch'in 李學勤 identified the geographic names mentioned in the oracle bone inscriptions that told where the royal household held various activities. The royal domain was located, according to Li, in the lower Yellow River Valley: in the area northeast of the Ch'in River, east of the T'ai-hang Mountains, north of the Shang-ch'iu 商丘, and west of Ch'ü-fu 曲阜. The "external territory," or *wai-fu* 外服, mentioned in the *Book of Documents* (*Shu-ching* 書經) consisted of enfeoffed domains under the control of Shang vassals. Li Hsüeh-ch'in claimed that at the time of Wu Ting 武丁, who reigned in the early thirteenth century B.C., the area under Shang control extended into central and southern Shansi to the border of Shansi beyond the Yellow River. The extent of the Shang domain fluctuated from time to time, but the farthest point west was likely in the Wei River valley. To the south, the domain extended at least to the Han River valley, where P'an-lung-ch'eng was recently discovered and excavated. The northernmost limit is not yet determined.[65]

Beyond the external territories were the domains of other states, some of which were friendly or even subordinated to the Shang, while others were independent or even hostile. Conflict as well as peaceful interactions between the Shang and these neighboring states were commonly reported in the oracle bone inscriptions. Disturbances were recorded in the states in southern Shansi, located to the west of the Shang domain. Most of the military confrontations occurred in response to intrusions into border towns and resulted in few casualties. The conflict with the Kuei-fang 鬼方, however, was larger in scale, for the forces raised to fight them numbered in the thousands. The *Book of Changes* (*I-ching* 易經) registered wars with the Kuei-fang that lasted for three years. Wang Kuo-wei identified the Kuei-fang as the pre-decessors of the northern nomads, and if he is correct, the conflict was a confrontation between farmers and nomads, a theme constantly repeated throughout Chinese history. Generally speaking, there was no strong southern challenge to Shang domination, but conflicts took place both in the north and the west.[66]

People who resided to the west of the Shang were collectively called the "Ch'iang" 羌 in the Shang records, among them was a western state that frequently collided with the Shang. Thousands were recruited to participate in battles against them, and Ch'iang captives were often sacrificed in rituals. In fact, most of the human sacrifices mentioned in

65. Li Hsüeh-ch'in, 1959:37–60, 95–98.
66. Ibid., 61–76.

the oracle records seem to be Ch'iang captives. Some were organized into special military units, probably units entrusted with the job of raising horses. In one particular oracle record, two state-chiefs were sacrificed. Allied forces of the Ch'iang 羌 and the Lung 龍 are described in collective terms ("three-fang" 三方, "four-fang" 四方, etc.) implying that the Ch'iang were organized into several states. The Ch'iang did not create as much trouble as the Kuei-fang. Ch'iang captives were enslaved by the Shang and were put to work in the fields, but no Kuei-fang slaves are mentioned.

The states to the east and south of the Shang are not often mentioned in the oracle records. An exception is Jen-fang, a large state on the east coast, with whom the Shang were engaged in full-scale combat. People in that region finally joined the Shang against the Chou in the early days of the new dynasty.

The Shang gradually expanded into the east and the west. The Shang city at P'an-lung-ch'eng was a southern Shang outpost. The Shang state incorporated the area of the modern provinces of Honan and some parts of Hopei, Shantung, and Anhui. Its boundaries in the east and the south are somewhat unclear, for rivers, lakes, and hills prevented the rise of large states that could strongly resist Shang expansion.[67]

In quite a few archaeological sites in the southern Yangtze Valley, Shang cultural influence may be noticed. The Wu-ch'eng 吳城 cultures distributed in the northern sections of Honan and Kiangsu bear strong Shang characteristics. The Hu-shou 湖熟 people lived along the Yangtze in Kiangsu and Anhui and were a bronze-producing culture emerging from the southern Painted Pottery culture. Nevertheless, this culture too was influenced by the Shang.[68] In summary, the Shang influence in the east and south took place in the form of cultural expansion, while in the west and the north, the Shang state competed against other political entities, including nomadic states.

State authority during this period evolved into an increasingly more complex form. By the late Shang dynasty, government organization was complex. The Shang king originally was a political-military leader, while sorcerer-scribe figures took the role of religious leadership. By the end of the dynasty, however, the stature of the king had changed: all state affairs were managed under his name, and deceased kings were thought to be associated with various deities.[69] In addition, the mechanics of governmental organization had changed. The *hsiao-ch'en* 小臣, or minor attendants, who originally were household servants, had become very

67. Chang, 1977:218.
68. Pei-ching ta-hsüeh, Department of History, 1979:136–43.
69. Ch'en Meng-chia, 1956A:202, 365, 580–81.

powerful courtiers by the late Shang. The terms "wife-*x*" and member of "numerous Tzu 子 clans" were associated with Shang leaders. Authority, however, was rather diffused, as we see from oracle bone inscriptions of the last period that mention departments of government and officials whose function was supervisory. The organization of spiritual government was structured on the secular model—for instance, the Shang god Ti 帝 had a messenger depicted as a phoenix, whose job was that of a supervisor. The government of Ti consisted of five departments, each of which had jurisdiction over a particular category of behavior. Human government paralleled its spiritual counterpart, or vice versa.

The military titles mentioned in the oracle record indicate rank (such as lieutenant) as well as function (such as archery, horse tending, and garrison tasks). There was not only a differentiation between the civil and the military but also a transformation of the armed forces from tribal units into specialized military entities.[70] Shang combat units were normally tripartite; infantry and archers were organized into companies of centuria belonging to left, right, or central divisions.[71] Shih Chang-ju 石璋如 has reconstructed the Shang army organization from the remains of soldiers buried near the royal tombs. The burial pattern of chariots and soldiers formed five units, each of which contained five chariots. Each of the chariots was occupied by a driver, an archer, and a soldier with a halberd. The infantry was organized into squads of ten, each under the command of a leader, who was buried in front of them and equipped with more and better arms.[72]

The army was well organized, equipped with bronze halberds, swords, knives, bronze arrowheads, strong composite bows, and chariots drawn by two galloping horses. This armed force must have significantly reinforced the authority of the state. Indeed, in the Shang period, bronze tools and implements were only a small portion of the total bronze manufacture. The larger share of the production was used for weaponry, which assured Shang authority. The Shang achieved a remarkably strong state government, which was developed even further by the Chou.

The Shang dominated the core of the Yellow River Valley, which they had taken over from the Hsia and enlarged and consolidated into a well-organized state. By the advent of the Chou dynasty the role of leadership in China was firm, and there was a solid political mechanism in place to further cultural integration and expansion.

70. Ibid., 277, 508–17; Chin Hsiang-heng, 1974.
71. Ch'en Meng-chia, 1956:513.
72. Shih Chang-ju, 1951.

AGRICULTURE

Remarkable changes in agriculture, especially in cereal crops, were attributed to the Shang in oracle bone inscriptions. The identifiable crops belonged to three groups: millet, wheat-oats, and rice.[73] Two of them, wheat-oats and millet, still constitute the main cereal crops in north China today, and these were the crops most often discussed in the oracle records. The prospect for future crops was the subject of divination in early spring, whereas in the fall the harvest was the topic. The process of farming consisted not only of seed planting, cultivation, and harvest, but also of storage. All four stages are frequently mentioned in inscriptions, and two particular words even suggest the use of organic fertilizer or of some treatment of the soil near the root.[74]

The Shang farmers worked collectively, as the use of the word *chung* 衆 as a form of address for a farmer indicates. For instance, in the oracle inscriptions, it is usual to read: "the King orders the mass to work together in the field."[75] In a late Shang storage pit, 444 stone sickles showing wear were discovered with gold leaves, stone sculpture, bronze ritual vessels, and jade artifacts. Such precious items would be found neither in the storage pit of an ordinary farmer nor in a stone workshop. The implements must have been stored there by a master, who could issue them collectively to his workers.[76] These *chung* farmers probably were the commoners who formed the general population of the Shang state. Ordinarily they farmed, but they could be conscripted at any time into the military. The *chung* were members of a kin group (*tsu* 族) who were attached to the aristocrats. When the *chung* worked in the fields, the *hsiao-ch'en* were entrusted to supervise them.[77]

Although the level of farming was more advanced in the Shang period than it was in the neolithic, preserving the land's fertility after continued use of the same fields was difficult. *Pou-t'ien* 裒田 was a term probably used to describe reclamation of new fields, a process essential for shifting-field farming. In this activity, collective use of labor was more effective than individual efforts. Chang Cheng-lang 張政烺 claims that *pou-t'ien* was initiated near the summer solstice, when grass and woods were burned, or during the cold days around winter solstice, when trees were debarked. The Shang farmers, using only stone implements, cleared large areas of wooded land. They then prepared the fields by burning or flooding the residue in order to return decomposed material

---

73. Yü Sheng-wu, 1957; Chang Ping-ch'üan, 1970.
74. Ch'en Meng-chia, 1956:532–38; Ch'en Liang-tso, 1971.
75. Ch'en Meng-chia, 1956:537.
76. Tsou Heng, 1980:89.
77. Hsiao P'an, 1981; Chang, 1980:225–27; Chang Cheng-lang, 1973.

to the soil. In this manner, the fields actually were fertilized. The third step involved ground-dressing, where ridges and ditches were formed on rows for planting. These three steps were described in the *Book of Poetry*: (1) *tzu* 菑, fields newly cleared; (2) *yü* 畬, fields readied for planting; (3) *hsin* 新, new fields readied for growing.[78]

Pou-t'ien probably evolved from the neolithic slash-and-burn technique of farming. In rudimentary form, some fields could have been put to use at the end of the second stage. After the third phase, a well-prepared field would accommodate more refined agriculture. Without elaborate irrigation and use of fertilizers, features not fully developed until the Eastern Chou period, the fertility of well-prepared new fields soon would be exhausted. Some system that allowed fields to lie fallow was necessary. *Pou-t'ien*, therefore, might have developed not only as a means to claim virgin land but also to prepare fields that had lain fallow for an extensive period.

Activities included in *pou-t'ien* were sometimes mentioned as team projects conducted in other states. Chang Cheng-lang suggested that reclaimed fields were observed in a foreign land.[79] Furthermore, it is possible that Shang established agricultural colonies that were protected by the armed forces. The leaders of the *pou-t'ien* teams often bore military titles.[80] If this was the case, the Shang people had already created the institution of military colonies known in later Chinese history as *t'un-t'ien* 屯田.

Pou-t'ien was carried out by farmers organized according to kin groups and led by royal kinsmen and other aristocrats, including the king. In Shang domains, farming communities were often scattered in or near the city, located next to buildings used by the nobility. It is likely that the farmers and their rulers were distributed on land collectively reclaimed by the *pou-t'ien* system.

Shang farming implements were made of stone, bone, and seashells; very few bronze objects were in use except in ritual. Flat spades made of bone, stone, or shell were quite useful for digging and loosening the sod. A kind of digging stick with a double prong was the most common tool in use from the Lungshan period forward. Its imprint has been found on the surface of walls of Shang dwelling pits and storage pits. Stone and shell sickles were the principal harvest tools introduced by the Shang late in the period, replacing the rectangular knife.[81]

78. Chang Cheng-lang, 1973:98–102; Ho Ping-ti regards such a system as already developed in Yangshao neolithic. Ho, 1975:51–52. Ho's supposition, however, is yet to be substantiated.
79. Chang Cheng-lang, 1973:107–08.
80. Ibid., 109–10.
81. Pei-ching ta-hsüeh, Department of History, 1979:38–39.

The advancement of Shang agriculture was a consequence of better organization and more effective methods, rather than of improvements in tools. Although bronze was available, it was not used to make farming implements. The rise of the state was the condition that led to improvements in organization and efficiency, which in turn affected all activities under state purview. The staples were millet and wheat-oats, the native crops of the north. Rice cropping, learned through interchange with the south, diversified the repertoire of plants available. Successful cropping was necessary for the maintenance of the state.

THE SHANG WRITING SYSTEM

Whether the marks that frequently appear on neolithic pottery should be regarded as writing is in dispute. The graphs that embellish the late Ta-wen-k'ou pottery, however, are definitely ideographs. First, the disposition of strokes that form them meets the general principles of Chinese character formation. Second, identical signs were found on pottery at distant sites, suggesting that a conventional symbol system was accepted. A writing system related to that of the Shang oracle bone script may have existed during the late Ta-wen-k'ou period, but actual evidence of it is lacking.[82]

The system used on Shang oracle bones was adapted to serve the particular function of writing on bone or shell. There must have been another script used for record keeping and general communication. The writing on Shang bronzes, on the other hand, was in a formal script that was first inscribed on the mold. The numbers of Shang bronze inscriptions are too few to allow for meaningful analysis, but the principles of character formation can be derived from study of their relatives in the oracle bone inscriptions. T'ang Lan 唐蘭 grouped Shang characters into three categories: simple pictographs, abstract descriptive pictographs, and phono-pictographs. Ch'en Meng-chia thought that the latter two categories actually evolved from the simple rendering of visual impressions. The objects described, however, were often represented by a shorthand. For instance, the head of the ox stood for the entire animal. Small dots symbolized a small quantity of something —sand, blood drops, and so on. An indexical strike or dot was placed at a given spot for emphasis. For example, a dot on the side of a knife pictograph indicated the cutting edge. Combinations of parts of two pictures formed the idea of another phenomenon—two tree signs standing for woods, for example, Finally, deviations from the concrete to the abstract were served by the principle of "loaning"—the sign of a

---

82. Shan-tung ta-hsüeh, Department of History, 1979:1–28.

solar disc meant sun, as well as day and date.[83] These basic principles
have continued to guide the process of character formation throughout
Chinese history.

Contrast between the oracle bone inscriptions and the Chou bronze
inscriptions points out the line of that development. First, few new
pictograms were created by the Chou, suggesting that the writing system was already settled by the Shang. Simplification of complicated
characters was evident in many examples, but this was a process of
refinement, not of invention. And in the reverse, the Chou elaborated
or embellished pictograms. Second, certain Shang signs had been
adopted as *pu-shou* 部首, or radicals, which were indicators of categories
of meaning. More of these indicators can be found in Shang inscriptions
than in inscriptions of the Chou, where the already conventionalized
forms were used. Third, the few new indicators developed by the Chou
were often ones with abstract connotations. For instance, the sign for
"heart" prefixed a whole group of words indicating emotion, sentiment,
or intelligence. Fourth, phono-pictographs and "loan characters"
appeared more commonly in the Chou writing system. Fifth, final
particles, used at the end of sentences or clauses, were introduced.

These five innovations in the Chou writing system may be regarded
as the end product of conventionalization, developed in part to adapt to
the spatial and temporal needs of a written communication system.
Speakers of a distinctive local dialect could use the phonetic compounds.
Also, the increase in the complexity of daily life demanded new words
to accommodate new concepts.[84]

In summary, the Shang writing system established the basic patterns
of Chinese written script. Since the Shang state dominated north China,
this system was used by their contemporaries as the standard. Although
other written signs have been found, for instance at the Hsia-chia-tien
sites in the north and at Wu-ch'eng in the south, those systems were not
long lived. Sentences on the oracle bones were syntactically organized in
a straightforward subject-verb-object order, as in Chinese today.[85]
Although there were numerous local dialects in China, as the cultural
influence of Shang spread, their language became the ancient *lingua
franca*.

SUMMARY

Several neolithic traditions developed simultaneously in China in the
third millennium B.C. They interacted with each other when geography

83. Ch'en Meng-chia, 1956:75–80.
84. Ibid., 80.
85. Ibid., 132–134.

did not block contact. Interaction caused stimulation, enriched the content of life, and also made fusion necessary and inevitable. The competition and stimulation between the communities created conditions from which emerged an organized political entity, the state. With this evolution, China stepped into civilization. This development first was noticeable in the Hsia, for the Hsia state possessed organizational power much greater than that of the village. The succession from the Hsia leadership to the Shang increased the amount of land under the control of the central unit until the Shang controlled much of the central plain.

The organizational potential of the state gave rise to bronze production and urbanization, both of which required the mobilization of human and natural resources. Bronze, when used to make weapons, allowed the utilization of resources to buttress the power of the state. Therefore, even stronger controls developed through bureaucratization and through adoption of unified symbols of authority and communication, for instance, a "state" art and a state writing system. Advancements in agriculture brought a surplus of food, one due to increased efficiency resulting from clever organization of workers, rather than from invention of new tools. Large numbers of workers were mobilized to increase the capacity of the land through reclamation.

Both northern and southern crops were cultivated by the Shang, as a consequence of cultural and commercial exchange between the regions. Shang architecture combined the use of stamped earth, a northern tradition, and wooden superstructures, in the style of the south. The Shang writing system, which had its origins in the Ta-wen-k'ou script, in use to the east of the Shang lands, was the foundation for all later written Chinese. It was these conditions and models that the Chou inherited and elaborated to shape the basic patterns of Chinese civilization during the first millennium B.C.

2   The Chou before the Conquest

By the time of the conquest, the Chou were a considerable force in north China. Operating from their base in the Wei River Valley, they already had a history as a nation. Traditional literature claims that their founder's lineage was both divine and actual. Hou Chi 后稷, an associate of the founder of the Hsia, was an agriculturalist. The group's life-style was not completely sedentary, for at several points in the pre-dynastic period they were forced to move their home base, and migration became an important pattern in the formation of their culture. Constant interaction with non-Chou peoples forced cooperation, assimilation, and toleration of other groups in order for the Chou to survive.

By reinterpreting ancient literature in light of the archaeological record, we can now reconstruct the route followed by the proto-Chou. We now know that the Chou culture was formed through involvement with many peoples—the Kuang-she 光社, the steppe dwellers, the Shensi Lungshan 陝西龍山, the Ch'iang 羌, and probably others. The Chou were not an isolated group, but one with an assimilative character. Such a group, found in the dynamic circumstances of the late second millennium B.C. had the opportunity to accumulate and absorb cultural as well as territorial assets.

THE LEGEND OF THE CHOU

The legendary founder of the Chou, Hou Chi, was thought to have come from divine descent and to have held the position of assistant to the Great Yü, the founder of the Hsia dynasty. To the Chou such a lineage was surely auspicious, for they thought of the legend as an account of their actual historical past. Whether Hou Chi was an historical figure or not, his name was tied to legends that recount tales of developing agriculture, and the Chou regarded his ancestry as the record of their clan origin and the impetus for their development. This chapter deals both with history as the Chou saw it and with their past as modern archaeology understands it.

33

The best-known account of the origins of the Chou is found in the ancient text, the *Shih-chi* 史記 (*The Historical Record*), by the Han historian Ssu-ma Ch'ien 司馬遷. The tales therein reveal the principal cast of characters, their familial relationships, and an account of the interaction of the Chou with other groups. In addition, the path the Chou followed before settling their clan in the Wei River Valley is described. Study of these tales yields insight into the actual identity of the Chou and the character of their life.

An initial reading of the *Shih-chi* tells us about the life-style of the Chou and their migration. The text claims that Pu K'u 不窋, the son of Hou Chi, deserted the camp of his father and the Office of Agriculture (*Chi*稷) to live among the "barbarians." Here the term *Chi* (literally, millet) is used to indicate the office in charge of agriculture. That position had previously been held by Hou Chi, who was also known as the Lord of Millet. Although the text connects these Pu K'u and Hou Chi through references to agriculture, their actual relationship has long been disputed. Ssu-ma Ch'ien is thought to have confused their genealogy and thus perpetuated a story of mistaken lineage.[1] In fact, the name Hou Chi may not be the title of an office but simply an indication that the Chou were people who farmed millet. Moreover, the phrase "deserting the work of Chi" may indicate that Pu K'u abandoned farming and led his people to live the life of the "barbarians," that is, of pastoral nomadism. Subsequently, the *Shih-chi* records, the Chou resumed the work of Hou Chi, presumably returning to a settled agricultural life. The text attributes the resumption of farming to the son of Pu K'u, named Kung Liu 公劉.[2] But could such a radical change in life-style have taken place in merely two generations? Moreover, can the route of the Chou migrations be recovered? Is it possible to associate these episodes with known events and places?

The succession of leaders from Kung Liu to King Wen 文王 (see appendix), the first named "king" among the Chou, includes fourteen generations. If each generation is assigned a period of thirty years, the span from Kung Liu to King Wen is over four hundred years. Further, if the Chou leader named Tan Fu 亶父 was a contemporary of King Wu I 武乙 of the Shang, as recorded in the ancient tradition of the *Chu-shu chi-nien*竹書紀年, and there were eleven generations between Kung Liu and Tan Fu, the time of Kung Liu would just precede the establishment of the Shang capital at Yin 殷, or An-yang 安陽.[3] The establishment of the last capital of the Shang was the accomplishment of King P'an Keng

1. *Shih-chi*, 4/4; Hu Ch'eng-kung, 1888:24/33.
2. Ibid.
3. See Ch'en Meng-chia, 1956A:292; and *Shih-chi*, 3/19–25.

盤庚, and this moment corresponds with the Chou leadership of Kung Liu. The long period preceding the establishment of the Shang capital at An-yang was one in which the Shang kings moved the seat of their court frequently, as many as seven or eight times.[4] Movement of the Shang leaders must have allowed the Chou people the freedom to develop on their own, outside the surveillance of their stronger neighbor. The Chou distinguished themselves, therefore, as a separate culture, but one that benefited from knowledge of Shang accomplishments. The nature of that interchange will be discussed in the following section of this chapter.[5]

The semi-legendary record of the Chou points out three salient features of pre-dynastic Chou life: (1) The Chou were a farming people at the time of Hou Chi and the establishment of their collective identity, (2) Pu K'u led them to a nonfarming, or "barbarian," existence, and (3) with Kung Liu, the Chou resumed an agricultural way of life. The Chou were not the earliest farmers in China, for neolithic communities that are more than seven thousand years old have been sited in north China.[6] What is significant in the *Shih-chi* account is that the Chou established a political and social entity under Hou Chi coincident with the adoption of agriculture and a sedentary life-style. Moreover, they traced their historic heritage to the period of Hsia prominence, the third millennium B.C. When this sedentary way of life was altered under the direction of Pu K'u, the Chou must have moved outside the known sphere of Chinese cultivation. This temporary shift in location must have taken them to a marginal zone where agriculture was not practiced consistently. From there they migrated to the Wei River Valley, the region traditionally thought of as their homeland.

Chinese scholars have long searched for the precise locations of Chou settlements prior to and during their occupation of the Wei Valley. Archaeological data have been consulted as a means to verify the ancient texts. Conventionally, Hou Chi's home was located at Wu-kung 武功, Kung Liu's base at San-shui 三水, and Tan Fu's settlement at Ch'i-shan 岐山. All these sites are located in the valleys of the Ching and Wei 渭 rivers in a small region in western Shensi.[7] (See map 3.) Archaeologists followed the lead of the textual scholars and sought to find the actual remains at those locations. Consensus among them suggests that the earliest sites are in the upper reaches of the central Wei

4. For a review of this issue, see Chang, 1980:4–6.
5. The chronology of the Shang kings is not agreed upon among Shang scholars. See Ch'en Meng-chia, 1956A:208–16, for a review of those references.
6. For a review of neolithic farming, see Chang, 1977:80–143.
7. Ting Shan, 1935; Ch'i Ssu-ho, 1946.

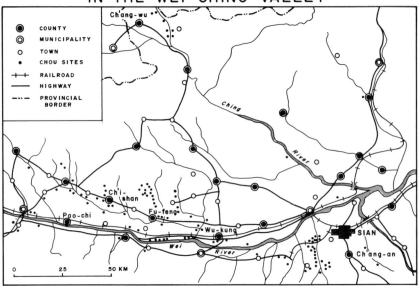

3. Distribution of pre-dynastic Chou sites in the Wei-Ching Valley

Valley. The move away from there took the group to the central Ching Valley and then finally back to the Wei.[8]

Another hypothesis, presented by Ch'ien Mu 錢穆, claims that the oldest home of the Chou is to be found in the south of the present province of Shansi.[9] He argued that because the names Pin 豳 and Ching 涇 were associated with activities of the Chou, they must be, in fact, the same as the sites Pin and Ching near the Fen 汾 River in Shansi (map 1.) He also argued that Tan Fu became known as the Duke of Ku 古 because he was associated with a place-name, presumably that of his home.[10] Ku is the name of a tributary of the Fen River, and thence Ch'ien Mu located the activities of Tan Fu in Shansi. In addition, in the Han period, there were still places near the Fen that used the title "Chi." What is more, even the character "*Chou*" could be found in use there. Ch'ien Mu also suggested that the presence of numerous fountains and springs in southern Shansi, especially in the country of Wan-ch'üan 萬泉,

8. Shih Chang-ju, 1954A:357–76.
9. Ch'ien Mu, 1931; Ch'i Ssu-ho, 1946, restated the conventional argument above in refutation of Ch'ien Mu's claim.
10. See the discussion of place-names and lineage in Chang, 1964:45–61.

recalled the landscape described in the poem "Kung-liu." The mountains named Liang-shan 梁山, which were supposedly crossed by Tan Fu as he retreated from the Hsün-yü 獯育, must certainly be the Liang-shan range in the northwest of Han-ch'eng 韓城 County on the west bank of the Yellow River. Ch'ien Mu, therefore, proposed that during the leadership of Kung Liu, the Chou lived in the area near the Shu 涑 River, east of the Yellow River, south of the Fen, and west of the salt pond called Hsieh-ch'ih 解池.

The occupation of the Ching-Wei valleys by the Chou at various times and in different locations is certain. Each move and each contact with other peoples must have brought knowledge of life that was comparable but distinct from their own. Both borrowing and reestablishing of known customs characterized the process of change at that time. Is it not possible then that place-names, too, were borrowed?[11]

PROTO-CHOU IN ARCHAEOLOGY

Investigation of archaeological information, independent of textual materials, avoids the methodological tangles so prevalent in philological studies of place-names. Such testimony may, of course, bear out the accounts of the ancients, but it also addresses the following questions. Where is there evidence of Chou occupation? Can the materials from excavation suggest an order for their migration? And, an even more fundamental question, how can we identify the Chou and thereby locate their presence in the archaeological record?

Study of the Chou homeland, the Wei River Valley, raises several critical issues. The Wei Valley of Shensi and eastern Kansu has yielded neolithic materials of the Shensi Lungshan type. It is directly over those levels that the Western Chou evidence rests. What, then, is the relationship between the two? Both the distribution of sites and the sequence of materials in the excavations allow us to assume that the Shensi Lungshan and the Chou were directly linked.[12] But how can the abruptness of the change of materials be explained? Although the cultures are associated through proximity, the nature of the transition is yet to be understood.[13] For instance, certain geometric marks and the low relief banding common on Shensi Lungshan pottery are absent on the Western Chou examples. Missing as well are the *ku*, the *kuei*, the *tseng* steamers, and the two-handled pots in the Chou assemblages.

11. Ch'ien Mu's proposal has met opposition from Ch'i Ssu-ho, 1946; cf. Průšek, 1971:25; Ch'en Meng-chia, 1956:292; and Chang, 1980:249−50.

12. Hsü Cho-yün, 1968.

13. Chang Chung-p'ei, 1980.

Shared in both strata, however, is the pottery *li*. In general, though, the morphology, ornamentation, and manufacturing techniques of the Chou clay pots are distinctive. Therefore, study of materials from excavations suggests that abrupt change took place between Lungshan and Chou and that the Chou were newcomers who quickly superseded the native Lungshan dwellers.[14] Where and how, then, did the Chou culture develop?

Some scholars suspect that the Chou become recognizable only after absorbing features of the Ch'i-chia 齊家 culture, known especially in Kansu. The immediate suppression of the Shensi Lungshan by the Chou must be interpreted as a direct succession, regardless of the impetus for change.[15] One need not accept that proposal fully to claim that the Chou borrowed from their western neighbors, for even in the easternmost regions of the Ch'i-chia the influence of Shensi Lungshan may be detected.[16] The choice of features found on the pottery is endemic to the Chou and thereby testifies to their identity, an identity separate from both the Ch'i-chia and the Shensi Lungshan. Chou pottery may be characterized as gray ware with relatively homogeneous color, wheel marks, angular rims, and clearly defined decorative cord marks confined to the body of the vessels. *Li* tripods with low feet, low collars, and nearly flat bottoms were common, as were basins, *tou*, and single-handled jugs with plain surfaces. In fact, that which we eventually know as the Chou culture was probably born out of the intersection of all three culture bases, and perhaps others as well.

Such a thesis has been presented by Tsou Heng 鄒衡. He suggested that the early phase of the pre-dynastic Chou period be named proto-Chou, and that that culture be seen as a conglomerate of several others. Tsou studied several types of clay *li* 鬲 tripods found in Shensi and used them as an index for periodization of the proto-Chou and early dynastic Chou phases (fig. 2.1). He designated four sequential periods: (1) those dated between Shang King Lin Hsin 廩辛 and King Ti I 帝乙 and Ti Hsin 帝辛; (2) those not earlier than Ti I and Ti Hsin; (3) ones not later than King Mu 穆 of Chou; (4) ones of the fourth period (and some of those from the third) roughly contemporaneous with Chou burials at Feng-hsi 灃西, near Hsi-an 西安.[17] The *li* of the first two periods are, therefore, proto-Chou in date. The stratigraphy of sites at Ma-wang-ts'un 馬王村 in Feng-hsi bears out the pre-dynastic date suggested by Tsou for the pottery *li*. Chou remains at Feng-hsi were few in the earliest levels, or Tsou's Period One; the numbers increased slightly in the next level,

14. Pei-ching ta-hsüeh, Department of History, 1979:144.
15. Hsü Hsi-t'ai, 1979.
16. Hsieh Tuan-chü, 1979.
17. Tsou Heng, 1980:314.

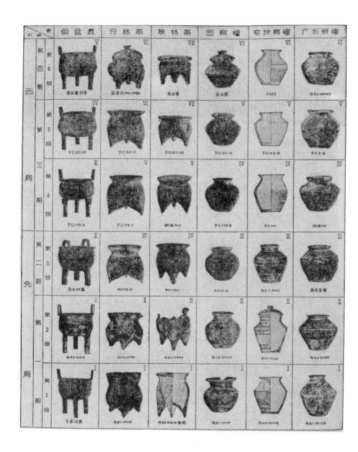

2.1 Proto-Chou
and Western
Chou pottery
types (from Tsou
Heng, 1980:304)

Period Two; then they dramatically increased in the upper levels. The sudden increase in quantity of Chou style remains in Period Three corresponds with the demise of the Shang. The dynamic Chou clan focused its attention at Feng-hsi, apparently when it became the western center of power.[18] That this transition takes place in Period Three is attested in excavations at Feng-hsi. During that time the Chou developed an identity of their own and eventually also saw themselves as politically separate from the Shang. They brought to the Wei Valley a momentum that allowed them to make that area their power base. Was that energy brought forth in response to interference from the Shang, or something else?

Distribution of proto-Chou sites in the Ching-Wei valleys is wide (map 3). They are found in the present counties of Pao-chi 寶雞, Feng-hsiang 鳳翔, Ch'i-shan 岐山, Fu-feng 扶風, Mei-hsien 郿縣. Wu-kung 武功,

18. Ibid., 297–315.

Hsing-p'ing 興平, Hu-hsien 鄠縣, Chou-chih 盩屋, Ch'ang-an 長安, Pin-hsien 邠縣, Ch'ang-wu 長武, Lin-yu 麟游, Ch'ien-hsien 乾縣, Yao-hsien 耀縣, Ching-hsien 涇縣, Hsien-yang 咸陽, and many other smaller localities.[19] The highest density of sites is found in three locations. One cluster is at Feng-hao near Ch'ang-an; another is near Fu-feng and Ch'i-shan; and the other is near Ch'ang-wu (see map 4). The most typical proto-Chou pots are found at these larger sites. The oldest artifacts are found at the northernmost site of the group, at Ch'ang-wu. The early date is suggested by the types of objects, decorative motifs and clay materials found at Hsia-meng-ts'un 下孟村, Ch'ang-wu. The pottery found at the other sites, at Ch'i-shan and Ch'ang-an, exhibits borrowed features common on Shang bronzes. These are typical motifs such as the circle or square spirals so recognizably Shang. The Ch'ang-wu pottery is decorated with simple squares.[20] A recent study of the evolution of the *li* confirmed the early date for Chou materials in the upper Ching

19. Ibid., 315; Hsü Hsi-t'ai, 1979:50.
20. Hsü Hsi-t'ai, 1979:57–58.

DISTRIBUTION OF CHOU SITES AT FU-FENG AND CH'I-SHAN

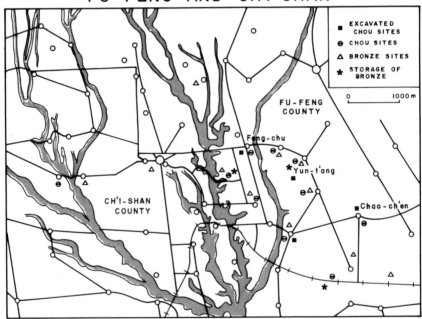

4. Distribution of Chou sites at Fu-feng and Ch'i-shan

Valley.[21] Ch'ang-wu is located in that valley on the upper reaches of the Ching, far from the center of Chou occupation of later days. Interestingly, that valley is a place where Tan Fu once took residence, according to legend. This archaeologically determined chronology puts the earlier proto-Chou sites in the north, not in the west as argued by most students of the classical texts. This provides an important clue when tracing the earlier Chou migrations.

THE RELATIONSHIP BETWEEN THE CHOU AND THE SHANG

Contact between the Chou and the Shang can be confirmed from study of many and varied sources.[22] Aspects of pre-dynastic Chou life reflect the widespread influence of late Shang culture, especially as it disseminated bronze-casting technology. Much beyond the political sphere of the Shang kingdom, regional cultures began to use bronze for weapons and other objects, especially those used for ritual purposes. Often the groups that adopted such technology were ones who had had contact with the Shang but were culturally distinct from the civilization centered at the Shang court. It may be that as the Shang authority waned, bronze technology became less easily controlled by them. To arm their allies with bronze weapons was desirable, but knowledge of bronze technology provided independence and power. Such was the case with the Chou as they began to develop bronze use for their own purposes.

Some bronzes found in Chou territory are faithful copies of Shang models, but others adapt metropolitan Shang forms and technology to an expression of very different taste (see fig. 2.2). Some of this second group may be called a mixed Shang-Chou, or provincial, style; others appear to have been invented by the Chou and may be called a local style. Tsou Heng has investigated the decorative motifs, the typologies of these objects and the clan emblems inscribed on the bronzes. He found that most of those of Shang-style examples were cast either in Shensi or in Shansi and therefore in Chou foundries. Others of that style were imported by Shang people at a later date. Those of mixed style were, according to Tsou Heng, a novelty. These are exemplified by spearheads, arrowheads, and halberds. Those bronze types invented by the Chou introduced new shapes and often bore motifs borrowed from proto-Chou clay objects. The unusual cross-shaped weapon called a *kuei* also seems to have been introduced by the Chou.

21. Hu Ch'ien-ying, 1982.

22. Emphasis here will be on what and how the Chou absorbed, incorporated, and assimilated, rather than on recording every bit of evidence.

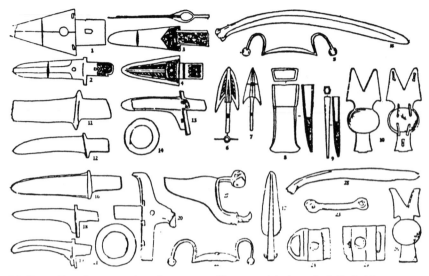

2.2 Proto-Chou bronze tools and weapons—Shang models (nos. 1, 5, 7–9, 13, 16, 18, 22, 24, 25); Shang-Chou mixed types (nos. 2–4, 6, 11, 12, 17, 19); Chou models (nos. 10, 20, 26, 27) (from Tsou Heng, 1980:323)

The greatest number of pre-dynastic Chou bronze objects bear the unmistakable mark of the Shang prototypes. Those of local Chou or of mixed heritage were small in number. According to Tsou Heng, the majority of Chou artifacts were cast in local foundries in which some of the artisans were captives from the Shang and others were Chou workers who had learned founding techniques from the Shang.[23]

Tsou Heng also observed that during the first recognizable period of proto-Chou culture, roughly parallel to the reigns of Shang Lin Hsin to Ti I or Ti Hsin, Shang-style bronzes predominated. Ones of mixed styles were fewer, and the purely Chou materials were primarily weapons and fittings for chariots. During the second period, when the Chou were settled in Ch'i-shan and found themselves a serious threat to the Shang, the number of mixed-style materials increased dramatically, as did purely Chou-style objects. The experimentation that was occurring in the industry reveals a heightened confidence among the artisans as they learned the craft, but also an expanded independence among the patrons. Apparently, as their local power increased, so too did their desire to exhibit an identity distinct from that of the Shang.

Interestingly, the opposite tendency can be noticed in the pottery industry. During the first period, pots bore the unmistakable mark of

23. Tsou Heng, 1980:309–33.

their Chou heritage. But in later periods, more and more foreign features were adopted.[24]

The Chou had become, perhaps, more "international," as both the intermingling of pottery styles and the development of the metal industry imply. The production of bronze, unlike that of ceramics, both afforded the Chou support for their military and enabled a fashionable and well-outfitted aristocratic ritual performance. But what can be said of the actual chronology of contact between the Chou and the Shang, given this evidence? Some materials recovered in the Ching-Wei valleys are comparable to the middle Shang objects from Erh-li-kang 二里頭, Cheng-chou 鄭州, Honan 河南, and suggest contact during the An-yang period. Vessels analogous to ones found in late Shang sites have been excavated at Hsi-an, Lan-t'ien 藍田, Lin-yu 麟游, and Fu-feng. Bronze artifacts resembling those found in Shang sites dating before Wu Ting's 武丁 reign have been discovered in a storage pit at Ching-tang 京當 at Ch'i-shan.[25]

Information on the whereabouts of the Chou is also found in the oracle records of the Shang. When a neighboring statelet impinged on the activities of Shang court, the question of what to do was put to the Shang gods, and sometimes that exchange was recorded on the bones. Recent finds at Ch'i-shan demonstrate that the Shang culture reached the Wei Valley in pre-An-yang times,[26] and that the site was not occupied at that time by the Chou. The first oracle inscriptions that mention the Chou date from the reign of Shang Wu Ting, who reigned in the fourteenth century B.C. Ch'en Meng-chia listed sixteen divinations from that time that mentioned the Chou. Twelve record military action taken against the Chou; that is, several *hou* 侯, or marquises, were ordered to join an expedition that included an agnatic unit of royal kinsmen. Other oracle inscriptions name the Chou in line to receive royal decrees and mention game catches obtained in Chou territory.[27] During this period the Shang frequently found it necessary to subjugate the Chou. The newly developed bronze industry and the increased sense of power it afforded must have created a threat of a magnitude quite noticeable at the Shang court. The Shang found it advantageous both to subdue the Chou by force and to grant their leaders titles in an effort to control them by association. Evidence of other sorts suggests that during the last reigns of the dynasty the Shang were increasingly aware and fearful of their independent-minded neighbors to the west.

24. Ibid., 309–33.
25. Tsou Heng, 1980:333–34.
26. Wen-wu pien-chi wei-yüan-hui, 1979/12:86–87.
27. Ch'en Meng-chia, 1956A:291–92.

King Wu Ting was one of the most colorful of the Shang monarchs. His reign, by historical convention and in the estimation of modern scholars, lasted about fifty years. During this period the Shang frequently interacted with foreigners.[28] They were in conflict with the Ch'iang, and King Wu Ting campaigned in the locale of the Ching, reportedly a land stretching to the west of the Chou. If the Chou were already in the Wei Valley at that time, the expedition would have had to travel as far as Kansu to reach the Ching. Such a lengthy trip is unlikely; it is more probable that the Ch'iang were living in areas much closer to the east, and that the Chou were still living in Shansi near the Yellow River as proposed by Ch'ien Mu (map 2).

Archaeological evidence of proto-Chou culture dates from between the reign of Shang Lin Hsin and the end of the dynasty. The active Shang monarch named Wu I 武乙 reigned in the middle of this period for about thirty-five years.[29] Among his deeds was the move of the Shang capital to Po, a site north of the Yellow River. Further, he daringly challenged the power of a Heavenly God by making a clay statue to symbolize the deity with whom he gambled. As the legend recounts, Wu I had a bag filled with blood hung above the clay surrogate. An archer shot the bag and allowed the blood to drip out, so that Wu I could claim to have shot into Heaven and caused the deity to die. By such a bold action Wu I claimed that he could challenge Heaven directly and that he had the power to overtake it. A declaration of that sort would not have been made by the Chou dynastic leaders, for to them Heaven was omnipotent.[30]

The *Shih-chi* recorded Wu I's death on a hunting expedition in the area between the Yellow and Wei rivers, that is, in Chou territory. Moreover, Wu I had apparently had contact with the Chou prior to his sporting activity. Life of the Chou during and after the reign of Wu I was by no means peaceful. As recorded in Mencius, the Ch'üan-jung 犬戎 were bullying Chou. Tan Fu, the great-grandfather of future King Wen of the Chou, led the Chou across Mount Liang and resettled them at Ch'i.[31] This particular legend was as important to the Chou in later times as the Exodus story was to the Hebrews. Nevertheless, no single leader in history has ever been able to relocate an entire population. A sizable number of the Chou must have stayed behind in Pin. This incident records the period prior to the migration of the Chou people under the leadership of Tan Fu. There is, indeed, a high mountain range

28. Ibid., 269–298.
29. Ibid., 210.
30. See chapter 3 for further discussion of the worship of Heaven by the Chou.
31. Legge, *Menius*, 174–76.

dividing the Ching River and the Ch'i region. The Han commentator Cheng Hsüan 鄭玄 actually recognized that range as Mount Liang and located it in the region bounded by the Ching, the Wei, and the Yellow River in Shensi.[32] The area left behind was in the land called Pin; the new location chosen by Tan Fu was reached after crossing Mount Liang. Further investigation of topography suggests an even more precise location for these sites.

The Wei Valley is level, the soil is fertile, the climate is mild, and there is an ample supply of moisture deposited on the face of the southern mountains. The region was well populated during the neolithic, as evidenced by the abundance of Shensi Lungshan remains there. The proto-Chou people under Tan Fu arrived at this fertile valley as newcomers and would have had to elbow their way into an already crowded lower Wei Valley. They would have met less resistance in the areas a bit north of the upper Ching in the highland between Shansi and Shensi (map 2). Ch'ien Mu proposed that Hou Chi came from the south; from there Pu K'u led them away, and during Kung Liu's leadership, the Chou once again resumed an agricultural life, presumably also in southwest Shansi. The area between the nomad-controlled region in the north and the farming culture in the south, or in the region of the highland north of the Wei River below the semi-arid desert of north Shansi to Shensi, is the logical spot for Kung Liu's occupation. Considered in this way, Ch'ien Mu's proposal has some validity. The Chou people for a few generations preceding Tan Fu were active farmers in the south and west of Shansi. Tan Fu reached the upper Ching Valley and resettled in Ch'i-shan, in the middle reaches of the Wei. Moreover, it is likely that some of the original group stayed in the previously occupied Chou territories of Shansi and Shensi.

Oracle inscriptions refer to the move of the Chou under the leadership of Tan Fu and to the location of their settlement at Ch'i. There they were to have built the city that consequently drove out the Ch'üan-jung, allies of the Shang. At that time the Shang ruler enfeoffed the Chou chieftain, giving him the rank of duke.[33] The Shang were again yielding to a situation in which they apparently had little direct control, for they conferred a title rather than attack and rule by force.

Later historians preserved the names of Chou rulers from this time onward: Tan Fu, Chi Li 季歷, King Wen 文, and King Wu 武, who reigned as the Chou king at the time of the conquest. Tan Fu, the Lord of Chou, was said by Ssu-ma Ch'ien to have "renounced the customs of the barbarians." The *Shih-chi* describes the building of permanent dwell-

---

32. *Shih-chi*, 4/7.
33. Shima Kunio, 1958:406–09.

ings and a walled city for the duke at Ch'i-shan. The passage records that the foundations were of pounded earth, a building technique commonly found at Shang sites. The Chou assimilation of the Shang culture must have been rapid from this time onward. The Shang kings must have become increasingly uneasy about the mounting power of their western neighbor. Later texts record lavish gifts given to Chou rulers, for instance, to Chi Li, Tan Fu's son. They also mention that Chi Li took a Shang woman as a wife and later was detained and died at the Shang court at An-yang.[34]

The next ruler of the Chou, King Wen, was equally troublesome to his neighbors, for he was supposedly held in captivity at the Shang court for six years. His reinstatement, as recorded in the histories, was as Lord of the West (hsi-po 西伯), a title bestowed by the last Shang king. The traditional accounts of this period are confirmed for the later period by the discovery of a Chou-date palace at Ch'i-shan. More than fifteen thousand oracle bones (fig. 2.3) were found hoarded in the palace, demonstrating that the Chou rulers practiced divination on a scale hitherto unknown except at the An-yang court. From these bones we learn that King Wen offered a sacrifice to the father of the reigning Shang king, a clear indication of feudal homage. Furthermore, the title, Earl of Chou (Chou fang po 方伯), could be conferred only by a Shang king. A visit by the Shang king to the court of a Chou retainer is also mentioned.

Wen's loyalty was, however, doubtful. The Shang designated him as an earl, but the oracle bones from Ch'i-shan record him as king during his own lifetime, and by his own people. The use of the title wang 王, or king, amounts to an usurpation of the Shang king's prerogative. Following this, King Wen moved eastward and established a new capital at Hsi-an, likely also an ominous move from the point of view of the Shang leaders.[35]

The excavation of some fifteen thousand oracle bones and fragments possibly of pre-dynastic and/or early Chou date from the Chou-yüan 周原 sites provides us with a new source of first-hand documentation. The bone fragments were found at two different times in storage pits in the back rooms of the Feng-ch'u palace remains. So far some two hundred pieces have been deciphered. The fragmentary inscriptions contain only parts of sentences but address a variety of topics that include ceremonies, harvests, travel, and military campaigns. The earliest inscriptions relate to the Shang royal house and date from before the

34. *Shih-chi*, 4/7–10; Fu Ssu-nien, 1952, vol. 4:221–23; Ch'en Meng-chia, 1956A:292–93.

35. Chou-yüan k'ao-ku-tui, 1979A:39–42; *Shih-chi*, 4/10–13, 16.

2.3 Oracle bones from Ch'i-shan (from *WW*, 1979 [10]:4)

conquest. The later ones, however, are clearly records of the Chou court, and they document religious or state affairs. The discovery of oracle bones of Chou origin has raised questions about the source of the bone fragments. Some scholars believe that those that mention events involving Shang monarchs are actually Shang records captured by the Chou armies during their occupation of the Shang capital. The consistency in style of characters and their small size, however, suggest that they are a single group of divination records, most of which bear a distinctive system of date-keeping and process of preparation. As a whole they are now considered a coherent group, produced at a predynastic Chou date.[36]

36. Chou-yüan k'ao-ku-tui, 1979A: Li Hsüeh-ch'in, 1981:10; Hsü Hsi-t'ai, 1982.

The Chou fragments describe important aspects of the relationship between the Shang and the Chou conquest.[37] In one inscription, for instance, the spirits of the Shang kings Ti I 帝乙 and Ch'eng T'ang 成湯 were sacrificed to by an offering of two females, three sheep, and three pigs. In another example, on the occasion of an investiture of the Lord of Chou, the spirit of Shang king T'ai Chia 太甲 was asked for a blessing. Altogether there are five examples that record Shang royal cere-monies.[38] Although the patronage of these bones is not agreed upon, important information can be extracted from them. The Chou leader was enfeoffed by the Shang court, and the Shang ancestors were vener-ated in Chou territory before the Conquest.

Moreover, the Shang dispatched troops to fight the Chou during Wu Ting's 武丁 reign, and at other times as well. Tung Tso-pin 董作賓 found an inscription that he has interpreted as the Shang giving orders to the Chou. That word "order," however, has also been interpreted to mean "giving appointment."[39] This record coincides with the record of the investiture mentioned above. Nevertheless, the Chou, even as a Shang subordinate, were probably a tributary state and not a member of the internal political domain of the Shang.[40]

On another of the bones from Feng-ch'u is recorded a hunting trip by the Shang king, thought to have taken place in Chou territory.[41] Although Li Hsüeh-ch'in has suggested that this inscription does not refer to the Shang at all, the *Shih-chi* does record that King Wu I was struck to death by lightning during a hunting tour in the land of the Chou.[42] That the first inscription referred to Wu I cannot be confirmed, but it is plausible that Shang kings were able to travel to the land of their subordinates.

The spirits of the Shang kings received Chou offerings as well. Two of the Shang royal ancestors were included in the Chou pantheon: a Shang progenitor worshiped by the Chou as a spirit who accompanied the Supreme God; and, Hsiang-t'u 相土, another Shang ancestor who was made the God of Earth.[43] Among the three Shang kings mentioned in the Feng-ch'u records, one was the founder of the Shang dynasty and another was also a great leader, whose position in Shang history was second only to the founder. These auspicious persons may have already

37. Chang, 1980:212—15.

38. Li Hsüeh-ch'in, 1981:10; Chou-yüan k'ao-ku-tui, 1981A:1—6; 1982:22.

39. Tung Tso-pin, 1929A; Ch'en Meng-chia, 1956A:291.

40. Chung Po-sheng, 1978:20; Chang Kwang-chih, 1980:210—12; Shima Kunio, 1958:408—09.

41. Chou-yüan k'ao-ku-tui, 1979A:39—41.

42. Li Hsüeh-ch'in, 1959:7.

43. Fu Ssu-nien, 1952, vol. 4:223—28.

been taken into the Chou assembly of great spirits before the conquest. The other, Ti I 帝乙, a lesser figure in Shang history, was worshiped along side of Ch'eng T'ang 成湯, the Shang founder. Such reverence was due probably because King Wen of the Chou had married a Shang princess from whom was born King Wu, the founder of the dynasty.[44] The princess, according to an episode in the I-ching (Book of Changes) was a sister of Ti I.[45] This poem also included information about the birth of King Wen, the son of the Shang royal house. The matrimonial ties between the Shang and the Chou must have legitimated the worship of certain Shang kings and ensured close ties between the two states. Political subordination and matrimonial ties reinforced each other at times. All such connections with the Shang must have allowed the Chou some measure of confidence in their early relations with the competitive and powerful Shang confederacy. As the Chou gained an internal identity, they drew on these connections with the mighty Shang to legitimate their bid for the throne.

These passages make it clear that both the Shang and the Chou were powerful groups in north China during the last hundred years of the Shang dynasty. Although there were other groups of formidable strength all around them at that time, the Chou had developed a considerable power base by the time they reached the Wei Valley with Tan Fu. The period following was one in which that base grew and flourished under Chi Li and King Wen. Sometime thereafter, King Wu, the son of King Wen, marched farther to the east and overran the Shang vassal statelets in southern Shansi, reaching the vicinity of An-yang. Leading a confederation of tribes from the west and southwest, King Wu captured the Shang capital in the twelfth year of his reign. The Shang king, unable to ward off the Chou advance, died in the ruins of his palace. Thus began the eight-hundred-year period known as the Chou dynasty.[46]

These circumstances attest to the interaction between the Chou and the Shang, especially during the last one hundred years of the Shang occupation of Yin. These two groups shared a common culture base and differed primarily in detail.[47] Those cultures with whom the Chou did not share a common heritage lived to their north. Comprehending the nature and content of their interchange will allow even further understanding of the assimilative character of the proto-Chou culture.

---

44. Shih-ching, 3-1-2; Legge, She King, 434−35, describes the wedding ceremony.

45. Wilhelm and Barnes, 1977:211−2. The translator misread "sister" as "daughter" and misidentified the king as Ch'eng T'ang 成湯. Fu Ssu-nien, 1952, vol. 4:222.

46. Shih-chi, 4/18−26.

47. See Chang, 1980:347−50, and the section below.

INFLUENCE OF THE NORTH ON THE CHOU

The period preceding the establishment of the capital at Ch'i-shan was one in which the Chou must have frequently come into contact with their northern neighbors, the Jung-ti 戎狄. Under the pressure of the Jung-ti, as tradition has it, Tan Fu moved his group south. Although the cultural impact of the nomads on the Shang has received some study,[48] the consequence of the nomadization of Inner Asia during the late second millennium B.C. has little been noticed in the proto-Chou remains.[49] Numerous groups who were located in or wandered through Shansi during the proto-Chou period belonged to the Ti peoples. They were both nomadic and seasonal pastoralists.[50] Moreover, the area in central Shansi and northern Shensi below the semi-arid desert was historically thought of as a seesaw zone, one that fluctuated between use by nomads and by farmers. Surely it was a place where the two groups met. And, as in the Zagros and Euphrates marginal zones of the ancient Near East,[51] the groups may have coexisted in a symbiotic fashion, each providing goods and foodstuffs that the other lacked. The archaeological record has yielded evidence of mixing and borrowing of features of weapons, tools, and gear for horses. The populations in the area manipulated the environment in different ways. The proto-Chou population specialized in sedentary food production, other groups in animal herding, adopting nomadic patterns of existence.

In the middle reaches of the Yellow River, immediately downstream from the river's great bend in western Shansi, archaeological investigation has provided evidence of distinctively local cultures in Pao-chi 寶雞, Hsin-hsien 忻縣, Shih-lou 石樓, I-tieh 義牒, Yung-ho 永和, Ling-shih 靈石 and P'ing-lu 平陸. In addition to Shang-style and mixed-style bronzes found in these sites, artifacts of steppeland heritage were unearthed. The most obvious features of nomadic heritage are animal-headed knives and spoons.[52] But it was the realistic style of animal heads with their movable tongues that was borrowed from a nomadic prototype, rather than the form of the objects. Such a mixture was not uncommon on decorated bronze vessels as well, and signifies a process of borrowing, perhaps without knowledge of or interest in the parent culture. Across the river on the west bank, finds were more distinctively

48. See a review of this material in Loehr, 1956.
49. See Watson, 1971:42–44 and 98 for a discussion of the interaction between the Shang and the Karasuk culture.
50. Průšek, 1971:7, 53–56.
51. See Lamberg-Karlovsky, 1979:61.
52. Wen-wu pien-chi wei-yüan-hui, 1979:57–88; Wu Chen-lu, 1972; Shen Chen-chung, 1972.

steppelike in manufacture and style. Both horse-headed knives and snake-headed daggers find exact parallels in the steppeland materials.[53] (See fig. 2.4.) The proto-Chou culture developed with knowledge of these other cultures, but how significant its debt was to them is unclear. Their primary interest may have been in trade, for there are few direct borrowings in the record as we know it today. The steppeland-style bronze plaque, for example, found in K'o-sheng-chuang 客省莊 is likely a trade item.

Study of the tripod named *li* has been used and may be used again as an index for the development of proto-Chou. Most archaeologists agree that the proto-Chou developed two types of *li*. A type with three set-apart legs is believed to have originated with the Kansu neolithic, especially with the Ssu-wa 寺洼 culture.[54] The other type, in which the belly merges into the legs, is associated with the Kuang-she 光社 culture (see fig. 2.5). These people were known in Shensi, east of the T'ai-hang Mountains, and throughout central Shansi, in eastern and northern Shensi, as far north as the great bend of the Yellow River, and south to the Lü-liang 呂梁 Mountains near the Fen River Valley. The earliest Kuang-she material has been dated before the reign of Shang Wu Ting, a second group has been placed contemporary with occupation of the Shang city of Yin under Wu Ting 武丁, and a final phase has been designated coincident with the last decades of the Shang power at An-yang.[55] The earlier two periods correspond to the first stage of proto-Chou development.

The Kuang-she assemblages from their earliest dates contained *li* with merged legs. Very similar ones have also been found at Tou-chi-t'ai 鬪雞台 in Pao-chi (fig. 2.5). A type of flat-based urn was also found in both locations and serves as additional evidence of shared culture traits. The earliest remains from the Kuang-she tradition predate the earliest evidence of proto-Chou. Their level of social and political organization was in advance of the proto-Chou. This situation suggests that the proto-Chou drew on not only the Kuang-she knowledge of clay but other cultural features as well.[56]

Contact between the groups is confirmed by the presence of a bow-shaped artifact made of bronze found in the Kuang-she remains and referred to in Chou inscriptions (fig. 2.2). This object whose use has yet to be understood, was found more commonly in the Kuang-she sites in Shansi, Pao-chi, Shih-lou, et cetera[57]; thus far the only locations that

53. Wen-wu pien-chi wei-yüan-hui, 1979:125; Hei Kuang et al., 1975.
54. Hu Ch'ien-ying, 1982.
55. Tsou Heng, 1980:258, 336.
56. Ibid., 336; Hsieh Hsi-kung, 1962:28–30.
57. Yang Ch'ing-shan, 1960:52; Kuo Yung, 1961:34; Wu Chen-lu, 1972:66.

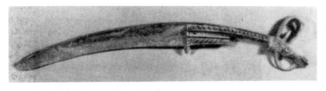

2.4 Animal- and snake-headed hilts (from *WW*, 1975 [2]: 82–87)

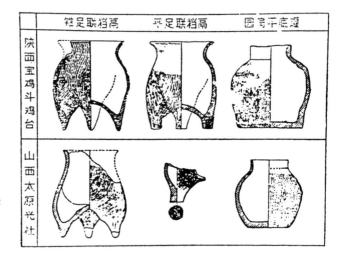

2.5 *Li* of proto-Chou (*above*) and Kuang-she (*below*). *Li* with pointed leg; *li* with flat foot (from Tsou Heng, 1980:337)

have yielded this object are Kuang-she sites. Curiously, however, pictograms bearing a bow-shaped design have been reported on bronze inscriptions cast into objects of Chou manufacture. Tsou Heng regarded these signs, which appear on sixty examples, as a *tsu* 族 emblem.[58] The locations of those sites in which these Chou bronzes were unearthed were widespread. They were found at T'ai-yüan 大原 in Shansi, at Ch'i-shan in Shensi, at Lo-yang and Chün-hsien 濬縣 in Honan, and at K'o-tso 喀左 in Liaoning 遼寧. Tsou Heng speculated that this bow-carrying people originated in Shansi, moved to Shensi, then dispersed

---

58. Tsou Heng, 1980:336–37. The word *tsu* used by Tsou Heng is not the equivalent of a "lineage" in later usages in ancient Chinese. A *tsu* was a social and political entity that was headed by a ruling house whose name often was identified also as the name of such an entity. A *tsu* in ancient China thus probably resembled a "nation" of early American Indians.

into Honan and as far north as Liaoning at the establishment of the Chou political dominance.[59]

Tsou Heng has also studied another character, *t'ien* 天 , which commonly appears on Chou bronzes. He claimed that this was also a *tsu* 族 emblem, whose distribution suggested more about the Kuang-she and the Chou. The character, a frontal, standing graph of a human body with outstretched arms and legs, has been documented on about fifty bronzes. These objects were found at Fu-feng, Ch'i-shan, Ch'ang-wu, Sui-te 綏德, Pao-chi, and Ling-shih, all in Shansi. One other was found in Honan. The distribution coincides with the area defined above as the homeland of the Kuang-she and the proto-Chou. The people with the *t'ien* emblem probably first lived in Shih-lou and the Sui-te region before migrating to the Ching-Wei Valley.[60]

Yet another clue as to the whereabouts of the proto-Chou may be found by reexamining the "Pin-feng" 豳風 odes. They were recorded in the *Shih-chi* and were traditionally thought to have been written in the east, as the text declared. The content of the odes, interestingly, recounts the early history of the Chou people. Why, then, were they thought to have come from the east, and not the west? In the thirties, Hsü Chung-shu 徐中舒 investigated the content of the odes and concluded that the musical instruments mentioned in the text were ones native to the region of western Shensi. He believed that the odes were songs sung by musicians at the eastern court of the state of Lu 魯, located in the present province of Shantung.[61] Moreover, the "Pin-feng" odes were listed in the ancient classificatory system as an eastern musical form, and it was in the state of Lu, an eastern land, that these songs were later preserved in ritualistic court music. This may not have been their place of origin. The words sung by performers may well have been adaptations created to replace an older set, a practice continued in Chinese performance today.[62] The ritualistic music of the court may reflect an older tradition than the one recorded in Lu.[63] Because the narration recorded the very early history of the Chou and the music was a common early tradition with most clans, these songs too were probably very old. They may have been regarded as "eastern" because they were created while the Chou were living in Shansi, to the east of Shensi. Therefore, the location of the writer of the text likely reflected the ancient location of the Chou in Shansi, not in Shantung.

This sort of reconsideration may also explain the classification of some

59. Tsou Heng, 1980.
60. Ibid., 338–39.
61. Hsü Chung-shu, 1936A.
62. Fu Ssu-nien, 1952, vol. 2:67–70.
63. Hsü Chung-shu, 1936A:443–44.

"northern" traditions of music. These forms were thought to have originated in the present province of Hopei.[64] Hopei is also to the east of Shensi. Archaeologically, the northern Hopei tradition during the pre-dynastic Chou period belonged to the Hsia-chia-tien culture, one covering a large area from Liaoning to northern Shensi at the bend of the Yellow River. They lived in a buffer zone between the steppeland and the region occupied by the proto-Chou tribes. If those who recorded their musical tradition lived in Shensi, as has been proposed, then they were truly a northern people.[65] Such rethinking suggests that the Chou ancestors were very active in Shansi before their eventual move to the Ching-Wei Valley.

THE HSIA-CHOU CONNECTION

Many have puzzled over the relationship between the Hsia and the Chou.[66] Were the Chou actually familiar with the Hsia, or was the Chou reference to the Hsia merely a way to legitimate their right to govern? If the Chou had come into contact with the Hsia, where did this contact occur? Moreover, why did the Chou claim the Hsia as their ancestors? In light of recent discoveries, some conclude that the Chou did actually come into contact with the Hsia. For instance, Li Min 李民 has suggested that the Chou were members of a Hsia confederation and that they lived in the area dominated by the Hsia. During the middle of the Hsia dynasty, Hsia domination was challenged by peoples who were members of the Hsia confederation living on the eastern plain. This was the time when the Chou people moved away from the Hsia in Shansi to the highland of Shensi under the direction of Pu K'u.[67] Li Min has asserted that there is a historical as well as a linguistic and an ethnic basis for the association of the Chou with the Hsia. Li Min argued that the Chou did not forget their association with the Hsia confederation, for it was useful in justifying their succession to the Shang as the masters of the central plain.

There is general agreement that the Hsia, the Shang, and the Chou shared the same culture, with differences only in detail. Chang Kwang-chih has pointed out that the succession of dynasties was sequential but that the states existed contemporaneously with each other. He suggested that the dynastic succession may be regarded as marking relative power

64. Fu Ssu-nien, 1952, vol. 2:69.
65. Wen-wu pien-chi wei-yüan-hui, 1979:39–40.
66. See Fu Ssu-nien, 1952, vol. 2:88–94; vol. 4:234.
67. Li Min, 1982.

changes among the three states. The Chou were located in the west, the Shang in the east, and the Hsia in the middle. Newly published carbon dates confirm the temporal overlap of these cultures in north China.[68] Geographic proximity argues for interaction as well. Both archaeological data and textual analyses allow us to confirm contact among all the states.[69]

THE CHOU AND THE CH'IANG

Evidence of contact between the Chou and the Ch'iang is substantial. Cross-marriage between the Chi clan of the Chou and the Ch'iang was recorded throughout Chou history. The mother of Hou Chi was a woman named Ch'iang Yüan. The wife of Tan Fu was also a daughter of the Ch'iang. In fact, it is quite remarkable that so many of the Chou royal line were bound to members of the Ch'iang clan.[70] In a recent excavation at Ju-chia-chuang 茹家莊 near Pao-chi, a Chi princess was recorded in an inscription as the wife of a noble with the Ch'iang surname. Even as late as the reigns of King Chao 昭 and King Mu 穆, the burials of the Ch'iang nobility included bronze artifacts both of the Chou tradition and of that related to the Ssu-wa culture, which was related to the ancient Ch'iang. The process of fusion of the Chou and Ssu-wa was presumably still taking place.[71] Materials found in Kansu and in Western Shensi, include bronze human figures (fig. 2.6), jade reindeer with affinities to the pastoralists (fig. 2.7), and non-Chou weapon decorations (fig. 2.8 and 2.9); all bear marks of the influences of the pastoralist culture. Nevertheless, the hierarchical order of the set of *ting* found in Ju-chia-chuang, Pao-chi, again reflects the fusion of the Chou and other cultures in the west.

The connection between the proto-Chou and the groups to their west has already been drawn. The presence of the *li* tripod in both proto-Chou sites in Shensi and in the Ssu-wa 寺洼 and An-kuo 安國 cultures in Kansu attests to a kindred relationship.[72] Tsou Heng has identified a *tsu* emblem that carried a pictograph of the *li* dating from long after the conquest of the Shang. Because this vessel was present in cultural areas at the borderland between Kansu and Shensi, he concluded that the ancient Ch'iang were related to the Ssu-wa and that they passed on

68. See Chang, 1980:350.
69. See Ch'ien Mu, 1931; Li Min, 1982; Tsou Heng, 1980.
70. Liu Ch'i-i, 1980A:89.
71. Chang Ch'ang-shou, 1980.
72. Hu Ch'ien-ying, 1982.

2.6 Bronzes from Kansu (from *WW*, 1976 [4]:pl.4)

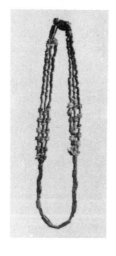

2.7 Jades unearthed in a Western Chou grave at Ju-chia-chuang, Pao-chi

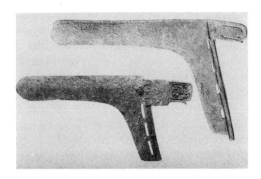

2.8 Chou weapons with atypical decoration (from *KK*, 1977 [2]:12)

2.9 Chou weapons with atypical decoration (from *KK*, 1977 [2]:13)

such elements to the proto-Chou.[73] The identification of the Ch'iang with the people in Kansu and the Tsinghai 青海 region as early as the neolithic has been suggested in studies of hairstyles and painted faces that appear on some painted pots. The hairstyles were identified as typical of the Ch'iang in Han-date descriptions.[74] More testimony about the Ch'iang can be found in the Shang oracle records, where they are often mentioned as enemies in war. Numerous inscriptions claim that Ch'iang captives were offered as sacrifices. Some of the Ch'iang surrendered to the Shang; these were named the To-ma-ch'iang 多馬羌, or Ch'iang who herded horses. Li Hsüeh-ch'in has proposed that there were two identifications for the Ch'iang during the Shang period. The term *Ch'iang-fang* 羌方, he has suggested, indicated a particular Ch'iang state, whereas the broader use of the term referred to a cluster of foreigners who resided in the broad area to the west of the Shang domain. The Ch'iang state was probably located fairly near the Shang, for the record shows that frequent conflict caused the Shang to mobilize subordinated *tsu* to fight them. In one battle, two chiefs of the Ch'iang state were captured by the Shang. These sources attest to the considerable military strength of the Ch'iang and to the possibility that there was more than one Ch'iang state. Li Hsüeh-ch'in located the Ch'iang in the territory just west of the Shang state, in the region used for hunting by the Shang nobility. This was located in the south of Shansi and west of Honan.[75]

Through study of the surname Ch'iang, Fu Ssu-nien attempted to identify the Ch'iang in ancient times. He proposed that they were mountain tribes that originally lived in the hilly areas in western Honan and the southern Wei Valley. And, indeed, most of the unnamed barbarians regarded as relatives of the Ch'iang in the Han records were to be found in precisely those geographic regions suggested by Fu.[76] Those Han-date Ch'iang tribes located in the provinces of Kansu and Tsinghai probably represented only one branch of a once much larger conglomeration of the old Ch'iang.

In summary, the Ch'iang were widely distributed geographically during the Shang period, living in a zone stretching from present-day Kansu to western Honan. Those of this group called the Ch'iang-fang lived closest to the Shang clan center. Another branch of the Ch'iang that occupied part of the Wei Valley and became close allies of the Chou

73. Tsou Heng, 1980:345–49; Hsia Nai, 1961:11–49.
74. Hu Shun-li, 1981; Chang P'eng-ch'uan, 1979:52–55. For the relationship between the Ch'iang of the Shang-Chou period and those of the Han period, see Pulleyblank, 1983:418–23.
75. Li Hsüeh-ch'in, 1959:77–80.
76. Fu Ssu-nien, 1952, vol. 4:13–22.

used the surname Ch'iang. Those groups who never organized as a state must be those known in the *Tso-chuan* 左傳 as the Ch'iang-jung. Those living at a neolithic level were people of the Ssu-wa culture of Kansu, who were the ancestors of the Ch'iang people, recorded as such in the Han period. Fu Ssu-nien correctly found a cultural parallel in the movement of peoples of the Tungus. Their branches repeatedly entered China, each time leaving some members behind in Manchuria.[77]

In addition, the importance of the Shang in the Wei Valley is now clearer. They must have strongly influenced the Shensi Lungshan descendants, for the Shang seem to have sent exploratory missions to the fertile Wei Valley in search of new lands to cultivate.[78] Frequent military exchange is documented in oracle inscriptions as early as Wu Ting, thereby recording active interaction between the Shang and the Chou. During the following century, between the reigns of Wu Ting and of Ti I, there is no mention of contact. This must have been the period when the Chou migrated to the northern Shensi highland. Their move to the Wei Valley was the second contact with the Shang bronze-using culture. It is not such a surprise, then, that the Chou emerged as a bronze-using culture at that time in the Wei Valley.

The proto-Chou culture combined many features of neighboring groups, with their own Chou base as the parent culture. The culture of the steppeland from northern Shensi, that absorbed from the Chou alliance with the Ch'iang, and repeated borrowings from the Shang example were the main additional components. The relatively indirect, and somewhat less significant, influence of the local Shensi Lungshan provided one more ingredient.

THE CHOU STATE IN LITERATURE

Under the leadership of Kung Liu, the Chou became a political entity. The story of that development was recorded in a poem by the same name, the "Kung Liu," found in the collection called the *Book of Poetry*. Although the interpretation of individual phrases and words of this poem is disputed, the general content is agreed upon. The song "Kung Liu" tells the story of an armed party migrating to a new land. They carried dried food and departed from the land of "hundreds of springs" to ascend to the highland. They stopped at Hsü 胥 and Pin 邠, where they offered sacrifices and established Kung Liu as their ruler and patriarch. In the new land they settled in temporary dwellings. They

77. Ibid., 22.
78. Chang Cheng-lang, 1973.

were organized into three regiments, each assigned to till the most desirable fields and each regulated by Kung Liu, who fixed some sort of taxation based on that occupation. The poem concludes that the Chou population grew until they decided to march beyond that place. The armed party was organized into units led by an elected patriarch who supervised the division of the land. A certain portion of the products was levied for taxation, presumably to sustain collective activities such as group ceremonies.[79]

The place-names in the poem are of great interest. The place called Pin was mentioned in relation to the area of the Fen River, as Ch'ien Mu proposed. "Hsü" has been interpreted both as a particle and as a geographic name. Since the term appears in another poem in relation to Tan Fu as a place-name, Ting Shan took it to be a variation of the title "Hsia." Furthermore, he located Hsü on the west bank of the Yellow River, near Ko-yang County in Shensi.[80] That location is midway between the Fen River Valley in Shansi and the Ching Valley in Shensi. It was, then, a logical place for the Chou to stop off on their way west toward the Ching Valley. Nevertheless, if the Chou had been among the barbarians for the century before the election of Kung Liu, they could not have departed from the old Shensi homeland. Although this issue is not entirely settled, we do know that the Chou established a military state under the direction of a patriarch named Kung Liu. His son, Ch'ing Chieh 慶節, led the Chou people to the upper reaches of the Ching River, a place called Pin then and now. This is the area where, in Period One, the proto-Chou are located.

Tan Fu, a direct descendant of Ch'ing Chieh, but eight generations later, led the Chou for the final time to the Wei Valley. A song in the *Book of Poetry*, this episode is narrated as follows:

> In a long train ever increasing grow the gourds.
> When (our) people first sprang from the country of the Tsu and Chi,
> The ancient duke Tan Fu made for them kiln-like huts and caves,
> Ere they yet had any houses.
> The duke Tan Fu came in the morning,
> Galloping his horses,
> Along the banks of the river westward,
> To the foot of Mount Ch'i;
> And there he and the lady Ch'iang
> Came together and looked for a site on which to settle.
> The plain of Chou looked beautiful and rich

79. Ting Shan, 1956:61–63; Hu Ch'eng-kung, 1888:24–40.
80. Ting Shan, 1935:92–93.

With its violets and sowthistles (sweet) as dumplings.
There he began with consulting (his followers),
There he singed the tortoise shell (and divined).
The responses were—There to stay, and then,
They proceeded there to build their houses.
He encouraged the people and settled them;
Here on the left, there on the right.
He divided the ground into larger tracts and smaller portions.
He dug the ditches; he defined the acres.
From the west to the east,
There was nothing which he did not take in his charge.
He named his superintendent of works;
He named his minister of instruction;
And charged them with the building of the houses.
With the line they made everything straight;
They bound the frame-boards tight, so they would rise regularly.
Up rose the ancestral temple in its solemn grandeur
Crowds brought the earth in baskets;
They threw it with shouts into the frame;
They beat it with responsive blows;
They leveled the walls repeatedly, and they sounded strong.
Five thousand cubits of them arose together,
So that the roll of the great drum did not overpower the noise of
    the builders.
They set up the enceinte:
And the gate of enceinte stood grand.
They reared the great altar (to the spirit of the land)
From which all great movements should proceed.
Thus though he could not prevent the rage (of his foes)
He did not let fall his own fame.
The oaks though thorny were thinned,
And roads for travelling were opened.
The hoards of the Huns disappeared,
Startled and panting.
(The chiefs of) Yü and Jüeh were brought to an agreement
By King Wen stimulating their natural nature.
Then, I may say, some came to him, previously not known
And some, drawn the last by the first;
And some, drawn by his rapid success;

And some, by his defense (of the weak) from insult.[81]

81. *Mao-shih cheng-i*, hereafter *Shih-ching*, 3-1-3; Legge, *She King*, 437–41, translation
revised slightly.

This poem depicts vividly the scenes of Tan Fu's arrival at the Ch'i-shan area and his effort to build a capital literally up from the bare ground. The description of the westbound route is interesting, for their old home was actually to the north in the Ching Valley. On the whole it appears that before Tan Fu the Chou were living in the upper Ching Valley to the east of the Ch'i region.

The description also mentions that the Chou lacked houses and dwelt in caves. This does not necessarily indicate that they existed at a low level culturally, but rather that they lived in semi-subterranean pit-dwellings, common in both Shensi and Shansi Lungshan cultures. The setting described in the poem was probably of an ordinary, and temporary, settlement established while the palace and temple buildings were being erected.

The most significant task completed by Tan Fu was reclamation of land from heavy woods and bushes. This sort of clearing impressed the ancient poets so much that they repeated descriptions about it at least twice in some poems.[82] The sentences regarding division of the land, ditch digging, and acre-making are reminiscent of the work conducted by Kung Liu when he settled at Hsü. Kung Liu also lived in temporary residences, but Tan Fu engaged in large-scale construction in order to build a capital. The endeavors differed not only in scale, but also in intent.

STATE ORGANIZATION OF PRE-DYNASTIC CHOU

In Tan Fu's time the Chou were organized as a tribe with a patriarch at the head. The *Shih-chi* records that Tan Fu had not only built palaces and temples but also created positions for officials in charge of five departments in the government.[83] In the song about Tan Fu presented above, two offices were listed: superintendent of works and minister of instructions.[84] In the Feng-ch'u divination record, the position of *shih* (scribe or historian), and the title of *shih-shih* 師氏, a military officer, were also listed.[85] Scribes were often cited in Shang inscriptions on oracle bones. The title of *shih-shih* (a commander) has not been found in Shang examples, but it is common on Chou bronze inscriptions. The *shih-shih* Commander, the Royal Attendant, and the Commandant of the Royal Guard (Tiger Guard) were the three most important Chou

---

82. *Shih-ching*, 3-17, 4-1-5; Legge, *She King*, 448–51, 574.
83. *Shih-chi*, 4/7.
84. Legge, *She King*, 439.
85. Chou-yüan k'ao-ku-tui, 1979B:39–40.

officials.[86] In other inscriptions, the Minister of Works, the Minister of Land, and the Minister of Horses (i.e., the Army) are specified as the "Three Ministers."[87] Although the later Chou administrative system is well known and elaborate, some features of that order were already apparent before the conquest. That there was clear division of functions is revealed in the titles of the three ministers. By contrast, the Shang government officials bore titles such as *hsiao-ch'en* 小臣, or junior attendant; *ya* 亞, a subordinate; *lü* 旅, men under a flag; even *ch'üan* 犬, literally "dog," a kennel attendant, actually a game attendant. Such titles were often derived from names given to household servants. In particular, the office of *hsiao-ch'en*, which was to become one of the most powerful positions in the late Shang court, carried out various functions. At the end of the Shang period, the population was still organized according to agnatic groups, although geographically divided administrative units had been in existence before. The Shang population distributed in the Chou vassal states were listed one by one according to their *tsu* unit.[88] The early Chou courts continued the Shang practices, but with significant changes. For instance, the practice of taking oracles and recording that exchange on a bone was borrowed from the Shang. The recent discovery of thousands of these bones at Feng-ch'u attests to the importance of the practice for the Chou. Until their discovery, Chou divination was thought to have been based on the use of the hexagram, a numerical system. Recent identification of sets of numerals found on the surfaces of pottery, bronzes, and bones affirms that the Chou were using that system as well in pre-dynastic days.[89] Thus, the Chou did make conscious decisions about the assimilation of the Shang practice.

The Chou political organization allowed for efficient operation. This may be evidenced in the creation of functionally differentiated offices that allowed the central government to mobilize human resources more efficiently. This capacity to organize surely aided the Chou in conquering a larger and more powerful state.

During the pre-dynastic period, the Chou had already acquired several vassal states, ones located near them. The Feng-ch'u inscriptions record at least twice that a Ch'u 楚 ruler had visited the Chou court or had sent an envoy to report his succession of the throne.[90] Ancient literature claimed that the Ch'u leader, during his stay at the Chou court, served as a night guard for the king. He was supposed to have kept the campfires burning at a special ceremony dedicated to the swearing of

86. Shirakawa Shizuka, *KBTS* 30:680–82.
87. Ibid., 19:316–17; Li Hsüeh-ch'in, 1957; Chou O-sheng, 1957.
88. Legge, *Tso Chuen*, 754.
89. Chang Ya-ch'u, et al., 1981:153–63; Chou-yüan k'ao-ku-tui, 1979B:41.
90. Chou-yüan k'ao-ku-tui, 1982: 17.

allegiance by the Chou to several other states.[91] In both records the Ch'u were in a subordinate position to the Chou. The *Kuo-yü* 國語 claims that these Ch'u were the forebears of the Ch'u of the Ch'un-ch'iu period.[92] A recent study has suggested that the Ch'u were not located in the south at this time, but rather in the western regions of Shensi, and probably near Mount Ch'u in Ch'ien-yang 汧陽 County.[93] The locations of the other two states, Shu 蜀 and Ch'ao 巢, mentioned in those inscriptions, have yet to be identified. The *Book of Documents* claims that Shu was among eight allies that sent troops to campaign against the Shang. The appearance of Shu in the archaeological record gives credibility to the ancient report.[94] The Feng-ch'u record also includes one mention of the Kuei-fang, known as a strong competitor of the Shang. The archaeologists at Chou-yüan believed that Kuei-fang 鬼方 was a nation in Shansi, to the north of the Shang.[95] Ch'en Meng-chia combed through the data in ancient literature looking for materal relating to the activities of the Chou in the northern frontiers. He managed to reconstruct a chronology for Chi Li's involvement in campaigns against northern "barbarians" during the reigns of Shang kings Wu I, T'ai Ting, and Ti I. He claimed that Chi Li, the father of King Wen, fought on behalf of the Shang, especially in the province of Shansi. His Chou troops won in most instances recorded. Chi Li was then given a Shang appointment as the Master of the Herds, the lord over a cluster of minor nations. The relationship was later to turn sour, for Chi Li was killed by the Shang soon after his military involvement.[96] The Feng-ch'u record did confirm, then, that the Chou were once subordinate to the Shang. Significantly, however, the Chou had stretched their involvement deep into Shansi, where the Shang felt intimidated, and in doing so moved even closer to the Shang domain. The death of Chi Li at the hands of the Shang shows that they found him a threat. All such activities in Shansi confirm Chou occupation in areas close to the heart of Shang power.

A SPECULATION

When in the pre-dynastic period the Chou people went from being a small tribe of obscure origin to a significant power, they came to pose a threat to the Shang. The most critical point in their development was

91. *Kuo-yü*, 14/7–8.
92. Fu Ssu-nien, 1952, vol. 4:193–94.
93. Chang Hsiao-heng, 1958; Liu Ch'i-i, 1982:44.
94. Chou-yüan k'ao-ku-tui, 1979B:40; Legge, *Shoo King*, 301.
95. Chou-yüan k'ao-ku-tui, 1979B:42.
96. Ch'en Meng-chia, 1956A:292–93.

their activity in the northern territories. Their conversion to a "barbarian," or "Jung-ti," nomadic livelihood in the early period, their migration to escape from the pressure of nomads under the leadership of Tan Fu, and their campaigns against the nomads in Chi Li's time all were important events that denoted periods of change in their history. The development of this pre-dynastic state was affected by pressures from massive migrations on the Eurasian steppes during the second millennium B.C. In the west in the seventeenth century B.C., the Kassites invaded Mesopotamia and established political dominance there. Around the same time, the Hyksos forced their way into Egypt. During the fourteenth to the twelfth centuries B.C., the Mediterranean coasts were alive with activities of so-called "peoples of the sea," according to Egyptian reports. Some of these activities were related to the people in the Caucasus, who were pushed southward and westward in this period. The Aryans, for instance, entered the Indus Valley and altered the Indian culture permanently. That activity took place during the long period from the fifteenth century B.C. through the ninth century B.C.[97]

It is generally recognized by archaeologists that the second millennium B.C. was a period of phenomenal dispersion of people across the Eurasian steppes. In Central Asia there were three waves of movement. The first stage began early in the second millennium B.C. In the second stage, during the latter half of the second millennium B.C., the nomads spread to areas near T'ien-shan, the Altai, and the Sayan Mountains, and reached beyond Lake Baikal. A widely known movement of the nomads that included the Hsiung-nu took place during the seventh century B.C. and may be counted as the third wave of migration.[98]

The early Chou were most affected by the second wave of nomadic wanderings. Climatic changes during the latter half of the second millennium B.C. may have been the impetus for that move from the north to the south and toward the borders of China. William Watson suggested that the northern boundary between the forest and the steppe lay along the 56th parallel in about 1500 B.C., and by 1250 B.C. that boundary stood at the 60th parallel, a move of some two hundred miles north.[99] A gradual warming before 1250 B.C. probably lifted the pressure from the northerners on the Chou, who then had the opportunity to recover the land in Shansi and Shensi for agricultural use. This time frame concurs with the episode recorded about Kung Liu. Yet according to climatologists, by the end of the second millennium a

97. See Clark, 1977:84, 89–91, 158–163, 275; Wilson, 1951:185–87, 244–60; Childe, 1942:167–71, 185–86; Oppenheim, 1977:61–62.

98. Sherratt, 1980:245–55.

99. Watson, 1971:42.

cooling trend continued and developed until the Ch'un-ch'iu 春秋 period. The colder temperatures began in the northeastern Pacific Coast region and moved westward, eventually reaching the Atlantic. A southern movement was also recorded and was thought to have brought cooler weather to China.[100] The conflicts between the Shang and the Jung-ti, the campaigns conducted in Shansi in pre-dynastic times, and the almost constant trouble recorded along the northern border throughout the entire span of the Western Chou dynasty may be considered reactions to disturbances in the steppes at that time, whatever the cause of that movement.

In all, the rise of the Chou was closely related to struggles between agricultural and nomadic peoples just below the northern zone and China's central plain.[101] The Hsia-chia-tien 夏家店 cultures, who were found along the line of the Great Wall in later days, represented that same interplay between two cultures. The forebears of the Chou people, who converted their economy from farming to pastoralism and returned again to farming, were probably simply reacting to the same seesaw movement of other peoples near them. When the Chou farmers finally moved to better farmland in the Wei Valley, they were responding to and taking part in a gigantic migration of peoples. Along their migratory route they absorbed the cultures of their neighbors and were the host to others. The result was that the Chou civilization at the beginning of the dynasty was assimilative, heterogeneous, powerful, and well organized, both internally and in relation to its allies.

In summation, in this chapter we have reconsidered the route taken by the Chou before they settled in Ch'i-shan and examined their cultural heritage and their political organization. In light of primary documents including traditional literature, inscriptions, and materials provided by recent archaeological investigation, we have refrained from drawing absolute conclusions. We offer our comments, rather, as thoughtful reinterpretations.

The proto-Chou were first located in the Shansi-Shensi highland, where they absorbed elements from the Kuang-she culture and from the steppe dwellers. Kung Liu moved his people to the lower Fen Valley and to the western bank of the Yellow River, where they resumed agriculture. His son, Ch'ing Chieh, led the Chou to the upper valley of the Ching River. They stayed there until Tan Fu (or T'ai Wang) moved again to the Wei Valley in order to avoid incursion by the Jung-ti nomads. During this period, the Chou mingled with the Ch'iang people, who provided them with a cultural inheritance derived from the Ssu-

100. Chu K'o-chen 竺可楨 , 1979:479–95.
101. Watson, 1971:65–66.

wa and An-kuo peoples and formed a political alliance with them. In all these stages, the advanced Shang bronze culture constantly imparted its influence on the Chou.

The Ch'i area was the region in which all these influences would come to fruition. The contact among the proto-Chou, the native Shensi Lungshan, the Ch'iang, and the northern steppe traditions, plus the tradition of the Shang, produced momentum for change and development. From that mix the Chou matured into a bronze-using culture with the political organization necessary to govern and to maintain their influence.[102]

The Chou did not, however, receive blindly. The Chou bronzesmiths first produced imitations of Shang pieces, and slowly began to infuse their own ideas on the technology, design, and use of ritual materials.[103] Chou potters, on the other hand, gradually let go of their native, local styles to produce a court-style pottery in the Shang tradition. By doing so they gave impetus to an evolving court tradition that was to continue throughout Chinese history.

Early Chinese political organization was also altered fundamentally by the proto-Chou. At the time of Kung Liu the lines of authority followed agnatic ties, with groups led by patriarchs. Groups organized in such a way were easily mobilized for military purposes and thus served the specific needs of the time. In the hands of Tan Fu, a more complex political order was initiated. The governing body was divided according to function, and departments formed a state machine that could administer from a settled capital. Under the leadership of Chi Li, the Chou expanded their territory again to include Shansi. The Chou, thereby, served the interest of their overlords, the Shang, while also paving the way for their own eventual takeover of the Chinese world from the Shang.

102. Franklyn, 1983:94–99.
103. Soon after the conquest, the Chou bronze vessels began to carry lengthy inscriptions recording investitures and the work of deserving nobles. That is a radical shift in use of such materials, for which there is no parallel in the Shang inventory. See Fong, 1980:193–203; chap. 9 below.

3 The Conquest of the Shang and the Mandate of Heaven

The *Book of Poetry* contains the following passage about the early history of the Chou people:

> Among the descendants of Hou Chi was King T'ai
> Dwelling to the south of (Mount) Ch'i,
> Where the clipping of Shang began.
> In the process of time Wen and Wu
> Continued the work of King T'ai.
> And (the purpose of) Heaven was carried out in its time,
> In the Plain of Mu.[1]

Even though their final triumph took place at Mu-yeh 牧野, in the minds of the Chou people the planning and preparation were done previously, during the time of Tan Fu 亶父, or T'ai Wang 太王 (King T'ai), when they were settled in Ch'i-shan 岐山. Within three generations, from T'ai Wang to his son Chi Li 季歷 and his grandson King Wen, the Chou moved their operational center step by step eastward toward the lower streams of the Wei 渭 River. The entire procedure gave them better access to the core area of China and resembled the attempt of the Ch'in 秦 state to unify China seven centuries later. Strategically, a move to the approximate center of power had obvious advantages. The Chou were finally successful in their attempt to conquer the heartland of China and through the Mandate of Heaven to claim themselves to be the rightful heirs to the throne of the Central Kingdom. The remarkable victory of this relative newcomer in North China was a major accomplishment. The feat by which the Chou amassed the strength, both military and moral, to overcome their powerful neighbors fundamentally altered the direction of Chinese political and philosophical thinking. Although the legacy of that change is well known, the motivations of the Chou and the cultural, social, and political conditions that existed during the century in which their civilization developed are less well known. Their complete victory was accomplished with a conviction not predictable from the ordinary context of village life in the northwest plateau, and their achievement provokes the following questions. Did the Chou have more and better material resources? Did special circumstances in that region allow them to develop an aggressive stance? Was their shift in thinking due to rethinking of older traditions that they themselves knew or borrowed from their more sophisticated neighbors, the Shang? Did their contact with others allow them more opportunity to reevaluate their own position? In other words, did the Chou policy and position derive from a natural evolution in perceptions, or did new thinking infuse from the outside?

PRODUCTIVITY OF THE CHOU PEOPLE

Many efforts have been made to explain the circumstances that allowed the Chou advantages over their adversaries. Hsü Chung-shu 徐中舒 believed that the Chou victory was due to their occupation of the fertile land of the Wei River Valley. From that position, he suggested, they could reach rich resources of the Szechwan 四川 basin in the south as well as the highland of Han-chung 漢中, which opened access to the Han 漢 and Yangtze valleys.[2] Indeed, the Wei Valley, known in Chinese history as Kuan-chung 關中, was considered the strategic point from which both the Ch'in and Han later set out on their east-bound campaigns to unify a fragmented China. The Chou, on the other hand, arose there as a regional power and challenged the unified and powerful Shang kingdom. The land area under direct Chou control was much smaller than the Shang core area in the middle and lower reaches of the Yellow River, with its extensions in cental Hopei to the north (at Kao-ch'eng 藁城) and central Hupei to the south (at P'an-lung-ch'eng 盤龍城). The Wei Valley was to the Shang a small fraction of their entire domain. The Shang population lived in a region that was densely inhabited continuously from neolithic times. The Chou adult male population is estimated by Li Ya-nung 李亞農 to have numbered about sixty to seventy thousand persons. Li examined the productive capacity of the Wei Valley and approximated the size of the adult male population needed to sustain an army of three hundred chariots, the apparent military strength of the Chou. Li Ya-nung cited a case mentioned in the *Tso Chuan* 左傳, where the state of Wei[3] sustained thirty war chariots with a

---

1. *Shih-ching*, 3-11-4; Legge, *She King*, 622.
2. Hsü Chung-shu, 1936B:141.
3. Not the Wei River.

population of about five thousand adult males.[4] Altogether, the Chou population in the Wei Valley was rather small.

Li-Ya-nung reached his conclusions by means of simple but crude deduction. He estimated that a ration of seventy-two infantrymen was attached to each war chariot—a quite arbitrary and not entirely accurate figure. Nevertheless, that the Chou population totaled less than the Shang was likely a historical reality.

Other historians argued that because the Chou were farmers from ancient times, their advantage was a consequence of advanced agricultural techniques and tools. Some have even suggested that the high yields of the early Chou were achieved by using iron implements. Others insisted that the Chou implement called the *ssu* 耜, a single-tipped digging stick, could be fixed with a metal tip. This would allow an advantage over the Shang two-pronged *lei* 耒, which could not be fitted with a metal tip. The Chou people were thought to be capable of clearing land more efficiently so as to secure more resources. Moreover, they were thought to enslave the people they subjugated and use them to till the land.[5] These arguments explain increased productivity through analysis of instruments and historical materialism. Such proposals are not, however, supported by archaeological evidence.

The findings at Chang-chia-p'o 張家坡 have been dated to a period around that of King Wen (figs. 3.1–3.6). The site provides appropriate data for investigation of the level of productivity during the early stages of Western Chou. The original reports list four categories of tools and implements found there[6] (fig. 3.7), which include cutting and hammering tools. In addition, there were sixty-five bladed tools, most of which were made of stone. Only one small bronze axe and fifteen small, short (20 cm.) bronze knives were found. A majority of the stone axes were crudely manufactured, and there were only seven polished examples among the total of fifty-one axes. All ten stone chisels, however, were polished. The stone hammers and clubs were made of natural pebbles, with limited reworking.

Farm implements found there consisted of digging and harvesting tools. There were 112 spades: 23 of stone, 7 of seashell, 82 of bone, either shoulder bones or lower jawbones of cattle and horses. The spade had a rather broad cutting edge and a relatively narrower base that was to be tied to a wooden handle. The marks of wear on it indicate that it was an implement used for preparing soil for cultivation. Two kinds of harvesting tools were discovered: a total of 246 knives and 90 sickles.

4. Li Ya-nung, 1962:666–69.
5. Li Chien-nung, 1962:17–20.
6. K'ao-ku yen-chiu-so, 1962:80–94.

3.1 Stone tools and implements discovered at Chang-chia-p'o (from K'ao-ku yen-chiu-so, 1962, pl. 40)

3.2 Stone tools and implements from Chang-chia-p'o (from K'ao-ku yen-chiu-so, 1962, pl. 41)

3.3 Bone implements
from Chang-chia-p'o
(from K'ao-ku yen-chiu-
so, 1962, pl. 45)

3.4 Bone implements
from Chang-chia-p'o
(from K'ao-ku yen-chiu-
so, 1962, pl. 47)

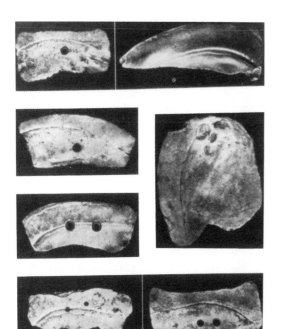

3.5 Tools from Chang-chia-p'o (from K'ao-ku yen-chiu-so, 1962, pl. 46)

3.6 Bronze knives from Chang-chia-p'o (from K'ao-ku yen-chiu-so, 1962, pl. 42)

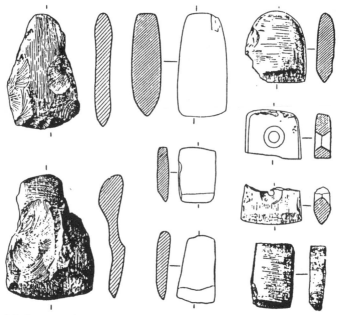

3.7 Stone implements found at Chang-chia-p'o (from K'ao-ku yen-chiu-so, 1962:82)

Most were made of shell, but some were of stone. Shell tools were popular in other Western Chou sites. The knives were polished into rectangular, somewhat thick, single- or double-edged blades. Small holes near the back of the sickle allowed it to be fastened to a handle with leather straps. Thus, the instrument could be used to cut off the ear, spike, or head of the grain. The sickle resembles modern Chinese models, which are attached to a wooden handle. Expected, but not yet unearthed, are examples of the single-tipped *ssu* 耜 and the double-pronged *lei* 耒. Such items are perishable and are not likely to appear except in unusual conditions.

Craftsmen's tools are the third category listed by the archaeologists at Chang-chia-p'o. They found clay molds for casting bronze bulbs, bronze edges, and stone tools used to work bone pieces. Clay pressers used for potting, and spinning wheels used for textile production, were also found. Awls and needles were made of bronze, bone, or horn.

Fishing and hunting equipment, the fourth category of tools found at the site, included 310 arrowheads made of deer antler or other animal bone. The arrowheads, generally described as dull, perhaps were used for killing small animals. One net weight was discovered. Fishing must have been a less important activity for procurement of food in this area.[7] The inventory did not include many large bronze tools or other metal-tipped implements. The yellow earth of the area is so soft that a spade made of bone or seashell is sufficient to penetrate it. The fact that harvest knives outnumbered sickles suggests that per capita labor efficiency and productivity were at a low level. Shell, a raw material needed for tools, must have been secured from the Ching, the Wei, and other rivers in the area. The bones were from cattle and horses, while antler came from deer. The large number of arrowheads and some of the fishing tools seem to have been used for obtaining raw materials, in addition to simply gathering food. The axes, as well as other tools, were employed for felling trees, clearing ground, and general carpentry.

Literary sources refer to productivity and living conditions and provide information consistent with the archaeological data. In the *Book of Poetry* one can find such passages as the following:

> The oaks and thorns were gradually thinned;
> And roads for travelling were opened.[8]

> King T'ai raised up and removed
> The dead trunks and fallen trees;
> He dressed and regulated
> The bushy clumps, and the (tangled) rows.
> He opened up and cleared
> The tamarix trees, and the stave trees.
> He hewed and thinned
> The mountain mulberry trees.[9]

The poets describe scenes of opening roads and land reclamation that would require the implements and tools found at the Chang-chia-p'o sites. In the poem that recounts King T'ai's settlement of the Ch'i-shan region, fertility of the soil is mentioned. "The plain in Chou looked beautiful and rich./ With violets and sowthistles (sweet) as dumplings."[10] The fertile yellow soil could easily be cultivated with bone and shell spades.

Fish and game were abundant. This is made clear in a poem dated from the Western Chou and recorded in the *Book of Poetry*.

> The King was in the marvelous park,
> Where the does were lying,

---

7. Ibid.
8. *Shih-ching* 3-1-3; Legge, *She King*, 441.
9. *Shih-ching*, 3-1-7; Legge, *She King*, 449–50.
10. *Shih-ching*, 3-1-3; Legge, *She King*, 438.

The does so sleek and fat
With the white birds glistening,
The King was by the marvelous pond;
How full it was of fishes leaping about.[11]

Apparently, many of the fish and animals were kept in ponds or in parks reserved for royal game.

Another poem of a later date described royal flocks and herds.

Who can say that you have no sheep?
There are three hundred in (each) herd.
Who says that you have no cattle?
There are ninety, which are black lipped.
Your sheep came,
Horned, but all agreeing.
Your cattle come,
Flapping their ears.
Some are descending among mounds;
Some are drinking at the pools;
Some are lying down, some are moving about.
Your herdsmen come,
Bearing their raincoats and bamboo hats,
Or carrying on their backs their provisions.
In thirties are the creatures arranged according to their colors;
For your victims there are abundant provisions.[12]

Such realistic account of herding is rather rare in Chinese literature, for the economy was based on farming, not herding. Even though this poem was attributed to the late Western Chou, the Chou people of early days must also have been familiar with these scenes. The Chinese characters for the names of close allies, for instance, the Ch'iang 羌, or their surname, Chiang 姜, both used a human figure and a sheep, indicating that the Ch'iang people were considered shepherds.[13] The vast region west of Ch'i-shan in the Wei Valley even today remains an important area for raising sheep and cattle.

Another poem reads:

Heaven made the lofty hills
And King T'ai brought it (the country) under cultivation.

11. *Shih-ching*, 3-1-8; Legge, *She King*, 457.
12. *Shih-ching*, 2-4-6; Legge, *She King*, 307–08.
13. Fu Ssu-nien, 1952, vol. 4:21–22; Liu Chieh, 1948:210–11; Wolfram Eberhard, 1982:65–66; Chu Chün-sheng, 1968:18/3534; Li Hsiao-ting, 1965:4/1325–40.

He made the commencement with it,
And King Wen tranquilly (carried on the work),
Till that rugged Mount Ch'i
Had level roads leading to it.
May their descendants ever preserve it.[14]

The task of taming the land was a continuous one that began with King T'ai 太王 and persisted throughout the reign of King Wen 文. The memory of their past remained in the minds of the Chou people, for the *Book of Documents* spoke of King Wen as a leader who dressed in coarse clothing and personally took to farming.[15] Such a description may not refer to a situation in which the king was actually in the fields every day; instead, it may allude to ceremonial farming. The emphasis on King Wen's direct participation probably recorded the memory of a non-differentiated farming life that existed before the established dynasty.

In summary, the situations reflected both in literature and in archaeological remains suggest that the Chou's material resources did not surpass those of the Shang. The productive capability of the Chou people seems to have equaled that of the Shang; no significant advantages or innovations are visible from the record thus far.

MILITARY STRENGTH OF THE CHOU

An investigation of the military strength of the Chou will determine if the balance of power was in favor of the Chou. If so, their victory may be more comprehensible. The Chou simply could not raise as many soldiers as the Shang, for they did not control as large a population. The Shang used a two-wheeled war chariot, drawn by two or four horses and occupied by two or three combatants who stood on a platform. They thrust with a composite bow from a distance; they pierced or struck with long weapons such as spears or halberds. The short weapons, such as daggers, could be used for combat on foot when in direct confrontation with another soldier; however, most daggers in Chinese archaeology date from later periods, with few from the Shang-Chou period.

The Chou weapon kit included a few distinctive items (figs. 3.8–3.11). The Chou *ko* 戈 was an improved striking halberd. It was more firmly fastened to a pole and more complicated than its Shang counterpart.[16] The Chou bronze sword was a new addition (fig. 3.12).

14. *Shih-ching*, 4-1-5; Legge, *She King*, 574.
15. Legge, *Shoo King*, 469.
16. Pei-ching ta-hsüeh, Department of History. 1979:82.

3.8 Western Chou bronze daggers and halberds (from K'ao-ku yen-chiu-so, 1962, pl. 48)

3.9 Western Chou bronze halberds and spearheads (from Pei-ching ta-hsüeh, Department of History, 1979)

3.10 Western Chou bronze daggers and Knives (from *KK*, 1978 [4]:234)

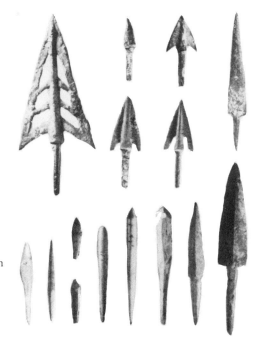

3.11 Western Chou bronze, stone, and bone arrowheads from Chang-chia-p'o (from K'ao-ku yen-chiu-so, 1962, pl. 49)

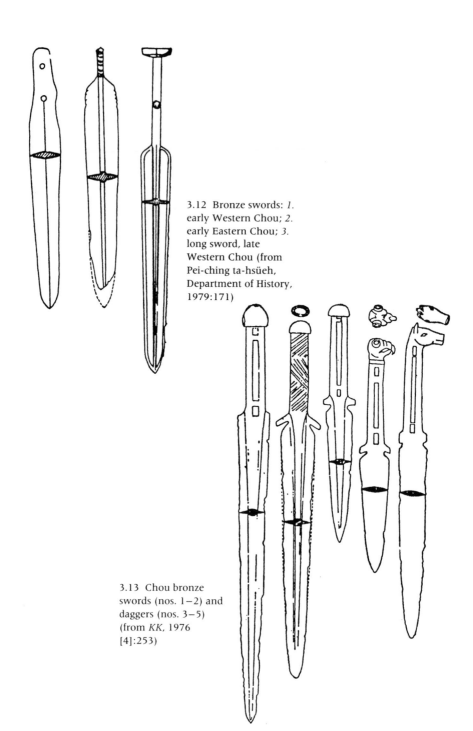

3.12 Bronze swords: *1.* early Western Chou; *2.* early Eastern Chou; *3.* long sword, late Western Chou (from Pei-ching ta-hsüeh, Department of History, 1979:171)

3.13 Chou bronze swords (nos. 1−2) and daggers (nos. 3−5) (from *KK*, 1976 [4]:253)

The oldest of these swords yet found was unearthed at Pao-te in north Shansi, a site coeval with the late Shang. The mixed assemblage of bronze artifacts in Pao-te demonstrates a legacy from the Kuang-she culture. Hollow-handled swords decorated with bronze jingles or balls in the head of the handle resemble the steppe "akinake" sword and its decoration (fig. 3.13). Bronze swords were widely distributed in early Chou sites in Shensi, Kansu, and Hopei. In general, the Chou specimens have leaf-shaped blades and no visible hilt.[17] Two gold, bow-shaped decorative pieces found there also belie nomadic influence. The Pao-te food and drinking vessels, on the other hand, are analogous to Shang examples. This northern Shansi group incorporated both steppe and central Chinese materials as they found them useful.[18]

The Chou sword was somewhat superior in certain types of combat to the short dagger used by the Shang soldiers. The *I-Chou-shu* 易周書 records a legend in which such a sword was used. King Wu, after winning a decisive victory, entered the Shang palace, where he shot three times each at the bodies of the Shang king and two court ladies. After this he struck them with a *ch'ing-lü* 輕呂, interpreted by the annotators as a precious sword.[19] The incident and the name *ch'ing-lü* are associated with sword worship in the steppes.[20]

Striking of the deceased with the sword has been interpreted as a ritual of sorcery rather than as an actual execution.[21] The use of the sword to conduct such a ritual probably testifies to the significance of the sword in the Chou mind. Nevertheless, the use of this weapon alone is not sufficient to explain the Chou victory over the Shang.

Chou armor was, however, somewhat more efficient than the Shang equipment (figs. 3.14, 3.15). Shang armor consisted of large pieces of rawhide, which protected the front of the warrior but greatly restricted his movement. Newly excavated fragments of Chou armor have allowed reconstruction of a different model. Three plaques of bronze were fastened to the front of the garment, and two were attached to the back. A bronze helmet, protective knee plates, and breast plates were the complete protective covering of the Chou warrior.[22] (See fig. 3.16.) This costume, although heavy, was flexible and provided more extensive protection than did Shang armor.

The war chariot played an important role in ancient warfare. The fast-moving chariot, pulled by two or four galloping horses, was

17. Ibid., 170–71.
18. Wu Chen-lu, 1972.
19. *I-Chou-shu*, 4/2–3.
20. Průšek, 1971:132–33.
21. Kao, 1960.
22. Yang Hung, 1977:84–85.

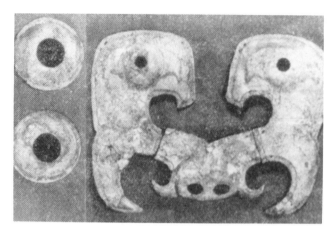

3.14 Bronze armor (from *WW*, 1977 [4]:71)

3.15 Chou-period bronze helmet (from *KK*, 1976 [1]:pl. 3)

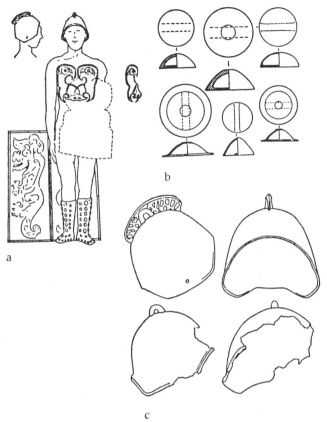

3.16 Suggested reconstruction of Chou armor: *a*. breast plate (from
WW, 1977 [5]:84); *b*. attachments (from *KK*, 1976 [4]:253); c. helmets
(from *KK*, 1976 [4]:253).

formidable to soldiers on foot (fig. 3.17). Even so, its hard wheels could
not move easily on unprepared road surfaces. Thus, even the most
expert archer could not be very accurate while riding in this bouncing
vehicle. The long weapons, the *ko* 戈 and *chi* 戟 halberd, were effective in
the hands of a mounted warrior. In order to engage in combat, chariots
had to pass one another, but the moment of exchange was extremely
brief. The more pragmatic use of the chariot was as a mount from which
a commander could view the battle and signal the soldiers by using a
store of flags and percussion instruments (drums, gongs, cymbals, etc.)
loaded in the chariot.[23] When the structure and size of recently
excavated war chariots were compared, the differences between Shang

23. Creel, 1970:263–82; Yang Hung, 1977:86–87.

3.17 Western Chou chariot burial in state of Yen at Liu-li-ho (from *KK*, 1984 [5]:pl. 1)

and Chou models were insignificant. Table 3.1 gives the sizes of several ancient vehicles.

The Chou chariot was similar to the Shang, and it did not provide a military advantage. The size of infantry under the command of one such chariot may, however, describe an advantage. The organization of the Shang combat units is clear from archaeological materials. Scholars of classical studies have long debated the ratio of infantry to chariot, concluding that from ten to seventy-two foot soldiers were led by one chariot. The burials of the royal guards near the Shang tombs at Hsiao-t'un 小屯 showed that combat formation consisted of a phalanx of infantry in the front and war chariots with attached foot soldiers in the rear. Five chariots made a squad, and each squad formed one of three columns. The infantry was organized into squads of ten, which were lined up into left, right, and central columns. Three hundred soldiers, therefore, constituted a functionally independent combat unit. In another cluster the infantry was organized into groups of five. Five such groups in turn formed a company of twenty-five soldiers with five corporals. Two companies were put under the command of a lieutenant; two of such units finally formed a combat unit of one hundred soldiers, plus twenty-five officers and corporals.[24] Since the war chariot was used as a movable command platform, its combination with the foot soldier was rather flexible.

Legendary accounts relate that the Chou army, with three thousand "tiger warriors" and a number of war chariots, actively took part in the battle of Mu-yeh. The number of chariots was reported differently: one hundred in the *Mo-tzu* 墨子, three hundred in the work of Mencius, and three hundred and fifty in the *I-Chou-shu* 易周書. Although there is no way to verify those figures, many of the "tiger warriors" had to be foot soldiers, and thus were probably outfitted with bronze armor, a halberd or spear, and a bronze sword. Creel based his conclusions on descriptions in the *Tso-chuan*, which emphasized the importance of the infantry in battle.[25] On one occasion (Ninth Year of Duke Huan 桓), there was a combined force of twenty-five chariots clustered in one unit, with infantry including five files of soldiers standing between each vehicle. The foot soldiers greatly outnumbered soldiers in chariots. In another incident from the *Tso-chuan* (First Year of Duke Chao 昭), the Chin commander in northern Shansi ordered all the mounted warriors to fight on foot in order to achieve better mobility in the mountainous terrain, the home of the Ti 狄 barbarians.[26]

24. Pei-ching ta-hsüeh, Department of History, 1979:76−79; Hsü Cho-yün, 1982:291−92.

25. Creel, 1970:276−91.

26. Legge, *Ch'un Ts'ew*, 46, 579; Hsü Cho-yün, 1982:372.

Table 3.1. Measurements of War Chariots

Locality	Period	Diameter of Wheel	Spokes	Track Width	Platform[a] W	D	Dashboard	Draft-pole[b] L	Dia	Axle[b] L	Dia	Yoke-bar	Horses[c]	Human sacrifices[c]
TSK-175	Shang	146	18	215	94	75	NR	280	11	300	NR	120	2	1
HMT-1	Shang	122	NR	240	134	83	49	268	7:8.5:6	310	5–8	NR	2	1
HMT-2	Shang	122	26	NR	100	NR	41[e]	260+	6:7.5:9	190	5–8	NR	2	0
HMT-South	Shang	133–134	22	217	129–133	74	45	256	9.5	306	13–15	110	2	1
CCP-1	W. Chou	129	22	NR	107	86	25	281	6.5	292	NR	240	2	1
CCP-2 (1)	W. Chou	136	21	225	138	68	45+	298	NR	307	NR	137	4	1
CPP-2 (2)	W. Chou	135	21	NR	135	70	20	295	7	294	7.8	210	2	0
CCP-3	W. Chou	140	22	NR	125	80	44	NR	NR	NR	NR	NR	2	1
LLH-1	W. Chou	140	24	224	150	90	NR	66+	14	308	8	NR	4	1
HA	W. Chou	140	18	224	164	97	29+	284	8,10	304	NR	138	4	1
STL-1227-2	Ch'un-ch'iu	125	28	180	123	90	33	296+	5.5,5.8	236	6.5	140	2	0
STL-1227-3	Ch'un-ch'iu	126	25	184	130	86	30[e]	250+	5.5,8.2	222	6.7	NR	2	0
STL-1051-1	Ch'un-ch'iu	107–124	25	166	100	100	NR	300	6.8	200	6	100	2	0
STL-105 1-7	Ch'un-ch'iu	NR	NR	200	NR	NR	NR	300	NR	248	7	NR	2	0
STL-180-1	Ch'un-ch'iu	117–119	26	164	130	82	NR	282	6.8	200+	8	NR	2	0
CCL	Chan-kuo	169	18[e]	200[e]	160	150	NR	340+	12	277	10	141	4	0
LLK-1	Chan-kuo	140	26	190	130	104	26,36[f]	170+	8	242[e]	10–12	170	0	0
LLK-5	Chan-kuo	95	26	140	95	93	22+,27+[f]	120+	4	178	7	140	0	0
LLK-6	Chan-kuo	105	26	185	120	98	30,42[f]	205	8	242	14[e]	140[e]	0	0
LLK-16	Chan-kuo	130	26+	182	140	105	40	210	10	236+	9–12	140	0	0
LLK-17	Chan-kuo	140	26+	180	150[e]	110	30,40[f]	215	10	242	14	150	0	0

Source: Adapted from Yang Hung, 1977:90.

Note:
TSK Ta-ssu-K'ung-ts'un, An-yang, Honan HA Hsi-an, Chiao-hsien, Shantung
HMT Hsiao-min-tun, An-yang, Honan STL Shang-ts'un-ling, Shen-hsien, Honan
CCP Chang-chia-p'o, Ch'ang-an, Shensi CCL Chung-chou-lu, Lo-yang, Honan
LLH Liu-li-ho, Fang-shan, Hopei LLK Liu-li-ko, Hui-hsien, Honan

The notation NR indicates that a measurement presumably could have been made, but none was reported. In some of these cases, evidence may have been destroyed. A plus sign (+) following measurement indicates that the object had at least the dimension or quantity recorded.

aW = Width; D = Depth.
bL = Length; Dia = Diameter.
cNumber found in pit.
dIn some cases, measurement of pole were taken fore and aft.
eMeasurement is approximate.
fMeasurement at low point and high point.

The troops that were aligned with the Chou in the battle of Mu-yeh were reportedly from eight "states," whose locations Hsü Chung-shu 徐中舒 traced mainly to the mountainous regions in the upper reaches of the Han River.[27] Those troops must have been infantry rather than mounted on chariots. The emphasis on infantry is a distinctive feature of the Chou military, one which allowed them the strength to overcome the clumsy formations of the Shang army and was a particular advantage in mountainous regions. And in addition to this emphasis on the foot soldier, they also benefited from their strategy and organization.

CHOU MILITARY STRATEGY

The Chou victory may in part be attributed to clever strategy, especially to their facility on broken terrain. The Chou flanked the Shang on both wings and then took advantage of the exhaustion of the Shang soldiers to attack on the other front as well. In addition, a series of events during the late Shang point out competition and confrontation between the Shang and the Chou long before the end of the dynasty. For instance, King Chi 王季 of Chou launched campaigns against the barbarians in northern Shansi on behalf of the Shang but was executed in spite of his success. Moreover, the Shang king Wu I 武乙 died in Chou territory. These incidents indicate that the Chou had become both a potential challenge and an ally to the Shang.

Another unusual event in the history of the Chou was the establishment of a state called Wu 吳, supposedly set up by the elder brothers of King Chi. When the two brothers were bypassed by King Chi for royal posts, they left for the south to establish a new state far from the Chou homeland.[28] Precisely why the Chou princes left has puzzled scholars for a long time. Whether the state of Wu was actually established has also been questioned. Ch'i Ssu-ho 齊思和 has doubted the validity of the legend, claiming that the state of Wu was not governed by descendants of the Chi 姬 clan at all.[29] The Tso-chuan, however, contains both formal and casual references to the Dukes of Wu using the royal surname Chi.[30] For example, the Duke of Wu claimed, "In relation to the House of Chi, we are the eldest branch."[31] This claim was made during a meeting attended by the major states when the Duke of Wu contended for leadership against the powerful

27. Hsü Chung-shu, 1936B:150–53.
28. *Shih-chi*, 3-1-3.
29. Ch'i Ssu-ho, 1940.
30. Legge, *Ch'un Ts'ew*, 757, 794, 828, 832.
31. Ibid., 832.

Chin 晉, a state also governed by descendants of Chi. With such tension between sister states, it seems unlikely that the Duke of Wu would present a false claim to the Duke of Chin, for he could challenge him if such a claim were fabricated. Recently, Hu Ch'ien-ying 胡謙盈 suggested that Wu was first established in the Ch'i-shan region and then in the southeast, after the Chou takeover of Shang.[32]

The controversy over the origin of Wu will remain open until more convincing evidence becomes available. Recent archaeological discoveries of blue-gray and yellow-green glazed ceramics at the Chou sites at Chang-chia-p'o indicate that there might have been contact between the Wei Valley and the lower reaches of the Yangtze. The glazed ceramics found in Chang-chia-p'o are comparable to those found at the sites in T'un-hsi 屯溪 and Tan-t'u 丹徒, both located in southeast China. The archaeologists who excavated the Chang-chia-p'o site reported that the ceramics were of the Wu-yüeh 吳越 type of blue pottery and that the Chang-chia-p'o specimens were probably imports from the southeast. The shapes of the Chang-chia-p'o pots are comparable to southern types that survived into the Ch'in 秦-Han 漢 period some one thousand years later.[33] The suggestion of contact between these northern centers and friendly states to the south raises further questions about the nature of the interaction.

Hsü Chung-shu has suggested two reasons for a long-distance expedition by the princes of Chi, T'ai-po 泰伯 and Chung-yung 仲雍, to a land which they called the state of Wu. He first suggested that the two princes were leaders of colonial troops in search of new land to settle. But instead, they may have been seeking asylum under the shelter of the Shang after they lost their bid for the throne. Hsü Chung-shu ruled out the second hypothesis by arguing that these contenders could hardly have been a constant irritation and threat to the Chou kings while they lived at such a distance. Hsü went on to suggest that the long march under the direction of T'ai-po was the result of the desire to avoid the strong control of the Shang in the Han River Valley and in the middle reaches of the Yangtze. The T'ai-po expedition penetrated deeper into the south beyond areas under direct influence of the Shang.[34] Although this proposition is plausible, the establishment of the state of Wu did not have much of an impact on the conquest of the Shang by the Chou. There is no historical evidence that Wu or any other southern state took part in the contest between the Chou and the Shang. The issue of the origin of Wu, then, may simply suggest that the Chou leaders took

32. Hu Ch'ien-ying, 1982:43−45.
33. K'ao-ku yen-chiu-so, 1962:94, 161−65.
34. Hsü Chung-shu, 1936B:143.

some preliminary measures to extend their influence beyond their homeland.

King Wen, on the other hand, did take an important step toward expansion. His efforts to keep the territories of the Chou free from trouble were recorded in a poem describing the early development of the Chou state.

> The hordes of the Kun disappeared, startled and panting.
> (The chiefs of) Yü and Jui were brought to agreement
> By King Wen's stimulating this natural virtue.[35]

The K'un-I 昆夷 were a "barbarian" group who lived near the Chou. They were probably related to other nomadic groups who later disturbed the northern and western borders of the Chou.[36] The Chou mediated between the Yü 虞 and the Jui 芮, the states in southwest Shansi, and their acceptance of the Chou intervention suggests that they were considered members of the Chi group. Several states of the Chi were apparently established in that region, and, even though they bore the surname Chi, they were considered barbarians along with the Jung and Ti. Might they have been branches of the family who stayed behind after the Chou moved to the Wei Valley?[37] If this had been the case, King Wen could have easily established suzerainty over them.

King Wen became ruler over the area to the west of the Chou, and he did so by conquering Mi 密.

> The people of Mi were disobedient,
> Daring to oppose our great country,
> And invaded Juan, marching to Kung.
> The King rose majestic in his wealth;
> He marshalled his troops,
> To stop the invading foes,
> To consolidate the prosperity of Chou
> To meet (the expectations of) all under heaven.[38]

The state of Mi, also called Mi-hsü 密須, was located in Ling-t'ai 靈台 in Kansu 甘肅. The Juan 阮 and Jui 芮 occupied the upper banks of the Ching River, and the campaign there against the Mi brought the highland under Chou's control. This event was a memorable occasion in the minds of the early Chou people, for a drum captured from the Mi became a precious item bestowed on a Chou prince when he was enfeoffed.[39]

35. Legge, *She King*, 441; *Shih-ching*, 3-1-3.
36. Průšek, 1971:43–48.
37. Hsü Chung-shu, 1936B:143, 155.
38. *Shih-ching*, 3-1-7; Legge, *She King*, 452–53.
39. Legge, *Ch'un Ts'ew*, 754.

In the same poem, following the description of the campaign against the Mi, is a passage relating the Chou attack on Ch'ung 崇.

> God said to King Wen,
> Take measures against the country of your foes.
> Along with your brethren,
> Get ready your scaling ladders,
> And your chariots of attack and assault,
> To attack the walls of Ch'ung.
> Against the walls of Ch'ung very strong;
> He attacked it, and let loose all his forces;
> He extinguished (its sacrifices) and made an end of its existence;
> And throughout the kingdom none dared to oppose him.[40]

The *Tso-chuan* also reported the seige of Ch'ung. After thirty days the Chou retreated, and only after another attack did the city fall.[41] The defeat of Ch'ung marked an important step in the eastward advance of Chou control, for no sooner was Ch'ung taken than King Wen moved the capital to Feng 豐. The actual location of Ch'ung is puzzling. Even though traditional opinion positioned it near the Wei River, the new capital of Feng was thought to have been built on Ch'ung.[42] Ch'en P'an 陳槃, however, identified Ch'ung as Sung 嵩, a region in the west of Honan near Mount Sung, which is midway between the Wei River Valley and the eastern plains.[43] If this identification was accurate, the capture of Ch'ung marked an important change in the balance of power in the Wei Valley. Ch'ung was an important outpost of Shang allegiance in territory between the Shang and the Chou. If Ch'en's proposition is true, the subjugation of Ch'ung by the Chou meant that they had reached the western edge of Shang by the time of King Wen. Surely the battle of Ch'ung meant a great deal in the Chou scheme.

In the year following the campaign against Mi, King Wen attacked Ch'i 耆, a place called Li 黎 in the *Book of Documents*. Li was located in the southeast of Shansi, near present-day Ch'ang-chih 長治 County, very far from the junction of the Wei and Yellow rivers. The advance of the Chou into Shang territory caused alarm among the Shang nobles, for they made special effort to warn their king of the imminent danger.[44] The next year Chou troops attacked Yü 邘,[45] located south of Li near the north bank of the Yellow River. Li Hsüeh-ch'in identified Yü as one part

---

40. Legge, *She King*, 454–55.
41. Legge, *Ch'un Ts'ew*, 177.
42. Ting Shan, 1935:111.
43. Ch'en P'an, 1969:379.
44. Legge, *Shoo King*, 286–72.
45. *Shih-chi*, 4/14.

of the Shang royal game lands, virtually within the royal domain. From Li and Yü, the Chou troops could look down from the highland upon the yellow earth plains of the Shang heartland.[46]

The *Shih-chi* puts the battle of Ch'ung one year after the fall of Yü.[47] Whatever the actual date, the Chou forces had advanced along both banks of the Yellow River. Further development in western Honan broadened their base of operation. Shirakawa Shizuka's 白川靜 study on the origin of the Chou associated this influential group with one called Shao-fang 召方 recorded in Shang divinations. He suggested that Shao was an ancient nation that spread across a vast territory to the west of Shang. It was there that the Shang were to have installed a Commissioner of the West to manage and control the land. Shirakawa noted as well that the Shao and the Chou shared the Chi surname.[48] The land controlled by the Shao was critical strategically. To their north and across the Yellow River was the early homeland of the Chou. The kinship between the groups allowed the Chou to advance on Ch'i and Li from that area. To the west, the Chou had already overcome the Ch'ung and were close to the Shang. The allegiance of the Shao and the Chou made the western front of Shang completely vulnerable. One may even suspect that the success of the Chou attack on Ch'ung was in part due to the positive nature of the relationship with Shao. From the west Honan base the Chou could stretch into the Han River Valley. Hsü Chung-shu cited an inscription on an early Chou bronze bell that stated that King Wen had already established some satellite states in the southern lands. It is not coincidental that the area south of the Shao region was customarily called "Shao-nan" 召南, or Shao's south, and that this area was under the supervision of Duke of Shao during the early reigns of the Chou dynasty.[49]

In pre-dynastic days the Chou probably maintained several "capitals." These included the old center at Ch'i-shan, Feng 豐 of King Wen, and Hao 鎬 of King Wu. The newly discovered ruins of palace buildings at Feng-ch'u 鳳雛 and Chao-ch'en 召陳 indicate continuous occupation there throughout the Chou.[50] By contrast, the sites at Feng and Hao look like military marching camps rather than centers with administrative or ceremonial capacities. Ch'i-shan retained its function as the true capital.[51] In other words, the Chou on the eve of conquest depended on the security of those military centers as essential to the

46. Li Hsüeh-ch'in, 1959:97.
47. *Shih-chi*, 4/14.
48. Shirakawa Shizuka, 1973:171–85.
49. Hsü Chung-shu, 1936B:144–46.
50. Chou-yüan k'ao-ku-tui 1979A:34; 1981A:21–22.
51. Ting Shan, 1935:107–10.

eastward campaign. They provided an important coupling in the encirclement of Shang territory.

Meanwhile, the Shang faced serious troubles along their eastern borders as well. The *Tso-chuan* twice recorded that the I 夷 people rebelled, causing the Shang king to launch a full-scale review of his troops at Li. The I eventually came under Chou control and became a serious threat to the Shang. The Shang exercise must have been made in preparation for the suspected attack by the Chou. But, unexpectedly, the Eastern I also revolted against the Shang. That rebellion was put down by the Shang, but at a heavy cost. The learned man who recorded this historical event in the *Tso-chuan* alleged that the Shang king lost his life as a result of that campaign.[52] Since the last Shang king did not actually die until the fall of the dynasty and after the Chou army entered the Shang capital, the allegations of his death in the battles with the I must be interpreted as the final, fatal blow to the Shang, the consequence of which was the fall of their capital city.

Although the Shang and their neighbors, possibly the descendants of the Ta-wen-k'ou 大汶口 neolithic, shared a cultural base, they belonged to different ancient nations. Their political relations must have been cordial, for few military actions are registered between them in the Shang divination records. Final subjugation of the I, however, was not complete. In an incident recorded in the *Great Declaration* 泰誓, the Chou claimed that the Shang king had control over hundreds of thousands of I people, but they were of divided mind.[53] In other words, the loyalty of the I people was dubious.

In summary, the contest between the Shang and the Chou gradually developed in favor of the latter when the attention of the Shang was drawn to the east. The Chou took advantage of this and extended their influence in areas on the western edge of the Shang domain. The *Tso-chuan* puts it this way: "When King Wen led on the revolted states of Yin 殷 to serve Chou 紂, his king, he knew the time."[54] The Chou obviously had brought into this camp those who were formerly Shang subordinates. The Chou already had control of the Wei Valley, the western half of the middle Yellow River in southern Shansi and western and southern Honan, and perhaps the Han River Valley as well. The Shang governed only the lower reaches of the Yellow River Valley and had recently dominated the coastal region of the I. The Shang were now completely encircled by antagonistic groups allied with the Chou.

52. Legge, *Ch'un Tsew*, 597, 633.
53. Legge, *Shoo King*, 292; *Ch'un Ts'ew*, 702. Legge translated "I" as "ordinary men." Here the term is taken to mean the I people.
54. Legge, *Ch'un Ts'ew*, 423.

THE FALL OF SHANG

King Wen was not alive to see the completion of the conquest, the job accomplished by his son, King Wu, known as the Martial King. The first attempt to directly attack the Shang was launched in the early years of King Wu's reign. The *Shih-chi* records that eight hundred lords from the Chou allies converged at Meng-chin 孟津, a ferry spot near the Shang capital.[55] The credibility of that account must be questioned, however, for the decisive battle was actually waged two years later, when Chou forces consisted of their army and troops from only eight allied states. An oath taken by King Wu and recorded in fragments of ancient works declared his determination to carry out the assault. There is no obvious reason why the Chou troops would withdraw before facing the Shang army.[56] Two years later, the battle of Mu-yeh 牧野 was waged.

In that battle the Chou king led an army of three hundred war chariots, three thousand "tiger warriors" (probably infantry), plus troops sent by the eight other states. In addition, four thousand war chariots from other allied nations were said to have joined the Chou. The Shang king allegedly commanded an army of seven hundred thousand men,[57] but the figures reporting the sizes of both armies appear to be highly exaggerated. The population of the Shang could not possibly have been large enough to raise 700,000 combat soldiers. The battles registered on oracle bone inscriptions never involved more than a few thousand recruits. After brief contact, the Shang army supposedly turned their weapons on their own king, and the victory was won by the Chou without much fighting. Such an allegation is included in the *Book of Documents* but was questioned by Mencius, who pointed out that the source described a battle that caused so much blood to flow that it could float wooden batons.[58]

In 1975 a bronze Li *kuei* 利殷 vessel was discovered at Lin-t'ung 臨潼 (fig. 3.18). The inscription on the vessel describes the battle of Mu-yeh and has been deciphered in several ways.[59] (See fig. 3.19.) In general the text can be summarized as follows: before the battle in which King Wu vanquished the Shang on the day of *chia-tzu* 甲子, in the morning, a ceremony of Sui 歲 was held and a divination was made. At dusk on the same day the Chou triumphantly occupied Shang. On the date *hsin-wei*

55. *Shih-chi*, 4/21.
56. Sun Hsing-yen, 1815:30 F/2–3.
57. *Shih-chi*, 4/24–25.
58. Legge, *Mencius*, 479.
59. Yü Sheng-wu, 1977; T'ang Lan, 1977A; Lin-t'ung hsien wen-wu-kuan, 1977; Chung Feng-nien et al., 1978; T'ien I-ch'ao, 1980:1–10; Chang Cheng-lang, 1978; Shirakawa Shizuka, *KBHS* 50:323–40.

3.18 Li *kuei* (courtesy of the Cultural Relics Bureau, Beijing, and the Metropolitan Museum of Art, Seth Joel, photographer)

辛未 (seven days after *chia-tzu*), King Wu conferred a blessing on Li, who cast the vessel in honor of his ancestor Lord T'an 檀. Although obscure and difficult to interpret, the middle section of the inscription is thought to refer to a divination performed by Li in honor of King Wu, the auspicious pronouncement that encouraged Wu to launch his attack.

This inscription has great historical value, for it confirms that the battle against Shang took place on the date of *chia-tzu* and that it lasted from morning to dusk of the same day. Both incidents are recorded in the *Book of Documents* and the *Shih-chi*. The combined evidence supports the notion that the battle was won by King Wu with some ease. Unfortunately, the year and the month of the battle were not recorded in the Li *kuei* inscription, and, due to the difficulties in reconstructing the Shang and Chou calendars, the precise year cannot be learned. Several dates have been given for the battle of Mu-yeh, and it must have taken place sometime between 1122 B.C. and 1027 B.C.

3.19 Rubbing of inscription, Li *kuei* (fig. 3.18 above) (Fong, 1980:203)

In 1965, the Ho *tsun* 何尊 vessel was unearthed at Pao-chi 寶雞 (fig. 3.20). The inscription on it gives a retrospective account of the events immediately following the battle of Mu-yeh (fig. 3.21). Although there are many different interpretations, a summary of the contents is as follows. The king (presumably King Ch'eng 成) was moving to a newly finished capital, and, in order to receive the blessing of Heaven, he offered a sacrifice to King Wu at a Chamber of Heaven (*T'ien-shih* 天室). On the date *ping-hsü* 丙戌 of the fourth moon, the king reminded the young royalty that their forefathers had served King Wen, the man who first received the Heavenly Mandate. King Wu, who conquered the great city of the Shang, reported to Heaven that he planned to reside in the Central Kingdom (*Chung-kuo* 中國) in order to govern the people. King Ch'eng encouraged the royal kinsmen to follow the example of their ancestors and serve the court well so that they too would receive Heavenly blessings. Ho, the maker of the vessel, was presented with thirty strings of cowrie shells. The date was in the fifth year of King Ch'eng's reign.[60]

The Ho *tsun* inscription reveals King Wu's grandiose plan to govern the civilized world of his day, and his desire to do so from the Central

60. T'ang Lan 1976A; Ma Cheng-yüan, 1976; Chang Cheng-lang, 1976; Yeh Ta-hsiung, 1980; Shirakawa Shizuka, *KBHS* 48:171–85.

3.20 Ho *tsun* (courtesy of the Cultural Relics Bureau, Beijing, and the Metropolitan Museum of Art, Seth Joel, photographer)

Kingdom in the old Shang domain, not from the previous Chou head-quarters in the Wei Valley. Such an attitude reflects the assumption that the Chinese world should be drawn together and integrated by the Chou, for whom he was a representative. He accepted this mission because he received a Mandate from Heaven, bestowed on him because he occupied the Central Kingdom. Itō Michiharu came to this conclusion by comparing the Ho *tsun* inscription to the statement in the "Tu-i-chieh" 度邑解 of the *I-Chou-shu* 逸周書 in which King Wu declared that he would reside in the Heavenly Chamber, the home of the Hsia, and thereby stay near to heaven. Itō believed that the similar tone of these documents strengthened the credibility of the *I-Chou-shu* as a

3.21 Rubbing of
inscription, Ho *tsun* (fig.
3.20 above) (from Fong,
1980:204)

useful historical source.[61] In any case, that there was such a message in
the minds of the Chou is confirmed by the coincidence of these two
pieces of information.

These bits of data are of special interest because the Chou felt that
they could legitimize their rule of China by governing from the old
home of Hsia. These assertions may be interpreted as an attempt to
establish a legacy for them in the dynastic succession, from the Hsia to
the Shang and then to the Chou. Also, emphasis on the notion of a
Central Kingdom is first made explicit in these documents. It must be an
extension of the Shang concept that the center of their domain was the
nucleus of the universe, the physical center of the world. The Chou
believed in the supreme authority of Heaven and thereby that the
Chamber of Heaven was symbolic of the zenith of the sky. Corre-
spondingly, on earth they regarded the Wei Valley as the old land and
took Lo-yang 洛陽 as their new capital and the new center of the world.

The Ho *tsun* inscription includes the line, "We repeat the Feng 豐
ceremony in which King Wu requested blessings from Heaven." T'ang
Lan regarded this particular ceremony as a ritual of worship of Heaven
and pointed out that the Chou considered three of their deceased kings
as attendants of the Heavenly God. T'ang Lan thus believed that the
Chamber of Heaven was literally the specific place where Heaven was
worshiped.[62] The term "Chamber of Heaven" also appeared in the
inscription on the Ta-feng *kuei* vessel cast in the early years of the Chou

61. Itō Michiharu, 1978:41−42, 51; *I-Chou-shu*, 5/3−4.
62. T'ang Lan, 1976A: 60, 61, n. 2.

dynasty and excavated in the nineteenth century. The Chamber of Heaven was named as the place where the great ceremony of Feng was held. But exactly what was it? Was the Chamber of Heaven a specific building, a shrine, or a sacred place? Could it have been a particular location that was regarded as the center of the land?[63] Our current information allows little further speculation. In fact, the Shang did have a "Great City" where the sacred ceremonies were held. That particular spot was not in the same location as their administrative center, for the latter was moved several times throughout the dynasty. Li Hsüeh-ch'in has suggested that "Great City" refers to the Shang domain in general as well as to a city near T'ang-yin 湯陰 County, a short distance from An-yang.[64] The Chou probably did build a shrine at a place that they thought was the center of the world. But where was it? The sacred Sung 嵩 Mountain was called the Central Yüeh 岳 (Peak) or the Grand Chamber in the "Treatise of Sacrifices and Rituals" of the Han-shu 漢書.[65] Is it not possible that Sung Mountain, which rises magnificently from the yellow earth plain, was the logical spot for the Chou to erect a shrine to Heaven? Or, is it possible that such a high-rising mountain was simply called the Chamber of Heaven because it was where the Heavenly diety resided?

The Ta-feng *kuei* inscription referred to a particular ceremony in which offerings were made to three, not four, directions. Itō Michiharu and Kuo Mo-jo agreed that the Chou considered themselves to represent the west, and that they had to secure the blessings of the other directions in order to legitimize their authority in all of China. The "Tu-i-chieh" of the *I-Chou-shu* also mentioned only three directions, omitting the west.[66] Thus, the Chou did seem to inherit and absorb the Shang notion that the central Yellow River Valley was "*Chung-kuo,*" the center of the civilized world. This claim was reflected in the Shang notion of their world-order, that is, a Shang royal domain bordered on all four sides by subordinate states.[67]

Another phrase in the Ta-feng *kuei* inscription is perplexing to scholars. There it is stated: "three times the worship of the King of Yin." Ch'en Meng-chia thought that an error had been made in the casting of characters.[68] Shirakawa Shizuka thought it meant that the Chou enjoyed reigns that were three times the length of the reigns of the

63. Itō Michiharu, 1978:48−49; Ch'en Meng-chia, 1955A: 152, 14−15.
64. Li Hsüeh-ch'in, 1959:8−15.
65. *Han-shu pu-chu*, hereafter *Han-shu*, 25A/14.
66. Itō Michiharu, 1978:49.
67. Ch'en Meng-chia, 1956A:269−312, 319−25; Chang, 1976:51.
68. Ch'en Meng-chia, 1955A:153.

Shang kings.[69] The oracle bones recently excavated from Chou-yüan do include inscribed pieces that record worship of deceased Shang kings.[70] If they are records of the Chou royal house, as we suspect, the kings did have reason to worship the Shang kings. The campaign against the Shang was declared by the Chou kings as a corrective measure against the crimes committed by the vicious Shang king Chou 紂. All the blame was put on him, not on the Shang people, who were given a new state where they could continue their own ancestor worship. Given this situation, the Chou kings could make offerings to the deceased rulers of a dynasty whom they succeeded.

Moreover, the chapter on post-conquest activities in the *I-Chou-shu* further explains the relationship of the Shang to the Chou. Five days after the execution of King Chou, Chou king Wu reported his great victory to his ancestors by recounting the crimes of King Chou. Three days later he communicated the same message to the Shang Supreme God, Shang-ti 上帝, at the Heavenly Shrine. Both rituals took place at the temple immediately following the victory at Mu-yeh, for the king was still in combat dress while conducting the rituals. The temple could not possibly be that of the Chou ancestors, for Wu was far from his homeland. There was no time for the Chou to erect a new temple, so he must have used a Shang royal shrine.[71] The Ta-feng *kuei* inscription also mentioned that King Wu conducted the Shang ceremony of *I-ssu* 衣祀, which collectively paid homage to all the Shang ancestors. In other words, King Wu probably took over the sacred services of the Shang in order to authorize himself as the legitimate successor to the Shang dynasty.

In summary, the conquest of Shang was symbolically proclaimed by the Chou not as a hostile act against the Shang, but rather as a pledge to continue the Shang level of domination over the world of the Chinese. Moreover, their commitment was countenanced by Heaven. The gesture made by the Chou king added coherence to rule and responded to a particular circumstance of the moment. The Chou had accomplished the nearly impossible task of allying and uniting the semi-independent and independent powers of north China. The small armed force that they controlled directly was not strong enough to hold the vast territory by force. Part of their solution was to maintain the ties established by the Shang and to legitimate them through moral decree. Compromise and cooperation were necessary to succeed, and the first Chou gesture for so doing was to adopt the sacred ceremonies customarily conducted by the

69. Shirakawa Shizuka, *KBTS*, 1:26.
70. Chou-yüan k'ao-ku-tui, 1979B: 39–40. Recall the discussion in chapter 2.
71. Li Hsüeh-ch'in, 1959:9.

Shang in their old, sanctioned center. The Chou could then be seen as generous and licit. They expressed such authority because they were obligated to do so by Mandate and by political and psychological reality.

THE MORALIZATION OF THE MANDATE OF HEAVEN

The results of the bestowal of the Mandate on the Chou in Chinese political life were far reaching and affected many aspects of life, especially the life of the aristocrats. Assessment of the conditions under which these changes occurred demonstrates how the overlordship of the Chou was gradually developed through military force and political alignments. With the adjustment came a shift in political, social, and spiritual order. The Chou altered their position in relation to the spiritual realm when they received the Mandate and accepted Heavenly authority as supreme and abandoned the pantheistic and shamanistic practices of the Shang in favor of a more abstract concept. But how can this change be explained? Did the design evolve from a Shang, or earlier, prototype, or from living conditions in China in the late second millennium B.C. that necessitated such a change?

The Shang notion of a power from whom blessings originated included a whole host of deities. They included those of the natural forces such as the Wind, Rain, Rivers, Mountains, et cetera, as well as many ancestors. Heaven (t'ien 天) was not considered extraordinary. In fact, the character t'ien was not distinguished from the character ta 大, meaning great. The character that often signified sky, or heaven, was shang 上 (up, above, upper) as opposed to hsia 下 (down, below, lower).[72]

The meaning of the word Ti 帝 also varied from one period to the other. As a noun, Ti was used in the Shang period as a posthumous title for a king. As a verb, it meant to offer sacrifices to those ancestors who were called Ti. Etymologically, Ti and ancestor worship were related.[73] The character Ti itself was interpreted as the stem of a flower and thus implied the origin of life. It was also used to signify a bundle of wood representing that used in ritual offerings.[74] Li Tsung-t'ung investigated the definition of Ti as a signifier of rituals such as those presented in the Li-chi (Record of Rites). He noticed that this ceremony was held to honor "those from whom the ancestors originated." He argued that the pro-

72. Ch'en Meng-chia, 1956A:580–81. These two characters should not be confused with the names of the two dynasties.
73. Ibid., 562.
74. Shima Kunio, 1958:186–89.

genitor was not an ancestor but a totemic figure and that the manifestation of that belief survived only in religious ceremonies.[75]

If further extended, the totem theory implies that the role of Ti in the Shang faith was specific to beings related to the Shang royal house. Ti was not a universal supreme being who transcended national borders or social status. The Shang version of Ti was one who extended special favors, offered blessings, and protected the Shang people. A tribal or national deity with such particular concerns need not and would not demand that the members follow a moral code. Ti was the guardian of the Shang, a particular ethnic group, not a deity with expanded, universal powers.[76]

Itō Michiharu, however, has argued that the early Shang did believe in a supreme being under whom lesser deities and the ancestors operated. He argued that the institutionalization of ancestor worship gradually incorporated the concept of ancestral protection and a group of nonancestral spirits into its genealogy. By the end of the Shang, the authority of the ancestral spirits was firmly established through institutionalization of ceremonies. Itō felt that such a trend was consistent with the establishment and incorporation of patriarchal authority under the Shang kings.[77] In the early years of Shang authority, their spiritual system had to expand to absorb guardians of other tribes with whom the Shang wished to associate. This expansion definitely helped consolidate the Shang kingdom.[78] Then, as ancestor worship was dogmatized and the ceremonies were codified, the Shang lost interest in including additional members. By excluding new participants, they lost the advantage of drawing diverse groups together. Itō suggested that the "new school" that excluded nonancestral beings from religious ceremonies actually represented the end product of that crystallization.[79]

Although argued on very different premises, the conclusions of Itō and Li Tsung-t'ung are strikingly similar—Shang worship of Ti and ancestor worship were merged. Moreover, both scholars concluded that the Shang deity Ti was not a universal supreme being. The fusion of Ti and the ancestral spirits was confirmed by the use of "Ti" as a term to describe the ceremony for worship of deceased Shang kings.[80]

For the Chou, worship of a national protector or exclusive guardian

75. Li Tsung-t'ung, 1954:266–67.
76. Hsü Hsü-sheng, 1960:199–201.
77. Itō Michiharu, 1975:45.
78. Hayashi Minao, 1970; Itō Michiharu, 1975:77–79.
79. The theory of dualism was first advanced by Tung Tso-pin, 1964, vol. 1:2–4; Itō Michiharu, 1975:112–17.
80. Shima Kunio, 1958:211.

of the Shang was not meaningful. Their miraculous victory over the powerful Shang was explained by them as an expression of sacred grace. There was a dilemma, however, for what would now happen to the protective powers of the Shang deities? The Chou were related to the Shang royalty through matrimonial ties as well as through political subordination, yet now they had received the sacred Mandate as a consequence of the Shang failure to govern justly. The moral demand to provide such care was sanctioned in the spiritual order created by the Chou. A supreme being who could make moral judgments appeared in their pantheon. Fu Ssu-nien has theorized that the changed Mandate necessarily provoked the moralization of political authority in the hands of the Chou.[81] The Chou were "chosen" because of their good conduct, not because of their specific ancestral affiliation. This attitude is recorded in the *Book of Poetry*.

> Great is God,
> Beholding this lower world in majesty,
> He surveyed the four quarters (of the world),
> Seeking for someone to give settlement to the people.
> Those two (earlier) dynasties
> Had failed to satisfy him with their government;
> So throughout the various states,
> He sought and considered,
> For one on which he might confer the rule.
> Hating all the (other great) states,
> He turned his kind regards on the West,
> And there gave a settlement (to King T'ai).[82]

The deliberations of the Great God were based on a moral obligation to stabilize the people with good government and secular rule. This song goes on to narrate the favors that the god bestowed upon three generations of Chou rulers (King T'ai, King Chi Li, and King Wen) as they attempted to fulfill the wishes of God. Through continued blessings from God, the Chou were successful in their preparation for a successful conquest.

Another poem, attributed to a Chou minister of later times, probably reflects an earlier work. Here again King Wen accuses the Shang king of crimes and faults that justify his action against the Shang.

> How vast is God,
> The ruler of men below.
> How arrayed in terrors is God,

81. Fu Ssu-nien, 1952, vol. 3:91–110.
82. Legge, *She King*, 448–49.

With many things irregular in his ordination!
Heaven gave birth to the multitudes of the people,
But the natives it confers are not to be depended upon.
All are (good) at first,
But few prove themselves to be at the last.
King Wen said, Alas!
Alas! You (sovereign of) Yin/Shang,
That you should love such violently oppressive ministers.
That you should have such extraordinary exactors.
That you should have them in offices.
That you should have them in the conduct of affairs.
Heaven made them with their insolent dispositions.
But it is you who employ them, and give them strength.[83]

The stanzas that follow accuse the Shang king of employing thieves and
robbers who had uttered false oaths. Lacking virtuous advisers, the
Shang are accused of indulging in heavy drinking, provoking foreign
wars, betraying good traditions, and ignoring past precedents. Such
activities certainly could not be seen as positive and, thus interpreted,
set the stage for the Chou to act with moral conviction. In the final
stanzas, King Wen declares that a giant tree was uprooted, just as had
happened to the Hsia when China yielded to the Shang.[84] It is especially
pertinent that the story of the succession from the Hsia to the Shang is
repeated, because the poet calls forth historical precedent to show that
God had not committed his will to a single ruling house. God is
described as a judge who took the Mandate away from the vicious and
gave it to the worthy and virtuous. Principles are rewarded before
personalities, and the same logic is to be applied to the Chou as rulers.

The Chou poets preach the message even more explicitly in a song
called "King Wen." The song praises Wen's achievements and warns
that the Mandate is constantly subject to review.

King Wen is on high:
Oh! Bright is he in Heaven.
Although Chou was an old country,
The (favoring) mandate lighted on it recently.
Illustrious was the House of Chou,
And the appointment of God came at the proper season.
King Wen ascends and descends,
On the left and right of God.

83. Ibid., 505–10.
84. Ibid.

Profound was King Wen;
Oh! Continuous and bright was his feeling of reverence,
Great is the Mandate of Heaven!
There were the descendants of (the sovereigns) of Shang;
The descendants of the sovereigns of Shang,
Were in number more than hundreds of thousands;
But when God gave the command,
They became subject to Chou.

They became subject to Chou.
The Mandate of Heaven is not constant.
Always striving to accord with the will of Heaven.
So shall you be seeking for much happiness.
Before Yin lost the multitudes
Its Kings were the assessors of God.
Look to Yin as a beacon;
The great Mandate is not easily preserved
Do not cause your own extinction
Display and make bright your righteousness and name,

And look at (the fate of) Yin in the light of Heaven.
The doings of High Heaven,
Have neither sound nor smell.
Take your pattern from King Wen
And the myriad regions will repose confidence in you.[85]

Chou is regarded as an "old country," meaning that the Chou thought of themselves as descendants of the Hsia 夏. The Mandate was, therefore, a renewal of the Hsia decree. King Wen, then already deceased, is not hailed as a deity as were the Shang kings. Instead, King Wen is regarded as merely an attendant or assistant to the Heavenly God. These three quotations from the *Book of Poetry* vividly illustrate the pious Chou attitude toward a supreme being. Such attitudes differ in kind from those of the Shang.

The *Book of Documents* includes twelve entries related to the history of the early Chou. Fu Ssu-nien found that the term *ming* 命, meaning both "order" and "mandate," appears 104 times. In seventy-three cases it refers to the Mandate of Heaven, especially in the context of discussions about the succession from Hsia to Shang, or Shang to Chou.[86] Clearly, this issue frequently occupied the minds of the early Chou leaders, and Fu explains that the Ti god of the Shang was considered their

85. Ibid., 428–31.
86. Fu Ssu-nien, 1952, vol. 3:31–38.

progenitor. In the legend of the birth of the Chou, Hou Chi 后稷 was only vaguely and indirectly related to a Ti god. Ti's giant footprint was stepped upon by the mother of Hou Chi, who by doing so became pregnant. Hou Chi was thus born through a miraculous incident; he was not the son of the god Ti. Fu argues further that when the Chou adopted the progenitor of the Shang his position was upgraded from his position as kin to the Shang into a more universal place. The Chou could not claim themselves as his kin, but they could incorporate him within the broader, more universal system.[87]

HEAVEN AS THE SUPREME BEING

Heaven, or the dome of the sky, was worshiped as the supreme being by the Chou. The word *t'ien*, or Heaven, did appear in their oracle inscriptions. *T'ien* was written as a front view of a standing figure. Sometimes *t'ien* was part of a proper name, sometimes it meant "great" or "grand," but in no case did *t'ien* carry an anthropomorphic meaning such as "sky-god."[88] Fu Ssu-nien thought that even though *t'ien* did not connote a sky-god, it did signify the solemnity of the dome of the sky. He emphasized the fact that oracle bone fragments are only a partial record of religion and that the appearance of Ti in the Shang record signals their recognition of a supreme being.[89] The oracle bones do contain considerable information about religious services and thus record several minor and major Shang deities. Many were the deities of natural forces or phenomena. If the rivers and mountains were worshiped and the services were recorded in the divination record, those dedicated to a sky-god should have appeared as well. Moreover, Ti was considered the progenitor of the Shang ruling house and his name should be distinct from a sky-god whose features had to be familiar in the context of the spirits of nature. The characters *hsia*, lower or below, and *shang*, upper or above, were often used in the Shang record as well as in the Chou. Their use often referred to spatial locations. The combination of *shang* and *Ti* into "Shang Ti" must have simply denoted the progenitor who resided above in the sky. Sky in this case was a location, not a phenomenon or personality to be worshiped in itself.

The use of the word *t'ien*, in early Chou literature and bronze in-scriptions, on the other hand, may be gleaned both as Dome of the

87. Ibid., 81–82; Hsü Hsü-sheng, 1960:201; Ikeda Suetoshi, 1964.
88. Shima Kunio, 1958:214.
89. Fu Ssu-nien, 1952, vol. 3:90.

Sky and as Heaven. Although this new use appeared abruptly at the beginning of the dynasty, it is doubtful that the concept for which the term *t'ien* was used developed suddenly. The term itself must have been borrowed from the Shang and used to name the already prevalent Chou concept of a supreme being.[90]

That adjustment in use, however, had a rather logical development. Wang Kuo-wei suggested that the bar or dot on the head of the front view of the standing figure indicated the sky above. The use of a bar or dot for emphasis in the structure of a character repeats a principle common in the creation of Chinese characters.[91] The dome of the sky, although sanctified, was still described as a physical space. In the *Book of Poetry* one poem illustrates that idea.

> The arrogant are delighted
> And the troubled are in sorrow.
> Oh azure Heaven! Oh azure Heaven!
> Look upon those arrogant men,
> Pity those troubled.[92]

The blue sky is addressed here as a phenomenon, not a deity.

We do know that the worship of a sky-god did continue in the area of the Chou homeland as late as the Han. Other incidences of the blue sky can be cited. The phrase, "O bright and high Heaven Who enlightens and rulest this lower world," appears in the *Shih-ching*.[93] In the "Treatise on Sacrifices" and the "Treatise on Geography" of the *Han-shu*, virtually all the shrines or sacred sites for worship of a heavenly god, other than the official or imperial ones, are located in the provinces of Shensi and Kansu.[94] They seem to be associated with the area of the big, open sky.

In addition, ancient legends preserve descriptions of the struggles between Ti and Heaven. In the mock gambling game between the Heavenly God and the Shang king cited in chapter 2, the Shang king created a wooden puppet to serve as a surrogate for the Heavenly God. The "God" lost the gamble. The king had a leather bag filled with blood hung in a tree. He shot at the bag, and in doing so was thought to be shooting at the sky.[95] A similar act was repeated by the last king of Sung

90. Some scholars believe that *t'ien* connoted a Shang deity in oracle inscriptions. See Sun Hai-p'o, 1934, vol. 1:1; Chin Hsiang-heng, 1959, vol.1:1; Li Hsiao-ting, 1965, vol. 1:13–21. Those opposed: Ch'i Ssu-ho, 1948A:23; Ch'en Meng-chia, 1954:93; Creel, 1970:495–96.

91. Wang Kuo-wei, 1959:262–63; Shima Kunio, 1958:215–16.

92. Legge, *She King*, 348.

93. Ibid., 363.

94. *Han-shu*, 25A/16, 25B/9, 28A/26.

95. *Shih-chi*, 3-24-25.

(ca. 920–880 B.C.), the state formed by the descendants of the Shang.[96]
The two incidents cannot be accidental or unrelated, and the Sung
leader must have copied the act of his ancestors, perhaps in a ritual of
sorcery. By doing so they reenacted a struggle between two nations,
using the Heavenly God to represent the Chou.

The *Shan-hai-ching* 山海經 , a treasury of ancient legends and myths,
records a story of struggle between gods for the position of Supreme
Being. The contest involved Ti and Hsing-t'ien 刑天 ("dissected T'ien"),
who had lost his head. Though his eyes were replaced by nipples and his
mouth by a navel, he could still dance with his weapons in his hands.[97]
This tragic hero probably represents a defeated sky-god who failed in
one round of the contest. As the *Shan-hai-ching* records heroes of the
east, it has been thought of as a collection of stories from eastern lands,
including the lands of the Shang. The previous story must record the
defeat of a western hero. Two other stories record the defeat of Hsia or
other non-Shang peoples.[98] These tales very likely reveal historical
struggles of the Hsia and the Chou with the Shang group. T'ien,
although accepted as the Supreme Being in Chou literature, must have
remained a contender, or even a pretender, for godly supremacy in the
minds of the Shang.

To the Chou people, the merging of Ti and T'ien was a logical
development that created alliances among the groups. The Chou
continued to use the name Ti in religious services when it applied to
Ti-ku, a Shang ancestor. Ti-ku 帝嚳, according to Fu Ssu-nien, was the
prototype of the Shang supreme being. In his view the Chou ancestor,
Hou Chi, was merely worshiped in the company of the Heavenly God,
but was not a god in his own right.[99] The Chou deceased kings were
thought of as "residents of Heaven," but none was considered the God
of Heaven. In early Chou works, Heaven ruled as the Supreme Being.
H. G. Creel found that *t'ien* was used 8 times in the *Book of Changes* and
104 times in the *Book of Poetry* (as opposed to 43 mentions of Ti), 116
times in the twelve early Chou chapters of the *Book of Documents* (in contrast to 25 instances of use of Ti), and 91 times in bronze inscriptions (in comparison to 4 appearances of Ti).[100] From this he deduced
the superior importance of the concept of *t'ien*.

Heaven was not tied to any nation as kin but was omnipresent. As
such, *t'ien* acquired the status of an impartial judge who could transmit
moral concerns to secular rulers. The messages repeated by the Chou

96. *Shih-chi*, 38/42.
97. *Shan-hai-ching chien-chu,* hereafter *Shan-hai-ching*, 7/2.
98. *Shan-hai-ching*, 6/4, 16/5.
99. Fu Ssu-nien, 1952, vol. 3:81–82, 91; Hsü Hsü-sheng, 1960:201.
100. Creel, 1970: 494–95.

leaders to their own people were included in the *Book of Poetry* and the *Book of Documents*.[101] These poems were confirmation of their readiness to apply a rigid moral standard to themselves. It was a means of ensuring good rule and virtuous conduct. This pious attitude was interpreted by Fu Ssu-nien as the dawning of humanism, the point at which the domination of mysterious powers of the spirit world was broken. That absolute power was ruptured because, if humans behaved morally, their will could actually influence the decision of the Supreme Being.[102] Furthermore, the Chou leaders drew their lesson from earthly, historical precedent rather than from theological or philosophical argument. Fu Ssu-nien listed the principles that were appropriate for the Chou: sincerity, consciousness of moral conduct, service to the people, care in use of punishment, diligence in governance, honoring good persons, honoring tradition, and abstention from abuse of alcohol. Fu summarized that the Chou, apparently preaching on the significance of the Heavenly Mandate, actually emphasized right conduct among men.[103] The position and power of the Supreme Being were not arguable, but human conduct was.

SOME REMARKS

The dawning of humanism, on the one hand, confirmed the importance of the sacred Mandate. On the other, it ratified the succession of ruling houses as a revelation of legitimacy determined by human will. The Chou effort to trace their succession to Hsia provided them with a double guarantee of legitimacy through their genealogical connection. The principle that combines the Mandate from Heaven and the will of man has operated in Chinese political theory since the Chou. The will of man has been interpreted as the interaction between the ruler's performance and the ruled's support. The model of political behavior was at odds with the notion of a divine will that was absolute and unpredictable.

The emergence of such humanism could not be merely a by-product of Chou propaganda developed to legitimate their succession. The idea must have had its inception earlier in the Shang period. Fu Ssu-nien observed that several phrases in the *Book of Documents* are referred to as quotations of ancient sayings. He suggested that Shang intellectuals, such as the scribes, must have based those sayings on historical knowledge derived from the wisdom of humanism. Quotations of that sort

101. Legge, *Shoo King*, 492–507; and other poems cited previously.
102. Fu Ssu-nien, 1952, vol. 3:91–92.
103. Ibid., 92–99.

should be regarded as seminal to a major philosophical breakthrough, one of few in human history.[104] The result was a new worldview.

The Shang ceremonies could be divided into two schools, according to Tung Tso-pin. The "Old School" offered elaborate services dedicated to a broad range of deities. The "new school" regulated ceremonies to a neat calendar and offered homage to only a limited number of deified, deceased kings and queens.[105] The "New School" probably reduced the number of Shang deities included, as Itō Michiharu has suggested. On the other hand, the New School divination practices demonstrated the routinization of a formerly mysterious aspect of divination. The influence of the will of the deities was no more taken so seriously, as long as the ceremonies were conducted regularly and correctly. That tendency to demythologize and rationalize may itself be taken as an indication of the humanization of ritual and belief. The exclusion of certain deceased from the list of worshiped spirits also reflects an increased separation between the spirits and the dead. The worship of ancestors was a measure of feelings for humanity, not of feelings toward the unknown.

The Old School started by including numerous already-deified characters and was possibly characterized by a certain tolerance that transcended the limits of kin. These two schools alternated in influence in Shang religion, but by the time of the conquest competition between them no longer existed. The Shang intellectuals, the scribes and priests, must have felt keenly the change in dynastic succession. Their ideas of humanism may have provided seminal stimulus for the Chou intellectual leaders, who were in need of a new ideology to explain and justify the dynastic succession. The emergence of a new ideology of humanism, in which human interests predominated, was built around the notion of a moral God of Heaven, and provided the nucleus of thought for Chinese philosophers like Confucius, for he too attempted to integrate the notion of a Heavenly Mandate with that of belief in the power of human will. The pivotal point in thinking about these issues was the juncture between the Shang and the Chou dynasties.

Finally, let us summarize the arguments in this chapter. The Chou were a small and culturally distinct, but inferior, state who managed to displace the powerful Shang and establish a new political authority that was to last for many centuries. The Chou's grand strategy of conquest was to establish alliances with states and culture groups, thus allowing them to surround the Shang domain. Meanwhile the Shang exhausted

104. Ibid., 99.
105. Tung Tso-pin, 1965:103–18; 1964, vol. 1:2–4. The phenomenon of dualism in the Shang period is dealt with in Chang, 1964:45–61.

themselves in foreign campaigns. The showdown between the Shang and Chou brought to the fore a profound question: Why had such a drastic change occurred? In the effort to answer that question, a fundamental change in thinking emerged. Justification of their own cause allowed the Chou to moralize—first about the will of God, and then about the new ideology of the Mandate of Heaven reflected in the will of man. This was humanism in its incipient form, a type of thinking that determined the subsequent orientation of Chinese thinking, both politically and philosophically. The Chou contribution provided the cornerstone for their own political legitimacy, but it also opened the course for the long Chinese tradition of humanism and rationalism and may be thought of as the first step toward a Jaspersian breakthrough.[106] Truth was seen as a very personal matter, apprehended by faith and communicated by an appeal to freedom of human will. Philosophical faith was attained in acceptance of the concrete historical situation (pragmatically) with its limitations and tasks and with the acknowledgment that at certain high moments in ultimate situations one could conform with the Heavenly will. That will was not logically or arguably existent, but lay beyond reason. Both humanism and rationalism lay on this side of truth, for they were human centered.

106. Jaspers, 1953.

4   The History of the Royal House

Ancient texts and inscriptions record the growing reputation of the early Chou royal house. King Wen 文 was the honored ruler of a multitude of states and the first true Chou king; Wu 武 campaigned in all directions and finally overtook the Shang. King Ch'eng 成 was both wise and successful in consolidating the territories under Chou rule. King K'ang 康 enfeoffed the land and was followed by King Chao 昭, who expanded the domain to the south. King Mu 穆 was thought to have developed a model to educate the Sons of Heaven in the wise ways of the early Chou rulers. And, indeed, by the time of the fifth reign, the Chou territories were governed by a well-developed feudal system. The security of a stable government must surely have allowed for reflection on the past.

The classical scholars considered each king worthy of a posthumous account of a particular accomplishment that could be considered an important piece of history. For them, the function of history was not only a matter of record-keeping but also didactic. They wished to record the impressive and appropriate ways in which the ancients behaved and how they contributed to the establishment of Chinese civilization in its proper place under Heaven.

The addition of bronze inscriptions to our body of evidence allows many of the specifics of this early period to be known. The new dynasty established its stability in a number of ways—by quelling uprisings and appeasing local populations, by moving large numbers of the formerly powerful Shang to new locations and using them as officials in new local governments, and by establishing a new capital farther east in a more central location. The middle Western Chou reigns expanded the borders of the Chou world, especially to the south, thereby testing the strength of the suzerainty. The court found the balance between royal power and that of the vassal states difficult to maintain. The royal house maintained its authority, even when threatened by increasing power among the nobles, as during the exile of King Li 厲, or when struggling to maintain its control of economic resources. By the end of the Western Chou a monarchy had evolved that both governed effectively and was resilient to changes in leadership.

112

MILITARY VICTORY AND THE RELOCATION OF
SHANG POPULATIONS

The victory at Mu-yeh 牧野, a site near to the Shang capital, was only the first step toward building a Chou nation. The ancient text *I-Chou-shu* 逸周書 gives accounts of the consolidation operations made by the Chou forces almost immediately after the victory at Mu-yeh. There the Shang were "officially" defeated, and there the Shang king committed suicide. The consolidation activities took place in various locations around the Shang capital and took somewhere between ten and twenty-three days. The results of these campaigns were the "destruction" of 99 "states," the amassing of enemy casualties numbering 170,300 captives and the subjugation of 652 "states." The date of this account in the *I-Chou-shu* has been argued, but most agree that the account is of Chou date and perhaps even contemporary with the event.[1] Even relatively conservative opinion would allow a date within the Western Chou.[2] Nevertheless, credibility of the report, especially of its figures, must be challenged, for the account was likely designed as propaganda by the Chou. The last campaign was near An-yang 安陽 in the present provinces of Honan 河南 and Shansi 山西, an area accessible on foot within a few days.[3] Each of the so-called states overcome by King Wu was probably not larger than a cluster of villages or settlements. The total number of destroyed and subjugated states was seven hundred and fifty, not many more than the figure of the eight hundred states allied with the Chou that is mentioned in the *Shih-chi* 史記. Each side claimed seven or eight hundred allied states. If the *I-Chou-shu* figure is taken at face value, there were almost half a million casualties and captives from the ninety-nine states. The population of each single state is given as approximately five thousand persons, but such figures were certainly inflated for propaganda purposes. Nevertheless, the largest portion of the population affected by such campaigns surely lived in the Shang domain. The total population of the area formally under Shang domination, including the satellite states, may have been considerably more, for this was the most densely inhabited area in China at that time. On the other hand, the Chou could claim a population of only sixty or seventy thousand in their home area. The density was far less than that to the east, and the Chou had to find a clever strategy to gain control over the more populous Shang domain.

The first task of the Chou was to establish their legitimacy over the new regime. New records of that process have come to light in recent

1. Ku Chieh-kang, 1963; Shaughnessy, 1981.
2. Ch'ü Wan-li, 1965.
3. Ibid., 329–30.

4.1 Rubbing from inscription on the Shih Ch'iang *p'an* (from *WW*, 1978 [3]:140)

a   b

excavations at locations where the Chou relocated some of the Shang population. In 1976 in one such area, 103 bronze vessels were discovered in a storage pit; seventy-four of them bear inscriptions. The vessels all belonged to a family named Wei 微 and had been accumulated over several generations. The oldest were of Shang style, manufactured at the time of the Chou takeover; the latest were cast in the style of late Western Chou. The most significant inscription for us contains a 284-word account by Shih Ch'iang 史墙 ("Ch'iang the historian"). It relates the major events under the six Chou kings from King Wen 文 to King Mu 穆 and records the deeds of Ch'iang's own ancestors (fig. 4.1). Shih Ch'iang himself lived in the time of King Kung 恭 and King I 夷, and the vessel was cast in the reign of King Kung.[4] Scholars generally agree on the main content of the inscription, but not on its details.[5]

4. Chou-yüan k'ao-ku-tui, 1978:4.
5. T'ang Lan, 1978; Li Chung-ts'ao, 1978; Ch'iu Hsi-kuei, 1978; Hsü Chung-shu, 1978; Ch'en Shih-hui, 1980; Shirakawa Shizuka, *KBHS*, 50:340−97.

The general content is as follows.

> In antiquity, King Wen reigned. God bestowed upon him virtues which allowed him to possess a multitude of states between Heaven and Earth. The powerful King Wu campaigned in four directions, took over the Yin 殷 (Shang) people, and quelled the troubles with (nomadic) Ti 狄 and the I 夷 peoples (on the east coast). The wise, sage King Ch'eng 成 was assisted by strong helpers and consolidated the Chou. The virtuous King K'ang 康 was the one who divided the territory (by enfeoffing feudal lords). The broad-minded King Chao 昭 campaigned southward in the region of Ch'u-Ching 楚荆. The brilliant King Mu 穆 developed a model to educate the current Son of Heaven in the ways of the old Chou kings Wen and Wu. A Son of Heaven who enjoyed long life and good health, who served the deities well, who glorified the previous kings and royal ancestors, who brought good harvest and made people of all places come to pay their respects was the model.[6]

Following this was the history of the Ch'iang family.

> "Our ancestor resided in Wei 微, at the time when King Wu conquered the Shang. Our great-grandfather was the historian of the Wei state and came to the court of King Wu. King Wu ordered the Duke of Chou to assign him a residence at Ch'i-chou 岐周. Our great-grandfather served the king and enjoyed his confidence. Our great-grandfather Tsu-hsin 祖辛 gave birth to many of the descendants of many branches. He brought them blessings and happiness. To him we should offer sacrifices. Our father I Kung 乙公, wise and virtuous, engaged in farming and managed well, for no one uttered criticism of him. I, Shih Ch'iang, who love my parents and my brothers, work hard all day and night. Ch'iang received grace from the king to cast this precious vessel. It is the fortune built by my forefathers that gave the Ch'iang their land. May good luck and blessings last until my hair turns white and my skin becomes dry. May we serve our king well. May the vessel be treasured ten thousand years.[7]

This rare inscription actually summarizes Chou history as they themselves saw it. It confirms that King Chao campaigned to the south and that King Wu faced troubles on both the northern and eastern frontiers. The unique part of it is, of course, the history of the Wei family. Three of the forefathers were named according to the

---

6. Shirakawa Shizuka, *KBHS*, 50:340–97.
7. Ibid.

Shang sequence of ten numerals—I and Hsin. There is little doubt that Ch'iang's ancestors surrendered to King Wu at the time of the Chou conquest and that one was court historian in the Shang state of Wei. Hsü Chung-shu even suggested that Ch'iang's ancestor was none other than the Shang prince named Wei-tze 微子.[8] Judging from the family emblem, which designates a scribe, and from other inscriptions in the cache that mention scribes, it is plausible that the positions of historian and scribe were hereditary assignments in the Ch'iang family. That ancestor must have been a scribe-historian in the Shang court, and once the Shang surrendered to the Chou, family members simply continued in the same position. As the inscription revealed, the Chou assigned the Wei family a piece of land at the old capital near Ch'i-shan. The storage pit where the bronzes were found was precisely in that area. Therefore, this family must have stayed in that region until the end of the Western Chou period. Names of seven generations are listed on these excavated bronzes. Since several vessels bear emblems with components describing two bundles of strapped tablets, presumably the Wei family considered themselves scribe-historians.[9]

It has not been uncommon to discover bronzes belonging to one family at more than one archaeological location. If the entire family migrated, those precious items were moved with them either as booty or as gifts. In the case of the Wei family treasure, found at one place, the inscriptions confirmed that their migration was a consequence of their surrender to the Chou court. It verified the assumption that some of the Shang population, especially the elite, was involuntarily moved.

Shirakawa Shizuka has suggested that many Shang-style bronzes discovered in Shensi were probably the belongings of Shang descendants who were moved to the region of the Chou capital. Good examples of such works are the bronzes found at Pao-chi 寶雞, Feng-hsiang 鳳翔, and Mei-hsien 郿縣. Shirakawa thought that the massive relocation of the Shang people to Shensi was an effort to develop the Wei River Valley by making use of knowledge of advanced technology carried by the Shang immigrants. He associated inscriptions recording land disputes as evidence of forced moves.[10] Because the Shih Ch'iang inscription explicitly described the farming activities of the Wei family and settled life, Shirakawa's thesis is seemingly confirmed. A comparison of farming implements from Chou sites in Shensi and Shang sites around An-yang reveals, however, few distinctions either in level of efficiency or sophistication. Archaeological data therefore show that Shirakawa's

8. Hsü Chung-shu, 1978:144.
9. Chou-yüan k'ao-ku-tui, 1978:3, 5, 7, 8.
10. Shirakawa Shizuka, *KBTS*, 46:18–19.

hypothesis may be applied to the upper classes, as judged by bronze artifacts, but not to the actual farmers.

Explanations for the movement of the elite address more immediate needs of the Chou. First, relocating the leaders of old enemies put them under immediate surveillance, and second, it made use of their special skills of writing and familiarity with ritual. In later Chinese history, members of the elite were repeatedly moved by decree from the capital for the sake of "strengthening the stem and weakening the branches." The transplanting of Shang people in the homeland of the Chou may be the historical precedent for such practices.

The Shang people who moved to Shensi went in groups of *tsu* 族, a social and political entity consisting of a ruling lineage and their relatives and subordinates. Such a unit remained intact throughout the Chou period. As late as the end of the Western Chou, there were still people in Shensi who were recognized as "I," the easterners known from the Shang period.[11]

The Cheng 鄭 were a group who moved to the Chou homeland. The name Tzu-Cheng 子鄭 is often mentioned in the Shang oracle records. Ting Shan 丁山 identified Tzu-Cheng as a Shang crown prince, although the identification of his father as King Wu Ting 武丁 or King Hsiao I 小乙 was uncertain. Tzu-Cheng's descendants later dwelt in an area to the south of the Shang capital known as Cheng-fu-chih-ch'iu 鄭父之丘 (or, the Mount of Father Cheng) near the River Yu.[12] The clan of Hou Cheng 侯鄭 (Marquis Cheng) was a powerful branch of Shang royal kinsmen. Shirakawa found in the oracle record evidence that the Cheng people often participated in royal ceremonies, military campaigns, and activities such as the construction of city walls. The royal oracle records also show that the welfare of the Cheng was a frequent topic for divination. These records point to the royal court's concern for this group. We know, for instance, that the Cheng were a very important group even outside the center of the Shang domain, for the following names designate the Cheng in the oracle records: the Nan-Cheng 南鄭 (Southern Cheng), the Pei-Cheng 北鄭 (Northern Cheng), and the To-Cheng 多鄭 (Numerous Cheng). The Cheng were apparently widely dispersed geographically and were differentiated into subunits. The areas in which they settled were to the north of the Wei, according to Shirakawa. The Hsin-Cheng 新鄭 (New Cheng) were settled to the south in a region in the center of the present province of Honan with their center at the present-day city of Cheng-chou 鄭州 .[13] After the conquest of

11. Ibid., 45:19–20. See chapter 8 below for further discussion.
12. Ting Shan, 1956:87–89.
13. Shirakawa Shizuka, 1973:367–414.

Shang, the Cheng were moved to Shensi, where their name was often recorded. In the reign of King Hsüan of Chou, a prince was enfeoffed as the Duke of Cheng. His fiefdom was near Hua-hsien 華縣, in Shensi. A bronze basin cast in the reign of King Li 厲, the father of King Hsüan and this prince, contained information about a marriage of a Chou princess to the Duke of Cheng. Shirakawa suggested that this earlier duke was not a member of the Chou royal clan but was probably ruler of the Cheng living in Shensi. In fact, the geographic name Hsi-cheng (Western Cheng) must have given the location of the group in relation to their old homeland. The Chou prince who received Cheng as his fiefdom was known in history as Duke Huan 桓 of Cheng. During the anarchic reign of King Li, Huan moved his people to the east and settled in the land of the Cheng. A legend in the Kuo-yü 國語 tells how he resettled his own people in a few localities that he "borrowed" from the reigning houses in that region.[14] It is not a coincidence that the new home of the duke was that of the Cheng people, for it is likely that the Cheng who went to Shensi kept in contact with the Cheng homeland. Thus the duke would receive the welcome of the brothers of his own subjects.[15]

The Tso-chuan contains a story about the special relationship between the Duke of Cheng and some people called "Shang-jen" 商人, a term that can be translated as either "people of Shang" or "merchant." It is said that there was an oath between the ducal house and the "Shang-jen" and because of it the duke was prohibited from imposing his will on them and the Shang-jen pledged not to betray the duke.[16] "Shang-jen" was translated by Legge as "merchant." But the Tso-chuan also said, "our former ruler, Duke Huan, came with the Shang-jen from Chou. Thus they (the Shang-jen) were associated with the cultivation of the land as well as the clearing and opening up of this territory by cutting its tangled woods and brush. Then they dwelt in it together, making a covenant of mutual faith to last through all generations.[17] Here "Shang-jen" refers to a group of people, rather than a single person, and to activities involving farming and clearing of the land, not commercial activities.[18]

In summary, a massive migration of Shang people to Shensi explains the frequent appearance of Shang names in the region. The discoveries

14. Kuo-yü, 16/6b.
15. Shirakawa Shizuka, 1973:422–24.
16. Legge, Ch'un Ts'ew, 664.
17. Ibid, with slight revision.
18. Ibid, 353. The use of "Shang-jen" to connote "merchant" is a later derivation; the word ku 賈 to mean "merchant" was common earlier. The term "Shang-jen" mentioned here probably did mean the Shang, for the Cheng did not enjoy their own "exodus."

of Shang-style bronzes excavated there, especially in the area known as Chou-yüan 周原, where the old Chou capital was located, also makes sense if they are thought of either as the property of the immigrants or as products of Shang technicians who accompanied their former patrons.[19] Many of the immigrants, such as the Wei family, were clustered in the Chou capital in order to serve the new leaders. The presence of these persons in Chou territory assured the Chou of direct surveillance of their former enemy and provided the new regime with a corps of experienced professionals such as scribes and historians, as well as skilled workers.

FORMING AN ALLIANCE WITH THE SHANG

In the beginning of the dynasty, the Chou tolerated the survival of the Shang ruling class, according to the *I-Chou-shu*, the *Shih-ching*, and the *Shih-chi*. A Shang prince named Lu Fu 祿父 was entrusted with the authority to govern the old Shang capital region and to maintain sacrifices to the Shang ancestors. The majority of the Shang population must have stayed in the east instead of moving to Shensi. Three Chou princes were assigned the task of overseeing the old Shang domain and were garrisoned in the nearby, newly established Shang state.[20] After the death of King Wu, two brothers, the Chou garrison commanders, challenged the legitimacy of the new royal authority. This power had been entrusted to the son of King Wu, whose regent was the Duke of Chou, yet another brother of King Wu. Several groups of the eastern peoples joined in the rebellion, and even in the homeland of the Chou there was unrest. No explicit information can identify the source of that unrest, and we can only suspect that the supporters of these three "overseers" rose up, as did the uprooted Shang, against the new king. It took the Duke of Chou and his colleague, the Duke of Shao, two years of fighting to put down the uprising. The Shang prince was driven to the north, and the eastern nations who took part in the rebellion were overcome by military force.[21]

Numerous incidents during this great campaign are recorded on bronze inscriptions. The inscription on a bronze *kuei* 殷 discovered in Shantung tells of T'ai-pao 太保 (Great Guardian) who was ordered by

19. Tu Cheng-sheng, 1979A:506–10; Ch'i-shan hsien wen-hua-kuan, 1976:26.

20. *I-Chou-shu*, 5/7; Legge, *She King*, 365; *Shih-chi*, 4/39.

21. *I-Chou-shu*, 5/7; Legge, *Shoo King*, 4/7, 357–58; *Shih-chi*, 4/38. For a concise summary of the situation in the eastern plain during the early days of the Western Chou, see Tu Cheng-sheng, 1979B:170–86.

4.2 Rubbing from inscription
on a *kuei* from Shantung
(from *KBTS*, 2:60)

the king to lead the expedition against Lu-tsu-sheng 彔子聖 and to pacify
the land of Hsü 徐.[22] (See fig. 4.2) In another, related inscription, this
person was addressed as "Sheng 聖, the Son of Heaven." He must be
none other than the Prince Lu 彔 of the Shang, who claimed the royal
title during the rebellion. The name of the Duke of Shao appeared in an
inscription on a vessel discovered in the same assemblage. He must have
been T'ai-pao 太保, an identification consistent with his titles in later
Chinese history.[23] In the inscription on the Pao *yu* 保卣, Pao (the
abbreviated form for T'ai-pao) received a royal decree to campaign in
the eastern land of Yin (Shang) and the territory of "Wu-hou" 五侯 (fig.
4.3). "*Wu-hou*" could mean either "five marquises" or the "Marquis of
Wu." In any case, the area of the campaign must have been the coastal
region formerly controlled by the Shang.[24] The land of the Hsü 徐 was
also the home of the Ying people, who were scattered along the eastern
seaboard and were probably the descendants of the Ta-wen-k'ou 大汶口

22. Shirakawa Shizuka, *KBTS*, 2:58–66.

23. Ibid., 60, 67; Ch'en Meng-chia, 1955B:96–99.

24. Ch'en Meng-chia, 1955A:157; Shirakawa Shizuka, *KBTS* 2:174–89; Huang Sheng-
chang, 1957.

4.3 Rubbing from inscription
on the Pao *yu*
(from *KBTS*, 4:175)

culture. Seven vessels known as the T'ai-pao bronzes were discovered in
Shou-chang 壽張 County of Shantung Province. The site was on the
major route from the central plain to the northern land of the Yen, the
northern part of Hopei close to the border later marked by a Great Wall.
It may not be a coincidence that descendants of the Duke of Shao were
the ruling class of this northern land of Yen. These vessels may have
been left while the Duke of Shao pursued the fleeing Shang prince, Lu
Fu 祿父, to this northern location. In the inscription on the Shih Ch'iang
史墙 basin, the northern nomads were called the enemy. The connection
between the nomads and the surviving Shang forces must have posed a
potential threat to the political authority of the Chou.

The participation of the Duke of Chou in the great campaign can be
validated by information contained in other bronze inscriptions. A Ch'in
kuei 秦毀 discovered in Feng-hsiang 鳳翔 County of Shensi was cast to
commemorate the victory the Duke of Chou over the Eastern I in the
land of Po-ku 薄姑 and Feng 豐.[25] Ch'en Meng-chia 陳夢家 identified
both places in contemporary Shantung Province and thought that these
peoples had joined forces with the rebel Lu-fu.[26] In another inscription
(fig. 4.4) Ming Kung 明公 led three groups of people to fight in the
eastern states, and another name appeared in the inscription—the
Marquis of Lu 魯.[27] Ming Kung has been identified as Ming-pao 明保,
one of the sons of the Duke of Chou.[28] The Marquis of Lu was his other

25. Shirakawa Shizuka, *KBTS*, 2:117.
26. Ch'en Meng-chia, 1955A:168.
27. Shirakawa Shizuka, *KBTS*, 2:133−39.
28. Ibid., 1:278−86; Ch'en Meng-chia, 1955B:88.

4.4 Rubbing from inscription
(from *KBTS*, 3:135)

son, who was enfeoffed to the land of the overpowered enemies. During the campaign, the marquis seems to have had some responsibilities to support his brother. In other words, the Duke of Chou and his two sons took part in the campaigns against the eastern people. Meanwhile, Ting Kung 丁公, the son of Lord Tai who led the Ch'iang people when they established an alliance with the Chou, also fought in Shantung as well as in the territory to the south, possibly in the Huai 淮 River Valley.[29] These troops served as the southern wing of the campaign army.

A bronze *yu* 卣, cast by a warrior named Ch'ien 趞, claimed that he was valiant in his attack,[30] and also that Ch'ien received orders directly from the king. If this is a factual statement, even King Ch'eng himself was at the front.

In the inscription on a bronze *ting* 鼎, a person named Chien-kung 濂公 was said to have two generals under his command. His assignment was to fight in an area in the southeast of present-day Honan.[31] One of these two generals was mentioned in the inscription on a *yu* as the commanding officer of the warrior Yün 痁, who had cast the vessel in commemoration of a victory in the old Shang territories.[32] This scattered information can be used to reconstruct the commanding hierarchy.

29. Shirakawa Shizuka, *KBTS*, 2:257−73.
30. Ibid., 206−09; Ch'en Meng-chia, 1955A:173.
31. Shirakawa Shizuka, *KBTS*, 1:217−21.
32. Ibid., 2:225−26; Ch'en Meng-chia, 1955A:174.

There were four levels of command. The dukes of Chou and Shao commanded two armies. Chien-kung was under one of them, and under him were two generals, each of whom commanded two units. Yün must have been a ranking officer, for he had the wealth to cast the bronze *yu*. The battle lines stretched far—troops of the Duke of Shao fought in the north as far as Hopei; the Duke of Chou and his sons fought in Shantung, where one of the sons established a feudal state called Lu 魯. The southern campaign reached the southern portions of the old Shang territories where Yün and his comrades fought. The Chou troops may have been active in the Huai River Valley as well as the southernmost part of present-day Shantung Province.[33] Consistent with the ancient text *I-Chou-shu*, the inscriptional evidence also suggests that the nations of eastern Yin (Shang), such as Hsü 徐, Yen 奄, and Hsiung-ying 熊盈, all had risen against the Chou.

From these scattered bits of evidence, we see that the great rebellion brought many top Chou leaders and many troops to quell uprisings across an extensive area as far north as Hopei and as far south as the Huai Valley. The revolt was a serious challenge to the newly established Chou kingdom, and amplified the need to develop effective ways to achieve rapid consolidation of the entire domain.

CH'ENG-CHOU, THE NEW CAPITAL

The strategic location of the eastern capital at Ch'eng-chou 成周 and the allegiance of the feudal states of the Chi 姬 and the Chiang 姜 on the eastern plain provided a solid foundation for Chou sovereignty. The acceptance and blending of the native populations of the eastern regions with the Chou were the basis for a united and stable cultural and political system. The chief inhabitants of these areas, who identified themselves as the Hua-Hsia 華夏, were the mainstay of the "Chinese" population. This identification was not apparent during the Shang period, for their focus was on the Great City Shang, a political rather than a cultural identity. The term Hua-Hsia, however, was associated with an agglomerated cultural tradition including the traditions of past and current Chinese populations. A conglomerate population was what the Chou accumulated through conquest; their goal when they established the dynasty was to find the proper political, philosophical, and social apparatus to manage this disparate population.

The Ho *tsun* 冏尊 inscription reports that King Wu planned to move the capital to the central plain as soon as the Mu-yeh 牧野 victory was

33. Shirakawa Shizuka, *KBTS*, 2:257–73; Ch'en Meng-chia, 1955B:78.

complete. The campaigns conducted by the Duke of Chou and his colleagues in the east alerted the Chou leaders to the necessity to establish another ruling center, which would assure proper control of these regions.

The new capital was built at the junction of the Lo 洛 and Yellow rivers, slightly west of the old Shang capital. Geographically, the site could control the east-west route along the Yellow River and the fertile farming land along one of its largest tributaries (map 2). The Chou gave their full attention to the task of building the new city. The dukes of Shao and Chou, the two most powerful leaders of the Chou, personally took charge of the construction. Shang people were mobilized to provide the labor, but, interestingly, the Chou did not organize them directly. The old Shang aristocrats were responsible for managing and organizing the labor force. That the Chou leaders issued orders to the Shang and achieved results indicates that Shang social organization was still functioning effectively.[34] As soon as the construction of the city was completed, Shang religious ceremonies were adopted by the Chou king, presumably in order to bless the new capital.[35] Moreover, the young King Ch'eng of Chou was advised by the Duke of Chou to "pay great honor to old statutes, and to the good and wise men of Yin (Shang)." Good government would in fact make him the new chief of the kingdom.[36] Keeping good relations with the Shang was, of course, necessary to provide longevity by the Chou sovereignty through allowing prosperity among the Shang.[37]

Two chapters of the *Book of Documents* are dedicated to a discussion of the Shang elite who were settled in the new capital. They were told, for instance, that they still possessed their own land and dwellings.[38] Because they were far removed from their home territory, the claim that they still owned their own land and dwellings may be understood in two ways. Either they were granted land and houses in the new location or they were able to maintain the status of landed lords in absentia. The second possibility was more likely, because there was simply not sufficient land near the new capital to parcel out to all these landed lords. It was important to maintain the status of the Shang elite so that they could effectively control their own people on behalf of the Chou. By doing so, the Chou would eliminate the problem of a burdensome, parasitic population. Archaeological evidence supports the second

34. Legge, *Shoo King*, 424.
35. Ibid., 438.
36. Ibid., 447.
37. Ibid., 450.
38. Ibid., 462, 463, 502, 503.

4.5 Rubbing from inscription
(from *KBTS*, 7:323)

hypothesis. There were some twenty Shang burials discovered at the Chou sites at Lo-yang 洛陽, the latter-day name for Ch'eng-chou. The style of tomb construction, the accompanying objects, and types of sacrifices all indicate that the nobles still practiced their own distinctively Shang burial customs.[39]

Ch'eng-chou is frequently mentioned in bronze inscriptions, with many references to the king's arrival at Ch'eng-chou, a ceremony held at the site, a royal audience with an important person, or other similar events. The city was sometimes called Ch'eng-chou, other times the "New City."[40] (See fig. 4.5). The king visited Ch'eng-chou quite often to conduct political and religious activities. The new capital had become, no doubt, a hub of activity for the eastern states.

A standing army was stationed in Ch'eng-chou throughout the entire Western Chou period. In bronze inscriptions these troops are called the eight Yin 殷 divisions and the six Chou divisions. Their mission often involved campaigns against uprisings of non-Chou states in the east and southeast.[41] The six Chou divisions were certainly armed forces under the direct command of the royal court and the eight Yin divisions must

39. Kuo Pao-chün et al., 1955.
40. Shirakawa Shizuka, *KBTS*, 2:311, 323, 341, 358–59, 366–68, 386.
41. Ibid., 13:721–22; 15:450.

have consisted of Shang soldiers. In the bronze inscriptions of the late Western Chou, the phrase "Ch'eng-chou eight divisions" appears, most likely referring to the same army. Because the eight Yin divisions were stationed in the new capital, they were called Ch'eng-chou divisions.[62] Moreover, the commanding officer was often called Ch'eng-chou *shih-shih* 師氏 , or Ch'eng-chou Commander.[43] He commanded troops garrisoned at strategic locations as well as led expeditions against the non-Chou peoples.[44]

Precisely who the soldiers in the Ch'eng-chou divisions were is not known. We do know that some of the soldiers were obligated to take part in military operations and required to report to a specific commanding officer who had standing jurisdiction over them. Failure to report for duty meant punishment. The inscription of the Shih-ch'i 師旂 *ting* 鼎 records one such incident. A number of soldiers who did not follow the king to an expedition were brought to the attention of the commander-in-chief, Po-mao-fu 伯懋父 . He penalized these violators by ordering them to pay a fine of three hundred pieces of metal. This was to be paid to Shih-ch'i, presumably the commanding officer of the "right" regiment to which these servicemen belonged.[45] This particular name, Shih-ch'i, appears at least twice on other bronze inscriptions. The associated emblem and the posthumous name of his father all tell that he was a Shang descendant.[46] Some Shang kin, therefore, formed military units in the standing army of the eight Yin divisions and were aligned through heredity. The eight divisions continued to be active throughout the Western Chou period. They were perpetuated through stong kinship ties to form a professional, aristocratic warrior class. The Shang army, naturally, fought under the Chou command system. Po-mao-fu, for instance, was one of the ranking Chou leaders who commanded not only Yin divisions, but was also commander-in-chief of the entire military operation registered in the Shih-ch'i *ting* inscription.

The new eastern capital of the Chou was not simply a garrison formed to oversee the subjugated. Instead, it was a hub around which the former Shang elite and the Chou ruling class coalesced. The royal domain in the west and the east thus formed the principal base of the Chou royal house. Feudalism acted as a network for the Chou royal house to extend its control beyond the nuclear areas.[47]

42. Ibid., 23:149; 28:514.
43. Ibid., 17:203.
44. Ibid.; Ch'en Meng-chia, 1955B:108—11.
45. Shirakawa Shizuka, *KBTS*, 13: 753—61; Ch'en Meng-chia, 1955B:85—86.
46. Shirakawa Shizuka, *KBTS*, 13:765.
47. See chapter 5 below.

EARLY CHOU REIGNS

During the time of kings Ch'eng and K'ang, the second and third reigns of the dynasty, Chou control was consolidated and stability was established. The Shih Ch'iang *p'an* 史墙盤 inscription claims that the deed of King Ch'eng 成 was to govern by established law, while that of King K'ang 康 was to divide and regulate the kingdom.[48] Such opinions are consistent with ones made by a Chou prince in 516 B.C., in summarizing the major features of Chou history: "King Wu subdued the Yin; King Ch'eng secured tranquillity throughout the Kingdom; and King K'ang gave the people rest. They (presumably Kings Ch'eng and K'ang) invested their brothers with the rule of states created as a defense screen for their rule. They also felt that they would not themselves alone enjoy the result of the achievement of Kings Wen and Wu and (reasoned) that if any of their descendants went astray or were overthrown and thereby plunged into calamity, (the vassal states) would succor and save them."[49] This statement leads us to surmise that the reigns of Ch'eng and K'ang were the period when feudalism was established.

Ancient texts often credit the Duke of Chou with having established the Chou feudal system. Sixteen sons of King Wen, four children of King Wu, and six children of the Duke of Chou were supposedly enfeoffed during his regency.[50] In the *Hsün-tzu* 荀子 the Duke of Chou is regarded as the one who established seventy-one vassal states, fifty-three of which were given to the members of the royal house.[51] There was, however, no actual disparity between the activities of kings Ch'eng and K'ang and those of the duke. The regency of the Duke of Chou and the reign of King Ch'eng overlapped; the duke is simply taken historically as the symbol of the early reigns of the dynasty.

The era of Ch'eng and K'ang is eulogized as a period of great peace, in which no punitive actions were recorded for some forty years. This was, however, merely a euphemized legend. Actually, during that time the Chou struggled to secure their hold and to expand their territories. On the northern front there were at least two major wars with the Kuei-fang 鬼方 nomads during the reign of King K'ang. Upon their triumphant return from one battle, the Chou troops presented the court with forty-eight hundred enemy heads, some thirteen thousand captives,

48. T'ang Lan, 1978; Ch'iu Hsi-kuei, 1978; Li Hsüeh-ch'in, 1978; Ch'en Shih-hui, 1980.
49. Legge, *Ch'un Ts'ew*, 717.
50. Ibid., 192.
51. *Hsün-tzu*, 4/1.

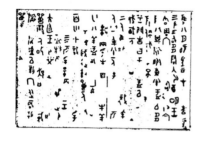

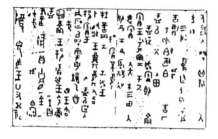

4.6 Hand-copied inscription from Lessor Yu ting

three hundred cows, and numerous horses, sheep, and chariots (fig. 4.6). In a second victory the Chou troops brought back one hundred and forty horses, as well as enemy heads, captives, and chariots.[52]

To the south, the vast territory of the Huai, Han, and Yangtze valleys was not brought into the Chou sphere of influence during the reign of King Chao. The inscription on the Shih Ch'iang basin specifically mentions that it was King Chao who opened up the Ch'u 楚 territory and made tours to the south, confirming the legend that he had done so. Several Ch'eng-K'ang bronzes were inscribed with notices of campaigns and names of towns in the south as well.[53] By then, a majority of the Chou vassal states, including the royal Chi 姬 and the Chiang 姜 in the central plain (such as Wei) as well as Lu 魯, Ch'i 齊, Chin 晉 and Yen 燕 etc., were already enfeoffed. The history of the Ch'un-ch'iu 春秋 period shows that only a few states were enfeoffed in the later reigns. The most obvious additions were Cheng 鄭, founded by a prince of King Li, and Ch'in 秦, made a feudal state in order to incorporate the old Chou capital district after the move of the political center to Ch'eng-chou. Chou feudalism, therefore, was not an extended effort but was accomplished in the early reigns. That it was put into place and made operative in those reigns suggests that resistance to it was rapidly averted.

52. Shirakawa Shizuka, *KBTS*, 12:648–714.
53. Ibid., 14:771–93.

THE REIGN OF KING K'ANG

The feudal system allowed the Chou to bring under their central control the loosely bound federation of nations allied to the Shang. The policies matured during the reigns of kings Wu and Ch'eng and the regency of the Duke of Chou. A much-quoted passage from the *Tso-chuan* attributed to a Chou prince states that King Wu conquered the Shang, King Ch'eng pacified the four quarters, and the third king, K'ang, gave the people rest and provided an opportunity to implement feudal policies in peace. King K'ang did so by sending his brothers to found vassal states that in turn served and defended the Chou.[54] The Shih Chiang *p'an* cited above bears an inscription that attributes redivision of territory to King K'ang.[55]

King K'ang's reign was probably more eventful than this statement implies, however. Reconstruction of the period was attempted by Ch'en P'an 陳槃, who tried to account for the background of the states of the Ch'un-ch'iu period. He counted thirty-four states of the Chi house established in the reigns of kings Wu and Ch'eng and the Duke of Chou, and only two additional states founded by the sons of King K'ang.[56] Based on that analysis, it is questionable whether King K'ang actually contributed much to the establishment of the Chou feudal network. But, why, then, did the Shih Ch'iang *p'an* inscription single out the redivision of the land as the significant deed of his reign?[57] The disparity may be explained by noting that Ch'en P'an's lists included only states which were continued into the Ch'un-ch'iu period. Chi states actually should have numbered far more than thirty, for the *Hsün-tzu* reports that the Duke of Chou established fifty-three vassal states that were governed by members of the Chi house.[58] Moreover, the Duke of Chou is frequently cited as the cultural hero to whose credit the establishment of most of the early Chou institutions is attributed. The thirty states of the Chi were located on both sides of the axis linking the old royal Chou domain and the new capital at Ch'eng-chou.[59] Where, then, were the other twenty?

They must have been those established to the south of the axis, probably founded in the reigns of kings K'ang, Chao, and Mu, during the expansion in that direction. Those were the states annexed by the

---

54. Legge, *Ch'un Ts'ew*, 717.
55. Shirakawa Shizuka, *KBHS*, 50:349–55.
56. Ch'en P'an, 1969.
57. Ch'iu Hsi-kuei, 1978:27.
58. *Hsün-tzu*, 4/1.
59. Li Ya-nung, 1962:627.

Ch'u during the Ch'un-ch'iu period as reported in the *Tso-chuan*. Chou descendants in those areas were thought to have been absorbed by the Ch'u.[60] As late as 640 B.C., however, the state of Sui 隨 led other states in revolt against Ch'u.[61] Whether the state itself was governed by a member of the Chi house has been at issue among scholars for some time.[62] Recent archaeological discoveries in the vicinity of the ancient Sui, from the state of Tseng 鄫, yielded bronzes whose inscriptions suggest that Tseng ducal house members were, in fact, descendants of the Chi house.[63] The artifacts of Tseng manufacture show a surprising level of sophistication and cultural achievement.[64] Nevertheless, this particular state does not appear in literature prior to the Ch'un-ch'iu. Those Chou states established near the Han Valley or south of the central plain must have been dissolved long before their names were entered into the sources on which Ch'en P'an relied.

Although the state of Tseng was governed by descendants of a son of King Mu 穆,[65] it was not one of the earlier-established feudal states. The Chou did not have full control of the valleys of Han and Huai until the mid-Chou reigns, those of Kings K'ang 康, Chao 昭, Mu 穆, and Kung 恭, when the Chou extended their power ever farther to the south.

The reigns of kings Wu and Ch'eng witnessed the conquest and consolidation of the east and the north. The southern front was divided into an eastern section along the Huai valley and a western one along the Han Valley. At the same time expansion did not halt toward the west and the north; there was simply a more aggressive effort in the south.

Strangely, there is little recorded about the Chou activities in the south. The sole mention of King K'ang's expedition there appears in the *Chu-shu chi-nien* 竹書紀年 (*The Bamboo Chronicles*), where King K'ang's tour to the south is chronicled in the sixteenth year of his reign, after an investiture of the Duke of Ch'i 齊. His travel reached both Chiu-chiang 九江 and Lu-chiang 廬江, located on the north bank of the Yangtze River. This event was, until recently, listed only in an obscure source. An inscription on a *kuei* (figs. 4.7, 4.8) claims that the king made an inspection tour of the east, and then moved the Marquis of I 宜 to a

60. Legge, *Ch'un Ts'ew*, 209.
61. Ibid., 178.
62. Ch'en P'an, 1969:209.
63. Li Hsüeh-ch'in, 1980A:55.
64. O Ping, 1973; Sui-hsien k'ao-ku fa-chüeh-tui, 1979.
65. Sui-hsien po-wu-kuan, 1980:36.

4.7 Bronze *kuei* (see inscription, fig. 4.8) (from *WWTKTL*, 1955 [5]:59)

new location. Since the bronze was discovered at Tan-t'u 丹徒 on the Yangtze, it is tempting to surmise that this was the location of the vassal state of I.[66] The tour must have included a visit to the state of Ch'i and lands to the south where new states were established as Chou military garrisons.

Notice of activities in the north can be found in two inscriptions, both found on *tings*, which are attributed to Yü and are dated to the reign of King K'ang.[67] The Ta-Yü *ting* 大盂鼎 inscription merely records that Yü

66. Shirakawa Shizuka, *KBTS*, 10:534–35.
67. Ch'en Meng-chia, 1956B:93.

4.8 Rubbing from inscription
(fig. 4.7 above)
(from *KBTS*, 10:532)

was given a chariot and clothes as royal gifts and that he was empowered to judge cases and to make inspection tours.[68] The heavily
corroded inscription on the Hsiao-Yü *ting* 小盂鼎 tells about a ceremony
held in the twenty-fifth year of the reign, at which Yü presented the
captives and booty of two campaigns against the Kuei-fang 鬼方. In one
campaign the captured amounted to 13,081 persons, 30 chariots, 355
cattle, 38 sheep, and other items not clearly delineated. In the following paragraph other items are listed, all fewer in number than their
counterparts in the preceding passage. The second list must have
reported another campaign, perhaps a follow-up after the main attack.[69]
The Kuei-fang were a major power in the north during the Shang, and
the victory achieved by Yü was an impressive one judging by the
number of captives taken. The reduced booty listed in the second
campaign probably attests to a decisive initial defeat of the Kuei-fang.
The total scale of the operation, if the captives numbered thirteen
thousand, must have involved tens of thousands on both sides. Why
was such a major campaign not listed in the historical record of King
K'ang?

King K'ang ruled twenty-six years according to conventional historical
sources. The Yü campaigns in the north took place during the twenty-

68. Shirakawa Shizuka, *KBTS*, 12:666.
69. Ibid., 691–93.

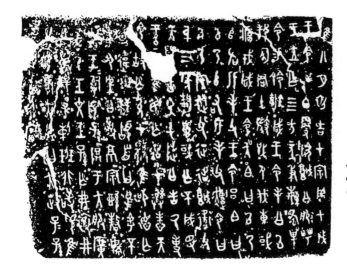

4.9 Rubbing from inscription on the Pan *kuei* (from *WW*, 1972 [9]:12)

fifth year. A rediscovered bronze, the Pan *kuei* 班毁(fig. 4.9), is inscribed with the following pertinent information. The Duke of Mao 毛 governed the eastern regions as well as led other state chiefs against aggressive non-Chou people in the east. The dukes of Ch'i and Wu were instructed to lead their troops to aid the Duke of Mao, both at his left and right.[70] The Pan *kuei* was cast by a person named Mao Pan 毛班 in commemoration of merits achieved by the Duke of Mao, who was either his father or his uncle. The date of the casting is apparently during the reign of King Chao or later, even though the actual event recorded took place much earlier.[71] The Pan *kuei* inscription does not report the conclusion of the campaigns, and, in contrast to the precise information listed on the Ta-Yü *ting*, the account of the activity of the Duke of Mao was quite vague. The campaign led by him, in spite of a mobilization of considerable scale, did not achieve much even after three years. Perhaps either the commander was at fault or the dynamism of the Chou had waned after the reign of King K'ang.

KING CHAO AND HIS SOUTHERN CAMPAIGN

King Chao was traditionally known as the ruler who was drowned in the Yangtze River while touring the south. In 656 B.C., when the duke Huan 桓 of Ch'i first led Chou troops against the Ch'u, he did

70. Kuo Mo-jo, 1972; Shirakawa Shizuka, *KBTS*, 15:34–58.
71. T'ang Lan, 1962:38; Huang Sheng-chang, 1981A:78.

4.10 Rubbing from inscription
that mentions "gold"
(from *KBTS*, 14:776)

so claiming revenge for the loss of King Chao. In response to the
accusation, the Ch'u envoy replied that the death of the king was not by
their hands, for they had not reached the river at that time.[72] Clearly,
the tragedy of the king's tour was common knowledge, and even the
Shih Ch'iang *p'an* inscription mentions the expeditions of King Chao as
memorable events.[73]

Inscriptions of four other bronzes describe royal campaigns to the
south against the rebellious Ching or Ch'u.[74] Although Ch'en Meng-
chia assigned the group of bronze vessels a date as early as the reign of
King Ch'eng,[75] both T'ang Lan and Shirakawa have argued that they
date from the time of King Chao. T'ang reached that conclusion by
analyzing the contrast in inscriptions, while Shirakawa did so after
examining the morphology and decorative styles of the bronzes.[76] All
four inscriptions mentioned that "gold" (i.e., metal) was captured in the
southern campaigns. (Fig. 4.10.) The interest of the Chou in the south
may be connected, therefore, with securing sources of metals, including
copper and tin.[77] The southern regions referred to here were probably
the valleys of the upper Huai and Han, but not the lake regions of the
Yangtze Valley.

72. Legge, *Ch'un Ts'ew*, 140.
73. Shirakawa Shizuka, *KBTS*, 50:349–55.
74. Ibid., 14:773, 776, 778, 782–84.
75. Ch'en Meng-chia, 1956B:77.
76. T'ang Lan, 1962:37; Shirakawa Shizuka, *KBTS*, 14:772, 782, 786, 792.
77. T'ang Lan, 1962:37; Kuo Mo-jo, 1957:186.

Another group of bronze inscriptions tell of Chou garrisons in the land of the Huai I 淮夷. At least six inscriptions record the presence of royal divisions from the eastern capital in the Huai region. The job of these divisions was to prevent invasion of the capital by the I. A state called Fu 甫, located in the present province of Honan, is often mentioned as the back-up base for those operations.[78] The bronzes all date from the reign of King Chao.[79] In 1976, several more bronze vessels were discovered that bear on this issue. Two of the inscriptions (see figs. 4.11, 4.12) charge an official of the royal guard at the capital with fending off the Huai I, who had invaded the royal domain in Shensi. On other inscriptions, the Chou commander claimed that he had taken 104 captives in addition to the casualities.[80] Judging by the location of the battles, T'ang Lan thought the invaders came from the upper Chung-Lo 中洛 Valley in Shensi.[81] The archaeologists who excavated these vessels, however, believed that the invaders were the Huai I, who lived beyond the Huai Valley.[82] It is difficult to determine whether these bronze inscriptions do give an accurate account of the invasion of the Huai I, since the location of the battle was far from the Huai Valley. If the invaders were the Huai I, they were already a very strong force by the mid-Chou.

New evidence suggests that King Chao had already subdued the southern lands at this time. An inscription on a bronze bell (fig. 4.13) mentions a southern people called the Pao-tzu 艮子 who had disturbed the Chou borders. After King Chao overpowered them, twenty-six state chiefs of the southern and eastern I people presented themselves for a royal audience.[83] Yang Shu-ta 楊樹達 identified the Pao-tzu as natives of the vast mountain areas in the mid-Yangtze Valley.[84] The name King Shao 召 in the inscription must refer to King Chao.[85]

On the northern front, however, the Chou probably were more defensive than offensive. On at least one occasion during the reign of King Chao the northern Jung launched a massive attack on the Chou states. Royal divisions were mobilized to reinforce the local troops of the state of Hsing   in order to fend off the invaders.[86]

The victory in the south probably marked the most glorious moment

78. Shirakawa Shizuka, *KBTS*, 17:154, 178, 184–86, 195, 199, 202–04.
79. Ibid., 17:229.
80. Fu-feng-hsien wen-hua-kuan et al., 1976:52–53.
81. T'ang Lan, 1976B:33–34, 38.
82. Fu-feng-hsien wen-hua-kuan et al., 1976:55.
83. Shirakawa Shizuka, *KBTS*, 18:260–69.
84. Yang Shu-ta, 1959:136.
85. Kuo Mo-jo, 1957:52.
86. Li Hsüeh-ch'in et al., 1979.

4.11 Rubbing from inscription
(from *WW*, 1976 [6]:57)

4.12 Rubbing of inscription
(from *WW*, 1976 [6]:58)

c   b   a

4.13 Rubbing, in three parts, from inscription of Chung-chou bell (from *KBTS*, 18:262–63)

of King Chao's reign, for twenty-six state chiefs came to pay homage. The conquest of the Po people perhaps intoxicated the king with victory such that when he entered the Han Valley later, he was neither defeated nor drowned simply by accident. The reign of King Chao also probably marked the peak of Chou power. After this they did not maintain their dynamism for long.

THE REIGN OF KING MU

King Mu's fame was tied to his travels. In the *Tso-chuan* he is described by his desire to leave his chariot track everywhere.[87] As the hero of the *Mu-t'ien-tzu-chuan (Biography of King Mu)*, the first fictional account written in the Chinese language, King Mu travels to a sacred mountain to visit the divine Queen of the West and seek immortality. In the same account, King Mu makes a chariot that is pulled by eight semi-divine stallions.

In fictional records, the non-Chou people in the Huai Valley were not submissive. For instance, in the *Hou-Han-Shu* an account of the King of Hsü 徐, a state of the Huai-I 淮夷, records an attack on the Chou by "barbarians" on the bank of the Yellow River. The king himself directed thirty vassal states, so King Mu rushed there, thanks to his wonder

87. Legge, *Ch'un Ts'ew*, 641.

horses, received the help of the Ch'u and attacked the Hsü.[88] Shirakawa Shizuka thought that the great expedition led by the Duke of Mao mentioned on the Pan *kuei* inscription was related to this legendary uprising.[89] Regardless, the person Mao Pan who cast the *kuei* wanted to honor his forefather, whom he believed had accomplished a great deed in the past. The expedition recorded on the Pan *kuei*, however, could only have occurred in the reign of King Chao, not in that of King Mu.

In epigraphic sources, the Huai I are mentioned as tributaries of the Chou court.[90] The names "Eastern I" and "Southern I," in both classical and epigraphic literature, usually refer to non-Chou peoples who inhabited the valleys of the Huai and the Han rivers. Some of them eventually established states that became part of the Chou feudal network and are mentioned as such in the *Ch'un-ch'iu Chronicles*. On the other hand, the independent and powerful Ch'u should not be counted as one of those eastern or southern peoples. The Ch'u envoy of 640 B.C. easily claimed innocence vis-à-vis the death of King Chao. In the early Chou, the area that repeatedly required defense was the east coast. During the reigns of King K'ang and King Chao, disturbances took place in the Huai region to the south and east of the royal Chou domain at Ch'eng-chou. After the reign of King Chao, that area was brought under Chou control. The Huai people did not trouble the Chou until the reigns of kings I and Hsiao.

The nomads in the northwest, however, started to threaten Chou order early in the dynasty. Several historical accounts record the confrontation between the Ch'üan-jung 犬戎 and the Chou in which King Mu is said to have planned to attack the Ch'üan-jung. A high-ranking official advised against it, claiming that the Ch'üan-jung were allies of the Chou and, furthermore, the Jung leader was capable. King Mu attacked anyway. The victory brought only a few captives to the Chou. After this event, those nomads no longer were submissive to the Chou.[91] This particular event does not appear anywhere in epigraphic materials, but if the account is true, the Chou action must be taken as an attempt to stop an uprising of the nomads. Such incidents were commonly documented in the first millennium B.C. across the Eurasian steppes.[92]

The legend of King Mu's eight wonder horses probably reflects some historical truth, for he was known to have raised good horses. In Mei-

88. *Hou Han-shu chi-chieh,* hereafter *Hou Han-shu,* 85/1–20.
89. Shirakawa Shizuka, *KBTS,* 46:67–69.
90. Chapter 10 will examine the relationship between the Chou and the Huai people.
91. *Shih-chi,* 4/43–46; *Kuo-yü,* 1/2–4.
92. Průšek, 1971:70–76.

4.14 Inscription on foal-shaped *tsun* from Mei-hsien. See Frontispiece (from *WWTKTL*, 1957:4).

hsien郿縣 an animal-shaped wine vessel has been unearthed that depicts a realistic representation of a young colt. The inscription on the body of the *tsun* 尊 (fig. 4.14) says that the king first handled a foal and then bestowed on the owner of the bronze two young colts. Two more inscriptions appear on the lid, each of which give the specifics of these two horses, facts probably related to their breeds.[93] The ceremony that is described, the handling of a new foal by the king himself, points to the importance of good breeding horses. The inscription on a bronze *ting* from the reign of King Hsiao registers that thirty-two horses were given as gifts.[94] Such horses, given in pairs or in fours, were harnessed to a chariot; they were not to be sacrificial offerings. A fragment from a later text tells that in the reign of King Yi the Chou attacked the Jung 戎 people at T'ai-yüan大原, located in the north of Shansi Province. From that battle one thousand horses were secured.[95] From the time of King

93. Shirakawa Shizuka, *KBTS*, 19:324–33; Kuo Mo-jo, 1961A:312–19.
94. Shirakawa Shizuka, *KBTS*, 29:583.
95. *Hou Han-shu*, 87/2.

Yi on, the Chou wanted to breed their own fine horses. The ancestors of the ducal house of the state of Ch'in, who became the masters of the Ching-Wei Valley after the close of the Western Chou, were entrusted by the Chou royal house with the raising of horses. The Ch'in ancestors had for a long time maintained friendships, and even marriages, with the Western Jung, the non-Chou people of this region.[96] One may suspect that both the emphasis on raising horses among the Chou and the interaction between the ancestors of the Ch'in and the Jung peoples resulted from nomadic movements across the Eurasian steppe. Some of the steppe population, probably farmers living adjacent to Chou territory in the north, were pushed into Chinese-held lands.

THE REIGNS OF KINGS KUNG, I, HSIAO, AND YI

The reigns of these four kings, though uneventful, were unusual because of the irregular order of their succession to the throne. The pattern did not follow the normal Chou father-to-son succession. King I 懿, who succeeded his father, King Kung, was followed by King Hsiao 孝, a brother of King Kung. After King Hsiao died, however, the Chou vassal states jointly supported King Yi 夷, the crown prince of King I, to succeed to the throne.[97]

King Yi must have been popular among his nobles, for it is said that when he suffered from a disease, the dukes of the vassal states sacrificed to their local deities and prayed for his recovery.[98] The authority of the Chou royal house was so strong that when the duke of the important state of Ch'i was executed—by being boiled in a cauldron—a new duke was appointed by royal decree.[99]

The reign of King Yi, however, witnessed the beginning of a decline of Chou central authority. In the *Li-chi* 禮記 (*The Book of Rites*), King Yi is recorded as the first Chou monarch who descended from the royal hall to meet the vassal dukes.[100] Because King Yi virtually owed his throne to his dukes' support, it is not strange that he was concerned about accommodating them. During the reign of these four rulers, many ceremonies of investiture and other bestowals took place. Appointments to government offices also point to a fairly complicated administrative

---

96. *Shih-chi*, 5/6–9.
97. *Shih-chi*, 4/51.
98. Legge, *Ch'un Ts'ew*, 717.
99. *Shih-chi*, 32/11.
100. *Li-chi chu-shu*, hereafter *Li-chi*, 25/14.

structure.[101] The king's general largess and the huge bureaucracy must have drained the Chou royal treasury and marked the beginning of the decline.

Along the northern boundaries, the nomads gradually gained strength. Although the ancient chronicles mention Chou victories, such as the one at T'ai-yüan, the Chou must have felt pressure to maintain peace on those borders.[102] Moreover, the royal domain in the Wei River Valley was exposed to nomads both on the west and the north. There was no buffer zone between the Wei farmland and the plateau near the steppe. It probably was under such conditions that the royal house had to rely on support from local forces. One such local group was the K'o 克 family, several of whose bronzes have been excavated in Shensi. Their members served in important posts in the royal court, as well as commanded troops stationed near the capital.[103] It must have been difficult for the Chou royal house to avoid the growing independence of such strong vassals, whose support had become indispensable.

Along the southern front, the Chou royal house took an assertive position. A cluster of bronze vessels from the reigns of King Mu and King Kung bear inscriptions telling that the Chou operations along the valley passages penetrated the mountains to the upper streams of the Han River. Such activities apparently were conducted in order to open up new routes to the Han River and the mid-Yangtze Valley.[104]

A lengthy inscription on a mid-Chou vessel (fig. 4.15) relates that the chief of a small state called Mei 眉, located at the eastern edge of the Szechwan 四川 Basin, surrendered after Chou troops were dispatched to his country. The subjugated chief went to the court to present tribute. He was entrusted by the Chou to take coats as a royal gift to the chief from K'uei 夔, a land located near the Mei homeland. The latter also surrendered to the Chou.[105] The surname of the K'uei chief happened to be that of the ruling house of the state of Ch'u. This particular inscription is the earliest known record of the Ch'u people. The operation, which opened routes south through the mountain passages, is related to the spread of Chou influence in this region.

---

101. Both subjects are discussed in the following chapter.

102. *Han-shu*, 94A/2.

103. Shirakawa Shizuka, *KBTS*, 28:505, 515, 536.

104. Ibid., 48:187–89. Ch'i Wen-t'ao thought these inscriptions related to the southern campaign during the reign of King Chao. See Ch'i Wen-t'ao, 1972. Chou Wen, however, based on decorations and morphology of the vessels, determined their dates from the reigns of kings Mu and Kung. See Chou Wen, 1972.

105. Shirakawa Shizuka, *KBTS*, 25:283–91.

4.15 Rubbing from inscription (from *KBTS*, 25:284)

In the southeast, the Huai I people remained subordinated to the Chou. The inscription on a bronze excavated at Wu-kung 武功 in 1974 relates that a ranking official was sent to tour the Huai region. He received a Chou official who was stationed there and was presented with tributes paid by various Huai I states, both large and small.[106] The archaeologists who first discovered this bronze vessel dated it from the reign of King Hsüan.[107] The person who carried out the mission lived during the reign of King Kung, and no later than the reign of King Hsiao.[108] The inscription also informs us that the Huai I maintained their political institutions in the form of a state and that someone from the Chou court was stationed there to supervise them. Moreover, it relates, the Chou court routinely dispatched agents to collect tribute from them. One Chou envoy returned to Ts'ai 蔡, a state located in the southern corner of the present province of Honan. Ts'ai, governed by descendants of a Chou prince, functioned as an outpost for the royal control in the Huai region lying directly to its south.

In summary, the Chou political control along the southern frontiers stretched beyond the Yellow and Wei River valleys to the edge of the Szechwan basin and to the Yangtze Valley in the east. The expansion achieved during the mid-Chou reigns was, of course, built on the

106. Ibid., 48:223–24.
107. Wu Ta-yen et al., 1976.
108. Shirakawa Shizuka, *KBTS*, 21:515–17.

foundation laid during the earlier Chou reigns. The eastern capital at Ch'eng-chou served as the base of operations to the south, and the vanguard could rely on the Ts'ai to support them in the Huai area and could count on the Fu in the Han region. The new route opened into the southern mountains led to Szechwan, while the Chou states of I and Wu were established in the lower Yangtze Valley and became the most distant outpost of Chou power. They were simply too far, however, from the nerve center of the Chou court to play any practical function in sustaining the gigantic Chou kingdom. Cultural influence of the Chou during this period went far beyond the political sphere.

THE EXILE OF KING LI

The expansion of Chou control over the Huai and Han region during the mid-Chou period brought increasingly more resources and territory under Chou management. Because of this there were administrative problems, which H. G. Creel characterized as a dilemma; the royal court could administer in a feudal fashion, partitioning the territories among vassals, or it could set up a centralized government regulated by functionaries who were directly accountable to it.[109] By the mid-Chou, expansion had stopped and the momentum of growth was diminished, leaving the administration of the domain as the major task, and most perplexing responsibility, of the government. Some vassal states were installed, indeed almost in the same manner as the others that had been founded in the early period of the dynasty. Resources in the form of tribute collected from the Huai region were stored in treasuries at Ch'eng-chou; thus, these assets were at the direct disposal of the royal court in the eastern capital, not at the disposal of the states. The Chou court must have found it hard to maintain the balance between royal power and the power of the vassal states. The mechanism of governance that emerged to meet the dilemma reached a fully developed form in the mid-Chou.

The effectiveness of the ruling body was tested especially when there was an abrupt change in leadership, and such was the case in the reign of King Li. His exile was brought about by his nobles, but the change did not bring down the government. The court itself continued to function for fourteen years in spite of the exile. The government was resilient and sturdy, more so than the king himself.

The particular episode that recounts the exile of King Li was set down

109. Creel, 1970:423.

in the royal Chou record by a Chou prince during the Ch'un-ch'iu period. In a brief sketch of the history of the Western Chou, the prince cited the accomplishments of the early rulers, kings Wen, Wu, Ch'eng, and K'ang. Then he omitted discussion of the mid-Chou reigns entirely, for apparently there were few spectacular events worthy of his attention during that period of consolidation and steady growth. Finally he gave rather detailed accounts of the last reigns of the dynasty:

> When [the throne] came to King Yi, he suffered from disease, and all the feudal lords hurried to sacrifice, praying for his recovery. Coming to King Li, he was found to be tyrannical and cruel. Myriad people found him intolerable, so he was forced to go into exile and live in Chih. The feudal lords removed him from the throne, so that there was an interregnum [during which there was no] royal authority. When [his son] King Hsüan [showed himself] possessed of character, [the feudal lords] handed over the government to him. Then [the rule] came to King Yu.[110]

The *Kuo-yü* lists the official reasons why the king was deposed. He was avaricious and his appointed officer of finance brought revenue into the private treasury or the royal household. The king was also thought to be cruel and tyrannical, and the "people of the state" criticized him. When the Duke of Shao, a high-ranking official, pointed out to him the widespread discontent and criticism, King Li assigned "witches" to search for the discontented people. Whoever the informant reported as a critic was put to death. A government of terror prevailed for three years until the aristocrats, or the feudal lords, stopped presenting tribute and jointly exiled the king from the capital in 841 B.C. The crown prince sought asylum at the residence of the Duke of Shao. This is the first reliable date in Chinese chronology, and from it Chinese history is accountable annually. At that time aristocrats organized a regency, which ruled the kingdom for fourteen years until the crown prince was enthroned.[111]

The period was known as the "Kung-ho" 共和 regency, literally meaning "jointly and coherently." There are two interpretations of the nature of this regency.[112] In one version, the regency was said to be jointly held by the Duke of Shao and the Duke of Chou, descendants of the two founding heroes of the Chou who held the same hereditary title of royal

110. *Tso-chuan*, 52/4; Legge, *Ch'un Ts'ew*, 717; translation revised slightly from Creel's version. Creel, 1970:426.

111. *Kuo-yü*, 1/4-6; *Shih-chi*, 4/53–57.

112. Ch'en Meng-chia, 1977:34–35.

counselor.[113] In the other version, a certain Lord Ho 和 of Kung 共 was said to be the Duke of Wei who actually served as the regent.[114] The first interpretation is not confirmed through study of bronze inscriptions, because no mention of the Duke of Chou is known throughout the mid-Chou period. The *Tso-chuan*, on the other hand, mentions the Duke of Chou frequently. The other version must also be doubted because the date of Lord Ho of Kung was simply too late to be contemporary with King Li. Neither position, therefore, may be supported reliably.

The Kung-ho regency may have been ruled by a group of influential Chou aristocrats, one of whom presided over the collective. The Duke of Shao may have been such a figure, since he played an important role in the court of King Li by providing shelter for the crown prince. Moreover, the Shao clan is named frequently in middle and late Chou sources including the *Book of Poetry*.[115] A person named Po Ho-fu 伯龢父 or Shih Ho-fu 師龢父 did occupy an unusual position in the mid-Chou period.[116] Shih Ho-fu may have presided over the collegiate regency as a leader of the loyalists who helped facilitate the restoration.

Although these are speculations, it is important to notice two issues in the episode involving the exile of King Li. First, in his effort to monopolize economic interests, the king took away some of the power of the feudal nobles. Because they resented that conduct, he was exiled. But, if the royal Chou domain had been available for the king to draw his own revenues, and his vassals had had their own fiefs from which to take their income, there would not have been a conflict between the king and the nobles. The overlap of their interests could have occurred only if royal authority actually did stretch directly into the domain of the vassals. In such cases the nobles would have had to take back some portion of the resources controlled by the royal court. If the royal authority actually reached into the vassals' territories, its power should be regarded as a monarchy, far more powerful than a suzerainty. In the case that an aristocrat received an emolument from the court he would be called a courtier, as opposed to a vassal. Only under such unequal conditions would King Li and his nobles have faced problems of sharing resources not monopolized by the throne.

The nobles managed to rule the kingdom for a considerable period. The regency, however it was constituted, did not claim the royal throne,

113. *Shih-chi*, 4/56.
114. *Chu-shu chi-nien*, B-8; *Shih-chi*, 37/5–6.
115. See chapter 5.
116. Yang Shu-ta, 1952:138, 255; Kuo Mo-jo, 1957:114.

for it was eventually returned to the former crown prince. The regency could not have worked effectively if there had not been a well-established administrative machinery. These two features of the coup d'état during the reign of King Li reflect an administrative network in ɩne Chou court consisting of nobility whose authority may have stretched to the enfeoffed domains as well. Interference in the Ch'i ducal succession by royal authority is thus explained.

Thus, the Chou royal house developed as the head of a coalition of several constituents (such as the Shang and other "nations"), gradually evolved into a suzerainty ruling over feudal vassals, and finally turned into a monarchy with a rather effective governing body. The increase of resources brought to royal control through military campaigns no doubt facilitated such a development.

5 Forming a Nation and Chou Feudalism

The dominant political power in north China at the end of the second millennium was the Shang. Although their actual strength was being contested by the Chou and other groups, especially those in the eastern territories, their government was the model on which the Chou based their own. Segmentation of kinship lineages formed the new line of Chou control, as it had with the Shang.

The Chou, however, amassed a larger territory to rule than their predecessors, and they continued to expand throughout the early period. Their constituency was larger and more diverse, and they were challenged with the possibility, as well as the necessity, of creating a system that could bring such diverse populations under one Chinese leadership (the Son of Heaven) with a single Chinese, or Hua-Hsia 華夏, as they would come to call it, worldview. What emerged was a multilayered feudal structure that accommodated both conformity in the ruling mechanism and diversity in practice as it was needed to allow participation of the annexed or subjugated members.

The *tsung-fa* structure of kingship, which ranked political authority, was the backbone of the new feudal system. Early in the dynasty local lords were incorporated into a vassal system that preserved and perpetuated the royal segmentation. Eventually systematization of feudal ritual developed in the middle Western Chou, as did stabilization of rank and function. The by-product of that process was the elimination of the flexibility and adaptability so characteristic of the early period. The feudal system was an institution of delegated authority made up of contractual feudal relationships. The combination of contractual and personal bonds ordered through the *tsung-fa* system was unique to China and the Chou.

The nature of the system and its regularization are discernible through examination of inscriptions on bronzes and oracle bones, through distribution studies of archaeological sites and objects, and through reading descriptions of court ritual in classical literature and secondary sources that analyze the ancient states.

147

SHANG RULING APPROACHES

The Shang kingdom included the lower and middle reaches of the Yellow River, an area large enough that effective methods of consolidation and control were needed to support their political unity. Chang Kwang-chih 張光直 has characterized Shang kingship as an institution having two basic components. First, the king occupied the top of a vast state structure and his position served as the central authority in a centripedal economy and enforced its rule by licit force and explicit law. Second, kingship was at the core of a vast kinship organization based on blood relationships, both actual and legendary, and was coupled with a strong state structure. The Shang state structure consisted of two social and political units: a geographic unit (*yi* 邑, or town), and kinship unit (*tsu* 族). Although the exact nature of the system of *yi* and how it was organized into nations have frequently been debated, most agree that the *tsu* kinship units were organized hierarchically.[1] Both Shirakawa Shizuka 白川靜 and Hayashi Minao 林已奈夫 noticed that the names of *tsu*, when written in pictograph form, often contained indices of rank.[2] This demonstrated that even the *tsu* were internally organized in a graded order, presumably parallel to the actual distribution of authority. Such a hierarchy was probably the consequence of segmentation of a kinship lineage into branches that formed the subordinated units of the main stem. Continuous segmentation resulted in a hierarchical network of several levels of branches within a *tsu*. From the Shang *tsu* emblems one can see such a hierarchy in the constituent branches (fig. 5.1).

But just what constituted a kinship unit during ancient times? Several terms could have connoted such a unit: *hsing* 姓, *shih* 氏, *tsung* 宗, and *tsu* 族. Originally, each must have designated functions. Li Tsung-t'ung 李宗侗 (Li Tsungtong) has suggested that a *hsing* was a group bound by common ancestry, one whose identity evolved from an ancient totemistic association.[3] *Hsing* was, therefore, a collective noun that referred to people who believed that they were of common origin, but who might or might not have been members of the same polity. A *hsing* was quite similar to a nation. *Shih* was a political unit that designated all people by surname who belonged to the same political authority. *Shih* was normally a subdivision of *hsing*. The character *tsung* combines the indicator for "rooftop" and for "offering table." It indicated a kin group in which the ritual of serving ancestors was regulated. A *tsu* sign

1. Chang, 1980:158–65.
2. Shirakawa Shizuka, 1951; Hayashi Minao, 1968.
3. Li Tsung-t'ung, 1954:7–10, 35–37.

5.1 Shang *tsu* emblems (from Chang, 1980:3, courtesy of Yale University Press)

included a flag and an arrowhead, most likely indicating a combat unit made up of people of the same identity and interest. By the time of the Ch'un-ch'iu 春秋 period, the uses of these four terms were already confused.[4]

In the Shang system, *tsu* was the unit on which the ruling apparatus was based. *Tsu* were attached to a prince, a queen, or a ranking aristocrat. They were charged with the responsibility of enlisting combat soldiers, participating in military campaigns, and engaging in farming. They were recorded as branches of the Shang royal family, or, in some cases, they bore other names and their own identity.[5] These were the people who inhabited the Shang domain. Beyond the royal area there were "marquises," who were probably the Shang garrison commanders. In addition, there were the *fang* 方 states, some of which were friendly to the Shang while others may simply have been neighbors, even hostile ones. More than thirty *fang* states were registered in Shang divinations.[6] They were normally states of other *hsing*. For instance, the *hsing* of the Chou 周 and the Shao 召 was "Chi" 姬; that of the Kuei-fang 鬼方 was "Huai" 槐, and that of the Jen-fang 人方 was either "Feng" 風 or "Yen" 奄. The Shang political sphere as it is known today covered an area largely populated by *Tzu* 子 people, or those whose *hsing* was *tzu*, represented by a swallow. The *tsu* and the *shih* were no more than subdivisions of the *Tzu hsing* 子姓. In other words, the *hsing* was the equivalent of a "nation"; the *shih* designated a "domain"; whereas *tsu* referred to an autonomous group of people. Outside the Shang domain, there were people who identified themselves as members of other *hsing* nations.

The Chou, by the time of the Shang period, were also organized into the same sorts of divisions. The Chi *hsing* was not a very large nation, and the Chou existed under the cultural shadow of the Shang. The Chou could not have maintained their control of the heartland of China, which they had gained through military triumph, without developing a sophisticated and effective ruling apparatus. An investigation of those characteristics of the Chou regime, which can explain their lengthy and enduring success as leaders in China, follows.

CHOU FEUDALISM

Several historical civilizations developed political and socio-economic institutions that were remarkably similar and have been called "feudal."

4. Yang Hsi-mei, 1954A, 1954B; Ting Shan, 1956:33; Etō Hiroshi, 1970:109–14.
5. Ting Shan, 1956.
6. Shima Kunio, 1958:384–85; Chang, 1980:248–59.

The obvious ones are medieval Europe and pre-modern Japan. Feudalism is, therefore, a meaningful term among historians.[7]

The existence of feudalistic society in medieval Europe induced historians in the West to study similar phenomena in the Orient. Feudalism has become the subject of comparative studies.[8] The Marxist historians define feudalism as one stage in the evolution of human society, one sandwiched between periods of slavery and capitalism. Marxists, therefore, have felt compelled to confirm a feudal period in Chinese history. The Chinese model was thorny for Marxist historians, for China was unified into a bureaucratic empire as early as the Ch'in 秦 dynasty in the third century B.C., but capitalism did not develop until the modern era. Feudalism, if understood as a system of subdivided units with considerable autonomy within a culture, ended in China with unification under the first emperor of Ch'in. The long post-feudal and pre-capitalistic period in Chinese history, therefore, posed a dilemma of definition for them. Some Chinese Marxist historians labeled the entire, long dynastic period as feudalistic. They called pre-Ch'in history a period of slavery, even though it was actually a period when the states were first enfeoffed.

Chou feudalization was interpreted by the T'ang 唐 scholar Liu Tsung-yüan 柳宗元 (A.D. 773–819) as a necessary development in the early reigns of the Western Chou, and not one of choice. He argued that human society could be brought to order only by instituting leadership among equals. Furthermore, he reasoned, leadership in communities of varying sizes was inevitably organized hierarchically. Capable, powerful, and appealing persons, ones with "charisma," in our current use of Weber's terminology, emerged into command positions at many different levels of the organization. Moreover, Liu claimed that because the organization of social groups and top leaders had changed as new dynasties replaced old ones, reckoning with power at the lower levels was especially and necessarily problematic.[9] He argued that the autonomy of social groups was so strong that it survived the application of external force brought by sanctioned political power. The dynastic leaders had both to subdue and to tolerate. Feudalization in the early Western Chou was, according to Liu Tsung-yüan, a form of governing that developed out of the political and social autonomy of local groups.

Hsü Tsung-yen 許宗彥 (A.D. 1768–1818), a Ch'ing scholar of classical studies, observed Chou feudalism in a similar way. He argued that King

---

7. Hsu, 1979:543–46; Lu Yao-tung, 1979:141–66; Li-shih-yen-chiu pien-chi-pu, 1957; Wang Ssu-chih, 1980:27–29; Fu Chu-fu, 1980:1–23.

8. Coulbern, 1956.

9. *Ch'üan T'ang-wen*, 582/2–5.

Wu's 武 alliances with the so-called eight hundred lords were all established before the end of the Shang and that kings Wen 文 and Wu inherited the affiliations. The best that the Chou kings could expect was peaceful coexistence with these old states, for they could not alter their state boundaries. The new states created by the Chou kings therefore had to be located within the old Shang domain and the territories of a few subdued states.[10]

Both Liu and Hsü justifiably claimed that the Chou realistically could not have imposed reorganization of nations and states in the newly conquered land. The Chou did not have much choice other than to tolerate and join hands with the local population.[11] The power structure consisted of an affiliation of the Chou (including the Chiang 姜), the Shang, and the native populace. The working principle of the new regime was one of cooperation.

In this situation, the principal initiators were the Chou royal kinsmen and their closest allies. They dominated the tripartite coalition, and they were intruders who invaded the central plain and established themselves as rulers. The Chou invaded, conquered, and reconstituted local structures by assimilating the local leaders into the power elite. By doing so they incorporated the conquered into the service of a united state, thus providing allegiance to the state and to the new dynasty. As suggested by Eberhard, the new ruling class was added to the old local social order to form a multilayered feudal structure.[12]

This multitiered arrangement could not remain stable if the members of the upper class remained culturally distinct from the others, unless rule was maintained by absolute force. The Chou, unlike their Shang predecessors, did not possess the military strength to do so. The differences among groups were too great, and some method of organization was needed to create fluency in the economy or the society would collapse. Evidence of cultural dualism, for instance, can be found in the state of Lu 魯, where there were shrines for religious services both for the local population and for the ruling class. Little evidence exists to suggest that the states founded during the early Chou lacked internal stability. On the contrary, throughout the Ch'un-ch'iu period, each state continued its local features and diversity thrived. To some extent, acculturation must have taken place whereby the new multilayered society was unified around mutually acceptable features.[13] Judging from history, we must argue that the differences between the Chou and those

10. Hsü Tsung-yen, 1829:1/36–37.
11. See chapter 4 above.
12. Eberhard, 1965:24–30.
13. See chapter 6 below.

whom they conquered were overcome through toleration and shared values, for the result of acculturation—the Hua-Hsia culture base—developed and continued.

In the core area of north China, interaction among native cultures had occurred since the upper neolithic, so the local cultures were already mixed. Moreover, the groups mingled with their neighbors across the borders and a congenial atmosphere was formed in the core area where the Hsia 夏 and the Shang dominated.[14] Likewise, the new states created during the Ch'eng-K'ang 成康 era were established with similar harmony.[15]

Expansion beyond the core area to the Huai-Han River valleys and farther south to the vast valley of the Yangtze during the reign of King Chao stretched Chinese culture into a region where native cultures were markedly different. From the neolithic Ta-hsi 大溪 cultures to the Ch'ü-chia-ling 屈家嶺 cultures, the native tradition was quite unlike its counterpart in the north. Shang influence reached the Yangtze Valley with limited success and the distribution of Shang colonies was scattered.[16] The process of assimilation in the south during the Western Chou was difficult, slow, and incomplete.

In summary, the dominance enjoyed by the Chou in the core area was provided by conquest of one nation over another. Its success rested on a reorganization across an extensive cultural sphere. Political and social structures were developed that accommodated both the local group and the intruders.

THE FEUDAL SYSTEM AND THE POPULATION

The substance of the new feudal states was of such interest to the ancients that it was often recorded in ancient documents, including passages in the *Tso-chuan* 左傳 (Fourth Year of Duke Ting 定), the songs "Sung-kao" 崧高 and "Han-i" 韓奕 in the *Shih-ching*, and bronze inscriptions on the I-hou *kuei* and the Ta-Yü *ting* 大盂鼎.

The passage in the *Tso-chuan*[17] lists the items bestowed on the dukes of Lu 魯, Wei 衛 and Chin 晉. They include ritual articles (chariots, flags, bows and arrows, weapons, armor, drums, and jades), groups of people (numerous Shang clans and the staffs of certain offices), and territories designated as the lands of certain ancient nations. The population

14. Chang Kwang-chih, 1978:287–306.
15. See chapter 4 above.
16. Chang, 1980:305–06, 320–21.
17. Legge, *Ch'un Ts'ew*, 754.

specifically assigned to the new dukes consisted of artisans, hereditary units specializing in certain crafts—potting and metal working, for example. They were supposedly organized according to their own agnatic group including a main clan and segmented branches. The paragraph concerning the gifts for Lu contained two baffling phrases: *t'u-t'ien* 土田 ("field" or "arable land") and *p'ei-tun* 陪敦 ("that attached thereupon"). The meaning of *p'ei-tun* was not clear at all, and Legge did not even render it in his translation. Yang K'uan 楊寬 correctly related this phrase to a similar one in the *Shih-ching* in which *t'u-tien* was connected to another phrase, *fu-yung* 附庸. Although *fu-yung* could mean "attached states," as Legge suggests,[18] Yang K'uan found that the use of *yung* on the bronze inscriptions often refers to a group of people in service. Therefore, he suggested that the Duke of Lu was actually given not only arable lands but also the farmers attached to them. In other words, these people were the original residents of the land bestowed on the Duke of Lu.[19] An enfeoffed lord would oversee three categories of subjects: the staff who had special knowledge of rituals and governance, the artisans and craft workers who commanded special skills, and the farming population attached to the fields.

The songs "Sung-kao" and "Han-i" describe the ceremonies that established the vassal states. The "Sung-kao" reads:

> Full of activity is the Chief of Shen
> And the King would employ him to continue the services (of his fathers)
> With his capital in Hsieh
> Where he should be a pattern to the state of the south.
> The King gave charge to the Earl of Shao
> To arrange all about the residence of the Chief of Shen
> Where he should do what was necessary for the reign of the south,
> And where his posterity might maintain his merit.
>
> The King gave charge to the Chief of Shen
> Be a pattern to the regions of the south.
> And by taking over those people of Hsieh,
> Who would be your servants
> The King gave charge to the Earl of Shao
> To make the statutory definition of the territory and fields of the Chief of Shen

---

18. Legge, *She King*, 623.
19. Yang K'uan, 1965:81–82; Itō Michiharu, 1975:232–36.

The King gave charge to his steward
To remove their private subordinate to the spot.

. . . .

The king sent away the Chief of Shen
With a carriage of state and its team of horses
"I have consulted about your residence,
That it had best be settled in the south,
I confer on you a great scepter
As the symbol of dignity.
Go my uncle,
And protect the country of the south."[20]

From this poem we learn that the Chief of Shen received ritual items
from the king (the scepter and carriage) as well as some "private
subordinates," who must have been assigned from the royal house. He
also received people in service from Hsieh, where he was to rule. The
forces of the Earl of Shao were dispatched to help the Shen Chief
establish the new state. Thus, the Chief of Shen had in his state the
king's men, men from the Earl of Shao's command, and the local
population of Hsieh.

In a similar fashion the song "Han-i" describes the court visit of the
Marquis of Han:

With his four steeds, all noble,
Very long and large,
The Marquis of Han came to court,
With the large jade scepter of his rank
He entered and appeared before the King
The King gave him
A fine dragon-flag, with its feathery ornaments;
A checkered bamboo screen, and an ornamented yoke;
A dark-colored robe with a dragon on it, and red slippers
The hooks for the trappings of the breast bands, and the carved
    frontlets
The learning board bound with leather, and a tiger's skin to cover it,
The ends of the reins, with their metal rings.

. . . .

Large is the wall of (the city of) Han
Built by the force of Yen

20. Legge, *She King*, 536, 539, with revision.

As his ancestor had received charge
To take over all the wild tribes (of the quarter)
The King now gave to the Marquis of Han
The Chui and the Mi
Forthwith to hold the states of the North
And to preside over them as their chief,
Making strong his walls, and deep his moats,
Laying out his fields, regulating his revenues,
Presenting his skins of the white fox,
With those of the red panther and the yellow grizzly bear.[21]

The state of Han was not newly established at the time of the court visit but had been secured earlier with the assistance of the forces of Yen, the northern state founded by the Duke of Shao as a stronghold of Chou power. The local people were called "wild tribes," because they wore the skins of wild animals. They were assigned to the charge of the Marquis of Han. The verb "to take over" (yin 因) appears in both poems to denote the takeover of local population. Similarly, the state of Shen was founded with the support of armed forces from a neighboring state. Feudalization, therefore, established the central government as the authority over a local population.

The I-hou *kuei* inscription (fig. 4.8) dating from the Ch'eng-K'ang period states that gifts of land were conferred on the marquis when he was transferred to a new territory in the Yangtze Valley. The gifts included ritual bows and arrows as well as land—both fields and settlements. Although the numerals in the text cannot be deciphered because the text is corrupted, the land given to I-hou is mentioned with precise measurements and boundaries. That I-hou's domain is well-defined is a surprise, for the record of the state of Lu is only vaguely described in the *Tso-chuan*. The people granted to I-hou are grouped into three categories. The king's men are listed according to surname; the people of Cheng 鄭 are described as a group led by seven chiefs; the common people are listed as a sum. The I-hou inscription confirms the information in the *Tso-chuan* (Fourth Year of Duke Ting) plus other specific data. Members of the elite, probably in agnatic groups, were collectively assigned to the vassals, while the local people were given as persons in service. For instance, the Shang-Yen 商奄 were assigned to Lu (mentioned in the *Tso-chuan*), the Hsieh 謝 to Shen 申, and the "wild tribes" to Han (in the *Book of Poetry*).[22]

The inscription on the Ta-Yü *ting* (fig. 4.6) charges Yü to succeed his

21. Ibid., 547–51, with revisions.
22. Shirakawa Shizuka, *KBTS*, 10:529–52

ancestor Nan-kung 南公. He first received ritual gifts such as clothing, horses, chariots, and flags. Then Yü was given four "chiefs of the state," six hundred and fifty-nine service people, thirteen chiefs and king's men, as well as fifteen hundred service people.[23] The distribution and ratio of peoples of various categories mentioned in the Ta-Yü *ting* inscription were consistent with those in the I-hou *kuei*. There were service people assigned from the local population, as well as king's men under the command of the "chiefs."[24] The exact status of the *jen-li* 人鬲 is yet to be determined, but it is generally agreed that they were some subordinated people who rendered services and were attached to the master. In the Ta-Yü *ting* inscription, fifteen hundred *jen-li* are listed as subordinates of the king's men. They probably made up the main body of the labor force given to Yü at the ceremony confirming his succession to an hereditary post.[25]

On another bronze inscription from the Ch'eng-K'ang period, we are told that the Marquis Hsing 邢 was granted the people of three old states of Shang, the residents of those localities near the Shang capital.[26] The Marquis of Hsing received them as his subjects because he was moved to the east plain. In the Ch'un-ch'iu period Hsing was in the same region. At least one of these localities is recorded in the *Tso-chuan* as part of the Hsing state.[27]

Based on this information, we see that the process of founding of Chou feudal states was remarkably consistent in manner and content. Both land and population were given to a vassal, along with other gifts. The area of land was often not specified carefully, and there were cases where a vassal was moved from one location to another. The groups of people given to a vassal were very clearly specified, for they were assigned according to the land of which they were a part. The collection of land and people, including residents of varied status and origin, made up a state. It was the people who were emphasized in these early documents, rather than the domain. Yang Hsi-mei 楊希枚 remarked about the composition of Chou feudalism that the people were bestowed, the domain was assigned, and the authority designated in the manner of creation of a new state.[28] Yang interpreted the term *tzu-hsing* 子姓, customarily understood as the bestowal of a surname, to be the bestowal of the "people," who provided a base for the newly

23. Ibid., 12:651–72; Kao Hung-chin, 1962.
24. Wang Ning-sheng, 1979.
25. Yang K'uan, 1965:100–10; Hsü Chung-shu, 1955; Kaizuka Shigeki, 1962.
26. Shirakawa Shizuka, *KBTS*, 12:592–603.
27. Ch'en P'an, 1969:266–67; Shirakawa Shizuka, *KBTS*, 12:588–99.
28. Yang Hsi-mei, 1952, 1954A, 1954B.

institutionalized ruling class. The ritual of creating a name for the new vassal state, *ming-shih* 命氏, according to Yang, should be regarded as part of the process of segmentation of the dominating group, that is, that of the lord. New units were created that remained subordinate to the old unit. Thus distribution of power was created in the hierarchic manner of continuous segmentation.[29] Such a phenomenon continued the Shang system, which had organized the kingdom according to basic units of *tsu* 族.[30] The vassal states of the Chou kingdom blended populations of different origins and reorganized them into a new population (fig. 5.2). After a long period these enfeoffed units acquired their own identity and attachments to the local area. Thus there evolved a system of localized states in the Ch'un-ch'iu period, which Richard Walker has called "the multi-state system."[31] It was possible for the Ch'un-ch'iu states to maintain features of the congregation of agnatic groups in the ruling class while simultaneously developing the characteristics of territorial states.

MOVEMENT OF CHOU STATES

In the early Chou, after the feudal system was in place, the vassal states became units that managed population rather than land. The Chou states were often not tied to given localities but moved from one place to another. Ku Tung-kao 顧棟高, a seventeenth-century scholar of classical studies, identified twenty Chou states, each of which had moved at least once. Ch'en P'an expanded the list to seventy-one by including other ancient states and some non-Chinese ones. Virtually all the Chou vassal states, both those of the Chi and of the Chiang, could be found in Ch'en's list. The distance over which they migrated, moreover, was often as much as several hundred to a thousand miles.[32] Let us look at the following examples as illustrations.

1. Lu 魯, a member of the Chi surname, was originally founded in present-day Lu-shan 魯山 County of Honan Province. After the great campaign against the uprising in the east, Lu was resettled in present Ch'ü-fu 曲阜 County of Shantung Province. The state of Lu, however, maintained a small pocket in Honan as late as the Ch'un-ch'iu period. The domain of Ying 應, founded by another son of the

---

29. Ibid., 1954B: 195–97.
30. Chang, 1980:163–65.
31. Walker, 1953; Hsu, 1965:78–100.
32. Ch'en P'an, 1969:16–17.

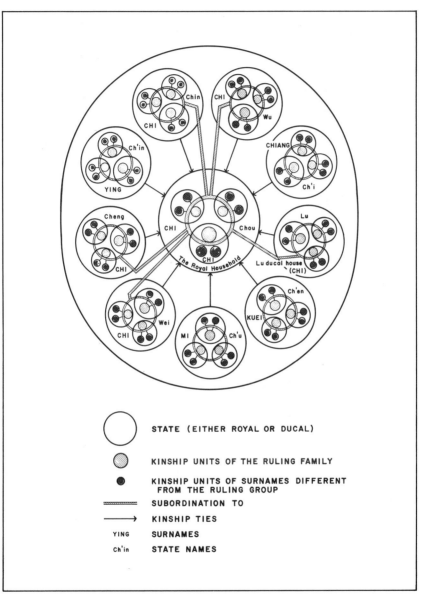

STATE (EITHER ROYAL OR DUCAL)

KINSHIP UNITS OF THE RULING FAMILY

KINSHIP UNITS OF SURNAMES DIFFERENT
FROM THE RULING GROUP

SUBORDINATION TO

KINSHIP TIES

YING   SURNAMES

Ch'in   STATE NAMES

5.2 Chou vassal states

Duke of Chou, was still located in the vicinity of Lu-shan during the Ch'un-ch'iu period.[33]

2. Wei 衛, also a Chi member, was traditionally regarded as a state established in the same location after the campaign in the east was over. Recent studies suggested that T'ang-shu 唐叔 was originally enfeoffed in the Chou domain in present Shensi. The Wei state was a new one created in the old Shang capital region by moving T'ang-shu there.[34]

3. T'eng 滕, a Chi member, was originally located near Wei in present-day Honan Province. Later it was moved to the present-day T'eng County of Shantung Province.[35]

4. Cheng 鄭, a Chi member, was not created until the reign of Li. The old territory of Cheng was at Hsien-lin 棫林 in eastern Shensi. At the time of the Western Chou collapse, Cheng moved its population to present-day Hsin-cheng 新鄭 in Honan Province.[36]

5. Wu 吳, allegedly a member of the Chi, was the only state located in the lower Yangtze Valley. Ch'ien Mu 錢穆, however, argued that it originally was enfeoffed in Shansi, on the east bank of the Yellow River.[37]

6. Yen 燕, was founded by the Duke of Shao in the general area of northern Hopei. Fu Ssu-nien noticed that Yen was originally located in Yen-ch'eng 郾城 County of Honan. Along with the campaign in the east in the early Chou, the Duke of Shao commanded the operation on the northern front. Yen was first moved to Yü-t'ien 玉田 County of Hopei Province, and then moved to a strategic position near Peking 北京.[38] Ku Chieh-kang 顧頡剛 suggested that Yen might have once been located on the upper reaches of the Fen 汾 River in Shensi Province.[39] Archaeological findings discussed in the previous chapters provide evidence to support the hypothesis that Yen was moved to northern Hopei as a newly organized unit.

7. Ch'i 齊, the most important member of the Chiang group, which allied with the Chi-Chou to achieve the conquest of Shang. Fu Ssu-nien suggested that Ch'i, originally named Lü 呂, was founded in Honan. The children of the Chiang were moved to Shantung after the campaign in the east.[40]

33. Ibid., 22.
34. Chou Fa-kao, 1951:24–27.
35. Ch'en P'an, 1969:33.
36. Ibid., 56–69.
37. Ibid., 76.
38. Ibid., 78–80.
39. Ibid., 694.
40. Ibid., 88.

8. Ch'i 杞, the descendants of an ancient nation located in what is now Ch'i-hsien 杞縣 County of Honan province. Before the Ch'un-ch'iu period began, Ch'i was moved to Shantung, at a location near Lü. Archaeological evidence has provided several bronzes inscribed with the character Ch'i.[41]

9. Chü 莒, a member of the Ying 嬴 surname. At the time of King Wu, Chü was located near Lang-ya 琅玡, on the coast of Shantung. Later, Chü was moved to Chu-hsien 莒縣 County of Shantung Province, and then to Chiu-hsien County. In Shantung Province, the name of Chü has been found at numerous locations. There was even a Chü at the west of the Chou capital, near the border between the present Shensi and Kansu provinces.[42] As a small state of non-Chou origin, Chü was vulnerable to the Chou orders and moved from place to place.

10. Shen 申, another important member of the Chiang, was located in the present Nan-yang 南陽 County of Honan Province. Ch'en P'an suggested that Shen was first located near Mount Sung 嵩, a sacred mountain in the legends of the Chiang. The distance between Mount Sung and Han-yang was considerable. Shen was moved to southern Honan, probably because the Chou needed some strong allies there to facilitate their expansion into the Han River Valley.[43]

11. Chi 紀, a small state of Chiang, was located in Shou-kuang 壽光 County of Shantung. Chi moved within Shantung at least twice.[44]

12. Kuo 虢, a Chi member, originally was in Pao-chi County of Shensi. In the reign of King Yu 幽, Kuo was moved to P'ing-lu 平陸 County of Shansi Province. Kuo bronzes were excavated near Feng-hsiang 鳳翔 in Shensi. It is possible that Kuo was once located there.[45]

13. Hsiang 向, a small state of the Chiang group, was moved from the present Meng-hsien 孟縣 county in Honan to Chu-hsien 莒縣 in Shantung. Several localities bearing the name of Hsiang were mentioned in the *Ch'un-ch'iu* and *Tso-chuan* and could be identified in Shantung, Honan, and Anhui 安徽 provinces. They might or might not be related to this small state.[46]

14. Hsing 邢, a Chi member located in Hsing-t'ai 邢台 County of Hopei Province. Bronze inscriptions yielded information on a Hsiang state near Pao-chi County of Shensi Province during early Chou times. In

41. Ibid., 123–25.
42. Ibid., 138–40.
43. Ibid., 153–54.
44. Ibid., 166.
45. Ibid., 171–75.
46. Ibid., 176–77.

the Ch'un-ch'iu period, Hsing was moved from Hopei to Liao-ch'eng 聊城 County of Shantung Province, as a consequence of nomadic invasions from the north.[47]

15. Hsi 息, a Chi member, was moved from southern Shantung to Honan.[48]

16. Kao 郜, a Chi member, was repeatedly moved. There were several Kaos in the states of Sung, Ch'i, and Chin during the Ch'un-ch'iu period.[49]

17. Teng 鄧, a member of the Man 曼 surname, originally was located to the north of the Yellow River. Gradually Teng was moved to the south, and established a capital in the present Yen-ch'eng 郾城 County of Honan and then in Hsiang-yang 襄陽 County of Hupei Province.[50]

18. Liao 蓼, a small state of the ancient nation of Chu-jung, which was moved from Ting-t'ao 定陶 County, Shantung, to T'ang-ho 唐河 county of Honan.[51]

19. Tseng 鄫, a member of the Ssu 姒 surname, was originally on the Tseng River, near Mi-hsien County of Honan Province, not far away from its sister state of Ch'i. It gradually was moved eastward from Honan to Shantung during the first half of the Ch'un-ch'iu period. Repeatedly Tseng faced the resistance and suppression by the Chou states along its migration route.[52]

20. Han 韓 was a Chi state founded at the time of King Wu. It was located in several places. Ch'en P'an suggested that Han was first founded near Yen and then moved to Jui-ch'eng 芮城 County of Shansi and finally to Han-ch'eng 韓城 County of Shensi.[53] But, if several Chou states were first established in the west and were moved to the east after the conclusion of the eastern campaign, Han must have been part of the same migration. Besides, during the reign of King Wu, Yen was not in northern Hopei. The previously cited poem, the "Han-i," claimed that the Han capital was built with the assistance of Yen troops. Therefore, the migration route of Han was most likely from Shensi via Shansi to Hopei. Then due to pressure from the north the state of Han was again moved to Shansi in the reign of King Hsüan.

47. Ibid., 181–84.
48. Ibid., 195.
49. Ibid., 197.
50. Ibid., 214–15.
51. Ibid., 243.
52. Ibid., 299–303.
53. Ibid., 340–45.

21. Lü 呂, a branch of the Chiang, was the original name of a powerful
    state of Ch'i in Shantung. After Ch'i was established on the east
    coast, some of the Lü probably stayed in Honan to retain the old
    name. The Chiang people originally roamed about in the corner of
    Honan and Shansi near the sharp turn of the Yellow River. They
    followed the expansion of Chou to stretch into the south of
    Honan.[54] At the time of Chou expansion into the Han River Valley,
    both Shen and Lü were Chiang states. They also moved to southern
    Honan, probably serving on the front line of Chou expansion.

The general pattern of Chou expansionism, thus, was for the
population to follow a vassal prince to a new locality and then form the
bulk of his subjects. These populations, either the Chi or the Chiang,
generally moved gradually from Shensi or Honan to the east or south,
where new supporting powers were formed by them "to screen and to
defend" the new Chou world order. In the new land, where these
immigrants constituted one stratum of the ruling class; they superseded
and were superimposed upon the native population. The *Book of Rites*
(*Li-chi* 禮記) records a sacrificial offering made to the ancestors of the
rulers of the "host state" (*yin-kuo* 因國), who had no descendants.[55] The
"host state", or "previous state," refers to the land and the people
whom the Chou governed. The distinction made between the "man in
the capital" (*kuo-jen* 國人) and the "man in the field" (*yeh-jen* 野人)
indicates a separation into two branches: the ruling group, who settled
in the capital, and the ruled natives, who lived in scattered settlements.
This bifurcation was a direct consequence of Chou feudalization.

THE TSUNG-FA STRUCTURE

To maintain solidarity among themselves, the *kuo-jen* stressed tight
organization in which the agnatic units of stratified kinship groups
fortified the system. In traditional terminology, this system was known
as *tsung-fa* 宗法. The hypothetical Chou structure that we see in table
5.1 illustrates the dual nature of this system. On the one hand, the
hierarchy of the political authority was reflected in ranks; on the other
hand, lineage was segmented into branches, each of which was regarded
as a subordinate to the line from which it divided. The principal line, of
course, was that of the kings. The *ta-tsung* 大宗, or major line, was only a

54. Ibid., 430–33.
55. *Li-chi*, 12/10.

Table 5.1.   The Tsung-fa System

Main Line	Branches	Secondary Branches	Tertiary Branches
King			
King	Dukes		
King	Dukes	Ministers	
King	Dukes	Ministers	Shih
King	Dukes	Ministers	Shih

relative term with regard to the segments. The *hsiao-tsung* 小宗, or minor line, was also a relative term with regard to its own main line.

The Shang population assigned to the vassals was constituted into groups according to *tsu* membership. The Chou nobles were solidly organized into agnatic *tsung-fa* units called upon for military purposes. The inscription on the Pan *kuei* (fig. 4.9) contains a royal directive for the vassals who were to take part in battle. It orders a lord to lead his own *tsu* (kinsmen) to protect the safety of the commander.[56] Likewise, in the inscription on the Mao-kung *ting* 毛公鼎, the Duke of Mao is assigned to guard and protect the king by using his own *tsu* as the royal guard.[57] These *tsu* were both units within the kinship structure and within the combat military. Even in the Ch'un-ch'iu period, in the great battle of Yen-ling 鄢陵 (574 B.C.), *tsu* were the military units on the battlefield.[58]

Traditionally, the Chou *tsu* was considered a typical case, one thought to be hierarchically organized according to the *tsung-fa* system. The members of the Chou nobility in the Ch'un-ch'iu period did appear to be constituted in that manner and to honor the ordered authority of such structures.[59] Bronze inscriptions yield limited evidence of use of the system in the early years of the dynasty.[60] It is known, however, that children of the Chou royal house filled most of the governing positions in the vassal states.[61] In at least one case the inscription of a bronze (fig. 5.3) of Ch'eng-K'ang period refers to a ceremony where a

56. Shirakawa Shizuka, *KBTS*, 2:132.
57. Ibid., 30:680.
58. Legge, *Ch'un Ts'ew*, 397.
59. Li Tsung-t'ung, 1954:192–96.
60. Creel, 1970: 380–81.
61. Ibid., 376.

5.3 Rubbing of an inscription (from *KBTS*, 15:9)

hereditary branch paid homage to the main line. Here Shen-tzu 沈子, the owner of the bronze, was the master of a subordinate branch of Lu, the ruling house. Shen-tzu prayed for the blessings from Lu ancestors to be extended to "brothers," those of a minor branch segmented from the main line.[62]

Differentiation in status between the main lineage and the segmented branches is reflected in two bronze inscriptions attributed to a person named Tiao-sheng 琱生, a subordinate of the Duke of Shao. After the duke bestowed gifts on him, Tiao-sheng cast the bronze. In one inscription Tiao-sheng is referred to as the son of a minor branch official related to the Duke of Shao. The duke's mother is addressed by Tiao-sheng as "Lady," counterpart of "Lord," and as "Aunt." Tiao-sheng's own position in the royal court was as *T'ai-tsai* 大宰, a very high-ranking official, but one subordinate to the Duke of Shao. In another inscription the duke terms himself "Elder Uncle," and asks common ancestors to give blessings. Tiao-sheng (fig 5.4) addressed the duke as *Tsung-chün* 宗君, "lord of our main line," an unmistakable sign that Tiao-sheng's

62. Shirakawa Shizuka, *KBTS*, 15:7–26.

5.4 Rubbing from inscription: Tiao-sheng vessel B (from *KBTS*, 33:861)

position was seen in relation to his lineage as well as to the feudal structure.[63]

The term *hsiao-tzu* 小子 ("the Junior") was commonly used on bronze inscriptions. Kimura Hideumi analyzed the use of this term and found that sometimes it was a description of the king himself. In most cases, however, "junior" was a term of address signifying oneself that was used by a member of the branch line when he spoke to the master of the main line.[64] In the Ho *tsun* 何尊 inscription, the term "*tsung-hsiao-tzu*" 宗小子 ("Junior of the Lineage") refers, according to T'ang Lan, to a person who was a member of the royal house.[65] The same use of the term can be found in several bronze inscriptions.[66] The very word "*hsiao-tzu*" implies not just junior in age but also subordinate status. Thus we may say that although the *tsung-fa* hierarchy within lineage is not explicitly recorded in epigraphic materials, its use can be detected.

Moreover, the very arrangement of tombs in Chou cemeteries indicates the lineage of the deceased. In the assemblage of Chou tombs at Tou-chi-t'ai 鬭雞台, smaller graves belong to a small group. Each

63. Ibid., 33:841–72.
64. Kimura Hideumi, 1981.
65. T'ang Lan, 1976A:60; cf. Shirakawa Shizuka, *KBTS*, 8:175–76.
66. Shirakawa Shizuka, *KBTS*, 14:783, 19:329, 49:268–73.

group consists of two rows of tombs facing each other in symmetrical order. These groupings in turn were located in the context of a large cemetery, apparently that of the entire extended family. We can surmise that at least two levels of kin were represented in that arrangement.[67] In the Western Chou burials at Feng-hsi 澧西 near Ch'ang-an 長安, Shensi, there were forty-eight tombs at Locality Four. These tombs were grouped into three distinct assemblages associated by proximity and lineage. In Locality One of the Chang-chia-p'o 張家坡 burials, also at Ch'ang-an, there were fifty-three tombs for adults, seventeen for children, and four for chariots and horses. These tombs were grouped into six sections forming a neat pattern. For example, in each section there were two rows of graves facing each other with a single grave in the center (fig. 5.5). These six sections represented the subdivisions of a family line.[68] It is worth noting that the cemeteries at Pao-chi and Ch'ang-an were for common people and thus the multitiered structure of ancestry was practiced by more than the aristocrats.

The state cemetery of Wei excavated at Hsin-ts'un in Chün-hsien 濬縣 County, Honan, was an extensive area consisting of eight large tombs, twenty-nine middle-sized ones, twenty-eight smaller ones, two for horses and chariots, and twelve for horses only. These tombs were arranged in neat patterns, and the sequence of burial was clearly marked out. The eight large tombs were located along an east-west axis; the middle-sized and small ones were distributed as if attached to the larger ones.[69]

The Huang-t'u-p'o 黃土坡 site at Fang-shan 房山 County, Hopei, contained Chou burials identified as those of the nobles of the state of Yen. Two sections have been excavated. In the first, forty-one tombs were arranged in two rows facing each other along an east-west axis. They were clustered into six groups, some of which were further subdivided. Individual tombs within each subgroup faced each other or were arranged in pairs (fig 5.6). Such patterns demonstrate a three-tiered structure of the noble line, while the larger tombs seem to be those of the patriarchs.[70]

The burial ground of the state of Kuo 虢, excavated at Shang-ts'un-ling 上村嶺, is one of the largest cemeteries of Chou date yet discovered. The 234 tombs, large and small, are arranged facing one another from

67. Su Ping-ch'i, 1954; Pei-ching ta-hsüeh, Department of History, 1979:189–90.

68. K'ao-ku yen-chiu-so, 1962:113–16; Pei-ching ta-hsüeh, Department of History, 1979:190–92.

69. Kuo Pao-chün, 1964:3–6; K'ao ku yen-chiu-so, 1979: 192.

70. Liu-li-ho k'ao-ku kung-tso-tui, 1974:309; Pei-ching ta-hsüeh, Department of History, 1979:193–94.

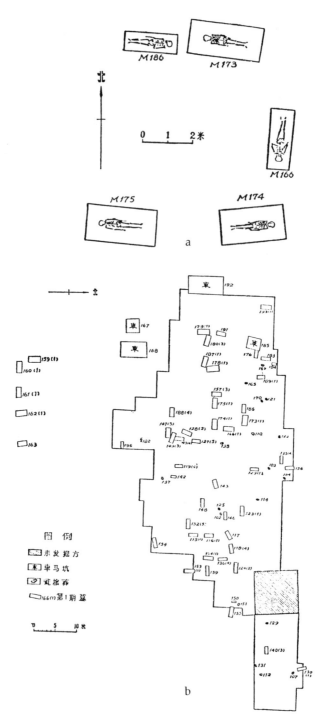

5.5 Burials at Chang-chia-p'o, Shensi: *a*. section of burials; *b*. assemblage of burials (from Pei-ching ta-hsüeh, Department of History, 1979:191, 192)

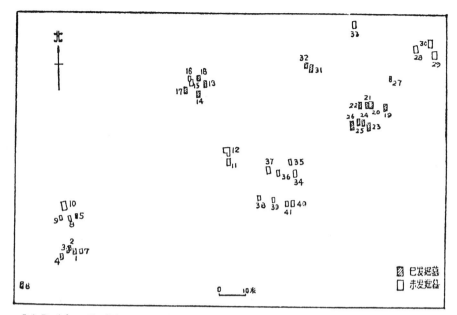

5.6 Burials at Liu-li-ho, Hopei (from Pei-ching ta-hsüeh, Department of History, 1979:193)

either the north or the south. The whole ground is organized into three sections. The southern section was dominated by a large tomb in which five tripod vessels (*ting* 鼎) were found. To the west of it were two more tombs, each containing three *ting*. Smaller tombs were dotted here and there in relation to the larger graves. The northern section was dominated by the large tomb of the Prince of Kuo, containing seven *ting*. To the north of this large tomb were two others, each containing five *ting*. The central section of the burial ground had a tomb with three *ting* and eight others with a single tripod each. These sections consisted of a large, richly endowed tomb in the center with several lesser tombs scattered nearby. In each location three branches of the line can be recognized in the burial site.[71] (See fig. 5.7.)

Tsung-fa, therefore, was broadly applied in the Western Chou society. Archaeological findings from various sites indicate that the dead were buried in an orderly fashion reflecting the ranked structure of kin groups. The Chou vassals, once dispatched to a new state, needed to

71. K'ao-ku yen-chiu-so, 1959, Plate I,B; Pei-ching ta-hsüeh, Department of History, 1979:194.

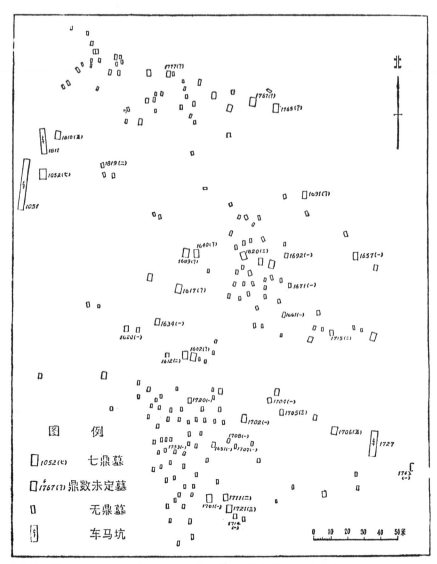

5.7 The Kuo cemetery at Shang-ts'un-ling (from Pei-ching ta-hsüeh, Department of History, 1979:195)

enhance and stabilize their relationships with various other groups in their domain. Moreover, a vassal had to retain close ties with the Chou royal house, and solidarity within the groups became an issue of paramount importance. The *tsung-fa* system assured absolute union between the main line and the segmented units. Even after Chou royal authority declined, the kinship system held the Chou feudal structure together and shaped the Chinese world throughout the Ch'un-ch'iu period.

THE FEUDAL HIERARCHY

Conventionally it has been believed that the Chou nobility consisted of five ranks: *kung* 公, duke; *hou* 侯, marquis; *po* 伯, earl; *tzu* 子, baron; and *nan* 男, vice-baron. The *Ch'un-ch'iu Chronicles* lists the titles of lords who appeared at an inter-state meeting in accordance with their ranked order. However, Fu Ssu-nien 傅斯年 long ago remarked that the five-tiered system did not appear in such ancient texts as the *Book of Documents* or the *Book of Poetry*. Rather, he said, the terms *kung* (old man), *po* (elder), *tzu* (son), and *nan* (male) were originally descriptive of status in a household. Historically, *hou* connoted a target used in archery. The later meaning, "warrior," was a derivative of that. Both *hou* and *po* were used in bronze inscriptions to indicate ranked titles. Fu Ssu-nien interpreted those two titles by noting that *po* was a general term for those who led their kinsmen while establishing new states and *hou* was assigned to those who defended Chou garrisons. Indeed, in the Chou feudal system, a *po* led kinsmen to a new state and *hou* were responsible to garrison and rule the territory taken over by the *po*. Of course, often these two functions were joined and the titles undifferentiated. But *nan*, on the other hand, were subordinate to *hou*, as were *tzu* to *po*.[72] Therefore, there was little distinction in status between the Chou feudal system and the segmentation of the Chou royal house into branches.

Feudalization, then, was the consequence of the Chou conquest and the dispatching of the children of both the Chi and the Chiang as a means to control the local regions and guard the Chou political order. Feudalization was not associated with a major change in production or tools, for the level remained virtually the same at it was in the Shang. Owen Lattimore argued that the process was related to the development

---

72. Fu Ssu-nien, 1952, vol.4:97–129; cf. Ch'en P'an, 1969:686–87; Creel, 1970:324–34.

of irrigation methods.[73] The area under Chou control extended to include much of present-day China and the geographic conditions have varied little since the Shang. The demand for water for different crops was met variously, as it is today. Millet, for instance, was the main crop in north China and required much less water than wheat. The need for irrigation was irregular so that its development was never central to the welfare of the Chou as a nation. More important, neither archaeological materials nor literary sources have provided any information to support the notion that extensive irrigation was in use during the Western Chou. Feudalization was related to economic factors insofar as it was a process that delegated political authority by parceling out power and resources to the vassals. Vassals, in turn, were able to maintain control of local areas on behalf of the Chou collectivity—the Chi, the Chiang, and their kinsmen.[74]

Although the bronze inscriptions do not precisely record the five titles of rank, the Chou feudal system was eventually institutionalized, as were aristocratic rituals which reinforced that ranking.[75] The hierarchy and ritual were regular in the middle Western Chou period, and burial practices reflected such institutionalization.

So far, no royal tombs have been excavated that can be dated from the Western Chou. The highest-ranking occupants of a tomb were the dukes of the state of Wei discovered in Hsin-ts'un, of Chün-hsien 濬縣 County, Honan. These were very large tombs with a deep chamber and two ramps leading to the south and the north. These graves were no doubt originally identified by an exterior marker, and numerous objects including horses and chariots accompanied the body of the deceased. Human sacrifice appeared only once at these graves. Smaller tombs were found in some twenty places, scattered at Pao-chi, Ch'i-shan, and Ch'ang-an, all in Shensi Province; Lo-yang 洛陽 and Chün-hsien in Honan Province; and Fang-shan 房山 and Ch'ang-p'ing 昌平 of Hopei Province. Some tombs (at Lo-yang, for instance) had ramps leading to the chamber, and most contained horses and chariots as well as ritual vessels—commonly *ting, kuei,* and *li*—and weapons. The masters of middle-sized tombs were no doubt middle-ranked aristocrats, whereas the small-scale tombs belonged to lower-ranked officials. These officials were buried in simple, deep, elongated pits with no ramp. No horses or chariots and fewer artifacts accompanied these officials in the graves. Masters of these third-class tombs were low-ranked aristocrats or

73. Lattimore, 1962:547.
74. Creel, 1970:342–45.
75. Ibid., 341–42.

wealthy commoners. There are more than one hundred and forty very small tombs now known to date from the early Western Chou. The poorest ones sometimes included no coffin, with only matting used to wrap the body of the deceased. These different sorts of burials attest to at least four different social levels: rulers, the aristocrats of a high level, low-class aristocrats, and commoners. From the burial rituals we can already discern rigid ritual application of the hierarchy of social and political ranking.[76]

After the reign of King Mu, about two generations after the end of Ch'eng-K'ang period, that ranking was widely in use. The most conspicuous example of its adoption is the appearance of rules governing the appropriate number of ritual vessels according to station. Generally there were two *hu* 壺 (wine containers) and one of the following: *hsien* 獻 (a steamer), *tsu* 俎 (a plate), *p'an* 盤 (a tray), *i* 匜 (a water container), *ting* 鼎 (a meat cooker and container), *kuei* 段 (a platter for grain), or *li* 鬲 (a cooker). They were combined in a regular way. *Ting* were found in odd numbers; *kuei* numbered one less than *ting*, and yielded an even total. The number of *li* also changed accordingly. In a single tomb the shape and decoration of the *ting* were often identical, only the size was adjusted to form a set.[77] The consistency in style tells us that the vessels were cast at the same time and in the same foundry, a practice necessitated by the increased use of bronzes and by the change in ritual.

The number of individual *ting* in a set was regulated according to the rank of the master of the tomb. The *Book of Rites* and other ancient texts are in agreement as to the number of *ting* appropriate to each rank. Nine were reserved for the king, seven for the rulers of vassal states, five for ranking ministers, three for the Shih, (the lowest-ranked warrior), while only one was allowed for daily use by the Shih.[78] The archaeological sites show the number of vessels discovered in Chou tombs coincides with the records in the ancient texts and the hierarchical arrangement of objects corresponds to the rank of the deceased in neatly regulated patterns.[79] (See table 5.2.)

Evidence from two tombs dating just prior to the reign of King Mu suggests that burial ritual was beginning to be regularized and institutionalized then. At Chang-chia-p'o, near Ch'ang-an, five pottery *ting* were found, and at Chuang-pai 莊白, near Fu-feng 扶風, a set of four bronze *ting* were found (fig. 5.8). That evidence indicates that feudal

76. Pei-ching ta-hsüeh, Department of History, 1979:196−202.

77. Kuo Pao-chün, 1959: 11, 43−59.

78. *I-li cheng-i*, hereafter *I-li*, 17/12, 19/11, 30/1-3, 36/12, 39/4; Legge, *Mencius*, 178.

79. Pei-ching ta-hsüeh, Department of History, 1979:204−05; Tu Nai-sung, 1976; Tsou Heng, 1974; Shih Ming, 1974.

Table 5.2. Hierarchical Order of the Chou Burials

		TOMB STRUCTURE			RITUAL BRONZES										WEAPONS AND ARMOR			
Locality	Period	Size of Chamber M[a] (Meters)	Ex. C	Int. C (Number)	Ting	Kuei	Li	Hsien	Tou	P'an	I	Hu	Ho	Others	K'o	Mao	Chien	Others
SHP-THM	W-E Chou	NR	NR	NR	9	7	9	1	2	1	1	2	1	3 P'eng	0	0	0	0
STL-M1052	W-E Chou	5.8 × 4.25 × 13.3	1	2	7	6	6	1	1	1	0	2	1	1 Chung, 9 Pien-chung	4	6	2	41 arrow heads
JCC-MIA	Mid-W Chou	NR	1	1	5	4	0	0	0	0	0	0	0	0	0	0	0	0
STL-M1706	W-E Chou	4.4 × 3.3 × 11.56	1	2	5	4	4	0	1	1	1	2	0	0	0	0	0	52 arrow heads
STL-1810	W-E Chou	4.4 × 2.95 × 15.2	1	2	5	4	4	1	1	1	0	2	1	0	2	1	0	0
TPH-CM	Early E Chou	NR	NR	NR	5	4	0	1	0	1	1	2	0	1 P'eng, 4 Fu,	5	1	0	0
CT-M3	Early E Chou	5.2 × 4.5 × 6.5	1	1	5	4	0	1	0	1	1	1	0	2 Lei	0	0	0	0
PTT	Mid-W Chou	4.2 × 2.25 × 3.56	1	1	1	2	2	1	0	1	0	1	1	3 Chung, 2 Ku,	0	0	0	0
HCLW	W-E Chou	NR	NR	NR	3	4	0	1	0	1	1	1	0	misc. 1 Fan-i,	0	0	0	0
STL-M1705	W-E Chou	3.62 × 2 × 9.15	1	1	3	4	0	0	1	1	2	0	0	misc.	2	1	1	15 arrow heads
STL-M1721	W-E Chou	4.2 × 2.7 × 8.50	1	1	3	0	0	0	0	1	1	0	0	0	1	1	1	20 arrow heads
STL-M1820	W-E Chou	4.5 × 3.55 × 8.35	1	2	3	4	2	1	1	1	1	2	0	2 Fu, misc.	0	0	0	0
FLP-M1	Early E Chou	3.75 × 2.1 × 14.5	1	1	3	2	0	1	0	1	1	2	0	1 P'eng,	0	0	0	0

Tomb	Period	Measurements[a]																
HCT-M5	Mid-W Chou	3.4 × 2.55 × 5.7	1	1	1	1	0	0	0	0	0	0	0	misc. 0	7	1	0	4 shields, 5 arrow heads
PTT-M2	Mid-W Chou	2.8 × 1.04 × 1.65	NR	1	1	2	0	0	0	0	0	0	0	2 Chüeh, 0	0	0	0	0
PFT-M2	Mid-W Chou	3.35 × 2.5 × 4.35	1	NR	1	0	0	1	0	1	0	1	0	misc. 0	18	1	2	shield, helmet, misc.
STL-M1702	W-E Chou	4 × 2.7 × 84	1	2	0	0	0	1	1	0	0	0	0	0	0	0	0	0
STL-M1707	W-E Chou	2.6 × 1 × 1-4	1	1	0	0	0	0	0	0	0	0	0	0	0	0	0	0

Source: Adapted from Pei-ching ta-hsüeh, Department of History, 1979: 205.

Note:
SHP   Sung-ho-pa, Ching-shan, Hupei 宋河壩，京山，湖北
THM   Burial of Marquis Tseng 曾侯墓
STL   Shang-ts'un-ling, San-men-hsia, Honan 上村鎮，三門峽，河南
JCC   Ju-chia-chuang, Pao-chi, Shensi 茹家莊，寶雞，陝西
TPH   T'ai-pu-hsiang, Chia-hsien, Shensi 太僕鄉，郟縣，陝西
ST   Sung-ts'un, Hu-hsien, Shensi 宋村，鄠縣，陝西
PTT   P'u-tu-ts'un, Ch'ang-an, Shensi 普渡村，長安，陝西
HCLW   Hsiung-chia-lao-wan, Sui-hsien, Hupei 熊家老灣，隨縣，湖北
FLP   Fu-lin-pao, Pao-chi, Shensi 福臨堡，寶雞，陝西
HCT   Ho-chia-ts'un, Ch'i-shan, Shensi 賀家村，岐山，陝西
PFT   Pai-fu-ts'un, Ch'ang-p'ing, Peking 白浮村，昌平，北京
CCL   Chung-chou-lu, Lo-yang, Honan 中州路，洛陽，河南
W-E Chou   Junction of Western Chou and Eastern Chou
Ex. C   External coffin
Int. C   Internal coffin
misc.   miscellaneous

The notation NR indicates that a measurement presumably could have been made, but none was reported.

[a] Chamber M is a designation for the main chamber, or pit. The order of measurements is length by width by height.

5.8 Bronze *ting* found at Chuang-pai, Shensi (from *WW*, 1972 [6]:24)

rituals must have been adjusted according to status.[80] The regulations
held only during the heyday of the Chou royal authority, however. In
the last phase of the Western Chou, the well-established hierarchy of
privileges was misused. From that Ch'un-ch'iu period, archaeologists
have found many obvious cases that testify to the abuse of hierarchy
and the collapse of feudal regulations.[81]

    80. K'ao-ku yen-chiu-so, 1962:122; Shih Yen, 1972.
    81. Yü Wei-ts'ao et al., 1978 (2):84–95.

The institutionalization of rank occurred as a consequence of a political authority that relied only in part on force to maintain control. Social order had to be made routine and acceptable in order to sustain political control. The regularization of ritual and status ranking reflected social stability, for privileges and obligations of individual members were known and regulated. Internal conflicts were minimized because everyone's place was known. Internal coherence enhanced stability and solidarity; it also cost the ruling group their flexibility and adaptability. The systemization of feudal ritual that emerged during the middle Western Chou grew too complicated, and even trivial, to be observed. Perhaps it was for this reason that the *Ch'un-ch'iu Chronicles* lists the rulers of states in rigid ranks of five.

DISCUSSIONS ON CHOU FEUDALISM

Did the Chou kings shower subordinates with gifts and glory primarily to assure obligatory behavior, after the manner of potlatch ceremonies practiced in Eurasian communities?[82] Or was there an actual contract made, as in the medieval European example? The Chinese ritual of investiture was one activity, apparently, in which a contract was made. *Ts'e-ming* 冊命 was evidence of that contract. *Ts'e* literally means written document, and *ming* means order or mandate; thus *ts'e-ming* means a recorded commission. Many bronze inscriptions describe such ceremonies and record the entire verbal commission. Summaries of some *ts'e-ming* are found in the *Tso-chuan*.[83]

Based on classical literature and bronze inscriptions, both Ch'i Ssu-ho 齊思和 and Ch'en Meng-chia reconstructed details of the *ts'e-ming* ceremony.[84] The observance was usually held in the main hall of the royal palace or in the ancestral shrine of the royal temple. On rare occasions, it was held in the residential hall of the vassal. Before dawn the Chou king would arrive at the assigned spot; at dawn he would grant an audience to the party who was to receive the charge. The main hall recently excavated at Chao-ch'en 召陳 included a building on a stamped-earth platform facing a courtyard, flanked by two side halls and a yard.[85] It would be an impressive site, indeed, for such a solemn occasion.

82. Keightley, 1983.
83. Good examples are Legge, *She King*, 554–55, in the poems of Ch'ang-wu; and the paragraph on Ts'ai-chung's charge in the *Tso-chuan*, Legge, *Ch'un Ts'ew*, 754.
84. Ch'i Ssu-ho, 1947; Ch'en Meng-chia, 1956B: 98–114.
85. Chou-yüan k'ao-ku-tui, 1981; Fu Hsi-nien, 1981B.

To begin the ceremony, the person to receive the instruction and gifts was led into the courtyard by an official usher. They stood in the yard while the king appeared in front of the hall, between two stairways which ascended from the courtyard. The *ts'e-ming* document was already written on tablets and was read aloud by a royal scribe-historian as soon as the king decreed to do so. Sometimes one scribe held the tablets while the other read it. The message was regarded as an oral decree to which the king might add an amendment, to be entered into the written document at a later time.

The *ts'e-ming* always began with the phrase, "The King said . . . " The content would include an account of the merit of the person who was to receive the honor and of the historical relationship between the royal ancestors and the predecessors of the honored one. It also included an inventory of the gifts, a paragraph about the charges of the new office, and, finally, some concluding remarks of encouragement to follow the good example of one's ancestors and serve the king well. The poem "Han-i" quoted previously is a good example of the style of these documents.

The content of the *ts'e-ming* above including descriptions and the location of the ceremony in formal surroundings and the citation of ancestors' achievements and their relationship to the king suggests that the *ts'e-ming* was a formal ceremony already made routine. In the reigns of kings Ch'eng and K'ang, the king conducted the *ts'e-ming* himself, as bronze inscriptions confirm. After that period, however, it was often a royal scribe or another person close to the king who was entrusted to administer such functions. From that evidence, one can conclude that ceremony was standardized.

The gifts included clothing decorated with symbols of privilege or in fewer instances, horses, chariots, flags, bows, and arrows. All bore rank and status significance. In a very limited number of cases, land, servants, slaves, and jade pieces were given.[86] In institutionalized ritual, even token gifts were treasured as much as objects of actual value. Gifts of symbolic merit dominated; these included dresses and decorations rather than practical or useful items. The hierarchy of privilege was simply being reiterated, not created.

Related to the subject of investiture is the question of subinfeudation. Did vassals also parcel out one portion of their own domain in turn to a retainer and thereby create vassals of lower order? This question is directly related to the nature and extent of delegation of authority in the political hierarchy. The notion of subinfeudation as a part of Chou feudalization has been disputed by scholars. Henri Maspero thought that

---

86. Shih Ming, 1974: 88, n. 4; Huang Jan-wei (Wong Yin-wai), 1978.

there was no such re-subordination in China and that that was a significant difference between Chinese and European feudal systems. Chinese historians, notably Ch'i Ssu-ho and Ch'en Meng-chia, think that they have found evidence of subinfeudation in the Chou records. H. G. Creel, however, did not agree that that evidence was conclusive.[87]

By looking at the *ts'e-ming* ceremony from a slightly different angle, though, one can see the lord-vassal relationship as a contract. Even without the exchange of land, a person who received charges and gifts from a lord was entering into an obligatory and subordinate position. If the charge was more than a request to carry out a simple mission, perhaps requiring long-term subordination to that lord, the case qualified as the establishment of a lord-vassal relationship. If the lord was the vassal of someone at a higher rank, the stratification must be regarded as a subinfeudation.

An inscription of the Ch'eng-K'ang period relates that a certain Marquis Hsing received a *ts'e-ming* with related gifts from the king. Marquis Hsing took the opportunity to bestow a *ts'e-ming* and a gift on his own subordinate, a person named Mai 麥, who cast a bronze to commemorate the occasion.[88] (See fig. 5.9.) Another bronze inscription (fig. 5.10.) tells of a person named Erh 耳 who received ten households from his marquis, who was addressed as Ching-kung 京公 (the duke of the capital). Even though there is no way to precisely identify that marquis, he definitely was not the king.[89]

The king could bestow a *ts'e-ming* on a ruler of a vassal state or on another ranking aristocrat. Those persons could in turn bestow a *ts'e-ming* on their own retainers and subordinates. This activity is yet another indication of the systematization that was taking place in the hierarchical ordering of Chou feudalism.

Other gift giving also may be viewed as symbolic of rank and obligation. For the subordinate there were rituals that formally symbolized yielding to a superior. The master-subordinate relationship was established at the moment a person submitted some tribute to the master. There was, in addition, the ordinary exchange of presents between equals to express good will and to establish or confirm friendship. The ritual of *ts'e-ming* and of *wei-chih* 爲質 were, however, different. In the *Tso-chuan* (Year Twenty-two of Duke Hsi 僖), Duke Huai 懷 of Chin held Hu T'u 狐突, a senior aristocrat in Chin, responsible

87. Maspero, 1950, vol. 3:133, 143−44; Ch'i Ssu-ho, 1948A:22; Ch'en Meng-chia, 1956B:105; Creel, 1970:372−73, 375.
88. Shirakawa Shizuka, *KBTS*, 11:629−44.
89. Ibid., 10:580−83.

5.9 Rubbing of an inscription
(from *KBTS*, 11:629)

5.10 Rubbing of an inscription
(from *KBTS*, 10:581)

to persuade Hu T'u's sons to surrender. The young men supported a contender to the duke's position. The father told the duke that "the ancient rule allowed that when a son was fit for official service, his father should enjoin him to be faithful. The new officer, moreover, wrote his name on a tablet, and gave a pledge of a dead animal to his lord, declaring that any wavering in his fidelity would be punishable by death. Now the sons of your servant have their names with Chung-erh 重耳 (the contending prince) for many years. If I should go on to call them here, I should be teaching them to swerve from their allegiance. If I, as their father, should teach them to do so, how should I be fit to serve your lordship?"[90] Here the "dead animal" (a catch of game) was a common ritual offering used as tribute for the ritual of *wei-chih*. It marked a subordinate's yield to a lord and a pledge of fidelity.

In another episode, after the Lord of Ku 鼓 was taken by the army of Chin, the subordinate of the captured lord followed his master into captivity. The Duke of Chin ordered him to stay in the city of Ku. He declared that once one pledged loyalty by presenting the gift of a game catch, he was to serve that master to his death. His loyalty was to the master, not to the city of Ku, for he was a subject of the lord, not of the land.[91] Yang K'uan 楊寬 also pointed out that the feudal relationship was between individuals, not the state and the individual.[92] In this context, the lord-vassal relationship was contractual. Moreover, it could not automatically be extended from father to son or between lineages.

If feudal ties between individuals overlapped between lineages, the new relationship had to be reconsidered. A son might receive an honor or gift due to the merit of his father.[93] The subordinated status of a junior branch of the main line had to be reconfirmed in such cases.[94] In one instance, even the subordination of a son to his own father was reiterated in the same feudal manner.[95] This son was probably not the heir of his father; he was both a subordinate to a master and son to a father. All these cases indicated that the hierarchical structure created and ordered feudal relationships as well as those resulting from *tsung-fa* segmentation of lineage.

Bronze inscriptions and the classics not only record the bestowal of gifts and declarations of fidelity, they give other information. Concrete job assignments are listed, such as one given to supervise the local chiefs

90. Legge, *Ch'un Ts'ew*, 186.
91. *Kuo-yü*, 15/1-2.
92. Yang K'uan, 1965:360–64.
93. Shirakawa Shizuka, *KBTS*, 15:31–33.
94. Ibid., 16:98.
95. Ibid., 86–89.

assigned to the Duke of Ch'i when he was enfeoffed in Shantung.[96] Other rather more specific jobs such as participation in military campaigns were outlined as well.[97] The vassal states were expected to provide assistance to other Chou states, as was mentioned in the poems "Han-i" and "Sung-kao." Providing a tribute was generally assumed as a duty among the peers. A learned minister of the Ch'un-ch'iu period cited an ancient rule during an inter-state conference: "Formerly, the Son of Heaven regulated the amount of contributions according to the ranks of the States. Where the rank was high, the contribution was heavy; this is the rule of the Chou. Cheng ranks as (the territory of) of an Earl or a Baron, and yet its contribution is on the scale of that of a Duke or Marquis. I am afraid we cannot render it."[98] These were all relatively obvious duties: military services and provision of contributions. But specific missions were also mentioned. The Duke of Mao was appointed to serve as chancellor of the royal court.[99] Another Chou noble was made responsible to command royal divisions and supervise the three departments in the royal court.[100] Another bronze inscription mentions a person charged with the care of forest land, pasture, and a cluster of service people.[101]

In literary sources, a jade token is very often mentioned to symbolize an assignment. For instance, the poem "Sung-kao" reads:

> I confer on you a great scepter
> As the symbol of your dignity.[102]

On the jade token, known as a *kuei* 圭 (fig. 5.11), might be inscribed the responsibility and authority of the owner. Not only was the vassal of the state given a *kuei*, ministers and lesser nobles were also entitled to such a token.[103]

Wang Kuo-wei believed that the vassal who visited the king carried his *kuei* and had to present it to the king. It had to fit another piece of jade held by the king.[104] The jade token verified sanction. In later Chinese history, the token *fu* 符 served the same function.[105]

Since a jade *kuei* was essentially a symbol of authorization, it is not

96. Legge, *Ch'un Ts'ew*, 140.
97. Kuo Mo-jo, 1972; Shirakawa Shizuka, *KBTS* 2:61, 3:133.
98. Legge, *Ch'un Ts'ew*, 652.
99. Shirakawa Shizuka, *KBTS*, 30.
100. Ibid., 20:314–17.
101. Ibid., 311.
102. Legge, *She King*, 538.
103. Yang K'uan, 1965:354–56.
104. Wang Kuo-wei, 1959:50–69.
105. Yang K'uan, 1965:358–59.

5.11 Jade *kuei*
(from K'ao-ku yen-chiu-so,
1962, pl. 102)

strange that in the poems of "Han-i," the ruler of the vassal state of Han carried his *kuei* for a court visit.[106] It is interesting to note that a bronze inscription (fig. 5.12) records a ceremony in which the Marquis of Han was reconfirmed as Marquis of the State as successor of his father and grandfather.[107] Both the poem and the inscription record a similar ritual: a royal *ts'e-ming* which recited the merits of ancestors, the bestowal of gifts, and encouragement to serve well. The court visit was a renewal of contracts between the court and the successor of the original vassal.

In a ceremonial court visit the first ritual began with presentation of the jade token.[108] Wang Kuo-wei interpreted that ceremony in the *Book of Documents* in the following way. The king kept the token until the mission was satisfactorily performed.[109] The poem "Chiang-han" 江漢 records a *ts'e-ming* to Shao Hu 召虎. His merits in campaigns in the Han River Valley are cited first, followed by a recitation of the merits of his

106. Legge, *She King*, 547.
107. Shirakawa Shizuka, *KBTS*, 22:29.
108. Ibid., 24:159–64, 25:357–61.
109. Wang Kuo-wei, 1959:50–69, 69–70.

a

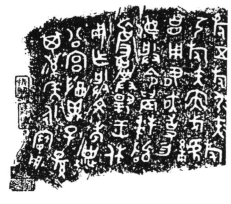

5.12 Rubbing, in two parts,
from an inscription
(from *KBTS*, 22:30–31)

b

ancestor, the Duke of Shao. Then it relates that Shao Hu was granted
the jade token, gifts, and land, which were given "accordingly as your
ancestor received his."[110] The entire ceremony of investiture given to
Shao Hu was a renewal of the contract of the Shao with the court after
Shao Hu had proven himself as a worthy vassal.

The phrase *mi-li* 蔑歷, as it appears on bronze inscriptions, has trou-
bled scholars of epigraphy for decades.[111] Only recently T'ang Lan suggested that *mi-li* meant "to record merit."[112] T'ang's interpretation
works especially well for the term as it appeared on bronzes. One
example relates that the king counted the merits of the second-ranked
noble who accompanied his marquis to court.[113] It was said that only

110. Legge, *She King*, 554.
111. Yü Sheng-wu, 1956.
112. T'ang Lan, 1979.
113. Shirakawa Shizuka, *KBTS*, 19:342–46.

the nobles of ministerial rank could claim their own deeds, while the ruler of state merely had a record of the services.[114] It was coincidental that the term *mi-li* did not appear on the bronze inscriptions related to the ruler of state. Nevertheless, the presentation and return of the jade token probably was a subtle way of keeping track of the performance of the second-ranked official.

In summary, the Chou feudal system was an institution of delegated authority; it assigned missions to trustworthy persons. Enfeoffment was not very different from dispatching garrisons and local administration.[115] Not unlike the European feudal system, the Chou relationships were contractual. The token, citation, charge of missions, and gifts were symbolic expressions of the contract between the involved parties. A court visit was a procedure necessary to reconfirm passage of authority from one to another.

Frequent ritual citing of old relationships respected tradition and demonstrated allegiance to and the routinization of Chou order. The vassals of the Chou were largely members of the Chi and the Chiang; those of other surnames were related through marriage. Infeudation reiterated the delegation of authority and graded order of both the political and lineage systems. The members of the Chou feudal structure, by the Ch'eng-K'ang period, were not strangers to one another. In medieval Europe, however, invaders had little trust or confidence to share with the conquered. Thus the relationship between the European lord and his vassals was built on a foundation of rather rigid and explicit contracts, in which rights and obligations of both parties were clearly stated and assumed by holy oaths. Here the European system departs from that of China. The combination of contractual and personal bonds through family ties between the *tsung-fa* units was peculiar to the Chou version, and regularization of procedures and ritual was probably a natural outcome of that system. The entire society relied on rituals to reinforce mutual dependence among individuals. Behind the ritual were personal promises and obligations, rectified through the social hierarchy. The elaborate ceremonies, including the bestowal of jades, gifts, and elegant words, embellished the structure of delegated authority.

114. Legge, *Ch'un Ts'ew*, 483.
115. Li Chih-t'ing, 1981.

6 Expansion of the Chou Political and Cultural Spheres

In the conquered areas the Chou newcomers and those whom they ruled had to make an effort to adapt to each other's customs and life-styles. We will focus on a few important vassal states to examine that accomplishment. We chose to study states with a prevalence of historical information available about them and which played strategic roles in the process of consolidation of Chou control during the early reigns of the dynasty. Cultural expansion beyond the political domain of the Chou is discussed as well, in an effort to explain the vitality and endurance of the Chou political and cultural systems.

THE CHOU STATES OF WEI 衞 AND LU 魯

The former Shang royal domain was divided into two parts. One was Sung 宋, governed by a Shang prince and his descendants after the great uprising led by Lu Fu 祿父 was quelled by the Chou. Immediately adjacent to Sung was the new state of Wei, which was given to K'ang-shu 康叔, a younger brother of King Wu 武 and the Duke of Chou (map 2). His mission was to oversee the Shang descendants in Sung and in the areas nearby. In the chapter "K'ang-kao" 康誥 of the *Book of Documents*, K'ang-shu was urged by the Duke of Chou to adopt the Shang laws and to honor the Shang traditions in order to achieve effective governance. He was also advised to enlist the services and assistance of the Shang elders and other worthy persons.[1] That the Shang cultural tradition was to be so tolerated is indicated as well in the Chou prohibition on drinking. The Chou people were not permitted to be drunk; the Shang, known to be fond of drinking, were to be spared from harsh punishment for intoxication.[2]

1. Legge, *Shoo King*, 386–91.
2. Ibid., 412.

6.1 Rubbing from an inscription,
K'ang-hou *kuei*
(from *KBTS*, 4:145)

An inscription on a vessel known as the K'ang-hou *kuei* 康侯毁 relates that the Marquis K'ang was ordered to establish himself in Wei and, with another named individual, to manage the territory after the king had overcome the Shang city. This part of the inscription (fig. 6.1) evidently referred to the reappointment of K'ang-shu from his old domain at K'ang to the newly established state of Wei.[3] The identity of the other official in charge of the land is not agreed upon by scholars. Ch'en Meng-chia 陳夢家 thought that he was another Chou prince.[4] Would it not be odd, however, to have two princes in one state? Tu Cheng-sheng 杜正勝 correctly noticed that the emblem at the end of the inscription was one found on Shang bronzes, so this person was likely a descendant of an old Shang family.[5] The territory referred to in the inscription can be interpreted as some portion of Wei, possibly a peripheral region.[6] If such interpretations stand, K'ang-shu of Wei indeed had followed the instructions to enlist the service of Shang elite as assistants.

In an often-quoted paragraph in the *Tso-chuan* 左傳 (Fourth Year of Duke Ting 定), a historian has recorded the land, people, and precious

3. Ch'en Meng-chia, 1955A:161–64; Chou Fa-kao, 1951:18–27.
4. Ch'en Meng-chia, 1955A:164.
5. Tu Cheng-sheng, 1979A:514.
6. Shirakawa Shizuka, *KBTS*, 4:156–58.

items bestowed on various feudal states. The state of Wei, founded by K'ang, was given a grand chariot, four flags, a bronze bell, seven *tsu* 族 of Yin 殷, and extensive territory. The charge given to him was contained in the "K'ang-kao" 康誥 (Announcement to K'ang), and the old capital of Yin was assigned as the center of his state. He was instructed "to commence governance according to the principles of Shang, but (to remember) that their boundaries were defined according to the rules of Chou."[7]

The instruction to govern according to the traditions of the conquered was consistent with that addressed to other Wei officials. The seven *tsu* of Shang people assigned to the Wei, judging by their names, were mostly artisans and technicians and included potters, flag-makers, manufacturers of decorative objects and ornaments, and metallurgists who cast cauldrons. Those of higher status, such as those mentioned on the K'ang-hou *kuei*, were not included there. The state of Wei, therefore, was formed through a coalition that brought together members of the Chou ruling class and Shang of varying classes.

In present-day Shantung Province where the non-Chou peoples called Yen rose to fight the Chou conquerors, the descendants of the Duke of Chou established the state of Lu. Because the duke and two of his sons had actively participated in the campaign that finally overcame the resistance, it seems logical to assume that some of the Chou leaders stayed on there in order to assure firm control of the region.

In the *Tso-chuan* passage (Fourth Year of Duke Ting), the establishment of Lu is mentioned, followed by an account of Wei and Chin. To the Duke of Lu was given a grand chariot, a flag with a dragon design, a great bow from an ancient state, and six *tsu* of Yin, whose clan heads were ordered "to lead the chiefs of their kin, to collect their branches in the remote as well as the near (lands), to conduct the multitude of their connections" for the sake of serving their duke. Lands were apportioned to the Duke of Lu, as were priests, superintendents of ancestral temples, diviners, historians and the tablets containing historical records, and various officers and their instruments. The state of Lu was set up as the governing body over the people of Shang-yen 商奄, in the territory of ancient Shao-hao 少皞.[8] The instruction given to K'ang-shu to govern in accordance with the Shang traditions was apparently applicable to the state of Lu as well.[9]

No bronze inscriptions now known describe the situation in Lu. Nevertheless, the *Tso-chuan* routinely reported that a certain Po-she 亳社

7. Legge, *Ch'un Ts'ew*, 754.
8. Ibid., 754.
9. Ibid.

(shrine of Po) was the site of many and varied religious activities. Human sacrifices were sometimes conducted at Po-she.[10] The name *Po* is the same as that of an old Shang capital and the eastern land of the Shang so often called Po. According to the Kung-yang 公羊 school of interpretation of the *Ch'un-ch'iu Chronicles* 春秋, Po-she were established in various Chou states as a "warning to their princes to guard against the calamity of losing their state."[11] Clearly the Shang people in Lu were permitted to have their own sacred shrines in order to continue their own religious practices. Since Po-she were not traditional religious centers for the Chou, the human sacrifices offered on the two incidents cited in the *Tso-chuan* must have been disapproved of by the Lu nobles.[12] Nevertheless, it is interesting to note that the local Lu house regarded Po-she and the shrines of the Chou as the two symbols of Lu sovereignty. When a Lu noble was born, the diviners predicted that "his place will be at the right of the Duke, between the two altars of the land."[13] After a coup d'état, a strongman of Lu imposed a covenant on the duke and his three ministers at the altar of the Chou and one on the people of Lu at the shrine of Po.[14] These two cases illustrate the religious potency of the shrine of Po as well as the political authority associated with the altar of the Chou in the state of Lu. This dualistic structure was indispensable both for the Chou and for the Shang. The *Record of Rites* distinguishes two kinds of shrines: one for the ruler and one for ordinary people.[15] The Po-she as well as other centers of native, local religious activities in the old Shang domain had survived the conquest and were the locus of religious practices for the local population. The dukes of Lu behaved in the same fashion as the Wei leaders, faithful to the policy of toleration of local custom. By doing so, they established a dualistic political and spiritual structure in the eastern realms of their Chou kingdom.

Ch'eng-chou 成周, Wei, and Lu were established in order to control Chou core areas in the central plain, the homeland of the Shang, and those territories closely allied with them. Cooperation between the Chou and local people was essential for the Chou to gain and remain in control. While the Chou were perhaps less sophisticated than the Shang culturally, they continued to develop the baselines of the Shang civilization in their new regime. The archaeological context in the core area,

10. Ibid., 629, 814.
11. Ibid., 805.
12. Ibid., 629.
13. Ibid., 129.
14. Ibid., 763.
15. *Li-chi*, 46/7.

therefore, shows both local homogeneity and temporal continuity among artifacts. In the Chou homeland, because of the immigration of the Shang elite—the scribes, historians, priests, and others—the cultural traditions of the Shang were visible and significant. And although the Chou respected Shang traditions, as strongly evidenced in production of and patronized use of Shang-style cultural artifacts, it was not as poor cousins that they maintained such customs, but as wise political designers. Early Western Chou bronze inscriptions reviewed above, for instance, show that the bronzes were used at rituals, ones commemorating political coups or illustrious family histories, and the like. The more secularized use of bronzes maintained the form of tradition; the bronzes were decorated and shaped like their Shang counterparts, but were changed in use. The dualistic use of an old form for a new function followed the spirit of the newly designed political units in these centrally located and politically sensitive areas.

THE PERIPHERAL AREAS

Although fusion between the Shang and the Chou occurred in the core areas, outside those regions, local people other than the Shang played a significant role in the shaping of Chou states. Etō Hiroshi 江頭廣 divided the people of ancient China into two groups: those who were in the mainstream (Hua-Hsia 華夏) and those who were non-Chinese. He grouped the Chinese according to surname such as Chi 姬 , Tzu 子 , and Chiang 姜 , and assumed that the names bore significance in defining who belonged to the in-group. Those names were consistently rendered in Chinese script. The non-Chinese were those whose personal names were variously transliterated in the texts. The non-Chinese, who were numerous, were named as follows:

1. The Ying 嬴 —states of Chü 莒 , Ch'in 秦 , and Hsü 徐 , originally eastern nations.
2. The Ssu 姒 —Ch'i 杞 and Yüeh 越 , from nations related to Hsia.
3. The Wu 吳 —in the south.
4. The Mi 羋 —state of Ch'u 楚 , finally a southern nation, originally in Honan Province.
5. The Ts'ao 曹 —state of Chu 邾 and Hsiao-Chu 小邾 , nations related to the Mi 羋 ; both members of the Chu-jung 祝融 group.
6.Miscellaneous groups—the Huai 隗 of the Red Ti 狄 , the Chiang 姜 of the Lai-l 萊夷 and the Chiang-Jung 姜戎 .

The groups were constituted as follows. For instance, the name of a ruler of the Chü 莒 was given as Mi-chou 密州 in the *Ch'un-ch'iu*

Chronicles, but in the *Tso-chuan* his name is given as Mai-chu-tsu 買朱鉏, a slightly different transliteration.[16] Or, in another case, the state of Tsou 鄒 was also known as Chu-lou 邾婁, a variation in pronunciation.[17]

These non-Chinese nations could be classified into four groups. The Chu-jung 祝融 group consisted of the surnames Chi 己, Tung 董, P'eng 彭, Yün 妘, Ts'ao 曹, Mi 芈, Chen 斟 and T'u 禿 and constituted a very large nation in some area of the central plain in the present provinces of Honan 河南, Shantung 山東, and part of Anhui 安徽. Those people eventually moved to the Yangtze Valley. The surnames Hsü 徐, Yen 偃, Yin 嬴, and Ying 盈 were descendants of ancient people in the eastern coastal region who later migrated to the Huai River Valley. The nation of Hsia, descendants of the Hsia dynasty leaders, originally lived in Shansi and later divided into several minor states in the central plain. The people of the state of Wu 吳, whose rulers claimed to be members of the Chi family of the Chou, remained in the south. Finally, the pastoralists along the northern and northwestern borders established states in areas away from the core area of Chinese civilization. All these groups shall be called "peripheral peoples" in contrast to the people of the nuclear area in the *chung-yüan* 中原, or central plain.

The Hua-Hsia groups resided in the central plain, where neolithic traditions of Yang-shao and Lung-shan prevailed. The peripheral groups were inhabitants of areas where various corresponding neolithic traditions are identified. For instance the Ch'ü-chia-ling 屈家嶺 culture flourished in places where the Chu-jung were active. Ch'ing-lien-kang 青蓮崗 cultures are known on the eastern seaboard, where the Hsü-Yen people lived. The Kuang-she 光社 culture in the north, located in Hsia territory, was a variation of the Lungshan. The nomads were related to steppe cultural traditions. The Wu-yüeh groups probably were natives of the coastal area of the lower Yangtze Valley, where the Ho-mu-tu 河姆渡 and the Liang-chu 良渚 cultures are known through excavation. Although one should not take for granted that the peoples in certain areas are descendants of the local neolithic cultures, the ethnic distributions and the neolithic cultures do, nevertheless, correspond in this instance. It is hardly a coincidence that the peripheral ethnic groups were distinctive culturally from the Hua-Hsia in the central plains.

The Chou could not adopt exactly the same model for cultural fusion with these peripheral groups as they did with the Shang people. There were greater differences between the Chou and these outside groups. In general, however, the Chou tried to assimilate and accommodate the

16. Legge, *Ch'un Ts'ew*, 563–65.
17. Etō Hiroshi, 1970:22–74.

local people when possible, and it appears that confrontation and high-handed suppression took place only when there were no other options.

THE STATE OF CHIN

T'ang-shu 唐叔, one of the younger brothers of King Wu, founded the vassal state of Chin in the former Hsia territory. The account of this development in the *Tso-chuan* states that "the charge was given to T'ang-shu 唐叔 as contained in the 'Announcement of T'ang' and the old capital of Hsia was assigned as the center of his state and he was to commence his governance according to the principles of Hsia, but his boundaries were defined by the rules of Jung."[18] Ch'en P'an 陳槃 traced the history of the Chin and concluded that their ancient settlements were in the southern part of the present province of Shansi, near I-Ch'eng 翼城 County, on the north bank of the Yellow River.[19] Ch'en's hypothesis is well-supported by archaeological discoveries in Western Chou sites including bronzes and inscriptions.[20]

During the Shang dynasty the states in the same area were more often challengers to Shang authority than peaceful neighbors. As observed in chapter 2 above, the route along the north bank of the Yellow River was an important road for Chou campaigns to the east. Finally, Chou groups flanked the northern borders of the Shang domain. T'ang-shu, who had played a significant supporting role in the campaigns as early as the days of King Wu,[21] was probably assigned to the task of surveillance and supervision earlier than the establishment of the states of Wei and Lu. His mission was a vital one, for it was the basis of security along the northern boundaries. The instructions given to him stressed governance according to the principles of the Hsia. Such emphasis on traditions of the Hsia validated their legacy in the region and confirmed once again the Hsia and Chou as historical kin. Settling of the boundaries according to the principles of the Jung, however, also accommodated local conditions.

Shansi was a farming zone standing between the steppe and the nomadic culture and the Chinese culture (map 1). As early as Wu Ting's 武丁 reign during the Shang, the Kuei-fang 鬼方, a powerful nomadic group, had caused a considerable disturbance in the northern

18. Legge, *Ch'un Ts'ew*, 754.
19. Ch'en P'an, 1969:1/36−47.
20. Shan-hsi sheng wen-kuan-hui, 1955, 1959; Hsieh Hsi-kung, 1957; Pei-ching ta-hsüeh, Department of History, 1979:155.
21. Ch'en P'an, 1969:1/36−47.

areas. Throughout the Western Chou period the resources of the state of Chin were focused on efforts to deal with the Jung-ti nomads.[22] The Chin rose to the status of a major power in Chou China largely because of the expansion of the Chou to include the non-Chinese regions of the Jung-ti in the north. The stress on the Jung tradition in the Chin state underlined the Chou's respect for them even though the main purpose of the state was to preserve the memory of the Hsia. The *Tso-chuan*, mentioned that "to T'ang-shu there was given a grand carriage, the drum of Mi-hsü 密須, the Chüeh-kung 闕鞏 mail, the bell of Ku-hsien 姑先, nine *tsu* of the name Huai, and five departments of government services."[23] The surname Huai actually was the equivalent of Kuei-fang, a Jung-ti nation.[24] The Kuei-fang, or at least some of them, were natives of the north bank of the river in southern Shansi and were incorporated into the state of Chin. In the old Kuei-fang territory T'ang-shu joined the Chou people, some officials of the royal government, and the native Jung-ti population to form his new state. The boundaries of the area assigned to him were not clearly listed, perhaps because his mission was to expand the territory into the land of the Jung-ti. The history of the Chin included continuous extension of the northern frontier during the entire Western Chou and into the Ch'un-ch'iu period.

The Fen 汾 River flows through an arid plateau of yellow earth where the Chin farmers could plant only crops that grow with limited water. Even in the Chan-kuo 戰國 period the staple products of the marginal, hilly areas of Chin were mainly lentils and some wild greens. The subsistence patterns in this region were, therefore, fundamentally different from that of the millet-growing cultures of central China.[25] Evidence of continuance of nomadic customs must record varied life-styles in the region necessary to support the enlarged population served by the new rule. Shang-date archaeological evidence yielded both Shang and nomadic style materials. Frequently, discoveries of Shang bronzes included knives, daggers, and small bells.[26] The daggers, with serpent and animal head terminals, as well as a mysterious kind of curved artifact, were products of steppe production (fig. 2.4). In the area known as the state of Chin, there had long lived a heterogeneous culture resulting from the juxtaposition of the Jung-ti and the Hua-Hsia Chinese.

The ducal house of Chin routinely had matrimonial ties with the

22. Legge, *Ch'un Ts'ew*, 660.
23. Ibid., 754, with minor revision.
24. Wang Kuo-wei, 1959:590–93.
25. Matsuda Toshio, 1965.
26. Wu Chen-lu, 1972; Yang Shao-hsün, 1981; Wen-wu pien-chi wei-yüan-hui, 1979:58.

Jung-ti. Duke Hsien 獻 and Duke Wen 文 , for instance, each had several Jung-ti wives. In the *Tso-chuan*, a Chin minister declared to the neighboring state that "the White Ti 白狄 and you are in the same regions. They are your enemies, while between us and them there have been intermarriages."[27] The lineage system of the Chin state was quite different from the systems of Lu and Wei. The ducal house never had strong branches, and the rule of succession in the Chin ducal house followed the Chou manner. Repeatedly, adult children were sent out to establish "vassal states," which then challenged the authority of the main-line dukes.[28] The Chin ducal house adopted the nomadic custom of sending adult children to herd in other places while the younger ones inherited the herd and tents of the aged parents.

The conglomerate culture developed in Chin was unlike mainstream Chinese civilization. The tenacious continuation of local customs in the state betrayed reciprocal tolerance between the Jung-ti and the Chinese interlopers. Such conditions exemplified the flexibility of the new Chou system of governance, perhaps in response to an economic interdependence between the nomads and farmers in a transitional zone. The sheer distance from the cultural centers of metropolitan China of the central plain must have contributed to the independence of each member group. The Chin state did, however, accomplish its mission. The Chin managed to maintain a firm hold on the northern land as well as bring the Jung-ti into contact with the Chinese culture.

THE STATE OF YEN

Founded in Hopei 河北 as a buffer zone beyond the northern territory (map 2), the original state of Yen was associated with the Duke of Shao and was moved from the central plain to the remote regions of the northeast. During his march to the north, the duke probably conducted campaigns along the coast of Shantung, for bronzes bearing the duke's name have been found there.[29] As cited previously, the bronzes named after T'ai-pao 太保 had inscriptions giving an account of contests with the Shang prince Lu Fu, who had fled to the north after he failed to overthrow the Chou. The Duke of Shao probably trailed him far to the north and his descendants finally became the ruling house of the state of Yen.

Recently discovered Western Chou burials in Fang-shan 房山 County

27. Legge, *Ch'un Ts'ew*, 382.
28. Utsuki Akira, 1965:134–37.
29. Ch'en P'an, 1969:1/79–82.

6.2 Yen-hou *yu* (from *KK*, 1975 [5]:279)

near Peking, dated 1120±90 B.C., yielded bronzes with inscriptions telling that they were gifts of the Duke of Yen. The burials found at
Pai-fu-ts'un 白浮村, Ch'ang-p'ing 昌平 County, near Peking resembled in
shape, in custom and in categories of artifacts those from Feng-hsi 澧西,
near Hsi-an 西安. From this evidence, it can be safely assumed that there
was a settlement of Chou people in northern Hopei near Peking as early
as the beginning of Western Chou.[30] As far as the northeast and the
Ta-ling 大凌 River, bronzes bearing inscriptions with the name of the
Duke of Yen have been found (fig. 6.2). The influence of the Yen
stretched beyond Hopei and penetrated into western Manchuria.[31]

Some of the clan emblems on the Yen bronzes found in the region
around Peking were Shang (figs. 6.3–6.4). Moreover, the system of
naming ancestors in the inscriptions followed a Shang practice which
used the so-called *t'ien-kan* 天干 numerals. A few of those individuals
named have been found to have been ranking officials, military figures

30. Pei-ching shi wen-wu kuan-li-ch'u, 1976; Liu-li-ho k'ao-ku kung-tso-tui, 1974.
31. Yen Wan, 1975; Pei-tung wen-wu fa-chüeh hsiao-tsu, 1974.

6.3 Po-chu *li*
(from *KK*,
1975 [5]:277)

who served the Duke of Yen. One general served both in the states of
Wei and Yen.[32] The burials discovered at Liu-li-ho 琉璃河 of Fang-shan
County yielded weapons, human sacrifices, and bronzes with inscriptions recording receipt of gifts from the Duke of Yen. The clan emblem
was, however, unmistakably a Shang one.[33] (See fig. 6.5.) Once again,
this evidence shows that some of the original Shang population were
encouraged and permitted by the Chou conquerers to preserve their
own clan identity. The rich content of these burials and the high status
of the deceased show that they were neither captives nor slaves. They

32. Yen Wan, 1975:277.
33. Liu-li ho k'ao-ku kung-tso-tui, 1974:314.

6.4 I-kung *kuei*
(from *KK*,
1975 [5]:277)

6.5 Rubbings from inscriptions,
Shang clan emblems
(from *KK*, 1975 [5]:3/4)

6.6 Shang vessels
from Liu-chia-ho
(from *WW*, 1977
[11]:pl. 3)

enjoyed status as nobilty and allies of the Chou in the state of Yen.[34]
Such a strong presence of Shang influence both before and after the
conquest leads to the assumption that the Shang had firmly secured the
area before they surrendered to King Wu. They had been successful
predecessors to the Chou and were afforded privileges accordingly.

Before the conquest these Shang stations served as military garrisons.
In 1977, a Shang burial was found at Liu-chia-ho 劉家河 in P'ing-ku 平谷
County; it was given a mid-Shang date. The bronzes unearthed there
are comparable to ones manufactured on the central plain, that is, their
shapes and decor are recognizably referent to metropolitan models (fig.
6.6). The combined variety of styles of vessels in the assemblage and

34. Tu Cheng-sheng, 1979A:522.

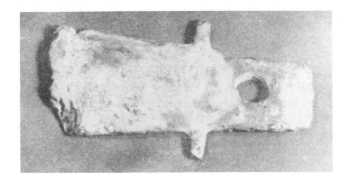

6.7 Bronze axe with meteorite iron blade from Liu-chia-ho (from *WW*, 1977 [11]:18)

the eccentricity of certain details of individual examples, however, are unlike other groupings of Shang manufacture. Whether imported or manufactured locally, such products when taken together reveal the taste of the new patrons: mindful of the past, somewhat flamboyant, and largely secular. A bronze axe (fig. 6.7), also of Shang date, found there had a meteorite, wrought iron blade and was manufactured in the same manner as the axe from Kao-ch'eng 藁城. Gold artifacts, including earrings and arm bracelets, are borrowings from the Hsia-chia-tien 夏家店 steppe culture.[35]

More impressive evidence of the presence of the Shang in this region before the Chou conquest was provided by the discovery of a Shang-

35. Pei-ching shih wen-wu kuan-li-ch'u, 1977.

date city at Tung-chia-lin in the Liu-li-ho area. At this site, one damaged
by the overflow of a nearby river, a section of the city wall some 850
meters in length was left running along the east-west boundary. On the
north, the east, and the west, the city was protected by a moat. The city
wall consisted of a primary, exterior structure, an inner, auxiliary support, and tabular surfaces along the wall. Because the wall remains were
broken by burials of early Chou date, the city is assumed to predate the
beginning of the Chou dynasty. Pottery, especially the *kuei*, closely
resembled examples discovered at An-yang. Near the city of Tung-chia-
lin 董家林 some two hundred burials have been sited at Huang-t'u-p'o
黃土坡. The excavated tombs were sequentially dated into four periods;
the earliest were late Shang and the latest perhaps as late as the middle
Chou. Because some of the inscriptions indicated that the vessels were
given as gifts by the Duke of Yen, some scholars believe that the site was
the Yen capital. The cemetery itself was divided into two sections. In
one, the accompanying artifacts were Shang products and the burials
contained both human and dog sacrifices. In the other, a large tomb has
been excavated where important bronzes were discovered but sacrifices
of any kind were lacking. Pottery was remarkably different section by
section, again underscoring the distinctly different burial practices.[36]

Tung-chia-lin settlement and the associated Huang-t'u-p'o cemetery
sites are distinguished by the mixed heritage of their components. Tung-
chia-lin city, with the elaborate defense structures, was probably a
significant stronghold even before the Duke of Yen established it as
capital. From the subdivisions in the cemetery we learn that two
groups distinguished themselves from one another. In the section including sacrifices and offerings of *li* 鬲, *kuei* 殷, and *kuan* 罐, Shang
customs were preserved. The deceased must have been in residence at
the northern front during the Shang dynasty. The other section, in the
large tombs, the bronze vessels were gifts from the Duke of Yen and
bore clan emblems of peoples from the central plain. The owners must
have followed the Duke of Shao and other Chou leaders to the north,
where they formed the core of the nobility in the newly created state of
Yen. The new Chou state was built on a secure foundation developed by
the Shang, and many of those former residents continued their own
burial practices even after the Chou takeover. Others rejected older
Shang burial customs, especially human sacrifice.

In addition, the Shang must have been in contact with the native
populations of the Po-hai 渤海 Bay region. Fu Ssu-nien long ago pro-

36. Liu-li-ho k'ao-ku kung-tso-tui, 1974.

posed that the similarity of Shang, Tungus, and Korean ancestor myths associated these people in some way.[37] The discoveries of daggers with eagle- or horsehead terminals in Yen sites reminds us of the wide distribution of these artifacts in the southern steppe from Mongolia to Manchuria. At several points these nomadic materials found their way into both Shang and Chou possession and finally into their burials (figs. 2.4, 2.6).[38]

The state of Yen was both comparable to and distinct in detail from the cousin state of Wei and the capital district of Ch'eng-chou. In all cases a combination of Chou and Shang elite formed the upper echelon, while Shang population was the main component in the rest of the state community. The northern, local people probably included a branch of the former Shang nation plus locals who had adopted Shang cultural manners. Through coalition between the Chou conquerors and the Shang, Yen was brought into the web of Chou feudalism. Yet, even as late as the Han period, the Yen dialect was still foreign to the Chinese ear and rather close to the languages spoken in the northern part of the Korean peninsula.[39] During the Ch'un-ch'iu period, the Yen seldom interacted with the other Chinese states. They retained many non-Chinese elements, such as those of the Hsia-chia-tien culture akin to the steppe rather than to China proper. They remained less incorporated into the mainstream than other states. Recent studies in historical geography note that the alluvial plain of the present southern Hopei Province was severely affected in ancient times by the inundation of various rivers, including the Yellow at the delta. Because such a condition existed until the Chan-kuo period, human settlements in this area during the neolithic through the Ch'un-ch'iu were sparsely distributed.[40] The relative isolation of the state of Yen from the Chou centers before the Chan-kuo period contributed to the survival of a heterogeneous culture ruled by a local elite.

THE STATE OF CH'I

Ch'i 齊 was the bastion of Chou power along the eastern coast from Po-hai Bay to the Huai 淮 River Valley, including the Shantung Pen-

37. Fu Ssu-nien, 1953, vol. 4:32–41.
38. Pei-ching shi wen-wu kuan-li-ch'u, 1976.
39. Ch'en Meng-chia, 1955B:126–27.
40. T'an Ch'i-hsiang, 1981; Ko Chou, 1982:141–42.

insula and the homeland of the ancient nations known as Feng-Yen 風偃 or Hai-Tai 海岱. In the Chou period this region was commonly regarded as the "Eastern Land" or as the "Great East," and such names were recorded in ancient songs (map 1.) The state was originally founded in Honan by the Grand Lord of the Chiang but was moved to this coastal region after he participated in the great eastern uprising.[41] Legend holds that on the very eve of the Grand Lord's arrival at Ch'i, he had to face the challenge of the natives called Lai-I 萊夷.[42] Not only was it important to secure peace with the Shang inhabitants there, but also with the local populace.

This legend mistakenly put the establishment of Ch'i as early as the time of the reign of King Wu and immediately after the conquest of Shang. But, throughout much of the Ch'un-ch'iu period and until the Ch'i annexed the Lai in 567 B.C., struggles between the Ch'i and the Lai were routinely recorded in the Ch'un-ch'iu. The Ch'i state was indeed located amidst hostile groups from the time of its inception.[43] The Book of Rites claimed that for five generations after the establishment of Ch'i, the bodies of Ch'i dukes were transferred to Chou territory for burial.[44] If this account was true, it reflected the lack of stability in Ch'i in the early years after its establishment.

After the campaign to overthrow the Shang, the Chou successfully reorganized their alliances on the eastern plain so that Lu, Wei, and Ch'eng-chou served to stabilize the formerly hostile population. In the land of the Great East, there were numerous small states of ancient origin whose ancestry could be traced back to legendary times before Hsia. During the Shang period, these nations probably coexisted with the Shang under their umbrella of influence and domination. Nevertheless, the arrival of the Chou from the west meant that an adjustment had to be made. The eastern peoples did not automatically accept the newly established Chou-Shang coalition. Thus, the state of Ch'i, ruled by Chiang nobility, developed along a course distinctly its own. The Shih-chi records that the first Duke of Lu took great pains to assimilate the local people into the Chou sphere while the first Duke of Ch'i allowed the local people to preserve their own customs. He even simplified the Chou rites in order to accommodate the local population. The legend then predicted that Lu would eventually be dominated by the Ch'i.[45] This story was certainly fabricated after the Ch'i dominated the

41. Fu Ssu-nien, 1953, vol. 4:1−11.
42. Shih-chi.
43. Uehara Tadamichi, 1956.
44. Li-chi, 7/1.
45. Shih-chi, 3/19.

Lu. Nevertheless, there is some truth to the notion that accommodation was characteristic of the new regime in Ch'i.

Archaeologically, the Shantung Peninsula has not yielded materials to indicate that it was part of the core area of Chou. During the neolithic, the Ta-wen-k'ou culture was separate from the Yangshao and the Lung-shan of the central plain.[46] The sites containing Shang-related materials are widely distributed over the peninsula. With the exception of the Ta-hsin-chuang 大辛莊 site, which is contemporary with the Erh-li-kang 二里岡 phase of Shang, virtually all the Shang sites were dated late in the dynasty.[47] It was not until its late phase that the Shang culture was absorbed into the Shantung Peninsula and that influence was not very well established, for the Shang were soon to be replaced by the Chou.

The state of Ch'i was established by subjugating the eastern people. The Lai-I who challenged them lived even farther outside areas influenced by the Shang. The state of Ch'i consisted of a complex of people of different cultural backgrounds: descendants of ancient nations, surrendered Shang people, and alien elements such as the Lai-I. The ducal house of the Chiang was allied with the Chou, but they were not children of the Chi even though the Ch'i ruling house must have included some Chi nobility. In the Ch'un-ch'iu period, two top-ranked ministerial houses of the Ch'i state, the Kuo 國 and the Kao 高, were addressed as "the two guardians from the royal house." These two persons held appointments directly granted by the Son of Heaven and made periodical visits to the royal court, presumably to report on the state of Ch'i.[48] These two ministers were probably members of Chi houses who accompanied the Chiang and represented the royal house in the new territory. In addition, the makeup of the existing ruling group was already complex.

In order to manage such a diverse group, the state of Ch'i began by initiating and then supporting policies of coexistence with and toleration of diverse customs. In addition, they formed coalitions among the local groups and stabilized their political authority. Two bronzes discovered in Huang-hsien 黃縣 County bear the emblem of a Shang noble house and one includes an inscription with the names of ancestors according to the Shang nomenclature system. Furthermore, one of the ancestors was mentioned as part of the royal entourage touring in Shantung and neighboring areas. These bronzes date from the reign of King Chao, four generations after King Wu. Even at that late date, the descendants of the

46. Shan-tung sheng wen-kuan-chü, 1974.

47. Shan-tung sheng wen-kuan-ch'u, 1959; Ts'ai Feng-shu, 1973; Ch'i Wen-t'ao, 1972:3–5; Wen-wu pien-chi wei-yüan-hui, 1979:190.

48. Legge, Ch'un Ts'ew, 159.

Shang continued to preserve their family identity and to participate in high-level political activities.[49]

The name of Marquis Chi 㠱 appears in inscriptions of at least eight bronzes discovered in Shantung, in the vicinity of Peking, and in other places. His surname was Chiang, as judged by the names of his daughters. On one bronze inscription, the troops from Chi and those from Ch'i and Lai were set against the I people of the Huai Valley.[50] The name of a Ch'i noble corresponded to Shang nomenclature, for he used Kan-chih 干支 to refer to his father and grandfather. The Shang people in Ch'i must have survived even the reign of King Chao, to whose time this particular set of bronzes is dated (fig. 6.8). The Chi seemed to be a active branch of the Chiang. Since numerous Chi bronzes were found in Huang-hsien County in the eastern part of the Shantung Peninsula, we may assume that the Chi were there to guard the eastern frontier. From there the troops were dispatched to the state of Yen as well.

In addition to the Chi, there were several small states, such as the Hsiang 向, ruled by members of the Chiang. Most of them were located in eastern Shantung.[51] The claim that the Lai were governed by the Chiang ruling house is, however, rather dubious. Shen Kang-po noted that the ruling houses of small states near Ch'i were often descendants of the Chiang, but they retained their independence instead of becoming vassal states of the stronger Ch'i. This situation was different from that found in the states of Lu and Wei, where segmentation of the ruling clan coincided with hierarchical feudal structure. Rather, each individual small state in Shantung was established in accordance with the distribution of native populations. In such a system their cultural heritage was continued.[52]

An interesting cultural blending did, however, take place in the state of Ch'i. The names of the early dukes were all selected from the *t'ien-kan* system, a common Shang practice, applied in Ch'i even though they were descendants of the Chiang. The policy must have been adopted to satisfy the old Shang population. Furthermore, the Ch'i people worshiped a cluster of eight deities, some of whom appeared in neither the Shang nor the Chou religious system. Worship of a sacred mountain, T'ai-shan 泰山, in Shantung Province was noticeable, Hou-shan 霍山, also known as T'ai-yüeh 大岳, was located in southern Shansi and was regarded as the progenitorial spirit of the Chiang people. When the Chiang moved to Honan, Sung-shan 嵩山 was made the sacred moun-

49. Ch'i Wen-t'ao, 1972:5–6; Shirakawa Shizuka, *KBHS*, 48:185–89.
50. Ch'i Wen-t'ao, 1972:8–9.
51. Tu Cheng-sheng, 1979A:517; Ch'en P'an 1969:164–66, 175–87.
52. Shen Kang-po, 1974.

6.8 Rubbing from an inscription (from *WW*, 1972 [5]:6)

tain. The name T'ai-shan must have resulted from the Chiang's move to Shantung.[53] After this imported culture was settled among the native population, members of both belief systems were adopted into the Ch'i collection of eight deities.[54]

53. Ch'en P'an, 1981:409, 1969:430–33.
54. Akatsuka Tadashi, 1977:75–176.

THE SOUTHERN STATES

The large area to the southeast of the Chou capital was populated by the descendants of an ancient nation known as the Chu-jung 祝融. They were inhabitants of the area before the demise of Hsia and Shang. By the time of the early Chou some of the eight subgroups of the Chu-jung had dispersed. Those who survived either formed small states in the central Chou core land or moved to the periphery. One of them, the Mi 芈, rose to become the Ch'u 楚, the most significant power in the Yangtze Valley during the Ch'un-ch'iu period. Some of the Chu-jung who mingled with the aborigines in the coastal region formed tribal states and were often confused about their own identity.[55] Such groups of mixed heritage formed the largest number of the population in southern Shantung, in northern Kiangsu and Anhui, and in the lake region of the lower Han River Valley.[56]

The Chou court enfeoffed many children of the Chi in order to establish vassal states in the south and the southeast. They were generally referred to as the Chi states east or north of the Han. The largest one of them was Sui 隨, and by 630 B.C. most of them had been absorbed by the Ch'u.[57]

The inscription on the newly discovered I-hou *kuei* 宜侯毁 (fig. 4.8) yields information about another southern vassal state of the Chou. This bronze was discovered in Tan-t'u 丹徒, a county on the lower reaches of the Yangtze River; it is believed to date from the Ch'eng-K'ang period. A certain marquis, the inscription reads, was ordered to move to the south. In addition to gifts bestowed by the king, such as bronzes and ceremonial weapons, he received a territory containing certain numbers of subordinated peoples.[58] From which state this marquis moved has not been settled by epigraphic scholars. This bronze is marked, however, with a Shang *tsu* emblem. Therefore, this southern state was actually the fiefdom of a descendant of Shang nobility who may have held a position in the Chou court until he was sent to govern the land in the south.[59] The actual size of that domain is unknown. The people assigned to him included three groups: the Cheng 鄭 people, the "King's men," and the people in the land of I. The new state entrusted to the Marquis of I was

55. Ch'en P'an, 1969:241, 269, 289; E. J. Pulleyblank suspects an association of the Ch'i with the Austro-Asiatic groups. Pulleyblank, 1983:427–28.

56. Tu Cheng-sheng, 1979A:525.

57. Legge, *Ch'un Ts'ew*, 178, 209.

58. Shirakawa Shizuka, *KBTS*, 10:531–53; Ch'en Meng-chia, 1955A:165–67, 1955C; Ch'en Pang-fu, 1955; Kuo Mo-jo, 1956; T'ang Lan, 1956; Barnard, 1958.

59. Ch'en Meng-chia, 1955A:167.

composed of Chou, Shang, and local people, a situation resembling that of Lu, Chin, and Wei as discussed above.

EXPANSION OF THE CULTURAL SPHERE—
THE NORTH AND THE WEST

In addition to deliberate political expansion, the Chou civilization had an impact on regions farther and farther away from their center. For instance, its cultural influence extended far to the north, along a front extending from the arch of the Yellow River to the edge of Manchuria, where in later years a section of the Great Wall was built. This was a transitional belt between the steppe and the northern Chinese farmlands.

In the decade after 1956, archaeologists gradually developed a system that recognized the local cultural assemblages found in eastern Mongolia, along the Great Wall. The common culture there was named the Hsia-chia-tien 夏家店 culture. The upper layer was approximately contemporary with the Western Chou but was not the immediate successor of the earlier Hsia-chia-tien, for little continuity can be discerned between these two layers. The lower Hsia-chia-tien was a northern, bronze-using culture, which produced items such as bronze helmets, short swords, and ornamental plates usually found in stone chamber burials. In addition, the upper Hsia-chia-tien was an agricultural community, one using animal husbandry and game hunting as supplements to food production (fig. 6.9). The people associated with the upper Hsia-chia-tien probably were the Shan-jung 山戎 (the mountain Jung) and the Hu 胡 (the proto-Tungus).[60]

In western Liaoning 遼寧, the lowest level of the upper Hsia-chia-tien could not be later than late Shang, while the upper limit could not be earlier than mid-Chou.[61] In other words, the transition period was in the early Chou, when the royal house stretched its influence into this region. Since the discovery of a Shang/Chou storage pit at Ma-ch'ang 馬廠 in K'o-tso 喀左 County in 1955, several other Shang/Chou remains have been excavated in western Liaoning on both sides of the Liao River. The Western Chou pieces found in K'o-tso and its vicinity were dated no later than the reign of King K'ang. The names of important *tsu* groups found there were related to those known in excavations in Yen sites near Peking. The style of these bronzes is similar to those of the central plain in the Chou core area; others exhibited local characteris-

60. Wen-wu pien-chi wei-yüan-hui, 1979:71–72; Hsia Nai, 1964.
61. K'o-tso hsien wen-hua-kuan, 1982.

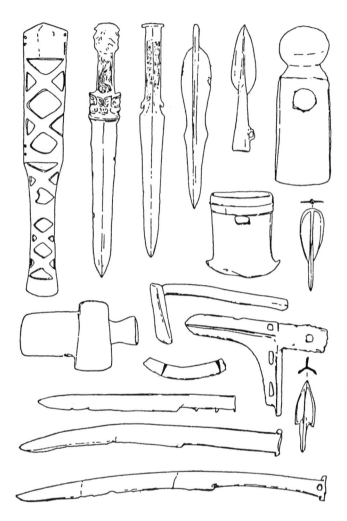

6.9 Bronze weapons and tools from Hsia-chia-tien culture (from Pei-ching ta-hsüeh, Department of History, 1979:222)

tics. The burials excavated at Fu-hsün 撫順 and Hsin-min 新民 yielded bronze weapons, ornaments for horses, and chariot fittings. They bore Chou features, although there were some decorative designs on the armor not found on materials from the central plain. Most of the Liaoning bronzes were compatible with the materials from the Chou stronghold near Peking. Red-brown pottery and three-legged vessels were common. Even though the influence from the central core area was strong throughout the Ch'un-ch'iu period, the Hsia-chia-tien cul-

6.10 Bronze sheaths from Liaoning (from *KKHP*, 1973 [2]:6−7)

ture in Liaoning persisted in using local styles. There were many short swords discovered and their genealogy can be followed (fig. 6.10). Field archaeologists generally agree that such weapons belonged to the Jung, who were likely the ancient Tungus.[62] The distribution of the Chou culture in the Liao River region should be closely associated with the establishment of the Chou state of Yen in the Peking area. By the end of the Western Chou, local, indigenous characteristics dominated the northern finds.

In the Hopei area, the Hsia-chia-tien sites were found mainly in the area near Peking where the state of Yen was established. Numerous bronzes discovered in Yen burial sites at Huang-t'u-p'o 黃土坡 confirmed that there was indeed a concentration of Chou cultural influence in the Peking region. On the other hand, the eagle-headed and horse-headed bronze knives unearthed in the three-layered chambered tombs at Pai-fu-ts'un 白浮村 in Ch'ang-p'ing 昌平 notify us that the steppe culture had left its mark on that local area (fig. 6.11).[63] In the Tientsin 天津 area of Po-hai 渤海 Bay, there was little sign of sudden cultural change following the lower Hsia-chia-tien. Some Chou features appeared on the pottery.[64] Such evidence reflected Chou colonization near the Yen state, stretching east to the Liao River valley near K'o-tso county. The political and cultural influence in this area must have been marginal in those colonies and on local cultures. The area where the Chou influence was most strongly felt was Ling-yüan 凌源 in western Liaoning, Man-ch'eng 滿城 and Yüan-shih 元氏 in Hopei in the south and Wei-hsien 蔚縣 in

62. Wen-wu pien-chi wei-yüan-hui, 1979:88−92.
63. Ibid., 4−5.
64. Ibid., 23−24.

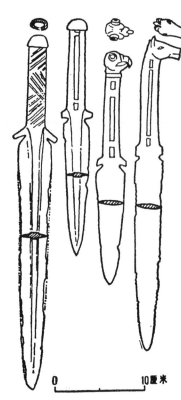

6.11 Bronze daggers from Pai-fu-ts'un
(from Pei-ching ta-hsüeh,
Department of History, 1979:200)

Hopei in the west. The hilly regions to the south of Yüan-shih were still in the hands of the Jung as late as the reign of King Chao.[65]

In the area where the upper Hsia-chia-tien cultures were discovered remains from sites in Ch'eng-te 承德, T'ang-shan 唐山, and Chang-chia-k'ou 張家口 are very different from those of the central plain. For instance, some one thousand artifacts excavated at Luan-p'ing 灤平 included steppe products such as bronze necklaces, bronze plates representing squatting tigers, frogs, sheep, and the like, as well as bronze short swords with animal-head terminals and bronze bulbs used as horse ornaments. The people associated with the upper Hsia-chia-tien were probably those who spread into the valleys of Lao-ha 老哈, Ta-ling 大凌, Luan 灤 and Ts'ao-pai 漕白 rivers during the early Chou and must have been a constant threat to the security of the Chou outpost at Yen.

In the early Ch'un-ch'iu period, the Jung (or the Shan-jung) from the

65. Ibid., 39; Li Hsüeh-ch'in et al., 1979.

Hopei hills were the most assertive group in the area. Duke Huan 桓 of the Ch'i fought with them to save the Chou state of Hsing 邢 from extinction. Obviously the Jung, who included some subgroups, enjoyed a prolonged period of dominance in the regions that formed a large part of the present province of Hopei.[66] Such conditions suggest that the Chou had developed a ring of colonies forming a corridor between the central plain and the northern state of Yen. The Chou cultural influence was competing with that of the strong, local Hsia-chia-tien culture. The furthest outpost of early Chou influence in the Liao River Valley must have suffered a loss of contact when the Western Chou power waned.

Even though Shansi Province is located directly north of the central plain, only rather sparse evidence of Western Chou influence has been found there. Bronzes have been discovered in Hung-tung 洪洞, Wen-hsi 聞喜, and Ying-ch'eng 應城 counties.[67] Most of the Western Chou finds were from areas in the south of the province, but not beyond the Fen River. The findings in the region along the Yellow River adjacent to the northern Shensi Plain, in Pao-te 保德 Ling-shih 靈石 and Shih-lou 石樓 counties, were largely steppe culture remains that can be dated as early as the late Shang.[68] The Chou states, including Chin, could barely hold the defense lines along the north bank of the Yellow River. That area formed a buffer zone in southern Shansi and shielded the Chou from the non-Chou who inhabited much of the Shansi plateau.

The western frontier was formed in the Kansu 甘肅 plateau. The local cultures that were contemporary with the Western Chou were the Hsin-tien 辛店 cultures of the valleys of the Huang and the T'ao 洮 rivers and the Ssu-wa and An-kuo cultures living between the T'ao River and the Lung-shan Mountains. Both cultures had a long neolithic tradition and were associated with the native cultures named the Ch'iang.[69]

Archaeological evidence there shows that the Western Chou culture penetrated beyond its western political borders. The most obvious are the Western Chou settlements in the Lung-hsi 隴西 region of Kansu. Numerous burials dating from the Western Chou were found in Ling-t'ai 靈台 and P'ing-liang 平涼 counties.

The sites at Ling-t'ai deserve special attention, for from these burials came bronze vessels typical of Western Chou production in the central plain. Also found were a bronze sword sheath decorated with cattle, serpents, and tangled vines and a ko 戈 halberd bearing an image of a tiger (fig. 6.12). The buried chariots and horses were sacrifices offered in

---

66. Wen-wu pien-chi wei-yüan-hui, 1979:40.
67. The well-known site at Hou-ma 侯馬 was later in date, from the Chin.
68. Wen-wu pien-chi wei-yüan-hui, 1979:58.
69. Hsia Nai, 1961.

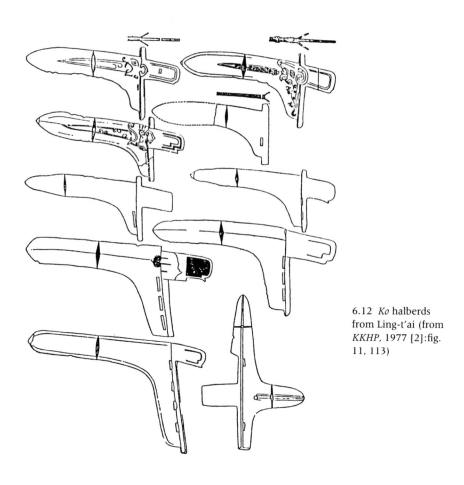

6.12 *Ko* halberds from Ling-t'ai (from *KKHP*, 1977 [2]:fig. 11, 113)

a bonfire ceremony. These features were not typical of Chou decoration. The Ling-t'ai sites may be dated in the mid-Chou, but not later than the reigns of King K'ang and King Mu. The burials of a later date were the Ch'in tombs, in which few significant bronzes were found.[70] More interesting were the stone carvings of human beings found at the Ling-t'ai tomb (figs. 6.13, 6.14). One of these was naked and standing and had a coiled hairstyle decorated with the tiger-head; another wore a double-pointed, high hat. Both of these figures had clothes and hairdos that were not typical of the Chou. The field archaeologists reported that

70. Wen-wu pien-chi wei-yüan-hui, 1979:144–45; Kan-su-sheng po-wu-kuan, 1976, 1977.

6.13 Stone carvings
from Ling-t'ai
(from *KKHP*, 1977
[2]:pl. 14, 3–4)

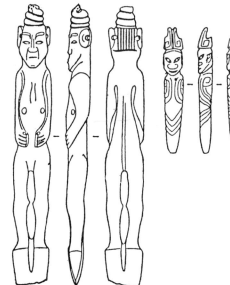

6.14 Drawings of stone
carvings from Ling-t'ai
(from *KKHP*, 1977
[2]:fig. 19, 20)

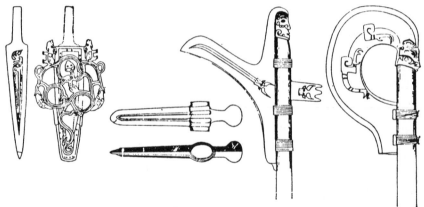

6.15 Bronze weapons from Ling-t'ai (from *KKHP*, 1977 [2]:115)

the figures were alien captives.[71] The statuettes might, however, have been imported from a non-Chou group who manufactured them for their own use.

Ling-tai was located in the upper reaches of the Chung River, in areas where the Chou people had been active, and in the west adjacent to the Ch'iang people. The mixed contents of the tomb suggest that this was the contact point between the Chou and the Ch'iang. The tiger held a special position in Ch'iang legends.[72] The tiger-headed objects from the Ling-t'ai burial are, therefore, not out of place. The sheath decorated with cattle, serpents, and ivy rested on a painted triangular base (fig. 6.15) and bore similarity to those swords used by the minority tribes in the mountains of southwest China (fig. 6.16).[73] The interaction between the Chou and their western neighbors is established without question.

EXPANSION OF THE CULTURAL SPHERE— THE SOUTH AND THE EAST

In the southwest, within the Szechwan Basin itself, there were two distinctive cultures—the Shu 蜀 and the Pa   (see map 2). The soaring mountains that surrounded the basin, however, did not stop the spread of Shang-Chou culture. The Shui-kuan-yin 水觀音 site at Hsin-fan 新繁 included both settlements and burials and cultural remains with tools

71. Kan-su sheng po-wu-kuan, 1977:125–27.
72. *Hou-Han-shu*, 87/4.
73. T'ung En-cheng, 1977:42–43, 52–53.

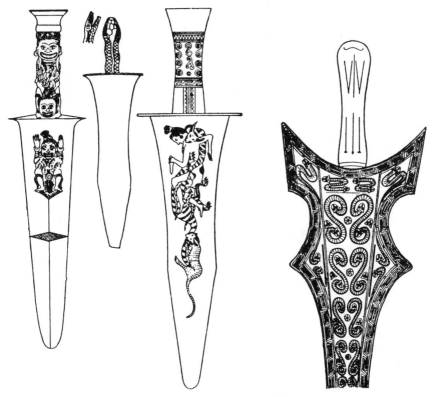

6.16 Bronze weapons from Yünnan (from *KKHP*, 1977 [2]:43)

and implements made primarily of stone. Hunting of game still supplied much of the food. The excavated bronzes included axes, chisels, spears, and halberds. The spears and the halberds resembled their Shang counterparts. From the storage pit discovered at P'eng-hsien 彭縣 came bronze vessels that bore comparable decoration and shapes to the Shang and Chou pieces in the central plain. The most interesting object discovered was a bronze jar whose shape, size, and lizard decor were similar to pieces discovered at K'o-tso in Liaoning (fig. 6.17). The inscription on the bottom of a bronze drinking vessel bore names in the Shang Kan-chih 干支 dating system. Some cattle bones and the turtle shells found at Ch'eng-tu were used for divination, for the drilling and burn marks were identical to materials from An-yang. The jade pieces unearthed from Kuang-han 廣漢 were also similar to ritual materials of Shang/Chou manufacture.[74]

74. Wen-wu pien-chi wei-yüan-hui, 1979:350–51.

6.17 Bronze vessel from K'o-tso, Liaoning (from *KK*, 1974 [6]:pl. 1)

6.18 Set of vessels
from P'eng-hsien
(from *WW*,
1980 [12]:pl. 5)

The relative date of the Hsin-fan find was determined by the discovery of Western Chou–style weapons there of the sort that were discontinued in the Ch'un-ch'iu period. The drinking vessel that carries the Shang nomenclature was probably imported from the central plain. The set of vessels (fig. 6.18), although similar to late Shang or early Chou bronzes in shape and decor, bears a strong local flavor and was probably produced in Szechwan.[75]

All these artifacts were found in the Ch'eng-tu plain, perhaps made for the people from the north who migrated to Szechwan and settled in the few desirable localities in the basin where they left their belongings. It is equally possible, however, that the Shu people secured the Shang and Chou bronzes either by trading or raiding, and in turn learned the

75. Feng Han-chi, 1980; Ssu-ch'uan-sheng po-wu-kuan et al., 1981.

technique of bronze casting. But generally speaking, the Pa-Shu aborigines were not intensively or extensively exposed to influence from the Chou core area until much later times, during the Chan-kuo period. Prior to that, cultural influence from the Chou was felt to a limited degree.

East from the Szechwan Basin are the regions of the present provinces of Hupei and Hunan. Neolithic cultures called the Ta-hsi 大溪 and the Ch'ü-chia-ling 屈家嶺 are known in the remains there, and the Shang established a base there. The Shang site of P'an-lung-ch'eng 盤龍城 yielded remains of palace buildings, burials, and city walls as well as Shang-style artifacts in the tradition of Cheng-chou. There is little doubt that P'an-lung was a stronghold of Shang power in the south in Hupei.[76]

Moreover, bronzes discovered in O-ch'eng 鄂城 in Hupei and Ning-hsiang 寧鄉 in Hunan are inscribed with the names formed by following the Shang system of nomenclature as are bronzes from the early Western Chou tomb at Chiang-ling 江陵. Such bronze vessels found in the Yangtze region may have arrived with the early Chou settlers.[77] The most amazing archaeological site was found in Ch'i-ch'un 圻春, in Hupei, where remains of a large building of wood with more than two hundred postholes scattered in an area of over five thousand square meters was unearthed. Wooden wall panels and wood stairs and the remains of grain were located at the site. The artifacts excavated included pottery, bronzes, lacquer, oracle bones, and turtle shells. The site dates from the Western Chou[78] and judging from the scale and the content of the site, it must have been an important base for the Chou in the Yangtze region. The large building must have served some kind of public function.

South of Hupei in Hunan Province, Western Chou bronzes have frequently been found, especially in the areas around the Tung-t'ing 洞庭 Lake. A bronze bell of the late Western Chou period was found at Hsiang-t'an 湘潭, for example (fig. 6.19).[79] The remains of Western Chou were generally excavated from burials, while the Shang objects in Hunan were often chance finds, perhaps intended as sacrifices offered to spirits of mountains and rivers, for they were found buried on hills or in water.[80] Because the Shang objects are not of a single provenance they are thought to have been imported. Western Chou artifacts from this

76. Chiang Hung, 1976:42.
77. Li Chien, 1963; Hu-nan sheng po-wu-kuan, 1963; Wen-wu pien-chi wei-yüan-hui, 1979:299.
78. K'ao-ku yen-chiu-so, Hu-pei fa-chüeh-tui, 1962.
79. Hu-nan sheng po-wu-kuan, 1966.
80. Heng-yang-shih po-wu-kuan, 1978.

6.19 Bronze bell from
Hsiang-t'an, Hunan
(from *WW*, 1966
[4]:1-2)

area were closely tied to the tomb master for whom they were objects of
daily use, a fact that suggests that those items were either brought by
Chou immigrants or manufactured by them locally following the manner of the central plain. For instance, a *ko* halberd of Shu style was
inscribed with the name Ch'u-kung 楚公 (Lord of Ch'u), a triple reference to the Chou, the Ch'u, and the Shu (fig. 6.20).[81]

In the provinces of Kwangsi 廣西 and Kwangtung 廣東, Western Chou
bronzes were occasionally found. Most come from the Pearl River Valley
where the bronze vessels discovered at Hsin-ch'eng 忻城 and Heng-hsien
橫縣 counties of Kiangsi 江西 and Hsin-i 信宜 County of Kwangtung were
finely cast examples comparable in quality to those from the central
plain. In addition, the bronze *tsun* wine vessel found at Lu-ch'uan
and Li-p'u 荔浦 of Kwangsi was very large and decorated with bold lines
in a local style. The bronze ko 戈 found at Jao-p'ing 饒平, Kwangtung, is
a type not found in other places. The workmanship is crude and unre-
fined, and it must have been locally cast.[82] Western Chou cultural

81. Kao Chih-hsi, 1959; Kao Chih-hsi et al., 1980:57.
82. Wen-wu pien-chi wei-yüan-hui, 1979:329, 341; Kao Chih-hsi et al., 1980:58;
Kuang-hsi Chuang-tsu tzu-chih-ch'ü wen-wu kung-tso-tui, 1978.

6.20 Bronze *ko* of Shu style
(from *WW*, 1959
[12]:60, 1−2)

influence in Kwangsi was probably made via Hunan, where its impact on local cultures was also limited.

Yet another route led south to the lower Yangtze Valley into Chekiang Province, the farthest point reached by Chou influence. Intermediate between the Chou core area and Chekiang was the Huai Valley. That region was dominated by the Ta-wen-k'ou culture during the neolithic and was occupied by Hsü and Shu people, descendants of the eastern coastal nations during the Shang. Many Shang remains have been found there. After the conquest, the Chou repeatedly collided with the Huai, or Huai-I as they were called in bronze inscriptions (map 2). Contact between the Chou and the Huai must have been frequent, for there were numerous Western Chou finds in Anhui Province, including the bronzes such as those found in Chia-shan 嘉山, Fei-hsi 肥西, and T'un-hsi 屯溪 counties. In general, the Western Chou objects in the Huai region were ones with features comparable to those from the central plain. Only some developed independent, local characteristics such as are evident on the bronze vessels discovered in T'un-hsi on the south side of the Yangtze, far from the central plain. They were decorated with geometric designs that copied matrix marks of the pottery. The glazed pottery found there and the ceramics with geometric imprints no doubt continued local traditions (fig. 6.21). Hard glazed pottery, on the other hand, resembled that found in Hsi-an and Lo-yang as did blue-glazed pottery found at the Tan-t'u site (fig. 6.22).[83] After the Western Chou period, the Ch'u culture dominated the region. The Chou influence in the Huai Valley faded so quickly that the Ts'ai 蔡 vessels of the Ch'un-ch'iu period already reflected the new Ch'u taste.[84]

In Kiangsi Province, the neighbor of Anhui to the south, Western Chou remains were found in various counties: Ching-chiang 靖江, Hsin-kan 新淦, Nan-ch'ang 南昌, Yü-kan 餘干, P'ing-hsiang 萍鄉, and Feng-hsin 奉新. All are located along the lower reaches of the Kan 贛 River or its tributaries and other small rivers which poured into P'o-yang 鄱陽 Lake. These river valleys were on the north-south route to the Yangtze.

The best Western Chou bronzes in Kiangsi were not very different from their central plain counterparts either in shape or decor. Most of the Kiangsi bronzes date from the early Chou and not after the mid-Chou. The pottery that accompanied the bronzes was often hard-paste with geometric imprints, a type widely distributed in the south and southeastern sectors of China. The center of production, however, was in Kiangsi and southern Anhui. Evidence of the indigenous cultures was frequently found throughout the area, but the distribution of sites showing influence from the Western Chou bronze culture is sporadic.[85]

A bronze found in Ching-an 靖安 bore the title of a king of Hsü 徐 (fig. 6.23). The Hsü were a large and major branch of the eastern nation and were the original inhabitants of the Huai region. As they were elbowed out of the Huai Valley by the expansion of the Chou, the Hsü gradually moved to the south. After the reign of King Mu of Chou, the Hsü people migrated to central Anhui on the Yangtze. By the seventh century, Hsü was a state located between the Huai and the Yangtze. The Hsü bronze found at Ching-an has been assigned a Ch'un-ch'iu date, thereby confirming their presence at that time.[86]

The coastal area of the Huai Valley is in the northern part of Kiangsi Province. In this area, the Ta-wen-k'ou and the Ma-chia-pang cultures intersected and formed what is called the Liangchu 良渚 culture, one of the largest culture groups in this area throughout the neolithic period. By the end of the Shang both the Hu-shou 湖熟 and a red-pottery-using culture were known in the lower Yangtze. The Hu-shou people knew bronze metallurgy, but only a few, rather low-level tools have been

83. An-hui sheng wen-hua-chü, 1959, 1964; Wen-wu pien-chi wei-yüan-hui, 1979:230–31; Li Hsüeh-ch'in, 1980A.

84. An-hui sheng wen-kuan-hui, 1956.

85. Wen-wu pien-chi wei-yüan-hui, 1979:234, 248–49; Hsüeh Yao, 1963; Kuo Yüan-wei, 1965.

86. Li Hsüeh-ch'in, 1980A:37; Chiang-hsi sheng li-shih po-wu-kuan, 1980.

6.21 Potsherds from Hsi-an
(from K'ao-ku yen-chiu-so,
1962, pl. 58)

6.22 Glazed jar from Tan-t'u
(from *KK*, 1964 [10]:478)

6.23 Rubbing of inscription
(from *WW*, 1980 [8]:13)

unearthed there. The Chou culture penetrated only rarely into this region at this time. The best known Chou-dated site is at Yen-tun-shan 煙墩山 in Tan-t'u where the I-hou *kuei* was discovered and a vassal state was located on the Yangtze River. The Chou burials at I-cheng 儀徵 and Chiang-ning 江寧 are sites that yielded evidence of the presence of the Chou as well. More common were earth mound burials of the local population. Those contained pottery and occasionally bronzes of late Western Chou date. The shape of the artifacts suggests that they were modeled on local types.[87] The provincial character of such bronzes reflected localization of the central plain tradition and testified to the strength of native cultures in the lower Yangtze.

Such is also the case in the present province of Chekiang, which shares the lower Yangtze valley and delta land of lakes and streams with Kiangsu. The distance from the central plain to Chekiang was formi-

87. Ni Chen-ta, 1959; Wu Shan-ching, 1973; Liu Hsing et al., 1976; Nan-ching po-wu-kuan, 1977; Chen-chiang shih po-wu-kuan, 1978, 1979, 1980; Wen-wu pien-chi wei-yüan-hui, 1979:201–03; Nan-ching shih wen-wu pao-kuan wei-yüan-hui, 1980.

dable, but even so, Chou bronzes found at Ch'ang-hsing generally were cast in shapes comparable to those in the northern plain. The decorations, however, were obviously influenced by the impressed pottery of local manufacture.[88]

Fukien Province was even farther from the central plain, and Chou influence there was almost absent. At the site of Min-hou 閩侯, a site probably of Western Chou date, the finds included nothing but imprinted and hard-paste pottery in shapes that were locally derived. Sites of a later date, such as the one at Nan-an 南安, dated in the Ch'un-ch'iu and Chan-kuo periods, contained bronze weapons and tools often accompanied by imprinted hard-paste pottery. The linear decorations on bronze weapons were similar to those found on the pots.[89] The deep south remained the home of the Yüeh 越 throughout the Western Chou.

CONCLUSION

The Chou began to structure their political network outside the capital after they had put down the great uprising in the east. Their special challenge was to gain control of the eastern populations, so diverse in cultural background and ethnic origin. Important members of the Chi and the Chiang were assigned official seats of command of vassal states in strategic locations: Wei, Lu, Ch'i, Chin, Yen, and so on. The location of the new capital at Ch'eng-chou complied with the Chou desire to create stability and the need for regular communication with the east. Within each new state a coalition was developed between the Chou and the Shang, on the one hand, and the native population on the other. The new ruling class often adopted both Shang and local dignitaries. The political composition of ancient China was reshaped from a set of numerous internally homogeneous and isolated nations into an interlocking network of fewer satellite states. Although the conglomerate population of each new Chou state was heterogeneous, the process of cultural fusion developed a common Chou conception of Chineseness, or Hua-Hsia. The diagram in chapter 5 above (fig. 5.2) outlines the pattern of organizing the non-Chou people into the new Chou order. For those who were Chou members, rituals of ancestor worship strengthened the consciousness of group identity. For those who were not members, exogamous marriages helped to incorporate them and to weld ties between member groups. Finally, at least in the minds of the

88. Ch'ang-hsing hsien po-wu-kuan, 1979: Ch'ang-hsing hsien wen-hua-kuan, 1973; Wen-wu pien-chi wei-yüan-hui, 1979:220.
89. Wen-wu pien-chi wei-yüan-hui, 1979:253–54.

political and social elite of the Chou, there developed a common Hua-Hsia identity. Sanctioned by the Mandate, the right to rule the Chinese and thereby to create a Hua-Hsia polity and consciousness was the basis of the Chou worldview. With such an outlook they could resist challenges from outside as well as expand Chinese cultural spheres farther and farther beyond the core area. The formation of the Chou order was sanctioned by Heaven and mandated to continue.

The early Chou during the reigns of King Wu, the Duke of Chou, and King Ch'eng witnessed the formation of this new Chou order. The mid-Chou period was one of growth. With the resources of China's core area, and the new strength of the Shang-Chou coalition, the Chou kingdom not only expanded its political sphere, the Chou extended their cultural influence in all directions.

Generally speaking, Chou expansion to the north was limited because of the strength of nomadic groups from the steppes. The Chou were barely able to hold their defense lines below the steppes. Only the states of Yen and Chin managed to hold firm. The movement of the Chou to the south, however, was more successful, for the Huai people surrendered, became subordinates, and paid regular tribute. In the lake region of the middle Yangtze, Chou advancement was limited, as the powerful Ch'u checked Chou intrusion toward the deep south.

Chou cultural influence in these areas did, however, reach farther than their political dominance. In the northeast, the contact between the Chou and the upper Hsia-chia-tien cultures did cause intermixing. Beyond, along the northern frontier, the line of demarcation between agriculture and pastoralism was not erased, for the Jung neither yielded nor mingled. In the northwest, the Chou cultural influence reached the upper Ching Valley until the Ch'iang of the Ssu-wa and the An-kuo cultures in Kansu blocked further encroachment. The mainstream of Hua-Hsia civilization, that is, the Shang-Chou culture, seemed not to penetrate beyond agricultural zones.

In the southwest, the Chou influence reached into the Szechwan basin but did not take root there. After the fall of the Western Chou, the local Pa and Shu cultures once again flourished there.

In the south, there were two routes across the Yangtze. In the middle reaches, where the Chou entered the Han Valley, they established themselves in the lake region and even reached the upper Pearl River Valley. The combination of Chou cultural features with local ones provided a rich basis for the development of the Ch'u culture there during the Ch'un-ch'iu period. In turn, the Ch'u influenced the peoples in the Chou states founded in the Han Valley.

Another route south was via the Huai region. The Chou displaced the local Hsü nation, who in turn moved toward the Yangtze. The native culture in the lower Yangtze, derived from the Hu-shou cultures, was one that made hard-paste and imprinted pottery. The remains of these Chou outposts were scattered, but their presence did introduce bronze production.

Chou culture, nevertheless, had a powerful impact on many local groups. After the fall of the Western Chou, a new dynamism stimulated some of those local cultures: the Ch'u, the Wu, and the Yüeh in the south; the Yen, Chao, Chung-shan, and the Ch'in in the north. That vitality was sparked in the mid-Chou.

7 The Chou Government

The process of development of the Chou royal government occurred in several phases. First, the king and his royal advisers made up an oligarchy, with power vested in a few. By the mid-Chou reigns, the government had undergone a process of differentiation that respected both heredity and merit as measures for job selection. There was also a gradual separation in power between private and public sectors in the Chou ruling apparatus. By the late Western Chou reigns, as the power of the inner court increased, an aristocratic monarchy gradually developed. Agnatic segmentation, so characteristic of the aristocratic Shang and early Chou government, was discarded in favor of differentiation and institutionalization of positions, thus setting into motion the process of bureaucratization. Although truncated at the fall of the Western Chou royal house, the routinization of government offices was refined through the next several centuries.

This process of change can be examined in several ways. Study of classical sources and bronze inscriptions yields titles of officials and suggests the relationships established among positions, both civic and military. Both sources also occasionally describe ceremonies that disclose the functions of these individuals. Together they help us to learn how the Chou ruled, what role the government played in organizing people's lives, and finally what the Chou believed appropriate to monitor, that is, the goal of government. The mechanism provided military protection, solved border disputes, allowed spiritual functions, and recorded many activities. The increasing effort of the Chou to create titled positions, appropriately ranked and charged, underscores their desire for an orderly society.

THE CHOU GOVERNMENT AS SEEN FROM CLASSICAL SOURCES

Among the classics, information found in the *Shu-ching* 書經 (*Book of Documents*) and the *Shih-ching* 詩經 (*Book of Poetry*) is relevant to the study of the royal government. In various chapters of the *Shu-ching*, titles of important officials are mentioned. For instance, in the "Mu-shih" 牧誓 chapter, in a speech supposedly delivered by King Wu 武 on the first day of the battle of Mu, he addressed many officials: the rulers of the allied states; his ministers in charge of instructions, war, and public works; his deputies; and the commanders of troops, including the captains of the thousands and of the hundreds.[1] The passage indicates that the structure of the government was apparently simple: there were three ministers, each having authority over specific tasks. The *ssu-t'u* 司徒, or Minister of Instructions, looked after land division and farming; the *ssu-ma* 司馬, or Minister of War, commanded troops; the *ssu-k'ung* 司空, or Minister of Works, was in charge of construction and manufacturing. The principle of divided labor was applied here to particular duties, suggesting that there was already a separation between the administration and an "inner court."

The "Li-cheng" 立政 chapter (Establishment of Government) lists two sets of titles of officials, both of which were components of a full catalogue of government offices that were sanctioned by the Duke of Shao. The list of the court attendants includes at least three ranks among the peerage—palace guards; inner officers belonging to the palace; government officers belonging to the administration. There were three divisions of government—staffs of the offices; officers of law and regulation; and pastors. The military included deputies, *equites* (masters of horses), petty officers, and personal attendants. In addition, overseers, treasurers, administrators of the cities both large and small, artisans, historians or recorders, chiefs of all directions, and finally the administrators of several specific ethnic groups as well as the Shang people are accounted for in the text.[2] Although actual titles differ from their counterparts listed in the "K'ang-kao" 康誥, the whole structure confirms the same principles suggested above. Namely, the *ssu-t'u* was in charge of human power; the *ssu-k'ung* was in charge of works; and the *ssu-ma* was in charge of "horses," or military affairs.[3]

The "K'ang-kao" chapter records royal instructions to Prince K'ang-shu 康叔 and was full of titles of the *wai-shu-tzu* 外庶子, the gentlemen or officers; the *chu-cheng* 諸正, the heads of departments; and the *hsiao-ch'en* 小臣, or petty officers. These titles did not denote actual positions, however.[4] Similarly, in the "Chiu-kao" 酒誥 (Instruction against Alchoholism), the government was collectively addressed as *shu-shih* 庶士, "numerous gentlemen"; as *shao-cheng* 少正, the "lesser ones" or "atten-

1. Legge, *Shoo King*, 301.
2. Ibid., 508–09, 514–15.
3. Creel, 1970:107.
4. Legge, *Shoo King*, 393–94.

dants"; and *yü-shih* 御事 or those who managed affairs. Neither status nor order of authority was described there. In another passage in the same chapter, however, the administrators were described in the following way: those in the exterior domains were the princes of the states (i.e., the vassals); those in the interior domains were various kinds of officers, the directors of several departments, their assistants, the heads of *tsu* 族 (i.e., kinship groups), and the ward leaders of the people. In yet another passage, in addition to the vassals and the ministers, the king addressed "the Great Recorder and his staff; the Internal Recorder and his staff," as well as "the Lord of Land," who deals with offenders, the Lord of Agriculture, who is the guardian of the people, the Lord of Work, who settles regulations.[5] From these passages, we may deduce that the government of the royal domain stood separately from that of the vassaldoms. In the royal government, there were several categories of functionaries, all of whom belonged to particular departments. There were administrators for the *tsu* as well as for the "wards," the archival staff with its two branches, and the lords. The Chou governmental system as constructed from the *Shu-ching,* on the other hand, is clear. The disparity between titles and divisions culled from these documents, if indeed they are contemporaneous, must be examined further.

The "Ku-ming" 顧命 (The Testimony of Change) and the "K'ang-wang-chih-kao" 康王之誥 (The Announcement of King K'ang) chapters recorded the death of King Ch'eng 成 and the enthronement of King K'ang 康. Those officials called upon to participate were recorded according to general titles. They included the title of head or chief of departments, *yü-shih* 御事 or "managers of affairs," and other officials with particular duties. Commanders of the army and the "Tiger Guards" were named as well. Three specific titles were given: *T'ai-pao* 大保, or Grand Protector; *T'ai-shih* 大史, Grand Recorder or Historiographer; and *T'ai-ch'ang* 大常, Grand Priest. These three were directly involved in the solemn ceremony of enthronement. Among them the Grand Protector was actually in charge, and he was conventionally identified as the Duke of Shao. He was the senior statesman in the early reigns of the Chou, and his status was only one step below that of the Duke of Chou. The Grand Recorder was the chief of the royal archives; the Grand Priest was perhaps either the Master of Ceremonies (as suggested by Creel) or the Minister of Religion (as suggested by Legge). One important function of this office was its special role in the administration of the affairs of the royal kin. In addition to these titles of individual offices and those designating collective offices, four feudal nobles were mentioned accord-

5. Ibid., 399, 407, 410–12, respectively. The translations are slightly revised.

ing to rank.[6] From these documents, we learn that the individual members of the nobility and the ceremonial functions that they carried out were specifically identified, while the remaining members of the government were mentioned collectively. The Chou government during the early reigns may have been conceived of as a collective body of guardian elders rather than as a structure composed of functions to be filled by nobles. Some division of labor was respected, but it was according to the individual, not necessarily the task. The group of those elders formed an oligarchy within the aristocracy.

The *Book of Poetry*, although an unlikely source of information on this topic, does list a few titles. As early as the pre-dynastic period when the Chou ancestor Tan Fu first built a city in the Wei Valley, the two officials in charge of construction were called *ssu-k'ung* (Minister of Works), and *ssu-t'u* (Minister of Land).[7] In a poem conventionally dated in the late Chou, some official titles and the names of the incumbents are mentioned: chancellor, minister of men, chief administrator of the household, chief steward, recorder of the interior, master of the horses (*equites*), and commander of the troops (or captain of the guards). The next stanza of the same verse, however, describes the administration in general terms with the phrase, "The Three Offices (or Departments)," presumably the Ministries of Men, of Works, and of War.[8]

More usual in the *Book of Poetry*, however, were records of the royal charges of individual nobles, and their feudal titles were used rather than titles describing their function.[9] In short, the classical sources do not contain enough information to allow for the complete reconstruction of the Chou governmental structure, so the functions of the offices chronicled above have been deduced literally.

THE CHOU GOVERNMENT AS MENTIONED IN BRONZE INSCRIPTIONS

From this source, dedicatory inscriptions on ritual bronze vessels, titles of officials can be categorized according to function. The divisions recorded include the household, departments, military, and secretarial personnel.[10] These groups may be described as follows:

---

6. Ibid., 544, 557, 563–64;Creel, 1970:106–07.
7. Legge, *She King*, 439.
8. Ibid., 322–23; Creel, 1970:107.
9. See, for instance, Legge, *She King*, 536–40.
10. Ssu Wei-chih, 1947.

7.1 Inscription from bronze
vessel, Ch'ai *kuei*
(from *KBTS*, 23:102)

THE HOUSEHOLD PERSONNEL

These titles probably evolved from actual positions, because etymologically the terms designated common household roles.

1. *Tsai* 宰, *t'ai-tsai* 大宰 (Interns).[11] In the inscription on a vessel called the Ch'ai *kuei* 蔡毀 (fig. 7.1), the person named Ch'ai was designated as the *tsai* of the royal household. He was instructed to cooperate with another *tsai* in managing the royal household by "taking and issuing the commands" of Lady Chiang 姜, evidently the queen or her equivalent. No one could enter the palace without first seeing Ch'ai, and he was commissioned to be in charge of *pai-kung* 百工, literally, "hundreds of craftworkers,"[12] persons ranked below the female servants.[13] The *tsai* is described as the head steward of the royal household in the inscription. This rank is echoed in the *Book of Poetry*, where a *tsai* is a high official in the court.[14]

2. *Shan-fu* 善夫, *shan-tsai* 膳宰 (Steward).[15] This title literally means cook or chief cook.[16] In one inscription, the *shan-fu* is listed with the

11. Creel, 1970:112−14.
12. Shirakawa Shizuka, *KBTS*, 23:103−06.
13. Ibid., 29:68.
14. Legge, *She King*, 322.
15. Creel, 1970:119−20.
16. Legge, *She King*, 323, 533; cf. Creel, 1970:119, n. 68.

7.2 Inscription from bronze vessel from the reigns of kings Ch'eng and K'ang (from *KBTS*, 16:125)

workers who handled the dogs; apparently they served as kennel attendants.[17] On another inscription, the K'o *ting* 克鼎, the *shan-fu* is listed as an officer who "delivered and brought in commands" of the king.[18] Ssu Wei-chih noticed that the office of *shan-fu* was often entrusted to summon the recipient for a ceremony of investiture or bestowal of royal gifts.[19] In another verse in the *Book of Poetry*, the *shan-fu* is listed as an officer comparable to those of other ranking countries.[20]

3. *Hsiao-ch'en* 小臣 (Minor Attendant). During the Shang period, the *hsiao-ch'en* had high status, even though the literal translation of this term suggests a servile position. In one Chou inscription, however, a *hsiao-ch'en* is ranked with the *shan-fu* and the Kennel Attendant.[21] Another *hsiao-ch'en* named Ching 靜, who lived during the reigns of kings Ch'eng and K'ang, was ordered to learn archery. He had also received royal gifts on various occasions (fig. 7.2) so he apparently was a courtier who enjoyed royal favor.[22] The political significance of his post, however, may only be guessed.

4. *P'u* 僕, *t'ai-p'u* 大僕 (Chamberlain, High Chamberlain).[23] The early use of the word *p'u* was simply to denote a servant. From the classics,

17. Shirakawa Shizuka, *KBTS*, 22:18.
18. Ibid., 28:498–500.
19. Ssu Wei-chih, 1947:3.
20. Legge, *She King*, 322.
21. Shirakawa Shizuka, *KBTS*, 22:18.
22. Ibid., 16:124–38.
23. Legge, *Shoo King*, 583–84.

we learn that *p'u* were often in charge of the chariots and because of that association, Legge suggested that they were charioteers.[24] Moreover, he suggested that because of their intimate relationship with the king, the *p'u* were entrusted with the job of conveying royal commands.[25] A bronze inscription named an individual who was appointed as a military commander of both *p'u* and archers.[26] Another epigraphic source recorded an incident where several *p'u* were punished by a commander-in-chief because they failed to follow their own "Commander of the Right Wing" in a campaign.[27] In the former case, the *p'u* was a military officer; in the latter, *p'u* were assigned to serve in military campaigns. In either case, the *p'u* were in service rather than in charge.

5. *Shih* 史, *t'ai-shih* 大史 (Tutor, Instructor).[28] This title is difficult to decipher, for it indicated many different roles. On several inscriptions it signifies both a military position and a musician. In one inscription, a person with such a title is appointed as a music assistant, a position passed on hereditarily. The same person is ordered to be in charge of percussion instruments, the bells and drums.[29] Throughout the Ch'un-ch'iu period, the title *shih* indicated an instructor or teacher, and it survives today with both musical and military associations. Shirakawa Shizuka suggested that the Chou, as the inheritors of Shang culture, entrusted the Shang learned men to teach the Chou youth of all backgrounds all kinds of topics, including music and religion. Thus, the title *shih* acquired several meanings.[30] The Chou, however, must have had their own tradition of educating their young people, even before they conquered the Shang. The title *shih* perhaps simply meant an elder who taught the young ones a broad range of topics, including music and martial arts. It should be noted that there were various uses of the term *shih*, even though it literally referred to musical experts who were retained by the noble households. Later the title of T'ai-shih was often given to a senior adviser to the throne.

THE DEPARTMENTS

These were the offices with titles beginning with the character *ssu* 司, meaning "to direct." In later history, officers of this category were the main functionaries in ministries and departments.[31]

---

24. Ibid., 583.
25. Ibid., 584.
26. Shirakawa Shizuka, *KBTS*, 16:115–16.
27. Ibid., 13:753–56.
28. Creel, 1970:111.
29. Shirakawa Shizuka, *KBTS*, 26:335, 31:770.
30. Ibid., 1973:290–300.
31. Creel, 1970:107–08.

7.3 Inscription from bronze
vessel, Mien *fu*
(from *KBTS*, 21:465)

1. *Ssu-t'u* 司徒. This title was written in two ways. An alternative form appears in bronze inscriptions with the second character, *t'u* 土, meaning land or soil. This person must have been a minister of the land. The term is used in the classics, however, to mean laborer or worker, and it must have meant Minister of the Multitude, or Instruction, as it did in Ch'un-ch'iu usage.[32] One bronze inscription mentions an appointment to the office of *ssu-t'u* in relation to the ceremony of tilling the sacrificial field,[33] a ceremony recorded in great detail in the *Kuo-yü* 國語 (*The Discourses of the States*). The Chou Minister of the Multitude apparently had the responsibility to mobilize workers. In another passage of the *Kuo-yü*, one regarding a statewide census, *ssu-t'u* has charge of coordination of the tasks of the working hands.[34]

The office of Minister of the Multitude only appears in inscriptions on two occasions, and in neither case is a specific assignment given.[35] On the other hand, in the Mien *fu* 免簠 inscription, Mien was appointed as *ssu-t'u*, or Minister of Land, in charge of fields, pastures, and game woods in the land called Cheng 鄭 (fig. 7.3).[36] Another inscription listed Wu 吳 as the person responsible for the fields, the pastures, and the

32. Ibid., 107, n. 19.
33. Shirakawa Shizuka, *KBTS*, 20:414.
34. *Kuo-yü*, 1/7, 9.
35. Shirakawa Shizuka, *KBTS*, 23:83.
36. Ibid., 21:460.

7.4 Inscription from bronze vessel mentioning Wu (from *KBTS*, 26:327)

woods in a region east of the Hu 滹 to the river and as far as Hsüan-shui 支水 (fig. 7.4).[37] There was no official title mentioned in the appointment of Wu; since his responsibilities were almost the same as those assigned to Mien, Wu must also have been a *ssu-t'u*. A *ssu-t'u* also could be attached to a military unit, such as the *ssu-t'u* of the Eight Divisions of Ch'eng-chou 成周, and they might also hold particular portions of land.[38] The same office could be attached to a vassal state or a particular area.[39] A long passage of the San-shih p'an 散氏盤 that records the settling of land disputes between two lords mentions *ssu-t'u* from both parties who took part in the settlement.[40] These *ssu-t'u* managed the land, at the state or subfief level. Since no one could make the land produce without human labor to work it, the *ssu-t'u* must have supervised the persons who worked on farms, in forests, and with the herds. Thus, perhaps, the *ssu-t'u* originally in charge of the land became the *ssu-t'u* in charge of the multitude.[41] Another bronze records *ssu-t'u* and a ceremony of tilling the royal fields.

2. *Ssu-k'ung* 司空 (Minister of Works, of Construction).[42] A bronze

37. Ibid., 26:330.
38. Ibid., 23:149.
39. Ibid., 4:153, 26:346.
40. Ibid., 24:199.
41. Ssu Wei-chih, 1947:6–7; Ch'en Meng-chia, 1956E:111–12.
42. Creel, 1970:107, n. 18; Ssu Wei-chih, 1947:13–14; Ch'en Meng-chia, 1956E: 121.

7.5 Inscription from bronze vessel naming a *ssu-kung* (from *KBTS*, 23:82)

inscription names a *ssu-k'ung* who was appointed to survey, assign places, and set up the marks for the area[43] (fig. 7.5). His range of duties was equivalent to that recounted in a more detailed description of the same ceremony in the *Kuo-yü*.

3. *Ssu-k'ou* 司寇 (Minister of Crime). This title rarely appears in bronze inscriptions and classical literature and when it does, no clear indication of judicial responsibilities is given.[44] Another person, the *ssu-shih* 司士, was the judicial official as evidenced in the Mu *kuei* 牧殷 inscription. Mu was told that because of the chaos and violence of the time he must expand the mission of the *ssu-shih* to include overseeing of all the officials as well as the commoners. The king also authorized him to use punishment to correct unconventional behavior.[45] Although the inscription is too corroded to allow a full reading, the text suggests that Mu was given much less power in his initial position as a *ssu-shih*. The original term literally meant "to be in charge of the *shih*," the lowest-ranked Chou officials. They were in position similar to that of a marshal who supervised warrior-nobles.[46] In the case of Mu's assignment, a *ssu-shih* was elevated to become a Minister of Crime.

4. *Ssu-ma* 司馬 (Minister of War). This office customarily belonged to the Three Ministries. Literally, *ssu-ma* meant "officer in charge of

43. Shirakawa Shizuka, *KBTS*, 23:82−83.
44. Creel, 1970:171.
45. Shirakawa Shizuka, *KBTS*, 20:364.
46. Creel, 1970:171, n. 62.

horses," including war chariots. Creel found, however, that there was not sufficient explicit description of the *ssu-ma's* office to suggest that he was actively responsible in war.[47] In one other inscription a *ssu-ma* is appointed to supervise justice and discipline in the army.[48] In yet another, a person named Yün 霣 is appointed as the commander of the "people of the city." The inauguration of Yün was held in the *ssu-ma's* office and a high-ranking aristocrat, the Earl of Hsing 邢伯, an incumbent *ssu-ma*, officiated.[49] The office in which Yün was to serve was commonly regarded as a military post. We do not know precisely what the responsibilities of the officer of the "people of the city" were, except that Yün was in command of a standing troop of "king's men." Because a ceremony was held in the *ssu-ma's* office, we deduce that the ministry of the *ssu-ma* was associated with military functions and that maintenance of a standing unit of draftees recruited from the "city population" was a duty of this state official. In other instances, the *ssu-ma* were called upon to administer justice within the military. They were also told to help the king by "pacifying the four quarters."[50] These clues do not lead directly to an explicit definition of the *ssu-ma* as the Minister of War, even though his duties were clearly associated with administration of the military. Since the Chou leaders were primarily warriors and any ranking official in the court could be assigned military duties, it is understandable that the demarcation between the military and nonmilitary roles is blurred. The *ssu-ma* were probably not strictly one or the other. In addition, the *pang-chün ssu-ma* 邦君司馬, the *ssu-ma* attached to a ruler of a vassal state (i.e., a *pang-chün*)[51] (fig. 7.6) was appointed by the Chou king. In the *Ch'un-ch'iu Chronicles* 春秋, these posts were still recorded in the state of Ch'i 齊, where they were held by descendants of the royally appointed custodians.[52] We have no record that identifies the officials by title, but leading aristocratic clans from the state of Lu had monopolized the three ministries of the state, one of which was a *ssu-ma*, for generations.[53] The Chou royal court apparently installed these custodians in the vassal states to control the army.

5. The Three Ministries; The Three Offices; The Three Left and The Three Right. These terms were used by the classical scholars to refer to various combinations of offices mentioned in the *Shih-ching* or the *Shu-*

47. Ibid., 107 n. 302.
48. Shirakawa Shizuka, *KBTS*, 16:115–16.
49. Ibid., 22:510–11.
50. Ibid., 12:664–68.
51. Ibid., 20:401.
52. Legge, *Ch'un Ts'ew*, 159.
53. Ibid., 599.

ching.[54] The term "Three Offices" is also used on bronzes as a collective term. An inscription (figs. 7.7, 7.8) on a *tsun* 尊 from Mei-hsien 郿縣 states: "The King appointed *x* in charge of six armies, the King's column, and the three officers: *ssu-ma, ssu-k'ung,* and *ssu-t'u.*" The king ordered him to "be in charge of the farming affairs of the six armies and the eight armies."[55] An inscription on a *ting* 鼎 (fig. 7.9) records the king's commission to the Duke of Mao 毛 to manage his state and his household and to supervise the staff. They were made up of the *ch'ing-shih* 卿士 and *t'ai-shih* 太史, apparently a secretarial staff, royal kinsmen, the "Three Offices," attendants, a commander, the Tiger Guards (the Royal Guards) and "others who serve us."[56] Similar statements are found on a *yi* 彝 in which Ming-pao 明保 and Ling 令 were entrusted by the king to supervise the "Three Offices, the "Four Quarters," and the "staff of *ch'ing-shih.*"[57] These three inscriptions all indicate that the recipient of such a commission was given overall authority to supervise both the military and the civil servants, in the royal government and household, as well as in the central government of the Four Quarters—that is, in the vassal states. In other words, the Three Offices represented the administrative organs of the royal government, as opposed to the military, the royal private secretariat, and the vassaldoms. In at least one case, "the three left and the three right" were mentioned,[58] perhaps referring to six offices in the government as an extension of the Three Offices,[59] or to two divisions of vassals.[60] By the Ch'un-ch'iu period the Three Ministers, the *ssu-ma,* the *ssu-k'ung* and *ssu-t'u,* were typically the highest-ranking triad in the government.[61]

6. Miscellaneous Offices. Some inscriptions include the specifications for jobs commissioned to appointees. An official might be authorized to take charge of the pastures, fields, and game woods at particular locations.[62] Others might receive assignments entrusting the lands of the six armies to their care,[63] and others were given the authority to supervise the farming affairs for the six armies as well as the eight armies.[64]

54. Ma Shui-ch'en, 1888:20/28–29; Hu Ch'eng-kung, 1888:318–20.
55. Shirakawa Shizuka, *KBTS*, 19:316.
56. Ibid., 30:680.
57. Ibid., 7:276.
58. Ibid., 12:685, 705.
59. Kuo Mo-jo, 1957:37.
60. Ch'en Meng-chia, 1956C:85.
61. Itō Michiharu, 1975:326.
62. Shirakawa Shizuka, *KBTS*, 26:328.
63. Ibid., 27:465.
64. Yeh Ta-hsiung, 1979:11; Itō Michiharu, 1977:59; Yü Sheng-wu, 1964; Kuo Mo-jo, 1961A.

7.6 Inscription from bronze
vessel naming a *ssu-ma*
(from *KBTS*, 20:402)

7.7 Li *fang-tsun* from Mei-hsien (courtesy of the Cultural Relics Bureau, Beijing,
and the Metropolitan Museum of Art)

7.8 Inscription from bronze vessel, the Li *fang-tsun* from Mei-hsien (from Fong, 1980:246)

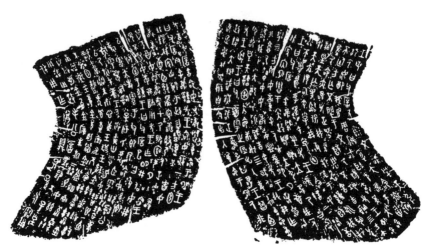

7.9 Inscription on a *ting* recording a commission to the Duke of Mao (from Wong Yin-wai, 1978:268, 269)

One inscription refers to the supervision of "nine reservoirs,"[65] and another mentions rice crops at another location. It is not clear from the context whether the officer was a granary manager or a supervisor of the production.[66] In another inscription, however, it is very clear a single official managed twenty storage depots at Ch'eng-chou as well as manufactured artifacts for palace use.[67] There is even an inscription in which the appointee was put in charge of the palace personnel as well as "the hundred artisans."[68] Since so many specific functions were not easily classified as regular offices or government organs, we learn that the Chou government was not fully institutionalized.

MILITARY OFFICES

In addition to the offices of *ssu-ma* (Minister of Horses) and *p'u* (*equites*) discussed in the previous section, other military offices included the following:

1. *Shih* 師; *shih-shih* 師氏. *Shih* generally meant an "army" such as the six *shih* or the eight *shih* armies. Shirakawa Shizuka suggested that the eight armies of Yin 殷 consisted mainly of Shang soldiers who surrendered to the Chou. Thus, he regarded persons with the title *shih-shih* (Commander of the *shih*) as descendants of the Yin. Shirakawa also suggested that these persons frequently occupied very high posts.[69] The Chou troops, however, included more than simply the surrendered Yin units, yet they still used the term *shih*. Even the eight armies who garrisoned at Ch'eng-chou must have included soldiers of various origins, not just the Yin and their descendants. The six "western" armies were supposed to have joined the eight Ch'eng-chou armies to fight the I people in the east and the south[70] (fig. 7.10). These six armies, according to the customary use of the term "west," were from the Chou homeland in the Wei Valley and they were the troops stationed in the royal domain near the capital. In fact, the royal troops directly under the command of the king are usually described in the *Book of Poetry* as "the Six Armies."[71] Also named are the "six Yang 揚 armies," who participated in the campaign in the southeast.[72] They must have been the six

---

65. Shirakawa Shizuka, *KBTS*, 25:302.
66. Ibid., 49:250.
67. Ibid., 28:195.
68. Ibid., 28:521.
69. Ibid., 1973:260–77.
70. Ibid., *KBTS*, 27:450.
71. Yeh Ta-hsiung, 1979:7, 12.
72. Shirakawa Shizuka, 1973:261

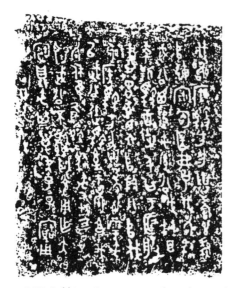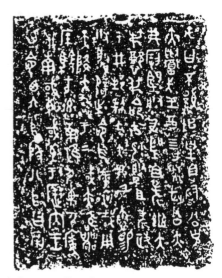

7.10 Rubbing, in two parts, from bronze inscription recording the six armies (from *KBTS*, 27:444–45)

units recruited from the people of Yang 揚, members of the Huai-I 淮夷 group. Those which were named simply as the six or eight armies, without identification of geographic or ethnic affiliation, were probably Chou troops. Among those cited by Shirakawa Shizuka, the majority simply were *shih-shih*,[73] presumably commanders of the armies. The most explicit use of the term was in an instruction related to the campaign against the Eastern I people where a high-ranking official ordered his deputies to enter combat duty with the *shih-shih*.[74] In another case, a person with the title of *shih* was in command of several ethnic units as well as the left and right Tiger Guards in a war against the southern Huai 淮 people.[75]

Other cases mentioning the "left" and the "right" *shih-shih* suggest that these detachments supported the main body.[76] Also outlined were left and right "units of horses," perhaps referring to horses harnessed to war chariots,[77] as well as left and right Tiger Guards, the royal bodyguards.[78] Even the palace attendants and artisans were divided into

73. Ibid., 268–76.
74. Ibid., *KBTS*, 5:219.
75. Ibid., 29:605.
76. Ibid., 19:356.
77. Ibid., 752.
78. Ibid., 28:543.

7.11 Inscription on the Shih-yu *kuei* (from *KBTS*, 31:703)

7.12 Inscription on the Shih-hsün *kuei* (from *KBTS*, 29:556)

west and east divisions.[79] Dualism was a basic organizing principle in Chou institutions.

The Chou standing army included special units recruited from specific ethnic groups. The inscriptions on the Shih-yu *kuei* 師酉毁 and the Shih-hsün *kuei* 師詢毁 (figs. 7.11, 7.12) reveal that both persons were

79. Ibid., 31:741.

commissioned to command the "city-people," the Tiger Guards, and several units of I peoples. In addition, the duties listed on the Shih-hsün *kuei* include ones for four more units that are described as "the surrendered and the subjugated."[80] The same inscription reveals that Yu's father was I-po 乙伯 and Hsün's grandfather was also I-po. They apparently held their posts through hereditary associations, either as father-son or uncle-nephew. The city-people were probably subjects in the capital who served in the regular army, while the Tiger Guards were the palace sentries. Together, these two regular units were probably Chou soldiers who guarded the capital. Units of the subjugated peoples stationed in the city formed special regiments. In all, Shih-yu and Shih-hsün commanded a large portion, or perhaps all, of the armed force at the capital garrisons.

From bronze inscriptions Shirakawa Shizuka identified twenty-four persons who had the title of *shih* attached to their personal names.[81] The number of troops commanded by each *shih* varied significantly, even though the *shih* was a high command post. The posts were differentiated into left and right commands. Further subdivisions belonged to the mid-Chou period after the reigns of kings I 懿, Hsiao 孝, Yi 夷, Li 厲, and even as late as the time of Li's exile. The trend to further classify ranks reflected a tendency toward greater differentiation in the late Chou government.

2. *Tsou-ma* 走馬, *ch'ü-ma* 趣馬. Literally translated, the titles mean "walking the horse" and "running after the horse" and suggest that these were equestrian officers. Although there was no cavalry in the Western Chou, the war chariot was an indispensable part of the Chou army and was drawn by two or four horses. Thus, raising and training of horses for combat duty had to be taken very seriously by the Chou leaders. Further, under the command of the *shih-shih* were equestrian officers named the left and the right *tsou-ma* and the *tsou-ma* of the five cities.[82] In another instance, the king ordered a *tsou-ma* by the name of Yen 雁 to bestow thirty-two horses upon Ta 大.[83] The inscription discloses Yen's duties as a horseherd even though the rank of *tsou-ma* was not a lowly one. That a *shih* was specially appointed to supervise these *tsou-ma* of the left, the right, and the five cities[84] indicated their special status. On the famous inscription of the horse-shaped *tsun* 尊 (see frontispiece), the king in person was described in the ceremony handling

80. Ibid., 702.
81. Ibid., 1973:274–75.
82. Ibid., *KBTS*, 31:752.
83. Ibid., 20:492.
84. Ibid., 31:752, 759; Yeh Ta-hsiung, 1977:2–4.

the young colt, so we know the importance of the horse in the Chou military.[85]

3. Tiger Guards. Literally translated, *hu-ch'en* 虎臣 means Tiger Attendants. In the inscription on the Shih-k'o *ting* 師克鼎, the Tiger Guards are described as a unit of the royal bodyguards including a left and right wing.[86] In the Mao-kung *ting* 毛公鼎 inscription, the Tiger Guards are listed with the *hsiao-ch'en* (the Lesser Attendants), both palace personnel.[87] The royal Tiger Guards were, however, also assigned to a field command or a field expedition and campaign.[88]

4. The Secretarial Services:

a. *Tso-ts'e* 作册 (Archivist). The pictograph *ts'e* has been interpreted as a bundle of tablets on which the script was written. *T'se* must have been documents, therefore.[89] Although Shirakawa Shizuka has argued that the original sign suggested a pen that retained domestic animals,[90] it is unlikely that the archivists would use such a word to describe documents. Bronze inscriptions indicate that a *tso-ts'e* was an official who participated in ceremonies of investiture or gift-giving. Occasionally, a *tso-ts'e* received royal graces. In inscriptions dated earlier than the mid-Chou reigns, the *tso-ts'e* prepared the documents of ceremony not only for the king, but also for the queen, the high ministers, or the vassal dukes. The royal house as well as the aristocratic households all retained archivists. The ceremonies in which they took part included casting of memorial vessels, making and receiving appointments, offering sacrifices, holding royal audiences, construction of temples, and a variety of other religious activities.[91]

Statistics show that after the reign of King Kung, *tso-ts'e* participated primarily in ceremonies of investiture. In addition, the title of *tso-ts'e* began to be qualified: *tso-ts'e-yin* 作册尹 (Chief *Tso-ts'e*), *yin-shih* 尹氏 (Chief), *ming-yin* 命尹 (Chief of Investiture Ceremonies), *Tso-ming-nei-shih* 作命內史 (Internal Historian, in charge of preparing investitures), *nei-shih-yin* 內史尹 (Chief Internal Historian), and *tso-ming-ch'en-kung* 作命臣工 (the attending staff who prepared documents of investiture). The differentiation reflected the functions of the *tso-ts'e*, including the role of a *tso-ts'e* and an "historian."[92]

85. Kuo Mo-jo, 1961A:312–14.
86. Shirakawa Shizuka, *KBTS*, 28:543.
87. Ibid., 30:680.
88. Ibid., 29:605.
89. Tung Tso-pin, 1929A:128; Creel, 1970:124–25, 128.
90. Shirakawa Shizuka, 1973:115–22.
91. Ibid., 150–55.
92. Ibid., 158–60.

b. *Shih* 史 , *nei-shih* 內史 , *wai-shih* 外史 , *tai-shih* 大史 . These titles designate the secretarial staff. Although *shih* came to mean historian in later days, the etymology of the character is not agreed upon. Among several meanings, *shih* does characterize "scribe" and "historiographer" in bronze inscriptions. The term also connoted "service," "office," and even "envoy." A simple, all-inclusive definition probably would be "functionary," for in the bronze inscriptions the terms *shih* (historian), *li* 吏 (officer), and *shih* (a function) were not clearly distinguished.[93]

In bronze inscriptions, a *shih* is most commonly mentioned as a participant in the ceremonies of investiture. Nevertheless, a *shih* still could be ordered to conduct functions other than ceremonial or scribal ones. For instance, a *shih* could be sent to supervise construction, to lead military units in combat, to tour in assigned areas, or to "comfort" the people on behalf of the king.[94] These duties were simply an extension of the role of recording orders issued by the king to the role of actually conveying orders to the parties that were involved. A *shih* could be told to delegate authority to a fief's office in a campaign[95] or to stay as a field supervisor in the army.[96] In a similar manner, a *shih* could conduct a religious ceremony on behalf of the king if he was dispatched to do so.[97]

The fundamental function of a *shih* was, no doubt, to record the documents and to keep them as references. Agreements signed by vassal parties involved in land disputes, such as the one recorded in the San-shih *p'an* 散氏盤 inscription, were concluded with the clause that the documents would be kept by the *shih*'s office.[98] Another inscription recorded a *shih*'s duty to do some sort of calculation.[99] The king naturally had a *shih* constantly at his side to consult about precedents as well as to keep records. The *shih* Mien 史免 even cast a vessel just to commemorate his participation in a long campaign.[100] The same person was entrusted to carry out various activities: for instance the *ssu-t'u*, who managed fields, pastures, and game woods, or the *ssu-k'ung*, who supervised construction projects.[101] The extension of roles of the inner court staff to include numerous functions was duplicated repeatedly in the history of the imperial Chinese court. The growth of the authority of the inner court emerged in the Chou period. The offices of *ts'e* and *shih*

93. Wang Kuo-wei, 1959:4, 263–69; Creel, 1970:170.
94. Shirakawa Shizuka, *KBTS*, 5:217, 223; 7:366; 24:179.
95. Ibid., 14:791.
96. Ibid., 23:97.
97. Ibid., 23:97.
98. Ibid., 24:199.
99. Ibid., 21:484–89.
100. Ibid., 21:477.
101. Ibid., 456, 459.

intersected. In the reigns of kings Ch'eng and K'ang, the tso-ts'e and the shih played two distinctive roles. The tso-ts'e only prepared documents, while the shih was responsible for reading decrees aloud at ceremonies. Attached to the titles of a shih were modifiers such as nei 內 (internal), wai 外 (external), or t'ai 大 (grand). After the Ch'eng-K'ang period, however, such distinctions disappeared, and instead, the combined titles of shih and ts'e began to appear. These scribe-officials who bore dual titles were responsible to read decrees in ceremonies in a fashion similar to the shih of the early reigns. The title yin 尹, meaning the chief, or principal, officer, was used to designate yet another member of the scribe-official group. In other words, the royal secretariat was gradually organized to include the scribes of both categories, and the group was so sizable that it required a supervisor of its own. Ch'en Meng-chia thought that the nei-shih (internal scribes) took over the role of issuing royal decrees after the mid-Chou reigns and the yin (chief of staff) appeared only in the late reigns.[102] The distinction probably reveals the change in the royal power from that sanctioned through ritual to one that institutionalized the king's authority by organizing an inner court that helped exercise the power. The growth and differentiation of the inner court, of course, were one more example of bureaucratization. In spite of institutionalization, royal authority was final; the king could alter the decree as he wished even after a written document had been read aloud by his scribal staff.[103]

5. Local officials. During the reign of King Li there appeared certain titles prefixed by the phrase wu-i 五邑, literally, "five cities." For instance, a person was put in charge of the soldiers and the functionaries of the Five Cities.[104] Another inscription mentioned the chu 祝, a sorcerer, of the Five Cities[105] (fig. 7.13). In a passage about the officer of the equites, the tsou-ma of the Five Cities were listed in addition to the left and right tsou-ma.[106] These officers of the Five Cities consisted of religious, field-managing, and military personnel, a fairly complete administrative unit. We do not know the names of these five cities, but since these tsou-ma were assigned to the same supervisor, we can guess that the cities were probably located near the royal capital. Throughout the Western Chou period, the royal residences were in Ch'i 岐, Ch'eng 程, Feng 豐, Hao 鎬, Hsi-cheng 西鄭, and Huai-li 槐里.[107] Five of these may have been counted as the Five Cities.

102. Ch'en Meng-chia, 1957:147–49.
103. Shirakawa Shizuka, KBTS, 26:335–37; Kuo Mo-jo, 1961A:328–32.
104. Shirakawa Shizuka, KBTS, 33:899.
105. Ibid., 31:737.
106. Ibid., 752.
107. Shih-chi, 4/15, 96; Chu-shu chi-nien, A/17, 18, 1; B/46.

7.13 Inscription mentioning the *chu* of the Five Cities (from *KBTS*, 33:900)

The archaeological site at Ch'i-shan 歧山 is generally regarded as the pre-dynastic Chou capital. It was continuously inhabited even after the captial was moved to other locations. The residential remains at Chao-ch'en are so impressive that they are regarded as palaces or residences of very important aristocrats. Other capitals must have been used and maintained even after the court was moved to other locations. The term "Five Cities" was likely one used to refer to the capital region, which was directly under the control of the royal court.

Another important district was the eastern capital at Ch'eng-chou. One inscription notes that a ranked aristocrat was in charge of "the city people of Ch'eng-chou, the vassal lords there, and their deputies." He was charged with judicial authority and could settle litigation by imposing fines.[108] In other words, the Ch'eng-chou region was managed by a high-ranking judicial commission, or a specially empowered judge.

In other cases, individual localities were assigned managers. One location was called *pi* 鄙, literally "suburb." Thus, even a low-level settlement could be defined as an administrative unit.[109]

The San-shih *p'an* 散氏盤 inscription records a dispute between two vassal states about estate boundaries that was settled through negotiation. Those who endorsed the settlement included fifteen officials on

108. Shirakawa Shizuka, *KBTS*, 25:271.
109. Ibid., 26:317, 346; 49:252.

one side and ten on the other. Some of these officials bore titles, others carried the names of the places they managed. Still others bore both titles of agencies and place-names of the local administrations in which they had specific tasks.[110] Thus, bureaucratic machinery at the level of local communities was already in place during the late Chou reigns.

It must not be coincidental that titles of the officer in charge of specific functions of the Five Cities and of those in charge of administrative responsibilities in local communities such as *pi* and of others all emerged during the late Western Chou. Such a phenomenon demonstrates the general trend toward greater bureaucratization.

SOME CHARACTERISTICS OF THE CHOU GOVERNMENT

The development of the Chou governmental system was characterized first by differentiation in accordance with the division of labor, second by bureaucratization leading to an increase in size of the government, and third by the institutionalization of royal authority and hierarchy. These changes were demonstrated above in the changes we noted in the grouping and naming of archivists and secretaries, that is, the *tso-ts'e* and the *shih* historiographers. Among the military, a parallel division of personnel developed. Some manner of military autonomy was maintained, for the army had its own fields and other resources. The aristocrats in the Ch'un-ch'iu period overlapped in both civilian and military roles, but professionalization *per se* did not occur until the Chan-kuo period. The fall of Western Chou probably brought the process of specialization and professionalization to an abrupt end. Changes in the Ch'un-ch'iu and the Chan-kuo, that is, in the Eastern Chou period, began anew rather than being continued from Western Chou. In the same manner, the appearance of local administrations in the late reigns of the Western Chou should not be taken strictly as a change from feudal to bureaucratic organization, for it was not until the Eastern Chou that the change was complete. The momentum that carried the trend toward bureaucratization in the Western Chou royal government probably disappeared altogether after the fall of the Western Chou. Such an interpretation is based on evidence of a rupture in that process of change caused by the fall of the ruling house and thereby the model for bureaucratization.

We should, nevertheless, take note of some other specific features of the Chou governmental system. First, the ruling apparatus was served

110. Ibid., 2:190–99.

by hereditary aristocrats, as the bronze inscriptions repeatedly demonstrate. The most commonly used phrases urge newly appointed officials to follow the good example of their ancestors, whose posts they were given. Both royal ancestry and the ancestry of the recipient recalled old relationships worth duplicating.[111] An alternate directive calls for a promise that the long-standing family tradition be carried on for generations in the future.[112]

A common practice recorded on bronzes was the reappointment of officials at the enthronement of a new king. The new oath acted as confirmation of the important relationship between the throne and the appointee and a reiteration of the earlier contract signed by the previous king.[113] In the *Book of Documents* the chapters "Ku-ming" 顧命 and "K'ang-wang-chih-kao" 康王之誥 describe the enthronement of King K'ang. All the vassals marched in procession to present gifts as a token of their submission to the new master.[114] In a similar ceremony, recorded in a bronze inscription, numerous chiefs are ushered in to have a royal audience at court in the capital.[115] The same ritual of renewal also was held in the households of aristocrats.[116]

In some cases, changes in responsibility are not explained. For instance, a musician was promoted from assistant in charge of small bells to assistant in charge of both small and large bells as well as drums. Yet in both inscriptions the phrase "giving you the posts of your ancestors" is included.[117] It is peculiar that each was thought to follow exactly the same career path as his ancestor. In another case, one military officer was commissioned to command several guard units. Later, another person, either his son or nephew, was also commissioned to command an expanded group including the same unit. Seven identical units were assigned to each man, but the latter had eight additional units under his command. Both inscriptions cite the same person as the exemplary ancestor.[118] Again, it would be quite coincidental if the person cited had thrice held assignments identical to those of his son and grandson. A third case involved a person whose original post was as Grand Diviner, a position held hereditarily. Later he was appointed to serve as a *ssu-t'u* (Minister of the Field) for the eight armies of Ch'eng-chou, and again he

111. Ibid., 28:543.
112. Ibid., 26:328.
113. Ibid., 21:510–11.
114. Legge, *Shoo King*, 544–68.
115. Shirakawa Shizuka, *KBTS*, 10:590: Ch'en Meng-chia, 1955B:111.
116. Shirakawa Shizuka, *KBTS*, 19:364.
117. Ibid., 20:335, 31:770.
118. Ibid., 29:555, 31:702.

was told to succeed his ancestor to this position.[119] All three incidents were recorded in the latest phase of the mid-Chou when flexibility in the procedure of personnel transference was possible.[120] The phrases concerning ancestors' positions probably were included ritualistically, as a formality.

Examination of a person's record of performance, as discussed previously, was an important consideration for promotion. A person named Mien, as the inscription records, was appointed to the post of Minister of Works after the king had "examined his record of performance."[121] Mien lived during the mid-Chou reign of King I. In that period the practice of holding government posts hereditarily began to be revised to allow selective appointments based on performance and qualifications.

In another mid-Chou inscription, an official expresses his gratitude to a ranked minister. Both were present at a ceremony to appoint the former as a supervisor of the affairs of the Five Cities. In fact, that bronze vessel was cast in honor of the minister's presence.[122] The appointment was to a post in the royal court, so the gratitude would customarily have been addressed to the king. This departure suggests that at that date no appointment could be taken for granted and that sponsorship of the minister was the crucial factor. Or perhaps the royal authority was less sure and the minister actually had more voice in determining the appointment.

Second, the bronze inscriptions suggest that for some career bureaucrats, expertise or knowledge was the primary sanction for holding their posts.[123] In the *Book of Documents* the chapter "Chiu-kao" 酒誥 mentioned the *yu* 友 of the *t'ai-shih* (the Grand Historiographers) and the *yu* of the *nei-shih* (Internal Historiographers). The character *yu* was translated as "friend" by James Legge to distinguish it from the two related offices of historiographers, which he called "recorders."[124] In fact, *yu* may be a collective term meaningful only when modified. In a bronze inscription, an official was told to succeed to the position of his father as well as the *yu*.[125] The character *yu* certainly should be read as more than "friend" in this instance; it probably meant "staff."[126] In the Ling *i* 令彝 inscription, Ming-pao 明保, the son of the Duke of Chou, was in charge

---

119. Ibid., 23:115, 148.
120. Hsu, 1966:519–20.
121. Shirakawa Shizuka, *KBTS*, 21:456.
122. Ibid., 33:899.
123. Hsu, 1966:520–21.
124. Legge, *Shoo King*, 410.
125. Shirakawa Shizuka, *KBTS*, 71:517.
126. Liu Chia-ho, 1981:129.

of "the three ministers and the Four Quarters." He traveled to the eastern capital to conduct a major religious ceremony, presumably on behalf of the king. Among the government personnel with whom he had been in contact, there was a group of department staff (ch'ing-shih-liao 卿事寮). After the ceremony, Ming-pao ordered two assistants to take care of "your department and their yu staff." Here the character yu was used to mean the staff (fig. 7.14).[127] Ming-pao had a personal secretariat who assisted him in managing the state affairs. The Ling i was an early Chou bronze and Ming-pao was the son of the Duke of Chou, probably a contemporary of King Ch'eng, and not later than King K'ang. Therefore, even in the early Chou reigns, there were career secretarial staff members in the Chou government.

In another inscription on the P'an-sheng kuei (fig. 7.15), dated later than the Ling i, P'an-sheng claimed to be a top-ranked assistant of the king. He was decreed to supervise the affairs of the royal kinsmen, the various departments (ch'ing-shih) and the t'ai-shih-liao,[128] the staff of the Grand Historiographer or the secretarial staff.

In a later inscription on the Mao-kung ting 毛公鼎, the Duke of Mao is virtually accorded the status of a head of government. Among several responsibilities, the duke is told that both liao of the ch'ing-shih and the t'ai-shih are to serve him.[129] Here, during a mid-Chou reign, two staffs, one for the administrative department and one for the secretarial office, are mentioned. This very likely represents the separation of an "outer" and "inner" court.

The members of the staff were the functionaries of various government agencies and were hardly more than instruments of the higher officials. They were located at the lower echelon of the aristocratic hierarchy. A poem in the Book of Poetry describes the status, the feelings, and the problems of these government functionaries. The verse "Pei-men" 北門 (North gate) reads:

> I go out at the north gate
> With my heart full of sorrows.
> Straitened am I and poor,
> And no one pays attention to my distress.
> So it is!
> Heaven has done it;
> What then shall I say?

127. Shirakawa Shizuka, KBTS, 6:276–303.
128. Ibid., 27:424.
129. Ibid., 30:680

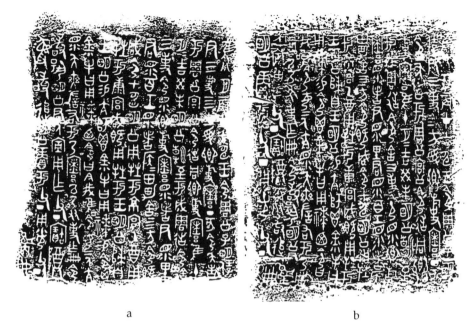

a   b

7.14 Rubbing, in two parts, from inscription from the Ling *i* (from Wong
Yin-wai, 1978:266, 267)

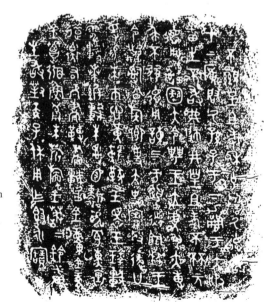

7.15 Inscription from
the P'an-sheng *kuei*
(from Wong Yin-wai,
1978:272)

The King's business comes on me
And the affairs of our government increases measures
When I come home from outside,
The members of my family all reproach me.
So it is!
Heaven has done it;
What then shall I say?

The King's business is thrown on me
And the affairs of our government are left to me more and more
When I come home from outside
The members of my family all thrust at me.
So it is!
Heaven has done it;
What then shall I say?[130]

The narrator here certainly does not have an impressive title. He is impoverished, overburdened with work, and totally helpless, and his lamentation is one of an underpaid clerk. These low-ranked bureaucrats were new members of the court whom the aristocrats of earlier days did not see fit to employ. The appearance of such a staff was an important ingredient in bureaucratization. Differentiation of the one staff into two probably prefigured the stage of development to follow.

The *t'ai-shih-liao* was a position that developed out of the system of "historiographers." These individuals, who came from families with a long tradition as diviners and priests who conducted and arranged religious ceremonies, had sacred knowledge of the names and powers of the deities as well as a background in the history of traditions. They survived the change of dynasties until the late Chou, when some members of them were assigned to activities such as commanding combat units in military campaigns.[131] The early historiographers carried out both religious activities as priests, diviners, and sorcerers and record-keeping functions as recorders and archivists. In either case they were intellectuals, with access to "knowledge." The intellectuals who had worked in the Shang court were employed by the Chou to continue their services. Shirakawa Shizuka probably was correct to suggest that many of the Chou "historiographers" were descendants of the Shang intellectuals.[132] One such eminent case was the family of Shih Ch'iang whose genealogy was cited above. The "historiographers" and other literates were the backbone of the government staff. In the case where

130. Legge, *She King*, 65–67. Translation slightly revised.
131. *Kuo-yü*, 18/1–2.
132. Shirakawa Shizuka, 1973:3–68.

the historiographer was asked to lead the military, the sacred tradition must have given way to a secularized bureaucratization after the mid-Chou. Therefore, even the hereditary diviner was commissioned to be in charge of land held by the army.[133] Along with the elevation of power of the inner court came the growth in influence of the *nei-shih* (Internal Historiographers) and the literate bureaucrats. In the *Book of Poetry*, Ch'eng-po 程伯 was regarded as a descendant of a diviner's family. He first served as a *yin-shih*, the chief secretary of the inner court, and then was ordered to supervise the royal army in a major campaign.[134]

Third, there was a general tendency toward institutionalization in the Chou government itself. Although that process was never completed, many bronze inscriptions list all the individual responsibilities of a new appointee. Some were standing jurisdictions, some seemed to be temporarily assigned tasks. Even though the post was hereditary, the inscription would reiterate the list, a fact suggesting that the government apparatus was not yet routinized. There were regular departments or ministries in the Chou government, such as the "Three Ministries," which reflected application of the principle of division of labor. Nevertheless, the appointed person may have been assigned additional tasks totally unrelated to the official title. In other words, the assignment of responsibilities was individualized rather than departmentalized. Since the principle of inheritance of positions was still observed in the Chou government, these individualized assignments represented a government bureaucracy not fully institutionalized.

In the Mao-kung *ting* inscription the king writes of "our household" and "our state,"[135] simultaneously mentioning the royal household and state. Another inscription lists two persons who concurrently held the title of *tsai* (chief steward). The king told them to manage "the exterior and the interior of the royal household" and that one of these two had to receive instructions from and report to the queen. He was also expected then to supervise her personnel.[136] This particular inscription is dated in the mid-Chou, somewhat earlier than the Mao-kung *ting*.[137] In other words, by the middle Chou the royal household was divided into private and public sections. In the late reigns the Chou people tried to make a distinction between the private aspects of the royal household and the public sector of the government.

As Ch'en Meng-chia suggested, the differentiation within the secre-

133. Ibid., *KBTS*, 23:115, 148.
134. Legge, *She King*, 18/2.
135. Shirakawa Shizuka, *KBTS*, 30:680.
136. Ibid., 23:101–07.
137. Kuo Mo-jo, 1957:103.

tarial staff and the emergence of an inner court symbolized the growth of the king's power.[138] In the Ling *i* inscription, Ming-pao is given the position of *ch'ing-shih-liao* and authorized to care for the three divisions making up the executive branch of the government.[139] The departments were part of the outer court, in contrast to the inner court, which was the personal secretariat of the king. The fact that the tendency to divide repeatedly asserted itself throughout Chinese history shows that the institutionalization did not take place all at one time in the Chou.

CONCLUSIONS

In the early days of Western Chou, several important leaders, the Duke of Chou, the Duke of Shao, Ming-pao, and others, occupied influential posts in the Chou ruling group, and usually bearing impressive titles such as Grand Guardian, Grand Protector, and the like. Early Chou documents such as the *Book of Documents* describe a relatively simple dualism: the royal domain as opposed to the vassal state. By the time of Ming-pao the Chou royal government had become more complex. There were department heads and staffs who belonged to the executive branches, the vassals of the Four Quarters, the royal secretariat of the *t'ai-shih-liao*.

Until the mid-Chou, the tradition allowing inheritance of office gave the Chou aristocracy opportunities to share power and privileges. However, the bureaucratization procedure grew more and more complicated and dispersed the literate to all branches of the government. Those people were bureaucrats whose forebears had performed functions held sacred, as diviners, priests, recorders, and historiographers. Thus started a process of institutionalization of government structure, which shook the foundation of the practice of inheritance of office. By the mid-Chou, division of the royal household and the government was accomplished, and each was served by a separate staff. Meanwhile, the inner court gained influence by having some of the former secretaries moved to prominent jobs, such as commanders in the army.

A verse probably composed in the late Western Chou tells of influential personalities who were dominated by those who were originally the stewards of the royal household.[140] This was not simply a primitive or unique circumstance, for it occurred after the separation of private and public sectors of the Chou ruling apparatus was complete. The re-

138. Ch'en Meng-chia, 1957:147–49.
139. Shirakawa Shizuka, *KBTS*, 6:276–303.
140. Legge, *She King*, 322.

emergence of these persons of the royal household in prominent positions can only be taken as a sign of the rise in power of the inner court.
It, in turn, signaled the gradual displacement of aristocratic government
by a monarchy. The exile of King Li was probably the result of conflict
between a strong king and his nobles. It was also the last performance of
the aristocratic government. Without a stable mechanism formed by
some degree of institutionalization, the Chou aristocrats probably could
not have maintained the Chou rule for a considerable length of time,
nor could the royal line have been restored without it.

8　The End of Western Chou

The great vigor that the process of feudalization engendered in the early reigns of the dynasty was lost in the last several reigns. The Jung 戎 nomads continued to challenge Chou control in the north and northwest, and Chou expansion to the south was met by rebellion. The center of gravity of Chou power shifted from the Wei homeland to the eastern capital at Ch'eng-chou. Continued territorialization increased the sense of autonomy among states, until finally Chou central authority was challenged. The diminished ability of Chou leaders to rule efficiently was exacerbated by the continued rearrangement of populations and the ever-increasing numbers of state officials.

Although social mobility was possible in the somewhat fluid society, it also signaled a decline in central control and an increasingly unpredictable social order. Natural calamities, in the form of drought and famine, earthquakes, and eclipses of the sun, seriously damaged the Chou's ability to care for and feed themselves. Poems that record the demise of the Western Chou court are sorrowful, lamenting the loss of prosperity, good fortune, and the blessing of Heaven.

CHALLENGE BY ALIENS IN WESTERN CHOU

The Chou were served by an institutionalized government, one that allowed them to survive the crisis of the exile of King Li 厲. The return of King Hsüan 宣 to the royal throne temporarily restored royal authority. The stability of this Indian summer was brief, however, for during the generation of Hsüan's son, King Yu 幽, barbarian invasions ended the Western Chou. The last two reigns were characterized by insecurity and change caused by challenges from outside. The *Kuo-yü* 國語, the *Shih-chi* 史記, and the *Hou-Han-shu* 後漢書 suggest that there was a seesawing pattern of dominance between the Chou and the nomads along the northern and the western borders even during the reign of King Hsüan. The ancestors of the dynastic Ch'in 秦 were commanders of the frontier defensive unit for the Chou, and they fought and fended off the western Jung 戎 people. At the same time, however, the Chou lost on the northern front. Even though the army of the vassal state Ch'in defeated the Jung on the Fen 汾 River, the Jung managed to capture Ch'iang 羌 cities which had belonged to the Chou. King Hsüan was victorious over the Shen Jung 申戎, but lost to the Chiang Jung 姜戎 in another battle.[1] Two verses in the *Book of Poetry* proclaim the merits of Yin Chi-fu 尹吉甫 and Nan-chung 南仲, defenders of the Chou territory against the invading Hsien-yün 玁狁 nomads. Battles were fought in the plateau region, and the Chou fortified the northern frontier.[2] Clearly the borders were under constant threat and surveillance. References to the reign of King Yu record several instances of trouble with the Jung. In one case, a leading warrior of the Ch'in garrison troops on the western front was killed in action while another was captured by the enemy as the Ch'in fought the Jung.[3] Finally an allied force of several groups of the Jung invaded the capital district and King Yu was killed.

The dramatic story of Yu's death and the fall of Chou is worth recounting to show how the historians accounted for the demise of Western Chou. In the second year of King Yu's reign, an earthquake hit the capital district. That was taken as an omen that the dynasty had reached its end. In his third year, the king took into his harem a beautiful women named Pao-ssu 褒姒, who was said in legend to be the incarnation of an evil spirit from an ancient time. To the couple, prince Po-fu 伯服 was born, and subsequently the king made Pao-ssu his queen and Po-fu his heir apparent. He dismissed the former queen and her son I-chiu 宜臼, the previous designate for the crown. The former queen's brother, the Marquis of Shen 申, was a Chou vassal near the royal capital, where he was in constant contact with the Jung people in defense of the royal domain. He naturally was enraged when his sister lost her position as royal consort. As the legend goes, Pao-ssu had not laughed since entering the harem and the king had exhausted every possible means to please her, but still she did not smile. Once, the story said, the king signaled an alarm by raising beacon fires and sounding the big drum. The vassal lords, including the Marquis of Shen, hurried in to defend the royal domain. To their surprise, there was no enemy presence, but simply the laughing Pao-ssu. In order to entertain her again, the king repeated the alarm. Of course, no vassal lords came. Moreover, King Yu had entrusted a minister named Kuo Shih-fu 虢石父 to raise revenues for the royal coffers. The Chou people considered the request to be motivated by greed. The Marquis of Shen then allied himself with Ch'üan-jung 犬戎 and other foreign forces and attacked the royal capital.

1. *Kuo-yü*, 1/8; *Shih-chi*, 4/59, 5/10; *Hou-Han-shu*, 87/3.
2. Legge, *She King* 261–64, 281–84.
3. *Shih-chi*, 5/10; *Hou-Han-shu*, 87/3.

8.1 Bronze inscription from
the reign of King Hsüan
(from *KBTS*, 32:787)

When the beacon fire was raised, no one came to rescue the king. The king was killed; Pao-ssu was captured; the city was looted; and the Western Chou period was concluded. I-chiu, the former heir-apparent, left the Chou homeland to re-establish a court at Ch'eng-chou 成周, the eastern capital. He was known as King P'ing 平 and reigned over only the eastern portion of the royal domain, which became known in history as the Eastern Chou.[4]

The account of the end of a kingdom belongs in the same category as stories of intrigue such as the story of Cleopatra in which the vulnerability of men to beautiful women is recounted. The naive and simple account of the fall of Chou did, however, record the central role of barbarians in their final demise.

Information drawn from bronze inscriptions substantiates the existence of such threats from alien groups. Three bronze vessels bear accounts of two battles between the Chou forces and the Hsien-yün 玁狁 people, one in the fifth year and another in the twelfth year, both probably in the reign of King Hsüan. In the battle of the fifth year an officer, Hsi-chia 兮甲, who had followed the king into the campaign was rewarded with four horses and a chariot for his merit in combat.[5] (See fig. 8.1.) In the battle of the twelfth year a ranking aristocrat, Kuo chi-tzu 虢季子, led troops to fight the Hsien-yün in a river valley close to the capital itself. He achieved victory by killing five hundred and capturing fifty. Because of his merit, the king bestowed upon him horses and ritualistic weapons such as bows, arrows, and war axes.[6] (See fig. 8.2.) The third inscription lists a citation given by Kuo Chi-tzu to one of his

4. *Kuo-yü*, 1/10; *Shih-chi*, 4/62–65.
5. Shirakawa Shizuka, *KBTS* 33:787.
6. Ibid., 32:802–04.

8.2 Bronze inscription recording the bestowal of horses and weapons (from *KBTS*, 32:802)

subordinate officers. He rewarded him with gifts including weapons, five households of servants, and ten fields. The officer achieved distinction by pursuing the enemy to the west and by capturing some of them.[7] In all cases, the threat to the royal domain is recorded.

These three inscriptions coincide with the incidents narrated in several verses in the *Book of Poetry*.[8] Both literary and epigraphic sources record two battles between the Chou and the Hsien-yün during the reign of King Hsüan, but the account in the *Book of Poetry* is embellished with more detail. The first battle took place in the fifth year and lasted from spring to winter. Yin Chi-fu led the main troop battalion; which included officer Hsi-chia and Nan-chung 南仲, who commanded a support force along the plateaus north of the capital in the Wei Valley. This area must have been near the great arch of the Yellow River, where fortresses were built to strengthen the defense line. The second battle took place in the eleventh year. The battleground was on the northwest front, along the Lo Valley. The commanding general there was Fang-shu 方叔 whose unit included three thousand war chariots, a very large number. Kuo Chi-tzu, mentioned in the bronze inscription above, was one of his divisional commanders. At the beginning of the twelfth year, Kuo Chi-tzu received a royal reward, and one year later, in the ninth month, he

7. Ibid., 817–29.
8. Legge, *She King*, 258–68, 281–88.

bestowed gifts upon his subordinates. In the second battle, the southern, non-Chou state of Ch'u 楚 was somehow involved, although no details are mentioned.[9] These Chou campaigns were defensive rather than offensive expeditions. The battlegrounds in both cases, were places fairly near the Wei 渭 Valley, where the Chou capital was located. The effort to build fortifications along the northern front indicated a desire to hold the line between farming land and the steppe to the north.[10]

THE CHOU IN THE SOUTHEAST

In contrast to the policy of defense in the north and the northwest, the Chou took an aggressive stance in the south and southeast. During the middle Chou reigns, as discussed in chapter 6, the Chou had expanded far into the south. In the reigns of kings Li and Hsüan, according to Fu Ssu-nien 傅斯年, the Chou had established states between the Yellow and the Yangtze rivers. The state of Shen 申 (map 2) was established in the southwest corner of the present province of Honan and served as the link between the southern states and the royal domain in the Wei Valley. These southern states flourished especially after the Chou homeland was lost, and they became new cultural centers of the Eastern Chou.[11]

The Huai and the Han valleys lying to the south of the central plains dominated by Ch'eng-chou had been under Chou control even during the mid-Chou reigns. During the reign of King Li, there was a major war between the Chou and these subjugated southerners. The Chou troops were led by the Marquis of O 鄂, a long-time Chou vassal who had hosted the Chou king during a royal tour in the south.[12] A marriage between the house of O and the royal house was recorded.[13] Later the same Marquis of O led a rebellion against Chou domination. Because the whole southern and eastern region was involved, the royal court mobilized six western divisions and eight Yin divisions just to suppress the rebellion. The instructions issued to the field commanders were harsh: "leave neither aged nor infant spared." One person in whose name a bronze commemorative vessel was cast led a detachment of one hundred war chariots, two hundred warriors, and one thousand combat soldiers. The total size of the forces was, of course, much larger, for the

9. Shirakawa Shizuka, *KBTS*, 32:834ff.
10. Wang Kuo-wei, 1959:595–99.
11. Fu Ssu-nien, 1952: vol. 2:34–38; Ting Shan, 1930A; Ch'ü Wan-li, 1971.
12. Shirakawa Shizuka, *KBTS*, 25:261–64.
13. Ibid., 263; Kuo Mo-jo, 1957:107.

battle line stretched across the entire southern part of the present province of Honan. Finally, the Marquis of O was captured and the rebellion was put down.[14] (See fig. 7.10.)

This particular rebellion is thought to have motivated the Chou to establish other vassal states near the state of Shen.[15] (Map 2) For instance, a person named Kuo Chung 虢仲 is cited as having fought the southern Huai people both in a bronze inscription and in the *Hou-Han-shu*.[16] Mention of southern expeditions in the *Book of Poetry* indicates that Chou generals such as Shao Hu 召虎 were extremely active in bringing non-Chou people into Chou domination during the reign of King Hsüan. The regions affected were the valleys of the Han 漢 and the Huai 淮 rivers from west of Honan to the coastal plain of southern Shantung 山東 and Kiangsu 江蘇 provinces.[17] The people who inhabited the vast land in the south bore many different names.

These southern people did not accept Chou domination passively. Not only was there a massive rebellion led by the Marquis of O, probably in the reign of King Li, the neighborhood of Ch'eng-chou as far as the I 伊 River Valley was also invaded. According to one bronze inscription, the southern Huai attacked at the time of a royal visit at Ch'eng-chou. Obviously they had reached the capital. On another, an officer was rewarded lavishly for his victory and the captives were presented to the shrine of royal ancestors.[18] Yang Shu-ta 楊樹達 correctly located the affected territory in the hilly areas of western Honan, near the axial route that linked the two Chou capitals.[19] It is no wonder, therefore, that a modest victory gained by the defensive force could have motivated the Chou king to celebrate it in the manner usually reserved for triumph in a major war.

Not only was the yoke imposed upon the conquered truly heavy, but the Chou conquerors executed their demands with brutal assurance. For instance, the subjugated Huai people bore the burden of regular submission of tribute to the Chou court. Special treasuries were established in Ch'eng-chou to store the staples collected from the Huai. An official was charged with supervising such treasures and demanded that the Huai people, called "our old tributary," serve as well as send their materials. Those who failed to do so were to be punished[20] (fig. 8.3). A special

14. Shirakawa Shizuka, *KBTS*, 27:450–56.
15. Hsü Chung-shu, 1959.
16. Shirakawa Shizuka, *KBTS*, 25:276.
17. Legge, *She King*, 551–58.
18. Shirakawa Shizuka, *KBTS*, 27:471–77.
19. Yang Shu-ta, 1959:25.
20. Shirakawa Shizuka, *KBTS*, 32:790–96.

8.3 Bronze
inscriptions
recording tribute
from the Huai
(from *KBTS*,
24:195)

division of garrisoned troops was ordered to take action against the Huai
and to demand that they yield their leaders, service, livestock, and
metals.[21]

COMPARISON OF THE TWO CAPITALS

The establishment of the new capital at Ch'eng-chou was intended to
control the non-Chou peoples in the central plain while the home base
of the Chou continued to be located in the royal domain of the Wei
Valley. Repeated aggression in the south and southeast throughout the
entire Western Chou period increased the importance of Ch'eng-chou,
for it served as the center for all south-bound compaigns. Wei T'ing-
sheng 衛挺生 speculated that the royal court actually moved to the
eastern capital because so many royal activities, including the dispatch-

21. Ibid., 29:601–09.

ing of troops and holding of investiture ceremonies, were recorded in Ch'eng-chou.[22] Even though the eastern capital was used for certain of these events, the official move did not take place until later.

The treasures stored at Ch'eng-chou were collected from the east and the south, making the center both valuable and vulnerable. One bronze inscription lists a particular person named Sung 頌 who was in charge of twenty such treasuries of newly collected tributes.[23] The eight military divisions commonly mentioned in bronze inscriptions were obviously a standing army regularly stationed at Ch'eng-chou. With both stored materials and standing troops readily available, it is understandable that the royal court, and even the king, who frequently visited Ch'eng-chou, used Ch'eng-chou as a base of operations for the east and the south.

On the other hand, conditions in the old Chou homeland in the Wei Valley were unstable, as nomads on the west and north constantly pressed into their territory. The Chou defense, notwithstanding the claims of victory in the bronze inscription, did not seem successful at all. Fortresses were built to maintain permanent defense, but battles often took place in the capital district itself. The story of King Yu raising a beacon to please his lover betrayed the fact that even the capital could be affected by threat of invasion.

The Chou had to gather additional armed forces to protect their homeland. Some eastern vassals were probably called upon to send in their combat units at a time of emergency. The ancestors of the ducal house of Ch'in, for instance, were officers of troops originally brought in from the east. Their surname, Ying 嬴, was one that belonged to an ancient coastal nation still independent during the Shang. When the Ying first appeared in Chou history the Ch'in ancestors were in charge of raising horses for the Chou royal court in the upper Wei Valley. For generations the Ying maintained matrimonial ties with the Jung nomads just as the Shen dukes had done. During the reign of King Li, the Jung attacked the Ying and almost extinguished them. Those surviving Ying members were armed by the Chou to fight the Jung during the reign of King Hsüan. Even so, the Ying continued to cross-marry with Jung chieftains' households in the Ch'i-shan 歧山 region. After the tragic ending of the Western Chou, the Ying fought alongside the Chou and escorted the future King P'ing to safety. They were then given the status of a royal vassaldom in the Wei Valley. This area was gradually re-covered by the Ch'in to form a new state on the ruins of the homeland of the Chou.[24]

22. Wei T'ing-sheng, 1970.
23. Shirakawa Shizuka, *KBTS*, 24:158−61.
24. *Shih-chi*, 5/12.

8.4 Inscription on the San-shih *p'an* (from *KBTS*, 29:616)

Thus well before the downfall of the Western Chou, the western territories were inhabited by non-Chinese and others whose allegiance to the Chou was unpredictable. The ancestors of Ch'in and the ducal household of Shen, related through marriage both to the Ch'in and the Chou royal house, had regularly established connections with the Jung people. Such marital ties between the Chou and the Jung people helped at times to maintain peace. On the other hand, Jung jointly attacked the capital and killed King Yu. By the reign of King P'ing, nomadic groups were dispersed widely through the entire Western domain from the upper valleys of the Ching 涇 and the Wei 渭 rivers east to the I-lo 伊洛 Valley.[25] (Map 2) The wide distribution of the non-Chinese pastoralist groups in China at the beginning of the Eastern Chou period confirms their deep penetration into the royal domain during the Western Chou period.

The history of the state of Tse 夨 illustrates this change in distribution of peoples in the western region. Tse was a non-Chou state located near the capital neighboring the state of San 散 (map 2). The San *p'an* 散盤 inscription (fig. 8.4) mentions a border dispute between San and Tse before their final settlement. Vassals who were subordinates of Tse were listed, for they occupied a wide area stretching to the west of the royal domain. Tse originally was located in the upper valley of the Ch'ien River 汧 and the region of the Lung 隴 Mountains, a few hundred miles northwest of the Chou royal domain. As the chief of Tse used the title

25. *Hou-Han-shu*, 87/3.

"king," we must assume that the state was not a part of the Chou feudal system at all. By the late Chou, however, Tse had established itself in the area juxtaposed to the capital.[26]

In addition, non-Chou people from the east were brought directly into the capital region. For generations the Ch'in group had dealt with the Jung either in war or in peace. The name of Ch'in does appear in the bronze inscriptions, describing an ethnic combat unit made up of I 夷 people, a name used collectively to designate non-Chinese, ethnic people from the east. One bronze inscription lists five I units while another inscription lists eight. Among them were the Ch'in, also named "the Ch'in garrison," and the "surrendered people and the subjugated I." All these ethnic groups were combat units assigned to the garrison commander at the capital, who also commanded the Tiger Guards and the "city-people."[27] A number of I soldiers, including the newly surrendered and subjugated, were brought to defend the capital. Their presence, or the necessity of their presence, must reflect the urgency felt by Chou royal court to strengthen their guard against the intruding Jung peoples. The dilemma, however, was that the limited resources in the Chou homeland had to defend against the intruders pressing in from the west and the ethnic units brought in from the east.

The difficulty faced by the Chou royal court was reflected in the San-shih p'an inscription, one of the longest epigraphs of the Western Chou period. The San-shih p'an inscription records an agreement on the boundary between the domains of two aristocrats, the Lord of San and the King of Tse. San and Tse were located to the south of the Wei River next to the capital. Initially, San was invaded by the Tse, but the Tse were soon defeated and San annexed land from them. New borders were drawn, and the fields and settlements to be annexed were handed over to San officials. All ten officials from the San and fifteen of their Tse counterparts swore to honor the agreement, which was to be kept in the royal archives as a permanent record. Ironically, Tse was not even part of the Chou feudal system.[28]

Wang Kuo-wei suggested that by the reign of King Li these two states had actually overtaken several Chou vassaldoms in the area immediately to the south of the Chou capital district. The people who occupied high posts in the Chou royal court also participated in the ceremony that settled the boundaries of the state of San; they appear to have been San officials. At the same time, the non-Chou state of Tse proclaimed a royal

26. Huang Sheng-chang, 1983:302–03; Wang Kuo-wei, 1968:2023–44; Shirakawa Shizuka, KBTS, 24:193–203.

27. Shirakawa Shizuka, KBTS, 29:555, 31:702.

28. Ibid., 24:193–203; Huang Sheng-chang, 1983:300–04.

title for themselves. In fact, after the reign of King Li the Chou court was so preoccupied with the problem of encroachment of the Jung and Hsien-yün peoples from the north that the vassaldoms in the southern valleys took the opportunity to expand on their own behalf and to struggle for supremacy over others.[29]

In summary, because of successful conquests in eastern China, Ch'eng-chou gained great significance as a new center. By contrast, the Chou homeland in the western sector of the royal domain in the Wei Valley was weakened and even exhausted by the intrusion of non-Chinese nomads and the burden of sustaining large defense troops. The heyday of the western domain was gone; the center of gravity had shifted to Ch'eng-chou and the east.

CHANGES IN CHOU FEUDALISM

Chou feudalism consisted essentially of a rearrangement of population of the Chou and various non-Chou groups. The Chou vassaldoms were mainly units in which people were combined to shape new, hetero-geneous entities that in turn formed the Chinese or Hua-Hsia nation. In this feudal system, states could migrate from one locality to an-other, and territoriality was of minor concern. Such a feudal system resembled a state established through military colonization.[30]

Study of the etymology of the word *kuo* 國 suggests a parallel to the development of the Chou state and nation. The original use of the word was to signify a fortified stronghold. In the *Tso-chuan* 左傳 chronicle, an interesting passage regarding the use of the term *kuo* in early Eastern Chou is included. In 718 B.C. the army of Cheng had already entered the external enclosure of the Sung capital. The Duke of Lu 魯, preparing to send aid to the Sung 宋, asked the Sung envoy how far the invaders had reached. The envoy replied, "They had not entered the *kuo*," so the Duke of Lu did not take action.[31] The duke understood *kuo* to mean the territory of the state of Sung, while the envoy defined *kuo* as the internal quarters of the capital. Based on this passage, a classical Ch'ing 清 scholar proposed that the term *kuo* defined three entities: (1) the capital, (2) the capital and its vicinity, and (3) the state, especially a vassal state of Chou.[32] Such definition may represent the process of

29. Wang Kuo-wei, 1968:2023–44.
30. Tu Cheng-sheng, 1979A:22–31.
31. Legge, *Ch'un-Ts'ew*, 19–20.
32. Chiao Hsün, 1888:1/13–14.

formation of a Chou vassaldom. A Chou vassal and his assigned forces, a combination of two (the Chou and the Shang) or three (the Chou, the Shang, and some other group) migrated to a designated area. They established an enclosed and fortified base from which Chou order was imposed upon the indigenous population. A *kuo* was formed; it was the enclosed city. By and by, the vassal prince, usually called the Duke or the Lord, stretched his rule into areas near the city, sometimes enclosing it with another fortified wall. The vicinity of the capital was guarded by detachments led by descendants or lieutenants of the lord. This constituted the second stage of Chou feudalism and the second definition of *kuo*. Those *kuo* stretched to incorporate satellite cities and territory. Under their control, neighboring vassaldoms and boundaries had to be marked. This extended unit formed a territorial state, which also was called a *kuo*.

In the first stage, the *kuo-jen* 國人 (people of the city, or citizens), included the colonial migrants and their descendants. From the viewpoint of the lord, they were his own men, the "in-group." To the local indigenous population, the *kuo-jen* were the ruling group. The migrants and descendants were called the *chün-tzu* (children of the lord, or gentlemen), while the indigenous natives were the *yeh-jen* (people of the field).

The distinction between the *chün-tzu* and the *yeh-jen* remained pronounced even in the time of Confucius or during the late Ch'un-ch'iu period. Confucius noted that the *yeh-jen* were civilized earlier than the *chün-tzu*.[33] This statement puzzled a great many classical scholars including Legge. His translation of this paragraph was ambiguous because, in his view, the term *yeh-jen* literally meant "wild people," who became "civilized" only after the arrival of the *chün-tzu* (the "gentlemen"). Judging from the etymology of the terms, however, the *yeh-jen* to whom Confucius referred must have been the indigenous population in the state of Lu, or that of the entire eastern plain. They were descendants of older nations that had developed advanced cultures long before the Chou "gentlemen" extended the Shang culture.[34] Moreover, the *kuo* people of the city and the *yeh* of the field had different privileges and obligations.[35] The citizens of a Chou "city-state," namely the *kuo-jen* and the *i-jen* 邑人, enjoyed the right to participate in state affairs[36] such as those involving the *i* 邑 (settlements), or satellites of the

33. Legge, *Confucian Analects*, 237.
34. Hsu,, 1965:158–67.
35. Yang K'uan, 1965:145–65.
36. Tu Cheng-sheng, 1979B:29–65.

main city. Some of them were developed from villages in which the "gentlemen," or *chün-tzu*, overtook the indigenous population.[37]

The Chou vassal state was built on a hierarchical structure. Above it was the Chou royal court. The capital cities of the states were not, however, autonomous as were the city-states of Sumeria, Mesopotamia, or ancient Greece. Below a vassal state were satellite *i* settlements maintained by the sub-enfeoffed great officials and ranked lower than the capital city, not only because of their subordinated position politically, but also because the capital was entitled to have temples for the deceased lords and was thus endowed with the blessings and protection of the ancestral spirits.[38]

In the Ch'un-ch'iu period, a great official might govern several tens or hundreds of *i*, some fairly small ones probably containing only a few households. Some of these *i* were simply villages.[39] Other *i*, however, were large and prosperous and challenged the status of the capital cities. It was commonly thought that a non-capital settlement enclosed by a wall exceeding one hundred battlements constituted a threat to the state security.[40]

In the early Ch'un-ch'iu period, it was common for large non-capital cities to belong to vassal states including Cheng 鄭, Wei 衞, Sung 宋, Lu 魯, Ch'i 齊, Chin 晉, and Ch'in 秦.[41] Typically, as in Cheng, the brother of the Duke of Cheng received a large city as his domain. He demanded that the Cheng people on both the western and northern *pi* 鄙 (border regions) of the state render him their allegiance as they had to the duke. Finally, a showdown took place in 721 B.C., and the Duke won and executed his brother.[42] In another case, three sons of the Duke of Chin were enfeoffed in 665 B.C. with three larger settlements. Later the state fell into a long period of civil war over the problem of succession.[43] In fact, the ducal house of Chin broke away from an enfeoffed ducal scion who had challenged and taken over the whole state after a military coup d'état.[44] These two cases illustrate the process of differentiation within the vassal states early in the Ch'un-ch'iu period.

The process of segmentation into multileveled structures within the vassal states should be regarded as a continuation of Chou feudaliza-

---

37. Yang K'uan, 1965:124–29; Tu Cheng-sheng, 1979B:56–64.
38. Legge, *Ch'un Ts'ew*, 115.
39. Tu Cheng-sheng, 1979B:57–59.
40. Legge, *Ch'un Ts'ew*, 5, 31.
41. *Kuo-yü*, 17:7–8.
42. Legge, *Ch'un Ts'ew*, 5–6.
43. Ibid., 114, 125, 130.
44. *Kuo-yü*, 7/1.

tion. In this case, it was developed through territorialization of garrison stations. As with the "five cities" mentioned in chapter 7, a similar internal differentiation of the royal domain developed in the cities and included specially assigned local officials.[45] Below the level of such cities was the sub-order community that was called *pi*, or border region.[46] During the latest phase of the Western Chou period, the process of Chou feudalization had undergone a change transforming it into a pattern that divided territory. Once the vassal states consolidated the control of exclusive territories, their capacity to secure resources within their territory no doubt was enhanced and their relative independence from the Chou suzerainty was advanced.

The inscription of San *p'an* lists twenty-five participants who were the officials of San and Tse involved in the boundary agreement. Several of these persons have geographical names attached to their titles.[47] These were local officials, such as sheriffs, magistrates, or others, and at least seven localities can be identified. These locations must have been situated along the unstable borders. One place, Mei 眉, appeared twice and was designated as a territory of both states. Thus, Mei was either a place conceded by one state to another, or one divided between parties. It is beyond doubt, however, that Mei was an identifiable entity; likely it was a settlement with its own historical background. Below the level of Mei, there was a settlement named Hsing 邢.[48] Hsing appears at least once referring to a settlement of the Hsing household and its attached fields.[49] The old vassal state of Hsing moved from the Wei Valley to the eastern plain of Hopei Province.[50] The place named Hsing was likely the former domain of the Hsing dukedom. Although there was no more a Hsing domain, the name survived to designate a city or a settlement.[51] On the San *p'an* inscription, at least three levels of administration are designated, that is, the state of San, the city of Mei, and finally the settlement of Hsing. An administrative hierarchy over such a territory is clearly implied in such a case.

Itō correctly pointed out that fields were attached to and identified with a settlement. A bronze inscription records that thirteen settlements and their fields were exchanged between two aristocratic households. The descriptive phrase always used is "the fields of the settlements of

45. Shirakawa Shizuka, *KBTS*, 31:737, 772, 33:899.
46. Ibid., 49:252.
47. Ibid., 24:199.
48. Ibid., 198.
49. Ibid., 28:505.
50. See chapter 4 above.
51. Itō Michiharu, 1975:185–95.

DISTRIBUTION OF WESTERN CHOU CITIES

(FROM PAUL WHEATLY, fig. 13)

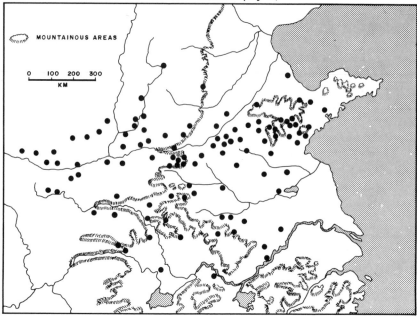

MOUNTAINOUS AREAS

0 100 200 300
KM

5. Distribution of Western Chou cities (from Wheatley, 1971, fig. 13)

. . . ,"[52] indicating that the fields belonged to the settlement where the local administrator or manager resided.[53]

In summary, the entire administrative pyramid in the Chou homeland resembled the structures of Ch'un-ch'iu states discussed above. A multileveled hierarchy prevailed throughout the entire Chou feudal system, and the process of differentiation continuously diffused the vassaldoms. At different levels, the sub-order stretched to create satellites. The dukedoms were the satellites of the Chou center, the fiefs or officials of the dukedom, and the settlements of the cities where such officials resided. The villages included the people of the field, the *yeh-jen*, and they were superseded by the towns of the gentlemen, the *chün-tzu*. The consequence of this structural process was a long-lasting development of urbanization, the momentum of which continued in the Eastern Chou period. Maps showing distribution of urban centers in the Western and the Eastern Chou periods clearly reflect such a pattern as it evolved throughout the dynasty (maps 5, 6, and 7).

52. Shirakawa Shizuka, *KBTS*, 29:615–22.
53. Itō Michiharu, 1975:198–200.

CITIES IN THE CH'UN-CH'IU PERIOD
(FROM PAUL WHEATLY, fig. 14)

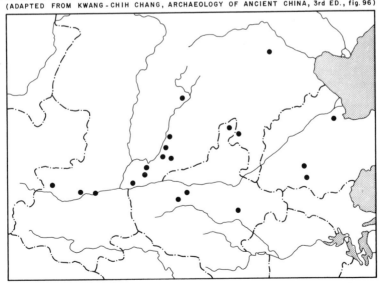

6. Cities in the Ch'un-ch'iu period (from Wheatley, 1971, fig. 14)

ARCHAEOLOGICAL SITES OF EASTERN CHOU CITIES
(ADAPTED FROM KWANG-CHIH CHANG, ARCHAEOLOGY OF ANCIENT CHINA, 3rd ED., fig. 96)

7. Archaeological sites of Eastern Chou cities (from Chang, 1977A, fig. 96, courtesy of Yale University Press)

8.5 Inscription from a K'o family bronze (from *KBTS*, 28:492–93)

In the late Chou the feudal institution no longer realigned population. Rather, both enfeoffment of territory and demarcation of boundaries were important. Two verses in the *Book of Poetry* clearly reflect such an attitude. "Sung-kao" 崧高 repeatedly used the phrases "to make the statutory definition of territory and fields" and "to make the statutory division of the lands in the south" where a new vassal of state was to be established.[54] The emphasis on land was related to revenues derived therefrom. Thus when the earl of the state of Han received confirmation from the royal court, the king decreed, "Making strong his walls, and deep his moats, laying out his fields, regulating his revenues."[55] Although in both verses, some group of people was cited as subjects to be assigned, the emphasis was clearly on the allocation of the territory.

The K'o 克 family produced several bronze vessels with interesting inscriptions that bear information further on this problem. In one inscription, K'o is bestowed both land and people. In another lengthy inscription (fig. 8.5), the king gives him numerous gifts, including ritual items, some groups of people who originally belonged to other households, and a list of domains located in careful detail.[56] The K'o finally

54. Legge, *She King*, 537–40.
55. Ibid., 551.
56. Shirakawa Shizuka, *KBTS*, 28:486, 501–04.

owned a domain stretching from the south of the Wei to its north, an extensive territory near the royal capital district.[57]

The boundaries between territories of neighboring estates were marked by tree-lines named *feng* 封, as well as by natural or man-made markers such as ridges, rivers, or roads. The phrases included in the San *p'an* inscription provide good illustrations. Notwithstanding the clear demarcations, however, border quarrels and raiding took place. The agreement mentioned on the San *p'an* inscription settled one such dispute. One bronze inscription, for instance, records an incident during a famine, in which twenty subjects of one aristocratic household raided the fields of a neighbor's estate and took away a considerable amount of grain.[58]

Exchange of fields commonly occurred, and such transactions were often the topic of inscriptions. Transfer of houses of superior quality for thirty pieces of land including a long list of names of localities and descriptions of natural terrain (such as woods, groves, ridges, etc.) has been recorded. Such transactions marked new boundaries, which were recorded with a clause indicating that the deed was kept in the archives.[59] The archives were presumably at the royal court. As the highest-ranked lord, the Chou king was the final owner of all land; a vassal received the right to use the enfeoffed domain from him. Registration of a transaction recognized that the deal was accomplished. Nevertheless, the direct transaction of land between vassals show that the vassals took the discretionary powers to dispose of the land they used. Land was taken as a valuable, if disposable, item representing wealth. Chou feudalism in its early stages established control by the elite over the non-Chou population. In the later days of Western Chou, feudalism became a mechanism to partition the land.

Two recently discovered bronze vessels belonging to the Ch'iu-Wei 裘衛 family reveal a fascinating story about how land could be secured from the older establishment by the social climber (fig. 8.6). The Ch'iu-Wei vessels were cast by a household of rather low social status. The first generation of Wei were probably furriers, or minor functionaries in the royal court in charge of furs (Ch'iu meant "fur"). A ranking aristocrat, an earl, however, lacked the means to provide himself with adequate ritual jade and ornamental furnishings for his chariot so he could attend a ceremony of raising the royal flag. The furrier provided the earl with

57. Wang Kuo-wei, 1959:887–88.
58. Shirakawa Shizuka, *KBTS*, 23:131.
59. Ibid., 20:426–32.

8.6 Rubbing from an inscription on Ch'iu-Wei ho (from *WW*, 1976 [5]:37)

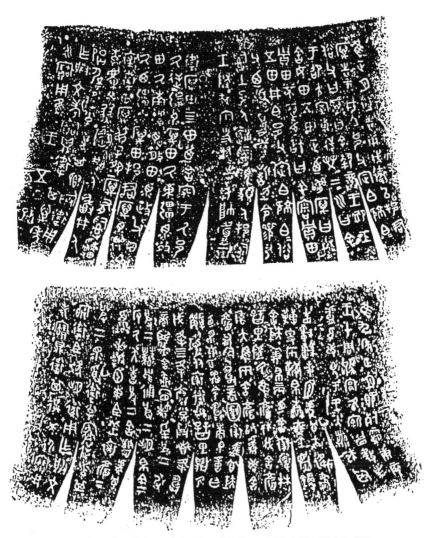

8.7 Inscription from the Ch'iu-Wei *ting* A and B (from *WW*, 1976 [5]:38−39)

such items and in exchange was given thirteen fields. The deal was reported to the three top-level ministers in the court, who verified the intentions of both parties and officially confirmed the bargain.[60] In the sister piece, the inscription mentions another noble who gave Wei five pieces of land (fig. 8.7). Wei reported the transaction again to the high

60. Ibid., *KBHS*, 49:257−59; Ch'i-shan hsien wen-hua-kuan, 1976:27.

ministers in the royal court. The deal was described as a *she* 舍 , "deposition." After verification with the original owner that he did intend to "depose" the land, the officials were instructed to supervise the transfer of land to Wei. Details of the location of such estates were described place by place.[61] The precise meaning of "deposition" was not clear. Some scholars suggest that it meant a lease, others a sale, and still others, an exchange.[62] It could not have meant purchase because the vassals were entitled to an incomplete right to dispose of the land which was entrusted and delegated by the Chou king, the supreme owner of all the land. Leasing to a "tenant" was unlikely, for it would confuse the feudal relationship, essentially a contractual agreement involving delegation of control from an authority. The arrangement mentioned in the above-cited inscription was a transaction de facto, although not a purchase in monetary terms but an exchange.

Acquisition of land by the Chou had declined by the late period of Western Chou. The major moves to establish vassal states took place early in the dynasty. Later, the Chou expansion to the Han-Huai valleys created conditions conducive to another wave of installation of vassal states. By the late Western Chou there was little open land available for establishing new states. The royal domain was especially crowded, due to the arrival of new troops brought in to defend against the nomads and the non-Chou from the north and the west. Thus, some land belonging to certain old aristocrats, such as the land of former estate of the Hsing, was given to new masters. More often, newly powerful or wealthy persons tried to secure land from the old households. Exchange was convenient and legal. In order to receive recognition of such deeds of exchange, the agreement had only to be reported to the royal court with the intention of original landlord verified. The cases cited above, therefore, include phrases about registration in the royal archives. After exchange became a common practice, the royal court apparently could not keep track of all the deals. Therefore, in another Wei family inscription an exchange is recorded in "the ninth year," but no royal investigation is mentioned at all. The previous record took place in "the fifth year," and verification by royal ministers was explicitly included. These vessels of the Wei household belonged to the reign of King Kung. The disparity in involvement of royal court probably reflects a transition in practical custom.

We do not have sufficient sources to investigate carefully what

61. Shirakawa Shizuka, *KBHS*, 49:262–63; Ch'i-shan hsien wen hua-kuan, 1976: 27–28.
62. Lin Kan-ch'üan, 1976; T'ang Lan, 1976B, 1976C; Chou Yüan, 1976; Huang Sheng-chang, 1981B.

happened in the eastern plain, where the bulk of the Chou vassal states were located. Nevertheless, the movement of the Cheng, for instance, from the royal western domain to the east must have involved exchange of land. The new state of Cheng was settled in territory formerly belonging to Kuo 虢 and Kuai 郐 .[63] What the Duke of Cheng paid to the host states is not mentioned at all in documents currently available. In another record, a piece of precious jade was given by the Duke of Cheng to the state of Lu in order to secure some Lu property located near the state of Cheng.[64] Here the arrangement between states was the same as the one mentioned in the inscription on the Wei vessels.

In summary, Chou feudalism went through a process of territorialization in which vassal states gradually extended their control to include a network of cities. There was unclaimed space between neighboring states, so competition was unnecessary. Later, however, such space was gradually claimed by one state or the other. Mutual assistance between the Chou garrison stations scattered across a vast area was transformed into a competition between neighboring landlords. The Chou feudal system, which had functioned as a network of mutual assistance, thus faced serious problems of internal conflict.

Within the royal domain, there was limited land available for regimentation, yet the demand of giving land to new members of the royal court, in every generation, continued. It resulted in the shrinkage of land directly at the disposal of the royal court, thereby continuously decreasing available resources. Meanwhile, the invasion of foreign peoples and the arrival of reinforcements to combat them compounded the problems of defense in the royal court. The exile of King Li and the revival of aristocratic collegiate regency was a political upheaval, one which weakened the Chou feudal system. The late Western Chou was indeed a time of great difficulty, in which any mishap could become a crisis, if not a catastrophe.

THE LAST REIGNS OF CHOU

The reign of King Hsüan allegedly witnessed the restoration of Chou royal authority, but in reality the Chou probably never regained full strength. Alien forces from the north and the west caused serious security problems for the royal court. Chou aggression in the Han-Huai valleys allowed them to collect tributes, which enriched the eastern capital at Ch'eng-chou. The drain on the resources of the Chou population, however, was costly.

63. *Kuo-yü*, 16/1–2.
64. Legge, *Ch'un-Ts'ew*, 35–36.

The *Kuo-yü* records a census planned by King Hsüan after the military loss in the south. His royal adviser, however, argued against it, pointing out that the demographic information could be easily gathered and verified from routine government activities such as large-scale seasonal ceremonies of farming and hunting. He remonstrated that a decrease of population, if revealed in the census, would adversely affect the royal domain. If it were not in top condition, the royal court would not be respected by the vassal states.[65]

This story is extremely revealing about the motivations of King Hsüan and his adviser. The decision to carry out the survey suggests that the king realized that routine government activities could not yield reliable information anymore. The process of bureaucratization taking place in the period preceding King Li's reign probably brought to the complicated government data collected by various government organs that could not fit together easily. If the decrease in population was readily visible to their contemporaries, it would prophesy diminishing central control.

A decrease in population could be caused by either natural calamity or social problems. A decrease of registered population could also be the result of evasion of registration or inefficiency in the system. We do not have sufficient information to assess the extent to which natural calamities contributed to the negative growth of population, but one bronze inscription indicates that displaced population in flight could have been a serious problem. The inscription on the K'o vessel records a gift of both land and people to K'o. Among the population received by him was one group called, "the people of Hsing who fled to the east." Shirakawa Shizuka interpreted this phrase as a reference to the subjugated who belonged to Hsing and who fled en masse.[66] If so, there had to have been massive escape, a capture, and a gift of them to the master. It was plausible that the census conducted in the reign of King Hsüan included such a population not previously registered.[67] Such a speculation, however, cannot be substantiated by currently available evidence.

During the reign of King Yu, the Western Chou collapsed after a series of catastrophes. In the second year of his reign there was a severe earthquake in the royal domain. All at once, the three rivers, the Ching, Wei, and Lo were dry. In the Ch'i-shan Mountains there were landslides.[68] The verse "Shih-yüeh-chih-chiao" 十月之交 in the *Book of Poetry* describes the calamity:

65. *Kuo-yü*, 1/9−10.
66. Shirakawa Shizuka, *KBTS*, 20:507.
67. Li Ya-nung, 1962:743−55.
68. *Kuo-yü*, 1/10.

At the conjunction (of the sun and the moon) in the tenth month
On the first day of the moon which was Hsin-Mao
The Sun was eclipsed,
A thing of very evil omen,
Then the moon became small,
And now the sun became small.
Henceforth the lower people,
Will be in a very deplorable case.

.   .   .   .

Grandly flashes the lightning of the thunder;
There is a want of rest, a want of good.
The streams all bubble up and overflow.
The crags on the hill-tops fall down.
High banks become valleys;
Deep valleys become hills.
Alas for the men of this time!
Why does (the King) not stop these things?[69]

Recently Liu Ch'i-i 劉啟益 suggested that this poem narrated an event that occurred in the reign of Li.[70] The *Kuo-yü* account about the earthquake of King Yu's time, however, records a major catastrophe as well. The text describes how the earthquake blocked the water source and thus rendered the soil unproductive.[71] Such problems could certainly occur in the yellow-earth plateau in the Ching-Wei Valley, for the earth there formed a thick stratum of fine-grained soil through which underground water was brought to the surface through capillary attraction. An earthquake moves and changes the texture of soil and the capillary system, so it would change the distribution of underground water. The millet crops in the Chou period depended solely upon the supply of water drawn from soil and from rainfall, which was rather low in Shensi. Thus, the effects of an earthquake on agriculture would last much longer than a single season. The significance of a crisis from natural calamities such as earthquakes appeared to be even more serious if it was associated with a eclipse of the sun, an inauspicious omen of disaster.

These events occurred simultaneously and created a crisis, perhaps even a feeling of doom. A verse entitled "Yün-han" 雲漢 in the *Book of Poetry* reveals the consequence of ruinous drought.

69. Legge, *She King*, 320–22.
70. Liu Ch'i-i, 1980B.
71. *Kuo-yü*, 1/10.

Bright was that milky way
Shining and revealing in the sky
The King said," Oh!
What crime is chargeable on us now,
Famine comes again and again.
There is no victim I have begrudged;
Our maces and other tokens are exhausted
How is it that I am not heard?

. . . .

The drought is excessive
And I may not try to excuse myself.
I am full of terror and feel the peril,
Like the clap of thunder or its roll.
Of the remnants of Chou among the black-haired people,
There will not be a man left;
Nor will God from His great heaven
Exempt (even) me.
Shall we not mingle our fears together?
(the sacrifices to) my ancestors will be extinguished

. . . .

The drought is excessive;
All is disintegration, the bonds of government are relaxed.
Reduced to extremities are the heads of departments,
Full of distress are my chief ministers,

. . . .

I look up to the great heaven;
Why am I plunged into this sorrow.[72]

The helpless lamentation was probably created by the poet on behalf of the king. The phrase referring to the "remnants" of the Chou people suggests that the piece was written after the fall of the Chou house. Neither an earthquake alone nor the sudden death of King Yu could have created such complete desolation. Sustained hardship, as from a long drought, must have led to such feelings of doom.

In two other verses from the *Book of Poetry*, the complaints are both natural calamities and social disorder. Some of the lines of "Chan-yang" 瞻卬 read:

I look up to great Heaven,
But it shows us no kindness.

72. Legge, *She King*, 527–34.

Very long have we been disquieted,
And these great calamities are sent down (upon us).
There is nothing settled in this country;
Officers and people are in distress.
Through the insects from within and from without,
There is no peace or halt (to our misery).
The web of crime is not addressed,
And there is no peace nor cure (for our state).
Men had their ground and fields,
But you have taken them (now).
Men had their people and followers,
But you have violently taken them from them.
Here is one who ought to be held guiltless,
But you snare him (in the net of crime).
There is one who ought to be held guilty,
But you let him escape (from it).
A wise man builds up the wall (of a city),
But a wise woman overthrows it.
Admirable may be the wise woman,
But she is (no better than) an owl.
A woman with a long tongue
Is (like) a stepping stone to disorder.
(Disorder) does not come down from heaven—
It is produced by the woman
Those from whom come no lessons, no instruction,
Are women and eunuchs.

. . . .

Why is it that Heaven is (thus) reproving (you)?
Why is it that the spirits are not blessing (you)?
You neglect your great barbarian (foes),
And regard me with hatred.
You are heedless of the evil omens (that abound),
And your demeanor is unseemly;
(Good) men are going away,
And the country is sure to go to ruin.[73]

An excerpt of the poem "Shao-min" 召旻 reads:

Compassionate Heaven is arrayed in anger
Heaven is indeed sending down rain,
Afflicting us with famine,

73. Ibid., 559–64.

So that the people are all wandering fugitives;
In the settled regions and on the border all is desolation.
Heaven sends down its web of crime;
Devouring insects weary and confuse men's minds,
Ignorant, oppressive, negligent,
Breeders of confusion, utterly perverse;
These are the men employed to tranquilize our country.
A pool becomes dry;
Is it not because no water comes to it from its banks?
A spring becomes dry,
Is it because no water rises in it from itself?
Great is the injury (all about),
So that my anxious sorrow is increased:
Will not calamity light on my person?
Formerly when the former Kings received their mandates,
There were such ministers as the Duke of Shao,
Who would in a day enlarge the kingdom a hundred *li*.
Now it is contracted in a day a hundred *li*.
Oh! Alas!
Among the men of the present day,
Are there not still some with the old virtue?[74]

Taken together these three poems repeat what must have been prevalent problems: famine caused by drought, injustice and poor administration due to incompetent, easily influenced officials, barbarian encroachment, loss of population to vagrancy, and a general upset of social order. All these problems, of course, were probably present in the reign of King Yu; thus, the dynasty was bound to fall. If foreign assaults alone had caused the death of the Chou king, order could have been restored as soon as a new king ascended to the throne. The most serious problem probably was the disintegration of the Chou feudal structures within the royal domain. The phrases "High banks become valleys; deep valleys become hills" depict not only changes in terrain caused by earthquake but also disturbances that altered the old, established social structure. The vessels of the Ch'iu-Wei households discovered recently reveal that the patrons detested the drastic social mobility taking place in the families of Chü-po 矩伯 and Ch'iu-Wei.

The entire group of vessels were found in a storage pit but were produced by members of a small family over time. Ch'iu-Wei was the first generation to cast vessels; Kung-ch'en 公臣 was the second generation; Lü-po 旅伯, Lü-chung 旅仲, and Chen 侁 were the third generation; while Ch'eng 再 was the last generation. Ch'iu-Wei was a furrier who

---

74. Ibid., 564–67.

lived in later mid-Chou, during the reigns of King Kung and King I. One part of his name, Ch'iu, meant "fur," and many objects made of fur are mentioned in the inscription to describe the products he supplied to others. Furriers occupied a fairly low place in the Chou social hierarchy. Lü-po, his grandson, was a Steward (*shan-fu* 善夫), which by this period could have been a very important position in the government. Lü-po and his brother Lü-chung were contemporaries of King Hsüan. Ch'eng, the great grandson, lived at the time of King Yu. Their surname, as judged from the inscription of wedding vessels, was Ying, which was one division of the ancient nation of the coastal region. It is not, then, coincidental that the ducal house of the Ch'in of a later day was also Ying and that the forebears of the Ch'in people served the Chou court by raising cattle in the Wei Valley and by fighting the nomads along the western front. The Ch'iu-Wei family was probably another branch of the Ying, who were brought to protect the royal domain. They engaged in husbandry and fur production[75] and became a powerful family.

As the chief of a vassal state, Chü-po was a ranking aristocrat of the Chou court. Even though he had a secretariat to serve him, he was so poor that he had to ask for a loan from Ch'iu-Wei. On a vessel attributed to Wei and cast to commemorate a ceremony to erect the royal flag, Chü-po gave some fields to Wei in exchange for jades, tiger skins, fur and leather outfits, and chariot furnishings. The total value of the jade pieces was eighty double-strings of cowrie shells, and that of the fur and leather items was twenty double-strings. The payment was not made in cowrie-shells, but by turning over four tracts of land.[76] Two years later, Wei secured four fields near two rivers as a deal with a person named Li, addressed as the chief of a vassal state. Wei turned over five fields in exchange.[77] Four years after that, Wei and Chü-po made another transaction. The king was to receive a state chief and Chü-po must attend the ceremony. Wei supplied Chü-po with a chariot with gold, fur, and leather furnishings. He also gave the wife of Chü-po three pieces of fine silk. Wei in turn was given woods and groves at a particular place. To the officials of that wooded locality and to persons who were entrusted by Chü-po to yield the woods, Wei gave two horses and numerous gifts of fur and leather.[78]

The content of these inscriptions reveals significant information about social interaction in the late Western Chou period. The chief of a vassal state was so impoverished that he had to search for materials necessary to mark his social status. Wei was a low-ranked furrier, but because he

75. Chou Yüan, 1976:45−46.
76. Shirakawa Shizuka, *KBHS*, 49:257−59.
77. Ibid., 28:262−63.
78. Ch'i-shan hsien wen-hua-kuan, 1976:28; Chou Yüan, 1976:48.

was in control of such materials he managed to enrich himself by securing land. The real estate he received included land between rivers, probably ideal pasture fields, and woods and groves that presumably provided him with the possibility of hunting game as well as sheltering domesticated animals. Ch'iu-Wei was so wealthy that he was able to provide the feudal lords with the materials they needed, to give gifts to the functionaries and to cast bronze vessels as commemoratives.

A FINAL REMARK

Social change, like metabolism in a biological entity, can engender vitality. Drastic change, however, often causes maladjustment of parts of previously stable systems. The Chou establishment, due to loss of domination, lost their confidence. Those new to power became frustrated because their own aspirations were yet to be fulfilled. Those who could not rise to high-status positions were even more frustrated. The poems of sorrow and lamentation in the *Book of Poetry* were almost all composed in the last period of the Western Chou, and reflect such frustrations. Those in the upper strata of the Chou society developed such a fear of crisis that they shunned it by escaping from the Western Chou domain. One poem reveals that aristocrats moved their wealth to new places, deserting the royal court.[79] The migration of the state of Cheng from the Wei Valley to the eastern plain even before the barbarian invasion reflected such an attitude.[80] Another illustration of the mentality of escape may be found in two stanzas of "Yü-wu-cheng" in which a Chou official cries:

> The honored House of Chou is (nearly) extinguished,
> And there is no means of stopping or setting (the troubles) aright.
> The Heads of the officers have left their places,
> And no one knows my toil.
> The three high ministers, and (others) great officers,
> Are willing (to attend to their duties) early and late.
> The lords of the various states,
> Are willing (to appear at court) morning and evening.
> If indeed he would turn to good,
> But on the contrary he proceeds to (greater) evil.
>
> . . . .
>
> I say to you, "Remove to the royal capital,"
> And you say that you have not a house there.

79. Legge, *She King*, 323–24, Ch'ü Wan-li, 1971:12.
80. *Kuo-yü*, 16/1.

> Painful are my inmost thoughts, and I weep blood;
> Every word I speak makes me hated;
> But when you formerly left to reside elsewhere,
> Who was it that made houses for you?[81]

There were some who did not leave soon enough, and they buried their treasures in haste at the time of great trouble. Several of those Chou treasuries have been rediscovered. One such storage pit was found in 1940, at Fu-feng 扶風; a deep chamber was discovered which contained one hundred or more Chou vessels. They were stored in a well-built pit, not casually thrown there and buried.[82] In 1961, fifty-three vessels made at different times were found in one pit at Chang-chia-p'o 張家坡, Ch'ang-an. They were purposefully stored treasures rather than offerings for a burial site.[83] The Ch'iu-Wei family treasures were found in 1975 at Ch'i-shan; thirty-seven vessels cast by four generations of the family were stored together there.[84] The rich findings of the Wei family consisted of one hundred and three vessels, among which individual objects dated from the reign of Kung to the end of Western Chou. A similar group of vessels was also discovered at Fu-feng.[85]

Indeed there were two major crises in the Western Chou. If such buried treasures were stored at the time of King Li's exile, they ought to have been recovered after order was restored. The vessels hidden away in the reigns of the last Chou kings were not discovered until the present day, suggesting that the owners of these treasures fled their homes in a great hurry and never returned to retrieve their buried wealth. These treasures must have been stowed away in the middle of the great chaos that killed King Yu and sent King P'ing away from the royal domain to the east. As the poet sang with deep sorrow:

> The grief of my heart is extreme,
> And I dwell on (the condition of) our territory
> To meet with the severe anger of Heaven
> From the West to the East,
> There is no quiet place of abiding.[86]

And so it was: the Western Chou had fallen.

81. Legge, *She King*, 326–28.
82. *WWTKTL*, 1951(10):143–44.
83. Kuo Mo-jo, 1961A.
84. Ch'i-shan hsien wen-hua-kuan, 1976A:266.
85. Chou-yüan k'ao-ku-tui, 1978:1.
86. Legge, *She King*, 521.

9   Western Chou Arts and Crafts

Archaeological evidence presently available that is dated to the Western Chou does not provide a complete picture of the entire three-hundred-year period. The excavations have provided, nevertheless, abundant information. The area around Hsi-an 西安 has received sporadic attention, and at least two (Feng 豐 and Hao 鎬) of the five Chou capitals recorded in literature have been identified. Sites along the river Feng, near Hsi-an, have been examined and remains of houses, burials, workshops, and bronze hoards have been recorded. The work of the Chinese archaeologists, especially Tsou Heng 鄒衡, has resulted in a complete typology of ceramic forms, and five main phases of occupation of this area have been delineated.[1] These excavations show that in many aspects, Chou culture retained elements of that of the Shang. Architecture, tomb construction, the use of ritual bronzes and jades in ceremony, and the use of the chariot and halberd in warfare exemplify the continuity. There are, however, notable changes revealed as well, for instance, in organization of palace grounds, in bronze decor, and, to some degree, in the shapes of ritual bronzes. Modifications either in bronze art or in the less sophisticated ceramic industry, for instance, make plain the blending of local traditions with those of the Shang and reveal the eclectic nature of Chou culture. No matter how subtle those adjustments were in the bronzes and other arts, the changes in material culture in the early Chou reflect, presumably, not-so-subtle changes in the social, political, and ritual atmosphere of the period.

The influence of the Western Chou can be followed beyond the main seat of power in Shensi 陝西 and Shansi 山西 to Honan 河南 and Shantung 山東. The walled city discovered near present-day Lo-yang 洛陽 was of military and administrative importance. This site yielded some of the most complete information on early Chou building practices. As far north as Peking, bronzes and a chariot burial have been excavated. In Liaoning 遼寧, metropolitan-style remains lie within what was the state of Yen 燕. To the south, extraordinary bronzes have been excavated at sites along the Yangtze 揚子; at Tan-t'u 丹徒, in

1. Tsou Heng, 1980:304.

Kiangsu 江蘇; at T'un-hsi 屯溪 in Anhui 安徽; at Ch'i-ch'un 圻春 in Hupei 湖北. The remains from the south show that the artisans there knew of northern, metropolitan activities and bronze styles, but their products often diverged from the standards in important ways, suggesting that Chou influence in the south was weaker than in the north.

In all, remains of architecture and material culture of various forms parallel the developments mentioned in other arenas. Continuity from earlier Shang local traditions is evidenced, and some previous practices were merely elaborated or adjusted to meet new standards and needs. The most significant change, that recorded in the *Shu-ching* and elsewhere, was in the focus and direction of the political system. The introduction of the notion of accountability, of the ethical pre-occupation introduced with the Mandate, moved the Chou government (and subsequent ones as well) and other aspects of Chinese life toward a more pragmatic position. This change is manifest in the arts of the Western Chou.

PALACE ARCHITECTURE

Recently two early Chou sites were excavated in Feng-ch'u-ts'un 鳳雛村 in Ch'i-shan 歧山 and at Chao-ch'en-ts'un 召陳村 in Fu-feng 扶風 (maps 1, 4). Both are in an area that the archaeologists call Chou-yüan 周原, or plain of the Chou. At Feng-ch'u the remains of wooden pillars of large buildings yielded material for carbon dating. A date of 1095±90 B.C. is given by the archaeologists, one coeval with the late Shang dynasty. The discovery of late models of pottery *li* 鬲 near the assemblage of large buildings suggests that the area was used continuously throughout the Chou.[2] The capitals built by King Wen 文 and King Wu 武 were, according to tradition, in Feng 豐 and Hao 鎬, much to the east of the Ch'i-shan region near the present city of Hsi-an 西安. The excavated palaces in Ch'i-shan and Fu-feng, therefore, are thought to be centers built by Tan Fu 亶父 or his son, Chi Li 季歷.

Large, elaborate dwellings were built above ground on raised platforms at Feng-ch'u. In the late neolithic, stamped earth, or *hang-t'u* 夯土, was introduced as a basic form of construction. The fine-grained yellow earth, once pounded, created a firm foundation as well as solid walls. The *Book of Poetry* cities the construction of palace buildings in this way: straight lines marked the contour of the foundation, "planks" were used to make frames to be filled with earth and pounded. The noise of hauling handbarrows of earth to the frames and dumping the soil, and the repetitive sound of stamping and pounding, accompanied

2. Chou-yüan k'ao-ku-tui, 1979A:34; Wang En-t'ien, 1981:77–78.

9.1 The site at Feng-ch'u (from WW, 1979; [10]:35)

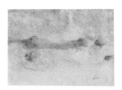

9.2 The site at Feng-ch'u: remains of foundations of houses (from WW, 1979 [10]:36)

the noise of scraping the rough walls in order to smooth the surface. All these activities were regulated by the rhythmic beat of a drum, as they are still in north China today![3]

The remains of large buildings at Feng-ch'u were probably the palaces that the Chou forebears built at Chou-yüan, perhaps the same type of construction that the verse "Mien" 緜 narrated. From the archaeological remains there, the original houses have been reconstructed (figs. 9.1, 9.2).

3. See chapter 2 above; and Legge, She King, 338–39.

The Feng-ch'u assemblage covered an area of 1,469 square meters, and revealed a large and sophisticated building complex. It consisted of a gate, a central passageway, a front yard, a main hall, a corridor divided into rooms, which led to the rear hall, and covered passageways flanking the central space (fig. 9.3). The main hall was built on a stamped-earth platform of 17.2 by 6.1 meters, which faced south and was marked by three rows of steps (fig. 9.4). The rear building was 23 by 31 meters and was reached by a hallway from the main hall. That corridor separated the yard between the main building and the rear hall into two smaller yards. The north wall of the rear hall was connected to the side walls, which stretched around to the front. The entire complex, therefore, was enclosed by a rectangular and continuous four-sided wall. The buildings were placed along a central axis within the wall and were symmetrically arranged. Along both the east and west sides were eight adjoining rooms, each connected by a passageway topped by a roof with eaves. Both the surface of the floor of the entire construction and that of the stamped-earth walls were covered with a layer of plaster. Clay drainage pipes were found underneath the structures, and pebbles served as a surface drainage system near the foundation of the platforms.[4] Based on the location of post holes, imprints of thatching bundles, and fragments of roof tiles, the basic shape of the buildings and their roofs can be reconstructed (fig. 9.5). Some of the structures had single, hipped roofs; the main hall had a double roof and the smaller ones had only one (fig. 9.6). Each roof was covered with thatching and was strengthened at the ridge with a line of clay tiles.

The Feng-ch'u architectural remains confirmed the descriptions of ancient buildings in the classics even to the most minute detail. The whole complex occupied an area of 45.2 meters south-west, and 32.5

4. Chou-yüan k'ao-ku-tui, 1979A:27–32.

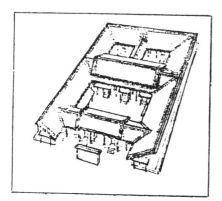 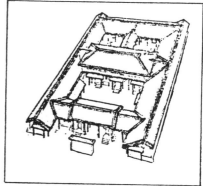

9.3 Feng-ch'u architectural reconstructions (from *WW*, 1981 [3]:72)

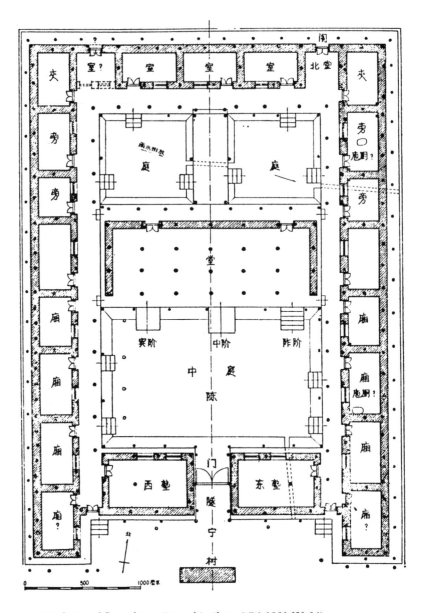

9.4 Rendering of floor plan at Feng-ch'u (from *WW*, 1981 [3]:24)

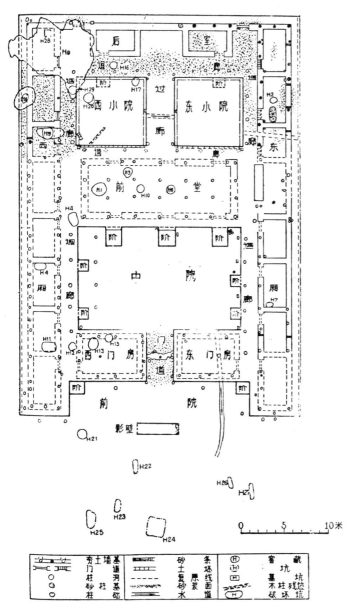

9.5 Alternate rendering of floor plan at Feng-ch'u (from Chou-yüan k'ao-ku-tui, 1979A:29)

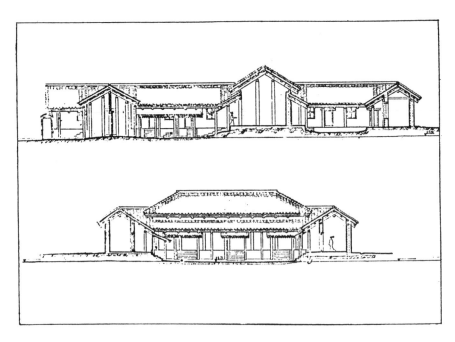

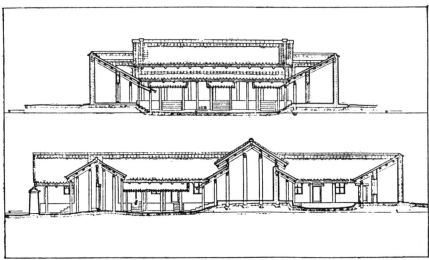

9.6 Reconstructed cross sections of the Feng-ch'u building (from Fu Hsi-nien, 1981A: 68, 71)

meters east-west, and consisted of eleven parts: the shield wall, the entrance, the gate, the vestibule, the central court, the grand hall, the side halls, the inner chamber, the rear gate, the side chambers, and the porch. The open space outside the shield wall stood in front of the entrance on the public square where ordinary people could gather. The courtyard between the front gate and the central grand hall was the location where the investiture ceremonies mentioned in bronze inscriptions took place. Three stairways led from the yard to the central hall, the very center of the entire complex. If the building was a residential palace, the inner chambers were bedrooms and living quarters; if it was an ancestral shrine, these rooms were used for offering food. Two gates located at rear corners were less formal entrances that led to the inner quarters. The side chambers were for officials' use. The main gate was flanked by two tall, supporting pillars and a broad beam that stood at the front of the entrance.[5]

To the east of Cluster A at Feng-ch'u a broad wall, perhaps the exterior wall surrounding the palace-shrine compound, indicates that the eastern section was also part of the complex. To the west of Cluster A was Cluster B; they were separated by a wall. The foundation of the main platform was larger than that of the central hall of Cluster A. No buildings were found, however, on the east and the west sides of the courtyard. In the classics, the main shrine is always located to the east of the residential palace. Cluster A, therefore, must have been the ruins of the ancestral shrine, and Cluster B the remains of the residences of the aristocratic inhabitants of the city. The very large structure most likely was the royal palace. If so, the appearance of Chou oracle bones at the site is explained, for they would have been essential to the royal activities and archives.[6]

Many special methods of building were used at these sites, suggesting that the Chou were concerned with questions of surface engineering durability of construction, and aesthetic form. To meet the problems of erosion and settling of the earthen foundation a drainage system of clay pipes and pebbles was used. Walls were built using the stamped-earth technique, and others were constructed from adobe or sun-dried mud bricks. Marks on the surface of the walls indicate that uneven places were trimmed with a knife, an action described in the *Book of Poetry*.[7] Wide use of plaster was made to cover surfaces of platforms, walls, and the inside and outside of rooftops. The amount of plaster used indicates that lime plaster was probably obtained by burning limestone. Although conventional opinion holds that the ancients obtained lime by burning

5. Wang En-t'ien, 1981:75–77.
6. Yin Sheng-p'ing, 1981:13, 15.
7. *Shih-ching*, 3-1-3; and chapter 2 above.

the shells of shellfish, such a cumbersome practice is unlikely here simply because of the large-scale use of lime plaster. Roofs were covered with tightly pressed thatching bundles, then plastered and reinforced with clay ridge tiles. The walls were decorated with mother-of-pearl inserts using designs taken from jade prototypes. The foundations reveal a four-sided outer wall that enclosed rooms along three of the four sides. These organizational patterns have dominated Chinese building practices for thousands of years.[8] The methods of construction found at Feng-ch'u are in accordance with the descriptions in the classics,[9] and the complex probably reflects the style of architecture of Tan Fu's time.

Excavated artifacts at these sites included thousands of different sorts of objects. Pottery *li* tripods and other clay urns bore cord-marks comparable to known early Chou styles, and some glazed ceramics appeared; bronze pieces included bulbs, arrowheads, and plaques. Residue of copper ore and remains of bronze indicate that bronze casting was done locally. Fine jade and stone artifacts were carved with geometric designs, as were ornaments of mother-of-pearl.[10]

The Feng-ch'u site is located within a larger area of 3 by 5 kilometers square, dotted with Chou sites. Two and a half kilometers away from Feng-ch'u is the Western Chou site of Chao-ch'en. At this large assemblage of ruins were remains of Chou palace-like constructions, ones occupied from the mid-Chou to the late period of the Western Chou (fig. 9.7). Thus, the Chao-ch'en complex was the chronological successor of the Feng-ch'u complex. The Chao-ch'en remains consisted of at least two sets of halls and chambers and one single hall.[11] The single hall, called H-3, was built on a platform standing 70 centimeters above the ground. The house occupied an area of 22 meters east-west and 14 meters north-south with four rows of pillar-bases containing pebbles. The postholes measured about one meter in diameter, indicating very large, tall pillars. The central hall was square, and at its center was an extraordinarily large hole measuring 1.9 meters in diameter. The column that stood in this enormous hole was the central supporting post for the roof. With eight auxiliary columns, a large double-layered roof-structure was supported. This hall probably was the so-called Grand Hall known from bronze inscriptions.[12] (See figs. 9.8–9.13.)

In the Chao-ch'en site were several pebble-paved surfaces near the building remains. The field archaeologists suggested that it was a kind of drainage facility comparable to that at Feng-ch'u. There were a great

8. Fu Hsi-nien, 1981A; Yang Hung-hsün, 1981:23–29.
9. Wang En-t'ien, 1981.
10. Chou-yüan k'ao-ku-tui, 1979A:32–33.
11. Yin Sheng-p'ing, 1981:13.
12. Fu Hsi-nien, 1981B; Yin Sheng-p'ing, 1981:17; Chou-yüan k'ao-ku-tui, 1981A.

9.7 Palace remains
at Chao-ch'en
(from *WW*, 1981/
3:1)

variety of baked tiles found at the site as well, flat ones and semicircular
ones, both of which were held in place with a knob or ring (figs. 9.14,
9.15). Not only were tiles discovered in Chao-ch'en, they were also
found in the Western Chou sites at K'o-sheng-chuang 客省莊 near
Ch'ang-an 長安 , Wang-wan 王灣 near Lo-yang 洛陽 , and Tung-chia-lin
董家林 near Peking. These were normally coiled and fired pieces,
although some unbaked examples were found in K'o-sheng-chuang.
Before the mid-Chou period the roof was generally thatched, and only
the roof ridge and other important sections were covered by tiles. Later
in the Western Chou, the roof was routinely tile-covered.[13] Recently,

13. Chou-yüan k'ao-ku-tui, 1981A; Pei-ching ta-hsüeh, Department of History,
1979:186−87.

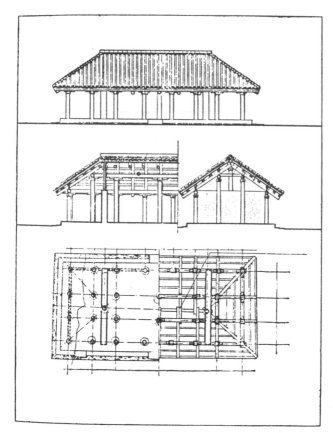

9.8 Reconstruction of Chao-ch'en hall (from *WW*, 1981 [3]:35)

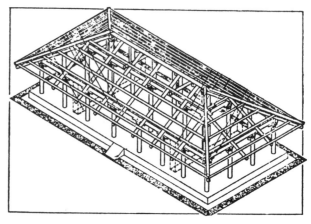

9.9 Reconstruction of Chao-ch'en hall (from *WW*, 1981 [3]:35)

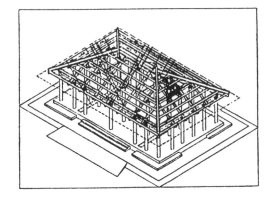

9.10 Reconstruction of Chao-ch'en hall (from *WW*, 1981 [3]:36)

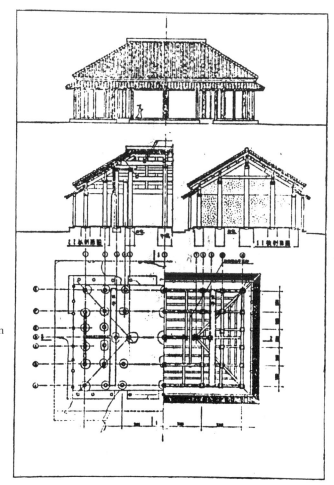

9.11 Reconstruction of Chao-ch'en hall (from *WW*, 1981 [3]:37)

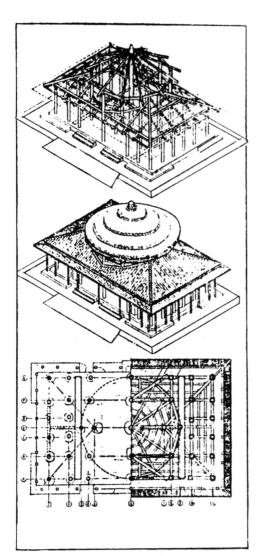

9.12 Reconstruction of
hall at Chao-ch'en (from
WW, 1981 [3]:38)

large baked clay bricks were found for the first time in Western Chou
ruins at Yün-t'ang 雲塘 of Fu-feng. Each brick block measured 36 by 25
by 2.5 centimeters and was fired to a very hard and solid state. On the
back of the brick were four protruding knobs, which would help fix the
bricks into the surface of the stamped-earth wall.[14]

The area between Feng-ch'u and Chao-ch'en is marked by remains of

14. Lo Hsi-chang, 1980.

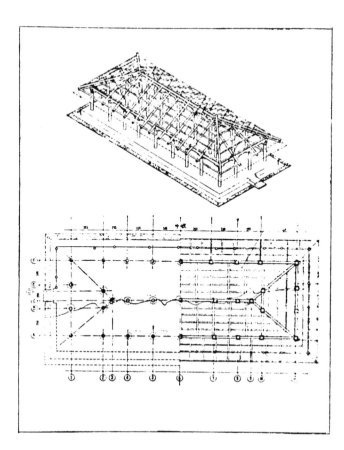

9.13 Reconstruction of Chao-ch'en architecture (from *WW*, 1981 [3]:39)

9.14 Roof tiles from Chao-ch'en (from *WW*, 1981/3:16)

9.15 Roof tiles from
K'o-sheng-chuang (from
K'ao-ku yen-chiu-so,
1962:pl.11)

other buildings: bronze foundries, potting shops, residences of ordinary people, as well as burials of early Western Chou date. The workshops for bone yielded tens of thousands of unworked animal bones. The potters' workshops yielded clay molds, and the bronze shops held large quantities of ores. The district was a large production center, and more than one thousand bronze artifacts were excavated in this small area. Tan Fu, called T'ai Wang 大王 ("Grand King") by the Chou people, must have been the patron of this large center. Even after King Wen moved the capital of Feng farther to the east, the Ch'i-shan settlement retained its importance. Ch'en Meng-chia 陳夢家 even claimed that the name "Chou" in ancient literature and in Chou bronze inscriptions actually referred to this particular city. Ch'i-shan continued to be a Chou city of considerable significance until King P'ing moved the entire Chou court to Lo-yang.[15]

OTHER HOUSING

The *Book of Poetry* describes the homes of the Chou forebears prior to the building of the capital as semi-subterranean pits covered by thatched roofs. In other words, they were typical neolithic dwellings such as those

15. Ch'en Meng-chia, 1955A; Ch'en Ch'üan-fang, 1979:45–49.

in An-yang, where the residences of the average inhabitants were nothing more than such pits. The neolithic levels directly under proto-Chou sites contain comparable evidence. In the Western Chou sites at Chang-chia-p'o 張家坡, fifteen early Chou half underground dwelling pits were found. These were of two kinds, either shallow or deep (figs. 9.16–9.19). Only one shallow pit-dwelling was sufficiently preserved to suggest contemporary living conditions. The modest room measured 2.2 meters by 4.2 meters (fig. 9.20). The depth from the surface level was 1.4 meters, barely reaching the shoulder of an ordinary person. In the center of the room, slightly to the east was found a round posthole in which a pole must have stood to support a circular roof. The walls of the

9.16 Pit-dwelling at Chang-chia-p'o (from K'ao-ku yen-chiu-so, 1962:pl. 36)

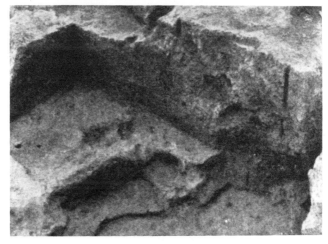

9.17 Pit-dwelling at Chang-chia-p'o (from K'ao-ku yen-chiu-so, 1962:pl. 39)

room and the floor surface were all hardened by fire. In the northwest corner was the sleeping area; on the northern wall, there was a storage niche; near the southern wall was an oval-shaped depression, probably a fireplace. The exit for this room was located on the central section of the northern wall, where a dirt ramp rose to ground level.

At the site were many deep, underground pits. The circular ones measured more than 5 meters in diameter and 2 meters in depth. Oval-shaped rooms had diameters of 7.8 to 9.5 meters, with depths of up to three meters. The oval-shaped residences were several times longer and twice as deep as the shallow pit dwellings and their exit ramps were on the south. A half-circular fireplace was located under the northern wall. The whole oval was divided into two rooms by a sectional wall, which stood a little to the south. An opening of 1.2 meters served as a doorway between the two rooms. There were several even

9.18 Pit-dwelling at Chang-chia-p'o (from K'ao-ku yen-chiu-so, 1962:pl. 19)

deeper pits, either elongated or oval-shaped. The openings were as small as 1.6 by 2.4 meters for the former and 0.7 to 1.05 meters for the latter, while the depth was more than 9 meters. Such pits, too small and too deep to be living quarters, were either wells or storage areas.[16] The foundations of Western Chou residences discovered at Tz'u-hsien 磁縣, in Hopei, were also semi-subterranean. Of the two elongated ones, the larger was 3.98 by 2.47 meters, with a depth of approximately one meter (fig. 9.21). The floor surface was plastered with mud and grass, then hardened by fire. The central posthole and numerous smaller holes around the four walls indicate the position of supports for the roof. A fireplace was dug into the southwest wall. A shallower pit was found

16. K'ao-ku yen-chiu-so, 1962:73–78.

9.19 Pit-dwelling at Chang-chia-p'o (from K'ao-ku yen-chiu-so, 1962:pl. 20)

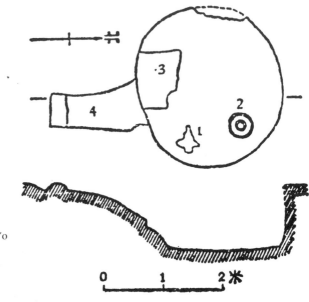

9.20 Chang-chia-p'o dwelling pit (from Pei-ching ta-hsüeh, Department of History, 1979:188)

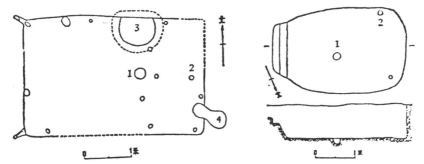

9.21 Dwelling pit at Tz'u-hsien (from Pei-ching ta-hsüeh, Department of History 1979:188)

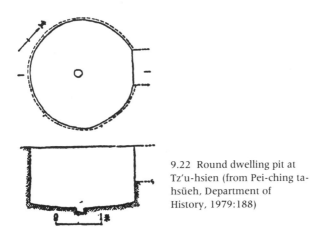

9.22 Round dwelling pit at Tz'u-hsien (from Pei-ching ta-hsüeh, Department of History, 1979:188)

outside, near the northern wall of the residence, and was strewn with stone tools suggesting that it was a storage pit. An irregularly shaped residence measured 3.4 meters in length, 2.13 meters in width, and 0.84 meters in depth. Its floor surface was fire-hardened, and two steps on its east wall allowed access into the house. The center and eight side postholes marked the locations of supports for the roof. In addition, there were three circular pits (fig. 9.22). One had a diameter of 2.5 meters, postholes, and steps. The walls were plastered with fine yellow earth. The remnant of the wall was 1.16 meters high, only part of the original height. A ramp led into an opening in the southern wall and served as an entrance. A fireplace was located near the eastern wall, where an earthen urn was half-buried. It was either a water container or a food vessel.[17]

Residential remains found in both Western and Eastern Chou sites are

17. Ho-pei sheng wen-wu kuan-li-ch'u, 1975:99.

numerous, and often include tools and simple utensils. The proximity of Chang-chia-p'o semi-subterranean residences to handicraft workshops suggests that such modest dwellings were occupied by Chou artisans or farmers.[18]

No Western Chou literature provides descriptions of the residences of people of lower social status. In the *Tso-chuan* 左傳, an aristocrat describes the poor as "people who lived in houses with wicker doors and open holes in the wall."[19] The walls with "open holes" must have referred to the short rim of stamped earth between the roof eaves and the ground. In Chan-kuo literature, the *Chuang-tzu* 莊子 depicts the residence of a poor man as a room with rim of short walls, a thatched roof, a broken wicker door hanging on a wooden axis, and two other openings framed by broken jars and covered with coarse felt. The room was wet because of a leaking roof and unsealed floor.[20] The description of the poor man's house in the *Chuang-tzu* and the archaeological information allow us to imagine that a majority of the Chou people lived in such low-roofed houses, half sunken into the ground. They were wet on rainy days, but could be warm in the winter. There were occasionally two rooms, but usually there was a single room that served both as the living quarters and the cooking area. That general standard of housing for the masses remained almost unchanged from neolithic until the Chan-kuo period.[21] Of course, the ordinary standard in the neolithic was comparable to that of the poor in the Chou.

Evidence of the most elaborate (palaces on platforms) and the most modest (semi-subterranean) dwellings of the Chou are well represented in the archaeological record. Simple houses built at ground level must have existed for the masses as well. Unfortunately, no archaeological data from the Western Chou period are available, but Shang houses may serve as examples. Ruins of nine such Shang houses were discovered at Shang-ch'iu 商丘 and they can be divided into three types. Dwellings of the first type were built on a slightly elevated foundation with all four sides inclined to facilitate drainage. One stamped-earth foundation supported three separated rooms, each of which had an individual entrance as would a row house. The middle room was higher and larger than the side ones. The walls were made of stamped earth that was smoothed, plastered, and then fired to harden. The reddened-earth wall surface was polished with a layer of yellow mud. The roof was supported by unfinished timber and covered with reed thatch. Onto the thatch, a layer of mud-plaster was added. The interior of the middle

18. Pei-ching ta-hsüeh, Department of History, 1979:188–89.
19. Legge, *Ch'un Ts'ew*, 448–49, slightly revised.
20. *Chuang-tzu*, 9/13–14.
21. Hsü Cho-yün, 1976:519.

room, measuring 3.3 meters north-south, and 5.4 to 5.8 east-west, contained a small chamber on the northwest corner enclosed by a short wall and an elongated fireplace in the southeast corner. The floor surface was smoothed, plastered, and then hardened by fire. Each of the two side rooms measured 2.6 meters east-west and 2.3 to 2.7 meters north-south, a much smaller space than the middle room.

The dwellings of the second category did not have a stamped-earth foundation (fig. 9.23). The floor surface, however, was fire-hardened. The ruins of the third category of Shang dwellings indicated small, round buildings, constructed directly on the ground. The typical house measured 2.6 meters in diameter and included a fireplace.[22] We cannot be sure that the Western Chou middle-level dwellings were the same as the earlier Shang ones, but judging from the semi-subterranean dwelling of the Chou period, its equivalent in the Shang, and the expanded Chou palace, we expect that the Chou middle-level houses were probably improved upon Shang models. Even so, the general method of construction, stamped-earth, elevated foundations and fire hardened floor surface, probably remained unchanged.

The stamped-earth and adobe construction was quite suitable for the north Chinese yellow-earth plain, where climate was arid. In the moist and rainy valley of the Yangtze River, wooden structures on posts were a more appropriate form of construction. In fact, the Western Chou site of Ch'i-ch'un 圻春 yielded some wooden buildings (fig. 9.24). In an area of 5,000 square meters divided into three clusters the houses each measured 8 by 4 meters (fig. 9.25). Wooden pillars were arranged in rows. Smaller pillars, wooden planks, floors, and stairways altogether suggested a multilevel building.[23]

We know little of the furnishings of houses except that the ancient

22. K'ao-ku yen-chiu-so, Ho-nan i-tui, 1982:49–54.
23. K'ao-ku yen-chiu-so, 1962.

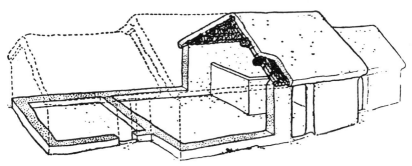

9.23 Reconstruction of a ground level dwelling from Shang-ch'iu (from *KKHP*, 1982 [1]:52)

9.24 Remains of wooden buildings from Ch'i-ch'un (from Pei-ching ta-hsüeh, Department of History, 1979:pl. 33)

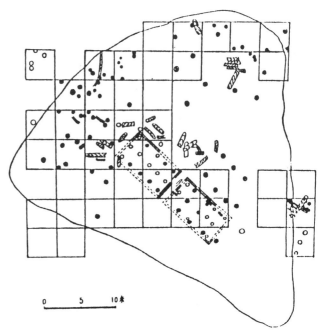

9.25 Ground plan of wooden buildings from Ch'i-ch'un (from Pei-ching ta-hsüeh, Department of History, 1979:163)

Chinese took off their shoes to enter a room or in the room in order to sit on mats. Therefore, we assume that the principal items of Chou furniture were various kinds of mats. Even the size of a room was measured in terms of numbers of mats, just as the Japanese do today. The size of each was nine square *ch'ih* 尺. In the chapter "Ku-ming" 顧命 (The Testamentary Charge) of the *Book of Documents*, the mats and tables set in front of guests are described in great detail. On a special occasion such as the succession to the royal throne, the furnishings in the hall of the royal palace must have been quite luxurious. The mats were made of woven bamboo, grass, or reeds, and either decorated with colored silk or simply painted with designs. The tables for people to lean against were wooden, lacquered ones decorated with painted designs, inlaid with mother of pearl, gems, or jade. A mat and a table formed a set to be displayed facing south near the window. The set at the north end was for the master, that is, the king; other sets were prepared for the dignitaries present. A screen shielded the entrance; curtains and draperies were hung on the wall. Such types of furnishings probably remained unchanged into the Eastern Chou.[24]

The living conditions of the people, therefore, differed according to wealth and social status. Building techniques improved upon and repeated those of the Shang. The Chou made extensive use of tile and bricks as well as stamped-earth foundations and walls.

THE BRONZE INDUSTRY AND TECHNOLOGY

The bronze industry was the centerpiece of the exclusive Shang aristocratic society. The bronze culture of the Western Chou period was in many ways a continuation of that of the Shang. By the time of the overthrow, the Shang bronze industry was highly developed and the Chou shared knowledge of metallurgy to the extent necessary to produce their own objects for local use.[25] After the conquest, the Shang technicians and skilled workers must have been brought to the Chou centers en masse and distributed to the newly established Chou vassaldoms as were experienced nobles.[26] In the Chou royal domain Shang artisans must have been retained to manufacture the vessels for the royal court.[27]

Interest in the industry, however, was in part politically motivated, for the continuation of Shang aesthetic ideals was proof of the Chou plan to

24. Hsü Cho-yün, 1976:519; Legge, *She King*, 551–53.
25. See chapter 2 above.
26. See chapters 4 and 5 above.
27. Satō Taketoshi, 1977:20–25.

accept, and assimilate, the Shang and their followers and to establish a unified Chou nation. The Chou had developed the skills necessary to produce and the desire for bronze weapons and ritual objects much before their conquest of the Shang. Both before the beginning of the dynasty and after, their own taste was apparent, though the models were Shang. For instance, their particular preference in the very early years of the Western Chou for lengthy inscriptions, for bases on which to display the vessels, and for expressive details (flanges, handles, animal tails, etc.) indicates that they were not merely copying but were developing their own idiom of expression within a very traditional industry. More exact continuation of Shang bronze styles may have had less to do with aesthetic choice than was previously thought.[28] It is possible that the Shang aristocrats who were relocated were the patrons of many of the bronze materials, which so clearly followed Shang models.

The bronze industry extended to the furthest corners of Chou political and cultural influence. It carried with it both the key to acceptance into the Chou orbit and the seeds of disintegration. A bronze-producing society was a highly differentiated one. The process required a coordinated effort from those who procured (miners and traders) and refined ores and fuel, clay workers who designed and made the models and molds, metallurgists who produced the molten bronze, as well as patrons who used the objects. The industry required many specialized workers and, once established, provided independence from the central Chou power structure by affording the states their own means (superior weapons) of defense.

The extent of the bronze industry can be understood by looking at an example such as Ch'eng-chou, the eastern capital, in the heartland of the former Shang royal domain where the Chou maintained bronze foundries. A very large Western Chou foundry site near Lo-yang was excavated between 1975 and 1979. The remains found at Lo-yang indicate that an enormous workshop existed there from early Western Chou until the mid-Chou period around the reign of King Mu. The whole area of this workshop measured seven hundred meters east-west and three hundred meters north-south. Although the excavated area was about 2,500 square meters, it was only a small portion of the whole site. The remains include foundations of houses, kilns, storage pits, several thousand fragments of clay molds, as well as a great variety of tools and implements.[29]

28. Loehr, 1953, contends that Shang designs developed from abstract patterns to coherent imagery.

29. Lo-yang shih wen-wu kung-tso-tui, 1983.

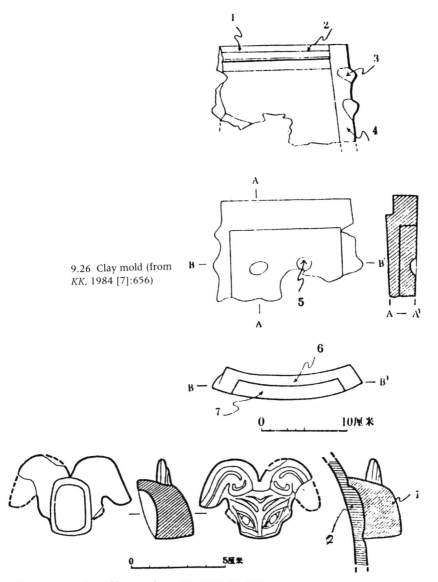

9.26 Clay mold (from *KK*, 1984 [7]:656)

9.27 Bronze casting of bosses (from *KK*, 1984 [7]:658)

The technique of bronze casting is well documented in the remains at Lo-yang. The procedure for casting bronze can be divided into three steps: creating a model, making a mold, and pouring the molten bronze into the mold (figs. 9.26–9.31). The model and the mold were both made of clay, and analysis of the Lo-yang remains showed that the clay

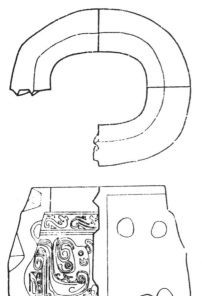

9.28 Sectional mold (from
KK, 1984 [7]:658)

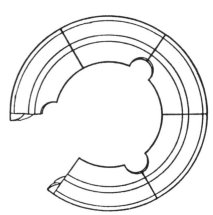

9.29 Sectional mold (from
KK, 1984 [7]:659)

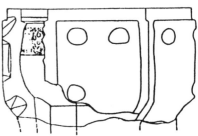

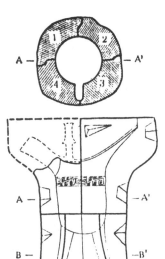

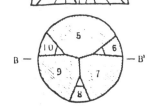

9.30 Model-mold assembly
(from *KK*, 1984 [7]:660)

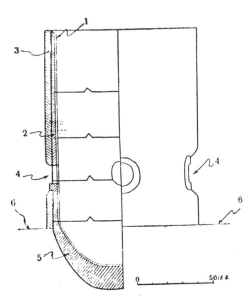

图八 大型竖式鼓风炉复原图
1.炉衬 2.炉壁层 3.保护加固层
4.鼓风口 5.炉底 6.地表

9.31 Furnace (from *KK*, 1984 [7]:662)

was finely sieved and mixed with silicon grains. Designs were carved in shallow relief or attached to the body by adding them on to the clay. The mold was fired in a well-built kiln, and sections of it were pieced together with tenon and mortice already built into the mold. A large, round vessel might need as many as six sections to frame it; four to eight were required to form the sides of a square shape. An irregularly shaped goblet might take more than ten sections, while small bronze pieces could be cast in a single mold. The molten bronze was held in crucibles on the top of a furnace. Although no crucibles were reported in the finds at Lo-yang, we may assume from the Shang model that the Chou crucible was conical, with a pointed bottom. The Lo-yang furnaces were generally made of clay and ranged in size from larger ones 1.6 to 1.7 meters in diameter, to smaller ones 0.5 to 0.6 meters in diameter. The clay interior of the furnace created resistance to high temperature. Three openings on the top of the furnace allowed a blast to create temperatures as high as 1,200–1,250°C.[30]

The Lo-yang remains of the Western Chou showed that bronzes were piece-mold cast, a method consistent with that of the Shang and one used widely until the later part of the dynasty.[31] Eastern Chou bronzes, for instance the *tsun* discovered at the Tseng-hou burial at Sui-hsien, were decorated with hollow fretwork as if they were engraved. Such a product was cast using the lost-wax method, a type of casting not documented archaeologically earlier than this late period.[32] In addition to the Lo-yang bronze workshop, several other workshops have been discovered in the Feng-hao, near the royal capital. These workshops were rather small, although division of labor can be observed in the remains. For instance, molds of ritual vessels were found primarily in the Ma-wang-ts'un workshop, while those of chariot fixtures were found in the Chang-chia-p'o workshop. Interestingly, a distinction was made based on the use of the product.

During and after the mid-Chou reigns, the use of bronze increased dramatically. Several storage pits have yielded hundreds of pieces. From large burial sites such as the Kuo 虢 cemetery at Shang-ts'un-ling 上村嶺, some one-hundred eighty ritual vessels were found. The total number of all categories of bronze items found at Shang-ts'un-ling exceeded five thousand. Not only did the Chou bronze industry produce more, the appearance of variations in style and decoration also indicated the Chou bronze industry had experienced some change. Technological changes in the mid-Chou period could be detected in two ways: a mother mold had

---

30. Ibid.; also Pei-ching ta-hsüeh, Department of History, 1979:472; Matsumaru Michio, 1977:66–90.
31. Shih Chang-ju, 1955; Chang Wan-chung, 1962:37–39.
32. Li Hsüeh-ch'in, 1980A: 63–64.

been repeatedly used to cast identical works, and the details of the large vessels had been separately cast and then welded onto the main body. These changes, no doubt, facilitated productivity as well as standardization of programs of decor.[33]

Not only did the royal court maintain bronze workshops, the vassal states did as well. Bronze vessels produced in the royal workshops, once received by a vassal as a gift, were copied by the workshop to produce identical or similar pieces. Adjustments in inscription were the clue to suggest that some were local copies.[34] Diffusion of bronze-casting technology was a catalyst that facilitated the development of the local bronze industries.

The increase of bronze production also implied that there was a tendency toward commercialization of otherwise "sacred" ritualistic vessels. That change in use, in turn, brought some deterioration in quality. Bronzes found at metropolitan centers and dated from the early Chou period were elaborate and finely cast. In the mid-Chou, the most noticeable new creation was the inclusion of large bird designs, which appeared in greater numbers during the reigns of kings Chao and Mu. Otherwise, the Chou bronzes were far less finely decorated than the Shang ones. On the other hand, the consequences of commercialization meant that the bronzes reached those who previously could not have obtained them. In the late period of Western Chou, less prestigious households, such as the Ch'iu-Wei family, also were able to cast bronzes for themselves to commemorate important occasions. Lengthy inscriptions were found on the late Western Chou bronzes more commonly than on the early pieces. These lengthy inscriptions, which were contracts or agreements of transactions between two parties, indicate that the sacredness of bronze vessels was reduced or even replaced by secularized use.

Secularization and commercialization were closely related, for bronzes were in each instance treated as commodities. Two almost identical bronzes of the late Western Chou period were discovered in two localities far apart, for instance. One was found in K'o-tso 喀左 of Liaoning遼寧, the other at P'eng-hsien彭山, Szechwan 四川.[35] Of course there is no absolute way to know whether such identical pieces were manufactured in the same workshop and then bestowed upon two different persons, or if they were simply shipped to two different destinations as merchandise.

The commercialization and secularization of the expanded bronze industry during the Western Chou period attest to the changes in social

33. Pei-ching ta-hsüeh, Department of History, 1979:169–70.
34. Matsumaru Michio, 1977.
35. Li Hsüeh-ch'in, 1980A:77; Ssu-ch'uan sheng po-wu-kuan, 1981.

and religious order in the communities as well. As the numbers of states established by feudal lords increased, so, too, did the aristocratic class. Ritual bronzes were no longer the guarded monopoly of the central, ruling class, as was the case with the Shang. As the feudal system was used to incorporate more and more regions and groups into the network well into the mid-Chou reigns, the venerated bronze vessels were produced in greater numbers and indicated that the in-group had increased. Inscriptions confirm their use as commemoratives. As a result the demands on designers must have changed rather dramatically. In some cases bronzes incorporated elements from non-official sources. The combination of non-native elements (for instance, animal-headed terminals from steppe models) with standard Chinese blade types was possible especially in the border states (fig. 6.11). But finally, by the end of the Western Chou, the artists broke free from the dictates of technology and custom or habit and created distinctive designs: fluid, not static, continuous, not bilaterally symmetrical. Such decor was patterned and regular and disregarded the character of the piece-mold process. Examples of the same pattern such as those found at Ying-shan County in Hupei Province represent the kind of uniformity in design that had developed (fig. 9.32). The other, perhaps more inventive, departure of this late period was the development of interlace designs (fig. 9.33). These patterns enriched the somewhat standardized and predictable expression of grooves and bevels of the previous century; but more significantly, they contained the germ of a newer, more radical change in interests among artists. They signaled an interest in creating the illusion of the third dimension by overlapping motifs. This visual formula is fundamental to the art of painting and is necessarily tied to the desire to record the visual world. This was the final departure from an art form that was exclusively ritualistic and otherworldly in its concerns (the Shang), to abstraction (grooves and bevel patterns), to the awakening of self-perception. Although artisans from the bronze industry were not the "inventors" of this perception, they experimented with the idea and finally conventionalized it into a motif.

BRONZE ART AND AESTHETIC, AN INTERPRETATION

The bestowal of the Mandate of Heaven on the Chou, their conquest of the Shang, and the formation of the Chou dynasty occurred in concert with primary changes in the intellectual life of the Chinese. The philosophic basis of those changes developed in the circumstances described above: dynamism evidenced in the intersection of cultures with varied ways of life, and motivation seemingly guided by self-confidence jus-

9.32 *Ho*, from the eighth century B.C. (courtesy of the Cultural Relics Bureau, Beijing, and the Metropolian Museum of Art)

9.33 Interlace design on handle of *ting* in the Shanghai Museum (courtesy of the Cultural Relics Bureau, Beijing, and the Metropolitan Museum of Art)

tified and supported through recognition of a broader spiritual base that separated the Heavenly and Earthly realms.[36] That separation and the reorganization of Chinese society marked a fundamental shift in patterns of responsibility among members and formed the nucleus of what the Chou perceived as the Hua-Hsia civilization. The revised worldview, naturally, was manifest in many aspects of early Western Chou life.

The process of change began during the late Shang, when the formerly mysterious aspects of ritual and belief were demystified and made routine. The Chou made the conduct of the Supreme Being and human beings, especially ancestors, separate and not enigmatic. Central to the intellectual maturation during the early Chou period was the emergence of abstract philosophic thinking in its incipient form: rationalism, as it would be labeled by later Chinese thinkers, and humanism. These ideas included the Chou conception that the universe was made up of at least two realms, that of Heaven and that of Earth. The system allowed interaction between domains, for the spirits were immanent. The system provided checks and balances, which assured assimilation of others' rituals, flexibility, and, thereby, perpetuity. One of the finest working examples of this thinking could be found in the

36. Chapter 3 above.

political system as it was applied to the process of forming a nation.[37] The Chou leaders approached the spirit world without anthropomorphizing and referred to "Heaven" (T'ien 天) rather than Shang Ti. Absolute authority was vested in Heaven, which had withdrawn its protection from the Shang and conferred it on the house of Chou, thereby deliberately shifting allegiance to a more virtuous line. The moral quality of a house was the rationale for imperial legitimacy. This reasoning was enlightened through receipt of the Mandate, but what evidence have we of this expanded worldview? The new political order, informed by humanism and rationalism, is one example. Yet another case in point is the modification in ritual and its associated artifacts. Did the changed social order alter values associated with ritual symbols and the bearers of such messages, that is, ritual artifacts?

The usual denominators of change in the visual arts, whether provoked by an individual artist, patron, or other influential thinker, are variations in imagery and style. An initial review of ritual materials made and used during the critical years of the shift in leadership yields no obvious evidence of radical adjustments. But how were the external symbolic forms adjusted to meet the difference in needs in the new regime? Those morphic changes are perhaps more subtle than their counterparts in the sphere of politics. Although the forms are similar, they could not bear their original Shang meaning any longer, because the social, political, and philosophical turns made new demands on ritual.

The period of juncture between the dynasties was a critical one, for the shift in ritual paralleled the evolution in philosophic worldview —older traditions were continued while newer expressions were formulated and began to be articulated in content and manner of observance. What one finds in this example was the shift from an art form that was integral first to solemn ritual, then to public ceremony as well. The bronzes were used regularly in spiritual communication with ancestors in the Shang and then were employed in public affairs as well as in their previous guise as markers of devotion to ancestors in the early Western Chou. The evidence for change in use appeared very soon after the political takeover by the Chou. Inscriptions such as the one on the Li *kuei* attest to the new use.[38]

Bronze art was the hallmark of Shang society. Its use and expressive character were an important ingredient in the ritual life of its patrons. Beyond local use, the production of bronzes reached a broader audience than simply their aristocratic makers. The bronze industry meant power

37. Chapter 4 above.
38. See chapter 3 and figure 3.14.

in Shang times. The industry was supported by a well-ordered, stratified society, and the patrons were aristocrats who had almost exclusive control over the use of bronze as ritual implements and weapons. Bronze to them was a necessary ingredient both for spiritual life and for military control. But the industry involved many others, all officially positioned under the Shang dagger. Skilled workers dug the ores and refined and transported them to the foundry sites. Priests and many others participated in ritual. Presentation of the objects must have signaled associations in societal structure and ritual content as well as an aesthetic response. When the context of production changed in the Western Chou, associations made by the viewers must have changed accordingly to include their new usage. When both political power and production were diffused over a broader area over which the Chou had hegemony, change in both imagery and style of the ritual bronzes occurred.

In late Shang society, centered at An-yang, ritual was well established and regularly operative. We do not know the exact content or disposition of that performance, but we do have the extant props from it: oracle bones, ritual bronzes, the tombs and their contents, and the like. We are informed through written documents—inscriptions on the bones and bronzes—that these rites were associated with ancestor worship and reverence for the natural phenomena.[39] The excavated materials from the intact tomb no. 5 at An-yang, known as the Fu-hao 婦好 tomb, may be thought of as representative examples from the capital. Much of this Shang court art was decorated with the image of the t'ao-t'ieh (fig. 9.34), which appeared on the majority of objects from the late Shang and was designated as the visual focus through its central position and relative size. Arrangement and dimension were controlled by the skillful hand of the artisan but also presumably through the desires of the patrons for a potent image: energized and sharply delineated without ambiguity. The t'ao-t'ieh and the vessel shapes are taut, closed compositions in which parts are conditioned by the whole, and in which there is absolute visual clarity to the subject. The intrinsic features of this bronze art, and its parallel expression in other media, were transmitted and replicated as Shang cultural and political influence stretched into regions beyond An-yang. Materials produced both nearby and at a distance from the Shang metropolitan center show a remarkable aesthetic and iconographic coherence (fig. 9.35). Some copy their An-yang counterparts; others imitate and introduce "new" elements, either in design or subject, and are "regional" in character (fig. 9.36).

39. Numerous studies of these documents are available and have been cited throughout the previous chapters. For bibliography and content, see Fong, 1980; Chang 1977A; Wen-wu pien-chi wei-yüan-hui, 1980.

9.34 Fu-hao *fang-ting* (courtesy of the Cultural Relics Bureau, Beijing, and the Metropolitan Museum of Art)

From the consistency in imagery on bronze materials we must assume that the emblems were acceptable. The presence of these vessels in ritual contexts, in burial, divination, and reverence to lineage, must have conveyed to the viewer information about Shang aristocratic authority and disclosed rules governing the observer's position in the society whether aristocrat, priest, worker, or otherwise.[40] There was little innovation or deviation from the accepted and well-known image. The *t'ao-t'ieh* was the most used image as long as the social structure was stable and the authority and role of the Shang leadership were

40. See Linduff, 1979:80–92; and Chang, 1977A:202–09 on the much-debated issue of how to interpret the specific iconographic meaning of the *t'ao-t'ieh*. A review of those interpretations may be found in Chang, 1983A:47–49, 66–74.

9.35 *Fang-ting* from An-yang (from Watson, 1973, no. 83:74)

unchallenged. Its use could be called, therefore, a restricted code, one that was tied to the authority of its Shang patrons and valid as long as they were in power. The images were simple, and direct, vital, and heraldic in appearance. They were not devalued through lack of understanding or irreverence. Psychologically, the images and the clarity and continuity of their presentation in the late Shang connected the ritual participants to their community and perhaps to their kin.[41] The effectiveness of Shang social control was evidenced in its developed ancestor worship and complex lineage system as the basis for power and position. The *t'ao-t'ieh* is tied to Shang political authority, according to K. C. Chang.[42]

Late Shang society did not remain stable, and their strength and right to govern were denounced by their Chou neighbors. The Chou not only

41. The theoretical framework for the discussion can be found in Douglas, 1982:3–30; Bernstein, 1965:165.
42. Chang, 1983A:47–74.

9.36 *Kuang* from Shih-lou (from Watson, 1973, no. 82:73)

defied the Shang military strength, they did so with the conviction that they were morally justified. The philosophic tenets nurtured during this critical period of change were germinated during the late Shang as their control waned. The Chou apparently realized that they were only part of a larger body of human existence. Too small and weak to challenge the Shang on their own, they accumulated strength through alliances with other groups. The population under Chou control was a conglomerate of many peoples with varying strengths and numbers. The Chou incorporated the most powerful groups, whether strong by reputation, tradition, military strength, or numbers, by offering respect and position to them. By doing so they gained control through accretion, assimilation, relocation, and surveillance.[43] This lack of Shang political stability must be reflected in changing ritual and ritual materials especially during the last reigns of the dynasty.[44]

The Chou belief system also seems to have been constituted in an eclectic manner. Older and respected traditions were incorporated under a new umbrella—the authority of Heaven including its attendant ethical preoccupations. Both group conduct and personal conduct, and presumably human existence, were justified and measured in accordance with moral standards. Such standards were to be further elucidated by thinkers, Confucius among them, throughout Chinese history. Good works, and the corollary personal success, were promulgated on behalf of humanity and judged on ethical grounds. The right to rule was both given and taken away by Heaven. This stratified belief system displayed a manner of thinking not usual prior to the early Chou. It was both abstract and elaborate. Their goal apparently

43. Chapters 4 and 5 above.
44. Huber, 1983:16–43.

was to incorporate and assimilate the Chinese under one unit—the Central Kingdom—and they did so under the aegis of Heaven.

The new establishment created new celebrations, rituals of state— ones relevant not only to one group, but to the aggregate. In government, as in social order, a two-pronged system developed; allegiance had to be accorded both to the state and to family. Older traditions continued and allowed a more personal access to the spirits associated with lineage. The Chou, for example, dealt with the Shang royal ancestors by endowing their sacrifices, by producing comparable artifacts, and by conducting rituals in the fashion of their predecessors.[45] The artifacts were made and used in a familiar guise, but the purpose of that ritual had to change—the Shang rites were neither entirely applicable nor appropriate to the Chou. Respect was still to be afforded to one's ancestors, but the public ceremonies also made use of artifacts modeled after the Shang bronzes. Lengthy inscriptions on bronzes commemorated allegiance and honorable response to duty as carried out by faithful members of the society. The content of inscriptions suggests a more philosophic, secular outlook toward observance.[46] Inscriptions often tell of deeds well done, of investitures, of historic events—all for the glory of the Chou federation and the faithful. The inscriptions attempt to connect good deeds with family and morality with an individual.

As the new Chou society was a conglomerate, and position and role were in a state of flux, selection of materials and imagery appropriate for their events came into question. Evidence for that can be found in various forms. For instance, food vessels predominated in the early Chou, unlike the late Shang preference for wine vessels. The use of the *kuei* increased during the late Shang and throughout the Chou. Sung Ch'ien proposed that a change in burial custom accounted for the increased use.[47] Traditional literature accused the Shang of indulgence in use of alcohol and accorded the Chou with the reassertion of temperance. The reduction in production of wine vessels would, therefore, be explained.[48] During the late Shang the *ting* and *kuei* were added only occasionally as a unit in tombs following the custom of placing *ku* and *chüeh* in pairs in earlier Shang sites. In the early Chou the *ting* and *kuei* combination was more popular and soon began to replace the *ku* and *chüeh* altogether.[49] Here, an occasional practice was made customary by the Chou usurpers. Perhaps that characterizes assemblages of bronzes

45. Chapters 4 and 5 above.
46. Chapter 5 above.
47. Sung Ch'ien, 1983, 77ff.
48. "K'ao-kung-chi" 考工記 of the *Chou-li chu-shu* (hereafter *Chou-li*); Wang Tsung-su, 1886; Linduff, 1977:7–16.
49. Kuo Pao-chün, 1981:136.

during the early Chou. For example, the tombs at Liu-li-ho, near Peking,[50] are filled with a rich assortment of contemporary bronze shapes and styles. Furthermore, individual vessels reveal changes both in shape and imagery. A vessel known as the I-kung *kuei* from that site will serve as an example (fig. 6.4). It is a standard *kuei*-shaped pot, but it stands on legs formed from elephant snouts, emerging from heads bearing elephant tusks, feline eyes, and bovine ears. On two sides of the vessel are bird-shaped handles, not unknown as a motif in the Shang, but here their presentation extends well beyond the belly of the vessel and describes a more fully rounded figure. That independence in choice of motifs is not characteristic of late Shang materials from An-yang, for instance, and surely would have appeared uncanonical to the Shang patrons and artisans. The flamboyant aspect of this vessel was especially preferred by the new patrons. The principal motif decorating the belly of the *kuei* is located in the standard Shang position in the center, is bilaterally disposed over a leg, and includes prominent eyes. The model is the *t'ao-t'ieh*, but this one is incoherent, a piecing together of parts of other motifs—connected in a somewhat arbitrary way. The relief design echoes the long snout, tusks, and feline eyes of the leg motif, but adds to it a bulky body formed by a raised spiral. The two elephant-like motifs stand facing one another across a hooked flange. Repeated on the lid these composite creatures stretch outside the boundaries of previous orders of design.

The sculptural techniques applied to the fashioning of this image are also varied and unusual by comparison to the Shang and assert the preference for the flamboyant so characteristic of early Chou taste. The raised spiraling lines that form the body and face of the animal rise over an otherwise unarticulated surface. The contour of the vessel is an altered version of the Shang model, but this one is shorter, with sagging sides to the belly. The aesthetic energy of the best materials from An-yang is not apparent in this example, but that quality is not missing from its companion pieces (figs. 6.2, 6.3).

These early Chou materials illustrate the range and character of the bronze vessels produced. The old imagery of the *t'ao-t'ieh* had lost its visual potency; it was diluted by distracting elements such as flamboyant appendages, legs, handles, flanges, bases (figs. 9.37, 6.3, 6.4); by splitting the image and separating its parts too far to maintain a single view of the animal face (fig. 6.2); or by adding playful passages to the central image: elephant trunks, spiral tails, and so on. Attention cannot be focused on a single image; instead, meaningful energy is manifest in another fashion. The *manner* of expression takes prominence. Cur-

50. Chapter 4 above.

9.37 *Kuei* from Shensi (courtesy of the Cultural Relics Bureau, Beijing, and the Metropolitan Museum of Art)

vilinearity, abstraction, and/or geometricization are more significant visually than any single image. Moreover, the vessels themselves were often objectified by placing them on cast bases (fig. 6.4). Observation was intended, and new psychological distance was introduced.

This material must have been appropriate to Chou ceremony and to its extended clientele. The establishment of Heaven as a moral God had "liberated" the Chou mind from the rigidity of taking mythical animals as sources of sorcerous power, and thus the Chou artisan had the freedom to rearrange the parts of the heretofore integrated animal images. The Western Chou kings were mediators and monopolized access to Heaven,[51] thereby confirming the separation of the worlds of ancestors, living beings, and animals.

Some decoration of the Chou bronzes focused more on the use of bird motifs, and occasionally on other recognizable animals. Although bird-

51. Chang, 1984:81.

shaped vessels and motifs were already apparent in the Fu-hao tomb at An-yang, and birds are prominent in clan signs during the late Shang,[52] birds were not as regularly chosen to decorate the outside of the vessels as were mythological animals like the t'ao-t'ieh and the k'uei. The usual exclusion of naturalistic animals from the main decorative zones of Shang bronzes underscores the preeminence of the fantastic animal designs and their importance as a symbol and divulges the close relationship among ancestors, animals and human beings.[53] Although the pre-conquest Chou material is comparable to the Shang, preference for bird decor and, perhaps, for naturalistic representation of other animals is already perceptible. For instance, the vessel yu was cast by both the Shang and the early Chou founders and with little discernible difference. Although these vessels are very similar in shape, those with a special graph 𝖶 have an association with pre-Chou foundries in the west[54] and suggest an early preference for programs of decor that focus on birds (fig. 9.38).

The use of the bird as a dominant motif began as early as the reign of King Ch'eng 成, according to Ch'en Meng-chia 陳夢家.[55] The Meng kuei from Chang-chia-p'o is used by Ch'en to illustrate this new decor (fig. 9.39). Pairs of long-tailed, crested birds face one another on the vessel, one very similar in shape to the early Chou-date Li kuei (fig. 3.18). The inscription suggests a date either in the reign of King Ch'eng or King K'ang 康, for Meng's father was a member of a regiment active in King Ch'eng's reign.

Many other Western Chou bronzes attest to the continued popularity of the "big bird" motif. The use of these motifs was catalogued by Chang Ch'ang-shou 張長壽 and Ch'en Kung-jou 陳公柔,[56] who note that the motif continued to be used through the reigns of kings Chao 昭 and Mu 穆. The remarkable yu discovered at T'un-hsi, Anhui, is dominated by "big-birds" facing one another with their tails intertwined (fig. 9.40). Weaving together of parts of decor was scrupulously avoided in Shang decorative schemes. Both the intertwine and the agitated movement on this vessel and many others from these reigns (figs. 9.41, 9.42) contrast with the more static quality of Shang and earlier Chou pieces (fig. 6.4). The preference for geometricized, regularized designs characterizes the vessels from the second half of the Western Chou.

Consonant with the regularization and routinization of the social and political systems during the middle period of the Western Chou, the

52. Tsou Heng, 1980:327.
53. Chang, 1977A:383–84.
54. Tsou Heng, 1980.
55. Ch'en Meng-chia, 1983:71.
56. K'ao-ku hsüeh-pao, 1984/3:263.

9.38 *Yu* from Hunan (courtesy of the Cultural Relics Bureau, Beijing, and the Metropolitan Museum of Art)

9.39 Meng *kuei* (from *KKHP*, 1951 [1]:91)

9.40 *Yu* from T'un-hsi, Anhui (from Watson, 1973, no. 97)

9.41 *Yu* from Kao-chia-pao, Shensi (courtesy of the Cultural Relics Bureau, Beijing, and the Metropolitan Museum of Art, Seth Joel, photographer)

bronze industry was secularized and commercialized. Flexibility and choice of vessel shape and decor, evident in tombs of the early period, ceased. The numbers of vessels were made routine, and the older order of decor was broken down into conventionalized patterns. Compression of *k'uei* dragons into supportive or decorative bands may be seen on such objects as the Li *fang-i* 方彝 discovered in Shensi at Li-ts'un

9.42 *Lei* from Liaoning (courtesy of the Cultural Relics Bureau, Beijing, and the Metropolitan Museum of Art). This *lei* is very similar to the vessel in figure 6.17.

李村 (fig. 9.43). The dragons frame a circular medallion in the center of the body. Hooked flanges and snout handles embellish the contour of the vessel in concert with the flamboyant styles of the early Chou

9.43 *Fang-i* from Mei-hsien (courtesy of the Cultural Relics Bureau, Beijing, and the Metropolitan Museum of Art)

period. Also favored are *k'uei* dragon designs such as those rear-facing ones of the neck of the Kung *yu* and those filling the blades of a *lei* (fig. 9.44) excavated at Fu-feng 扶風, Shensi, and dated approximately to the reign of King Hsiao 孝.[57] On the belly of the *lei* the animals are diminished to a dependent role, for it is the blade shape and its repetition that dominate the composition. Compression of *k'uei* dragons into continuous patterns in bands introduced a motif consisting of repeated figures and one that included ornament for its own sake. These motifs made up the entire ornament on materials now known from the reigns of the late Western Chou. Others are decorated with simplified, continuous bands of decor filled with modified animal designs (fig. 9.45) or with simple grooves or wave patterns (fig. 9.32). Finally, entwined bodies and tails of snakes and dragons were accented with symbolic eyes. This visual theme and the taste for pattern had transformed the old symmetry of the Shang and the early Western Chou canon of decor. The

57. Watson, 1973:81.

9.44 *Lei* from Fu-feng (from Watson, 1973, no. 95)

9.45 *Fu* from the eighth century B.C. (courtesy of the Cultural Relics Bureau, Beijing, and the Metropolitan Museum of Art)

repeating designs were employed and reiterated throughout the rest of the Chou period.

Emphasis on regularizing earthly affairs and the commercialization of the bronze industry were the result of the unifying efforts of the Western Chou kings. The consolidation of their rule was slow, but as it came together in the later reigns bronze decor became more and more predictable. Perhaps that regularization of an official bronze art reflected the attainment of a more uniform Hua-Hsia culture in the minds of the Chou patrons.

Along with the regularly designed vessels, however, grew an interest in naturalistically rendered, animal-shaped bronzes. Such a tradition existed as well in the Shang, but increased emphasis on this-worldly affairs in the later Western Chou must account for a new liveliness found in some pieces. The *tsun* in the shape of a foal (see frontispiece) unearthed at Mei-hsien 郿縣 and dated to the reign of King Yi may be seen as an example.[58] The natural pose, erect ears, and appealing expression on the foal and other naturalistic renderings on animals, along with the appearance of the interlace, reveal the interest in recording nature. These two very different traditions of patterning and naturalistic depiction also characterize the arts of the Eastern Chou.

Another feature of Chou art is the increased emphasis on calligraphic style of written characters. The increase in length and use of inscriptions allowed the middle Chou artisan, or scribe, to experiment even more daringly to produce beautifully displayed characters. Bold and wavelike, simple and direct, elegant scripts developed in a variety of styles during the period (figs. 6.23, 9.46, 9.47). Their development stood at the head of the art of calligraphy and underlines the attention given by the Chou to the word as the bearer of significance. In fact, many of these artifacts may be seen largely as a support for verbal charges, and, although the messages in these cases are not especially high-minded, this combination of well-formed shape and word prefigures the identification of idea and form so important to later Chinese calligraphy and painting.

The maturation of calligraphy may be seen as an imaginative departure from the earlier traditions, and one that was born out of a social situation in which the sister arts were being codified and redefined. The strictly conservative tendencies in the ceremonial arts left little to the imagination. These artifacts and the rituals in which they were used confirmed a social order already in practice. Writing was, of course, a restricted code and one comprehensible only to the literate, the aristocracy, and the scribe-historians. The development in formal writing at

58. *K'ao-ku hsüeh-pao*, 1957/2:3.

9.46 Rubbing from an inscription on a *fang-ting* from Liaoning (from *KK*, 1974/6:3)

9.47 Rubbing from the Yi-kung *kuei* (courtesy of the Cultural Relics Bureau, Beijing, and the Metropolitan Museum of Art)

this point seems to be a matter of emphasis. For the already limited audience, the artisans embellished the words aesthetically. Those who could not read could at least relish the form of the words as well as recognize their position in relation to the group in power. The creative energy formerly focused on ritual materials in bronze was, here, transferred to new media. Calligraphy became the bearer of vital messages. Although the bronze arts were continued throughout the Western Chou, their significance had changed. As official art, they bore official designs—ones geometricized and systematized.

OTHER CRAFT INDUSTRIES

There is rich archaeological information regarding the potting industry. The kiln, for instance, at the type-site Chang-chia-p'o was not very large. From a firing area below ground level, a fire-passage and a chimney brought heat to the whole kiln. Clay objects were placed on shelves in the furnace. In the early Chou period, unbaked clay pots were finished on the potter's wheel after rough shapes were made either by hand or in molds. After the mid-Chou period, the general use of fast-wheel rotation enhanced the productivity and standardization of production of pottery. This change coincided with development in commercialization of bronze production. In the early Chou period, primitive glazed ceramics were produced in sites in Shensi, Honan, Shantung, and Hopei. The ceramic fragments discovered in Chang-chia-p'o were covered with blue and yellow-green glaze that was fired with a temperature estimated by experts at 1,200°C. Such ceramics reached a high degree of hardness with a mineral composition that was similar to the primitive blue ware produced in the Yangtze Valley.[59]

Animal bones and shells were used by the Chou people to make various kinds of tools and weapons, ornaments, and other items of daily life (figs. 9.48–9.51). From a bone workshop at Yün-t'ang at Fu-feng, some twenty thousand half-finished items were excavated. These pieces bore marks of sawing, cutting, or polishing with bronze tools and instruments found *in situ*. Manufacturing bone objects consisted of at least four steps: (1) selection of good, fresh raw bones; (2) sawing the piece such as a shoulder blade into a proper shape suitable to the material; (3) cutting and filing the rough cut into the desired shape; (4) smoothing by polishing on a grindstone. If the product was to be a refined piece such as a hairpin, further touch-up or inlaying of colored gems and stones might be required. The half-finished bone pieces found at the Yün-t'ang workshop demonstrate a high degree of uniformity in cutting marks, suggesting that a standard production procedure was followed by a group of skilled laborers. The products of the Chang-chia-p'o workshop consisted of mainly hairpins (90 percent) and arrowheads. Specialization in production was reached. The number of bones found at the Yün-t'ang 雲塘 site was enormous. From storage pit no. 21 alone, there were some eight thousand pieces of raw bone taken from at least 1,306 cattle and 21 horses. The Chou obviously had a considerable number of animals ready to relinquish for such use.[60]

It is interesting to note that in a small area between the ruins of the palaces of Feng-ch'u and Chao-ch'en, there were special workshops to produce bronze, pottery, bone objects, as well as jade pieces. The close proximity of these factories to the palace buildings implies that the aristocrats retained artisans to produce the objects for daily life.[61] Archaeological information substantiated the existence of such individuals and industries because of the appearance of housing at these sites.[62] Another industry, chariot making was quite sophisticated.

Manufacturing a complete chariot probably necessitated the most intricate technology available at that time. The cabin and the wheels were made of wood; the strings that fastened the numerous parts together as well as the reins were made of leather. Various fixtures on the chariot, such as axle caps and decorative bulbs, were made of

59. Pei-ching ta-hsüeh, Department of History, 1979:171–72; K'ao-ku yen-chiu-so, 1962:appendix 2.
60. Chou-yüan k'ao-ku-tui, 1980:29–35.
61. Earlier in this chapter.
62. Satō Taketoshi, 1977:25–29.

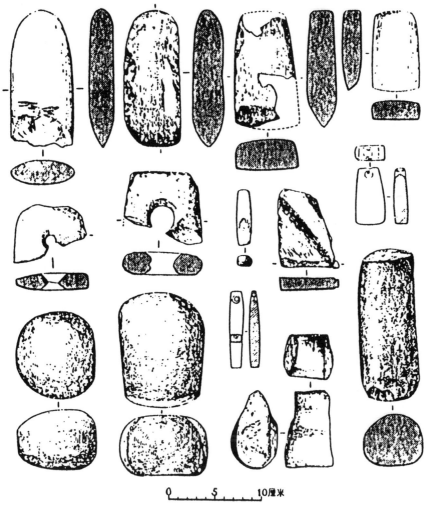

9.48 Stone tools discovered at K'o-sheng-chuang (from K'ao-ku yen-chiu-so, 1962:20)

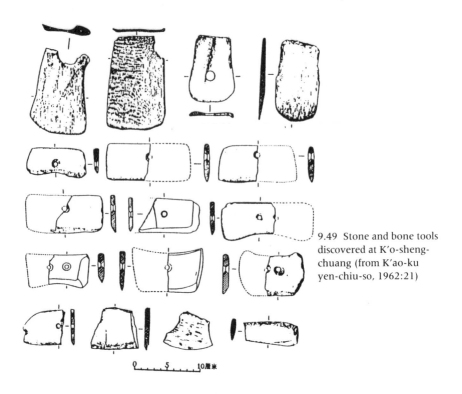

9.49 Stone and bone tools discovered at K'o-sheng-chuang (from K'ao-ku yen-chiu-so, 1962:21)

0   5   10厘米

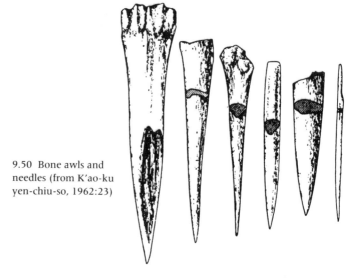

9.50 Bone awls and needles (from K'ao-ku yen-chiu-so, 1962:23)

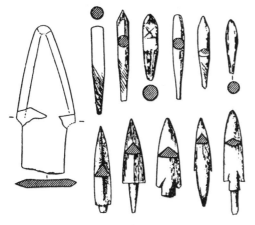

9.51 Stone *ko* and bone arrowheads (from K'ao-ku yen-chiu-so, 1962:23)

bronze. The parts were fixed together not only by fastening with leather straps but also by gluing and fitting tenons and mortises. In addition to bronze fixtures, chariots were decorated with jade inlay and lacquered painting. Chariot manufacturing required the cooperation of carpenters, bronzesmiths, leather workers, painters, and artisans who worked in jade—many of the handcrafts were brought in. A detailed description of chariot manufacturing was included in the "K'ao-kung-chi" chapter of the *Chou-li*.[63] This particular classic, however, was not a Western Chou work,[64] and cannot be taken as a fully reliable reference to the chariot of ancient China.

Archaeological discoveries of chariots, including horse skeletons, were made in Chou burials in Ch'ang-an 長安, Pao-chi 寶雞, Lo-yang 洛陽, Chün-hsien 濬縣, and Shang-ts'un-ling. The Chou chariot included a wooden boxlike cabin mounted on an axle with two wheels (fig. 9.52). It was drawn by two or four horses harnessed on a bar attached to a slightly curved shaft. The wheel was somewhat concave, supported by spokes. The number of spokes of the Western Chou chariot was twenty, more numerous than the Shang, and less than the Eastern Chou models.[65]

The Western Chou models discovered were all war chariots that took three riders: a driver, an archer, and a combatant. A verse in the *Book of Poetry* gives a vivid description of the movement of a chariot in gaming exercises:

Of the officers in charge of the hunt,
The voices resounded as they told of the men

63. Juan Yüan, 1829; Wang Tsung-su, 1888.
64. *Han-shu*, 30/11.
65. Hsü Cho-yün, 1976:522–23; Kuo Pao-chün et al., 1954:115; Hayashi Minao, 1959.

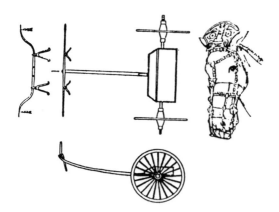

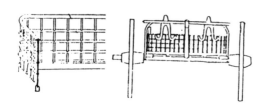

9.52 Chou chariot excavated at Chang-chia-p'o (from Pei-ching ta-hsüeh, Department of History, 1979:179)

They set up the banners, with oxtails displayed,
And we proceeded to pursue the chase in Ao.

With their four-horsed chariot (they came),
forming a long train,
In their red knee-covers and gold adorned slippers,
Princes gathered in accordance.
The bowstring thimble amulets were fitted on;
The bow and arrows were adjusted to one another;
The archers acted in unison
Helping us to form a pile of game.

Of the four yellow horses of each chariot,
The two outsiders inclined not to either side.
No error in driving was committed,
And the arrows went forth like downright blows.[66]

Another verse also contained a depiction of the chariot:

In his carriage drawn by four piebalds,
Four piebalds orderly moving
Red shone his grand carriage,
With its checkered bamboo screen, and quivers,

66. Legge, J., *She King*, 289–90.

With the hooks for trapping of the breast-bands,
and the rein ends.
Fang-shu led them on,
The naves of his wheels bowed with leather,
and his yoke ornamented.
Tinkle-tinkle went the eight bells at the horses' bits
He wore the robe conferred (by the king);
His red knee-covers were resplendent;
The gems of his girdle-pendant sounding.[67]

The color and the sound give the impression of a Chou chariot and its rider moving in the field. The fixtures and weapons were also depicted:

(There is) his short war carriage;
With the ridge-like end of his pole, elegantly bound in five places;
With its slip wings and side straps;
And the traces attached to the gilt wings to the marked transverse;
With its beautiful mat of tiger skin and its long naves;
With its piebalds and horses with white left feet.

Side by side are placed the dragon-figured shields;
Gilt are the buckles for the inner reins

There are trident spears with their gilt ends;
and the beautiful feather-figured shield
With the tiger-skin bow-case and the carved metal ornaments on
the front.
The two bows are placed in the case,
Bound with string to their bamboo frames.[68]

These poetic descriptions of war chariots and equipment are impressive, but the wagons must have carried freight and moved slowly on other occasions. In one verse, such a wagon was described as rumbling along, slowly and heavily. The heavy wagon seems to have been drawn by oxen.[69] No archaeological findings are available yet to substantiate the details of the structure of such wagons hauled by oxen. A bronze model of a wagon drawn by horses was found in the Ch'in burial site; this chariot is dated third century B.C., too late to confirm our discussion of Chou rigging.[70] This Ch'in model had a special way of harnessing the horses that placed the weight of the yoke resting on the animals' shoulders. It is done in the same manner as the breast-harnesses that

67. Ibid., 285–86.
68. Ibid., 193–95.
69. Ibid., 121, 413.
70. Ch'in-yung k'ao-ku-tui, 1983.

were used in the Ch'in-Han period, as opposed to harnessing horses along the neck as was common in West Asia. Sun Chi argued that harnessing the shoulder blades was a unique system developed in the Shang-Chou period.[71]

In summary, Chou technologies were developed on Shang prototypes. Improvement and change, however, could be detected in all the industries. In the late reigns the industries were commercialized and became conservative. Creative changes were in the art of writing, in naturalistic representation, and perhaps in other arts.[72] Divergences from the styles of art patronized by the central court signal the development of independent regional industries that were less conservative. As political allegiance waned, the "official" aesthetic conventions of the central court were less preferred and experimentation could be observed.

71. Sun Chi, 1983:27–29.
72. Kane, 1974/75:77–107.

10   Daily Life in the Western Chou

The extreme care with which early Chinese authors recorded political life extended to include ceremonial activities as well. From those early sources come insights into cooking and eating. The cuisine was simple, including cultivated fruits and vegetables as well as meats and fishes, all from local sources. The addition of herbs and a variety of cooking styles enriched the rather plain diet.

The regular, symmetrical organization of palace complexes at Feng-ch'u implies a regularized ceremonial life early in the dynasty. In fact, the *Book of Documents* describes ceremonies in which dress codes are apparent. Differentiation by political or social rank was as evident in burial as it was in life.

As an agriculturally based people, the Chinese were sensitive to the turn of the seasons. This is reflected in the *Book of Poetry*, where seasonal rituals of planting and harvest are recorded. Stages in one's life were marked with rites of passage—at birth, at puberty, at marriage, and at death. All such life rituals seem to confirm a communal attitude toward life, with ancestors, children, and adults participating in a coherent, self-perpetuating Hua-Hsia culture. The regular expression of ceremonies that celebrated that cohesion must surely have reinforced familial as well as cultural ties.

FARMING LIFE

The principal food crops in the Western Chou included millets, wheat, rice, hemp seeds, peas, and beans.[1] The most important subspecies of millet was *Setaria italica*, known as *chi* 稷 and very likely an indigenous domesticate, given its long history in China. The founding ancestor of the Chou was even called Hou Chi 后稷 (Lord of Millet). According to legend, this title designated him as an hereditary officer in charge of agriculture. Another subspecies, *Panicum miliaceum*, known as *shu* 黍 in

1. Ch'i Ssu-ho, 1948A; Wan Kuo-ting et al., 1959:35; Hsü Cho-yün, 1971; Ch'ien Mu, 1956.

ancient China, was no less significant as a cereal grain.[2] The character
mai 麥 for wheat, in other than geographical names, appears only about
a dozen times in the Shang oracle bone inscriptions. Its related
character, *lai* 來 appears no more than about twenty times. On the other
hand, the characters *chi* and *shu* can be counted by the hundreds.
Because of its rarity, wheat must have been reserved for consumption
by the privileged class, for the Shang commoners consumed very little.[3]
Nevertheless, wheat is commonly mentioned in the classics, and failure
of the wheat crops is regularly entered into historical records,
underscoring its considerable importance. Ch'ien Mu 錢穆 claimed that
the millets, *chi* and *shu*, were the principal crops in China from the
neolithic through the Western Chou period, while thereafter wheat and
a larger and better-tasting millet called *liang* 粱 gradually became more
popular. Wheat is mentioned more frequently, therefore, in most
classics.[4]

The *Book of Poetry*, a product of north China, mentions rice fields and
rice harvesting even though rice was a southern crop.[5] The major areas
where it was produced were the valleys of the Han 漢, the Huai 淮, and
the Yangtze 揚子 rivers. In a site of the Western Chou period at Ch'i-
ch'un 圻春, Hupei, *keng* 粳 rice was discovered, possibly from a food bin.[6]

Flax and hemp are now mainly cash crops used for their fibers and
their oil-producing seeds. In the Western Chou period, hemp seed was
regarded as a kind of cereal food, comparable to millet, beans, and
wheat.[7] The *Book of Rites* mentions hemp seed as an offering to the
king as a new crop in the early autumn.[8] The character of the bean 未
in bronze inscriptions was a pictogram of the tuberculated roots
characteristic of root systems of the bean family.[9] During the Ch'un-
ch'iu period, only in the Shansi highland were beans regarded as a
major foodstuff; in the Chan-kuo period, most ordinary people routinely
consumed beans.[10] The Chou people adopted agriculture in their earliest
pre-dynastic period. In fact, the great task attributed to Hou Chi was his
role in developing agriculture. Some historians suggested that in the
early Chou, there was fairly large-scale collective farming, and an often-
quoted verse in the *Book of Poetry* illustrates the point:

2. Hsü Cho-yün, 1971:804–06.
3. Yü Sheng-wu, 1957.
4. Yü Ching-jang, 1957:83–89; Ch'ien Mu, 1956:27.
5. Legge, *She King*, 184, 231, 379, 417.
6. Pei-ching ta-hsüeh, Department of History, 1979:168.
7. Legge, *She King*, 232, 469.
8. *Li-chi*, 16/10, 13.
9. Hu Tao-ching, 1963.
10. Hsü Cho-yün, 1971:807–08.

Lead your husbandmen
To sow their various kinds of grain ...
all over the thirty *li*.
Attend to your plowing,
With your ten thousand men all in pairs.[11]

The "ten thousand" farm laborers may merely describe a huge number. In another verse, for instance, a similar phrase is "one thousand pairs."[12] It is also possible that the twenty-thousand farm laborers were the whole labor force of this particular domain of thirty *li* 里 (either 30 *li* square or a circumference of 30 *li*). In either case, it represented a rather extensive farming operation. If such a phrase referred to massive collective farming, it probably was a description of gang-labor activities on the arable field belonging directly to the feudal lord.[13]

In addition to such large-scale operations, individual farmers worked on small farmsteads, which are described vividly in the "Ch'i-yüeh" 七月 of the *Book of Poetry*:

In the seventh month, the Fire Star passes the meridians;
In the ninth month, clothes are given out
In the days of (our) first month, the wind blows cold;
In the days of (our) second, the air is cold.
Without the clothes and garments of hair,
How could we get to the end of the year?
In the days of (our) third month, they take the plow in hand.
In the days of (our) fourth, they take their way to the fields.
Along with my wife and children,
I carry food to them in those south-lying acres.
The surveyor of the fields comes, and is glad.

In the seventh month, the Fire Star passes the meridian;
In the ninth month, clothes are given out,
With the spring days the warmth begins,
And the oriole utters its song.
The young women take thin deep blankets,
And go along the small paths,
Looking for the tender (leaves of the) mulberry trees.
As the spring days lengthen out
They gather in crowds in the white southern wood.
That young lady's heart is wounded with sadness,
For she will (soon) be going with one of our princes (as his wife).

11. Legge, *She King*, 584.
12. Ibid., 600.
13. Amano Motonosuke, 1959:95; Kaizuka Shigeki, 1962; Li Ya-nung, 1962:70–75; Hu Yü-huan, 1959:242–43.

In the seventh month the Fire Star passes the meridian;
In the eighth month are the sedges of reeds.
In the silkworm month they strip the mulberry branches of their
   leaves,
And they take their axes and hatchets,
To lop off those that are distant and high;
Only stripping the young trees of their leaves.
In the seventh month, the shrike is heard;
In the eighth month they begin their spinning;
They make dark fabrics and yellow.
Our red manufacturer is very brilliant
It is for the lower robes of our young princes.

In the fourth month, the small grass is in seed.
In the fifth, the cicada gives off its note.
In the eighth, the crop is reaped.
In the tenth, the leaves fall.
In the days of (our) first month, they go after badgers,
And take foxes and wild cats,
To make fur for our young princes.
In the days of (our) second month, they have a general hunt,
And proceed to keep up the exercise of war.
The boars of one year are all for themselves;
Those of three years are all for our prince.

In the fifth month, the locust moves its legs;
In the sixth month, the spinner sounds its wings
In the seventh month, in the fields;
In the eighth month, under the eaves;
In the ninth month, about the doors;
In the tenth month, the cricket
Enters under our beds.
Chinks are filled up, and rats are smoked out;
The windows that face (the north) are stopped up;
And the doors are plastered.
Ah! my wife and my children,
Changing the year so we do these;
Enter the (winterized) house and we dwell!

In the sixth month they eat the sparrow-plums and grapes;
In the seventh, they cook the k'uei 葵 and beans
In the eighth month, they knock down the dates;
In the tenth month, they reap the rice,
And make the spring wine
For the celebration of longevity of the elders.

In the seventh month, they eat the melons;
In the eighth, they cut down the bottle-gourds;
In the ninth, they gather the hemp seed;
They gather the sowthistle and make firewood of the Letid tree;
To feed the husbandman.

In the ninth month, they prepare the vegetable garden for stakes,
And in the tenth, harvests are stacked
The millets, both the early sown and the late;
With other grain, the hemp, the beans, and the wheat
O fellow husbandmen,
Our harvest is all collected
Let us go to the house of the prince to work.
In the daytime we collect the grass,
And at night twist it into ropes;
And get up quickly on our roofs:
Soon we shall have to recommence our sowing!

In the days of (our) second month, they hew out the ice with
   harmonious blows
And in those of (our) third month, they convey it to the ice-houses
(Which they open) in those of the fourth, early in the month
Having offered in sacrifice a lamb with scallions.
In the ninth month, it is cold, with frost;
In the tenth month, they sweep clean their stack-sites.
The two bottles of wine are enjoyed,
And they say, Let us kill our lamb and sheep,
And go to the hall of our prince,
And raise the crop of rhinoceros horn,
And wish him long life—that he may live forever![14]

The year-round activities of a farming household were expressed in terms of two calendars—that of the Hsia 夏 and that of the Chou—and the verse seems to adopt the point of view of a farmer. He was in servitude, and his daughter could be taken by the lord. His corvée duties required him to work during a leisure month at the house of the lord, repairing houses and engaging in a variety of household chores. No sign of collective farmwork involving large numbers of laborers is described. Other than farming, the farmer's household carried out a variety of activities: gathering fruits, growing vegetables, repairing houses, making clothes, and hunting small game. All these tasks seem to be organized around his own humble residence, together with his wife and children. He made most of the decisions on production, and, although he

14. Legge, *She King*, 227–33, with slight revisions.

probably received a ration of clothing issued by the lord, he and his family provided the necessary items for themselves. This person in servitude was a serf with his own assigned field and residence, rather than a slave who lacked an independent household.

The two different calendars used throughout the text[15] reflect a cultural dualism common in the Chou feudal vassaldoms, made up of a Chou ruling population and native people. Although it is still uncertain whether such a verse can be attributed to those dualistic feudal vassaldoms, the modifier "our" preceding one calendar system probably indicated that this serf was a member of the Chou, while the other, the Hsia, was probably a native. Chou princes normally brought some Chou people with them to the enfeoffed domain, where they were subjects of the ruler, received assigned fields to sustain themselves, and submitted a portion to their lord as tribute.[16] It was this group of the Chou population who were main supporters of the vassaldom, and probably the principal productive forces in the estate of the lord.

The well-field system, which Mencius described, may have operated in the Western Chou. In his description, eight farming families were responsible for tilling a unit of one hundred *mu* 畝. The harvest from that land belonged to the lord, while that of the one hundred *mu* assigned to each of these eight households was its own. The total of nine fields formed a checkerboard pattern that resembled the Chinese character for a well, *ching* 井.[17] Ever since Mencius wrote of this allegedly ancient pattern of land-holding, varying interpretations of its system have been espoused.[18]

The status of the farmer in the verse "Ch'i-yüeh" quoted above suggests that the Chou colonial population, or *kuo-jen* 國人, settled in vassaldoms and were assigned land-lots near the city to till. They produced from the assigned lots for themselves and jointly for the granary of the lord. In addition, they were required to fulfill other corvée duties as named by the lord. This possibly was the prototype of the well-field system. It cohered to the principle of reciprocity implicit in Chou feudalism. The lord and his subordinates each had a set of obligations and privileges in the form of land and protection on one side and tribute and services on the other. The property still belonged to the lord and although the farmer had the privilege of using a lot given to him, he could make most decisions about crops and production of other mate-

15. Hua Chung-yen, 1959.

16. See chapters 3 and 6 above.

17. Legge, *Mencius*, 244–45.

18. The issue was a focus of dispute among historians because of ambiguity in the definition of the well-field system in Mencius. Various propositions on periodization of Chinese history have developed. See Hsü Cho-yün, 1971:823, nn. 69 and 70.

rials necessary for subsistence. This was the form of operation and management of small, individual farmsteads.[19]

Although the date of the "Ch'i-yüeh" verse is disputed, it probably was composed during the late Western Chou period.[20] The passage on land-holding suggests that there was a tendency during the late Western Chou for those who had direct use of the land to gradually gain permanent control. Perhaps the same phenomenon prevailed at the level of the farmstead. Theoretically each individual farmer had to receive a new lot at one time, but a prolonged, continuous assignment of the same lot within a particular household might eventually give an individual farmer a considerable amount of autonomy only a little short of a private claim on the farm. The appearance of full private ownership, of course, was not noticeable until the Chan-kuo period.[21]

Now let us investigate the farming implements available to a Western Chou farmer. The term "pair" often appears in the classics, such as ten-thousand "in pairs" or one-thousand "in pairs." In the *Tso-chuan* 左傳, a scene of reclamation of land is described in which people stood in pairs in rows to cut clear the bushes.[22] Until the invention of the plow in the late Ch'un-ch'iu period, the standard way of breaking the earth was through cooperation of two persons. There were two possible ways for these persons to coordinate their actions. They might face each other to loosen earth clods or to dig up root systems of plants by jacking them up, using digging-sticks for leverage. They might also do the work by standing shoulder to shoulder to open up irrigation troughs or pile up ridges for planting.[23]

The digging-sticks, either single-tipped or double-pronged, were made of hardwood with a handle and a stepping-bar. The digging-stick normally was slightly curved in order to provide leverage.[24] Spades were also used for digging and were made of stone, bone, or shell. Many samples of these tips, made of various materials, were unearthed at Western Chou archaeological sites (fig. 10.1). The most-used materials used for digging tools represented in the findings at the Feng-hsi 澧西 sites were oxen and horse jaws and shoulder blades; stone was less common, while shell was the least common. Bronze tips were found, but they were very rare (fig. 10.2). In the early Chou site at Ch'i-ch'un 圻春, a U-shaped bronze digging tip was found. It resembled both an

19. Amano Motonosuke, 1959:105.
20. Hsü Cho-yün, 1971:822, 66; Hsü Chung-shu, 1936A; Fu Ssu-nien, 1951:95; Kao Heng, 1980:9.
21. Hsu, 1965:110−16.
22. Legge, *Ch'un Ts'ew*, 662.
23. Ch'eng Yao-t'ien, 1829:43−44; Sun Ch'ang-hsü, 1964:51.
24. Hsü Chung-shu, 1930; Sekino Takeshi, 1959, 1960.

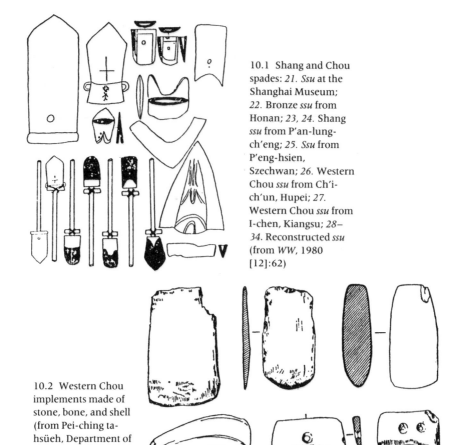

10.1 Shang and Chou spades: *21. Ssu* at the Shanghai Museum; *22.* Bronze *ssu* from Honan; *23, 24.* Shang *ssu* from P'an-lung-ch'eng; *25. Ssu* from P'eng-hsien, Szechwan; *26.* Western Chou *ssu* from Ch'i-ch'un, Hupei; *27.* Western Chou *ssu* from I-chen, Kiangsu; *28–34.* Reconstructed *ssu* (from *WW*, 1980 [12]:62)

10.2 Western Chou implements made of stone, bone, and shell (from Pei-ching ta-hsüeh, Department of History, 1979:166)

earlier counterpart from the Shang period and a later model from the Ch'un-ch'iu period (fig. 10.3). Little change or improvement had taken place in its development. Similarly, other implements, such as the harvest tools, did not change in shape. They were most often made of bone, stone, and shell.[25]

Bronze implements were rarely found at this early date. Recently, there were discoveries of a variety of bronze tools, such as spades and sickles, from Eastern Chou sites in Anhui 安徽, Kiangsu 江蘇, and Chekiang 浙江 provinces. Some were fragments found with unprocessed copper. Such findings suggest that there were workshops specializing in recycling worn-out bronze objects. Discoveries of such workshops provide an explanation for the rare appearance of bronze tools and imple-

25. Pei-ching ta-hsüeh, Department of History, 1979:167.

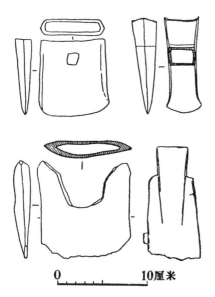

10.3 Chou bronze implements (from Pei-ching ta-hsüeh, Department of History, 1979:166)

0   10厘米

ments in more ancient archaeological sites. In the Chan-kuo period, iron tools were generally used and only a few bronze specimens survived. In the Western Chou period the most useful metal was bronze, and worn-out pieces were probably melted down to produce new objects. This procedure left little chance for early bronze implements to survive.[26]

In summary, the agricultural implements of the Western Chou were relatively simple. There were only two types: digging and harvest tools. Further differentiation and specialization to meet specific needs did not take place until the late Ch'un-ch'iu or even the Chan-kuo period. By then the appearance of cast or wrought iron had significantly altered agricultural advancement.[27]

Irrigation of considerable scale was not a significant factor in agriculture until the later half of the Ch'un-ch'iu period.[28] Western Chou farmers probably depended on wells to obtain their water supply. At the Chang-chia-p'o 張家坡 site of Feng-hsi, for instance, the well was more than nine meters deep. The opening of the well was elongated or oval-shaped suggesting that two buckets could be used side by side. We may further speculate that some pulley system had developed to allow these two buckets to move up and down alternatively.[29]

The Western Chou farmer had developed a system of field reclama-

26. Li Hsüeh-ch'in, 1980B:39.
27. Hsü Cho-yün, 1971:810–13; Liu Hsien-chou, 1963:58–62.
28. Hsü Cho-yün, 1971:815–16.
29. Liu Hsien-chou, 1963:46–48; K'ao-ku yen-chiu-so, 1962:77–78.

tion. There were three terms to identify conditions of fields. In the *Book of Poetry*, there are two references to such an arrangement:

> They were gathering the white millet,
> In those (*hsin* 新) new fields,
> And in these (*tzu* 菑) acres brought only one year under cultivation.
> When Fang-shu 方叔 came to take command.[30]
> And, ... Ah! Ah! ye assistants,
> It is now the end of spring;
> And what have ye to seek for?
> (only) how to manage the new fields
> And those (*yü* 畬) of the third year.
> How beautiful are the wheat and the barley,
> Whose bright produce we shall receive![31]

Clearly, there were three different kinds of fields. Legge interpreted *hsin* as a new field, *tzu* as a field brought only one year under cultivation, and *yü* as a field in its third year under cultivation. Hsü Chung-shu thought that the three-part division was no other than a three-field fallowing system used to recover fertility.[32] Yang K'uan 楊寬 agreed with Legge that *tzu* was newly reclaimed land, that *hsin* was a new field, and that *yü* was a well-cultivated field.[33] The existence of well-cultivated *yü* fields suggests that the three-field fallowing system was merely one step beyond primitive slash-and-burn agriculture. Within the core area during the Western Chou period there was a considerable density of population, yet the agricultural technique was still at a low level given the lack of differentiation of implements. To meet the problem of feeding somewhat densely packed population the answer was to increase usable acreages by continuously reclaiming erstwhile unused land. The *yü* field, once it was well-prepared for cultivation, need not lay fallow again until its fertility had been exhausted by a few years' continuous cultivation.

According to Ch'en Liang-tso 陳良佐, animal waste, including human waste, and green manure were used by the Shang farmer to enhance soil fertility.[34] Chang Cheng-lang 張政烺 also suggested that the Shang farmer practiced reclamation and carrying out consecutive stages including a final well-cultivated field.[35] Indeed the fallow rotation system was not only possible but necessary when land was abundantly available.

30. Legge, *She King*, 254.
31. Ibid., 582.
32. Hsü Chung-shu, 1955.
33. Yang K'uan, 1965:12–14, 45–48.
34. Ch'en Liang-tso, 1971.
35. Chang Cheng-lang, 1973:98–102.

Although Ho Ping-ti 何炳棣 interpreted the three technical terms (*tzu,*
hsin, and *yü*) as Yang K'uan did, he overestimated the neolithic agricultural conditions and implied that the *yü* field was continuously under
cultivation even then.[36] Judging from the large number of neolithic
tools used for felling trees and clearing underbrush, it is more likely that
primitive slash-and-burn agriculture and its immediate deviation, the
alternative fallow system or two-field system, was adequate for the
neolithic farmer. The relatively limited availability of potentially suitable
land within the Chou core area, where settlements were densely distributed, must have compelled the Chou farmer to use continuously the
already-cultivated field.

FOOD AND COOKING

The principal cereal foods in ancient China consisted of various subspecies of millet, wheat, rice, hemp seed, and a broad range of pulses
(beans and peas). Among them *shu* (*Panicum milleium*) was regarded as a
better foodstuff than *chi* (*Sectonra italica*), although both *shu* and *chi* were
commonly mentioned together as foods. Ch'ien Mu pointed out that in
later days other better-tasting subspecies of millet, as well as rice and
wheat, one after another became the preferred staples in the diet.[37] In
the Western Chou period, the most precious food was rice and it was
presented at state banquets and other extremely important occasions.
Although wheat was known to the ancient Chinese, it was not popularly
cultivated in north China until as late as Han period; instead, beans and
peas are routinely mentioned in ancient literature. In the Chan-kuo
period, pulses were a common food, but there is little explicit evidence
that the Western Chou people gave pulse a significant place on their
dining table.[38] The Western Chou cooked their cereal food in two ways:
by boiling or by steaming. The most ancient tripod, the *li* 鬲, was a
cooking utensil in which water and cereal were brought to boil by
placing the vessel directly over fire (fig. 2.5). A vessel called a *hsien* 甗
with perforated rack placed above boiling water was used to steam food.
Chan 饘 was a kind of thick rice porridge, while *chou* 粥 was diluted
congee. Neither one was as firm as the cooked rice, or *fan* 飯, which the
modern Chinese eat every day.

In a verse, steaming of grain is described:

> Take the good water from a distance;
> Draw it into one vessel and let it flow to another,

36. Ho, 1975:50–52.
37. Ch'ien Mu, 1956:10.
38. Hsü Cho-yün, 1976:509.

And it may be used to steam rice millet
(How much more should) the happy and courteous sovereign
Be the parent of the people.[39]

Although the aristocrats preferred steaming to boiling, the *li* tripod was
more common than the *hsien* steamer. Perhaps because both congee and
porridge required less grain than did steamed grain, only the aristocrats
could afford to consume steamed grain.

   Of course, any kind of grain could be crushed or ground into flour.
Mortars and querns have been found in neolithic sites. Although stone
mills have not been discovered in the Chou sites, flour was produced by
crushing the grains with rods or rolling pins.[40] The dishes on the Chou
dinner table do not seem to have been prepared in a sophisticated
manner. Boiling, broiling, baking, and roasting were the most common
ways of cooking meat. Meats eaten included beef, pork, mutton, rabbit,
and poultry. For instance, the *Book of Poetry* contains these lines:

With correct and reverent deportment,
The oxen and sheep all pure,
We proceed to the winter and autumnal sacrifices
Some flay (the victims): some boil (their flesh)
Some arrange (the meat); some adjust (the pieces of it).[41]

Of the gourd leaves, waving about it,
Some are taken and boiled;
(then) the superior man, from his spirits,
Pours out a cup, and tastes it.
There is about a single rabbit.
Baked, or roasted.

Roasted, or broiled ...[42]
Sauces and pickles are brought in,
With roast meat and broiled.[43]

And how as to our sacrifices (to Hou Chi)?
Some hull (the grain); some take it from the mortar;
some sift it; some tread it.
It is rattling in the dishes;
It is distilled, and the steam floats about.
We consulted; we observe the rites of purification;
We take southern wood and offer it with the fat;

39. Legge, *She King*, 489.
40. Amano Motonosuke, 1962:80–81, 843–50.
41. Legge, *She King*, 369.
42. Ibid., 420–21.
43. Ibid., 473.

We sacrifice a ram to the spirit of the path;
We offer roast flesh and broiled—
And thus introduce the coming year.[44]

Although much of the *Book of Rites* records Eastern Chou practices, the report must reflect the culinary customs and the cuisine of earlier days. Formal ceremonies preserved traditions, and, for instance, dishes presented in religious rituals included beef, mutton, pork, dog, chicken, pheasant, rabbit, and fish. A state dinner offered by a duke to his high officials included the above-mentioned meats and fish prepared in various ways by roasting or broiling in large chunks, or mincing into small pieces with mustard sauce and other spices.[45] A formal banquet for the king included nine meat dishes served in *ting* 鼎 tripods. (See table 5.2.) The dishes were beef, mutton, pork, fish, dried meat, stomach, skin, raw fish, and cured meat. As in burial, the number of *ting* tripods presented depended on one's rank. Seven *ting* were appropriate for dukes, five for ministers, three for great officials, one for *shih* 士 functionaries, and a single *ting* for the lowest-ranking aristocrats. The servings to the *shih* contained only broiled fish. A banquet for commoners merely included vegetables, for white fish was offered as sacrifice only during religious occasions or ceremonies dedicated to the ancestors.[46]

Other than such food for formal occasions, a broad range of animal meat (domesticated or game), fish, seafood, birds, and even insects (bees, ants, cicadas, snails) were used by the Chou chefs. Fish was the most usual source of protein for the Chinese people, and even the common people probably enjoyed fish as an occasional special dish. Numerous kinds of fish are named in the *Book of Poetry*, such as yellow jaws, sand-blowers, bream, tench, mud-fish, carp, sturgeon, and many more.[47] Beef, mutton, and various game meats were commonplace in the western Chou kitchen, but from the Chan-kuo period on, the Chinese gradually restricted their meat consumption to fewer choices— mainly pork, chicken, dog, and fish. The ideal life preached by Mencius was one in which an ordinary farmer kept some hogs, dogs, and hens in his own farmstead and secured fish from local ponds and rivers.[48] Changes in diet were probably the consequence of continuous rec- lamation of arable land in the Chou period at the cost of reducing the wooded areas, pasture lands, marshes, and swamps.

44. Ibid., 471.
45. *Li-chi*, 27/7–8.
46. I-li, 17/12 *Kuo-yü*, 18/2–3.
47. Legge, *She King*, 269, 589.
48. Legge, *Mencius*, 130–31, 461.

The list of vegetables consumed by the Chou people varies according to the sources one reads. The *Book of Rites* names a number of spicy items (mustard, ginger, leeks, onions, scallions, cinnamon, smartweed). These were served with meat and produced a strong odor.[49] The vegetables mentioned in the *Book of Poetry* included numerous kinds of leafy ones still grown domestically today and wild ones gathered from meadows and forests. In the former category, there were radishes, gourds, hot peppers, celery, and bamboo shoots. Of the latter type there were several kinds of water plants, such as cress and duckweed, as well as edible grasses, such as shepherd's purse, turnip greens, rape-turnip, thorn ferns, pigweeds, sowthistle, bracken.[50] The Chou people did not have a wide choice of domesticated vegetables and ate more wild ones than the Chinese do today.

Scattered mentions of fruits, berries, and nuts appear in the *Book of Poetry*. Also mentioned are several kinds of plums, peaches, pears, jujubes, caramabolas (or kiwi), melons, mulberries, and wild grapes, oxlips, sparrow-plums, chestnuts, and hazelnuts.[51] The *Nei-tse* 內則 chapter of the *Book of Rites*, mentions fruits, nuts, and berries which include the pear, melon, peach, plum, apricot, persimmon, jujube, chestnut, water caltrop, and chick-head: the list generally overlaps the one in the *Book of Poetry*.[52]

Some of the vegetables, fruits, and nuts that appear in the classics have been identified botanically; very few of them, however, have been archaeologically attested.[53] Most of the fruits and vegetables were collected instead of grown domestically. A passage in the *Book of Rites* says that during early winter months people should be taught to collect the vegetables still available in the woods and marshes.[54]

Even though cooking methods were not much more varied than boiling, steaming, broiling, and roasting, and even though the available ingredients were relatively limited, the ingenious Chou people developed a cuisine that made the best use of their resources. The *Book of Rites* includes recipes for the so-called eight delicacies that demonstrate the versatility of their gourmet dishes:

1. The most complicated preparation, roasted piglet, was roasted on the fire, deep-fried in a flour batter, and then steamed for three days and three nights.

49. *Li-chi*, 27/7–8, 28/1.
50. Legge, *She King*, 1, 8, 14, 22, 25, 53, 55, 136, 179, 188, 226, 232, 258, 270, 373, 401, 437, 465, 546, 614.
51. Ibid., 12, 26, 30, 35, 48, 61, 97, 217, 231, 437, 510.
52. *Li-chi*, 27/8.
53. Chang, 1977B: 28–29; Li Hui-ling, 1969, 1970.
54. *Li-chi*, 17/11.

2. A blended mince consisting of lean flank of five animals (beef, mutton, and versions of moose and muntjac) was hammered to a sinewless paste and eaten raw. It seems to be the most primitive way of preparing a meat dish.
3. Beef steak, sliced and soaked in wine, was served with plum jelly.
4. Beef, hammered to rid it of sinew and salted with ginger and cinnamon, was served after being thoroughly dried.
5. Beef and mutton, minced and mixed six times with rice flour to make patties, were then fried.
6. Dog-liver was deep-fried.
7. Rice porridge was served with animal fat, preferably wolf-fat.
8. Cooked rice or millet was topped with minced meat.[55]

These dishes, of course, were served only at the tables of the privileged and were probably eaten only occasionally. In daily life, soup of meat and vegetables was the most ordinary dish, for nobles as well as for commoners. Nevertheless, the *Book of Poetry* says that food for peasants was merely old, stale grain and leaves of wild greens.[56] They probably never even dreamt about the "eight delicacies."

Available seasonings were limited, so much so that no salt was added to soup even for formal ceremonies and religious occasions. Ordinarily, fish was seasoned with vinegar, pickles, salt, and plum, in an effort to reach an "harmony of flavors."[57] Spices, mainly the leaves of wild plants, were widely in use to supplement the seasonings. For instance, leaves of bean stalk would be added to beef; sowthistle, a kind of bitter herb, was added to mutton; and thorn fern was mixed with pork. Especially with meat, spices were routinely used.[58] Cane sugar was not known to the Chou people, nor was honey widely used. The sweetener was normally malt sugar made of grains.

Chou beverages were largely grain products, including a slightly fermented starch-water made of grain gruel. In addition, there was a "cool congee," probably a jellied drink. The "wines" were actually grain beers, for distillation of liquor was not well known during Chou times. The beer's sediment was drained by pouring the liquid over a bundle of rushes produced in the south.[59] The Chou people customarily added herbs to wines in order to enhance the flavor, and some of the fragrant herbs are often mentioned as gifts in royal decrees.[60]

55. *Li-chi*, 28/4−6.
56. Legge, *She King*, 231, 376.
57. Legge, *Ch'un-Ts'ew*, 684.
58. *I-li*, 19/30−31; *Li-chi*, 28/1.
59. Legge, *Ch'un Ts'ew*, 140; *Li-chi*, 27/7.
60. Huang Jan-wei, 1978:166−68.

The Chou did not consume as much alcohol as their Shang predecessors. The Chou often charged the Shang people with being alcoholics, and they prohibited the Chou people from indulging in drinking alcohol. Archaeologically, it is clear that there was much less drinking among the Chou than among the Shang. In the early Chou period, bronze ceremonial vessels were organized into sets of individual items similar to those of the Shang. After early Chou, the proportion of food containers increased, while drinking vessels decreased. By the late Western Chou period, a typical set would consist mainly of food containers such as tripods, trays, and water basins. The drinking vessels (fig. 10.4) occupied a secondary position.[61]

Thus, on the Chou dining table, there were only limited items, probably because Chou agriculture was rather unsophisticated and horticulture was not developed. Moreover, husbandry had been sacrificed to continuous land reclamation, which converted pasture and grazing land to farming fields. Chou culinary arts were not highly developed either, perhaps because of these secondary factors.

DRESS AND CLOTHING

There are few archaeological data from which to reconstruct the dress of the Chou people, but literary sources give abundant clues about fashion. Let us start with head coverings. In the "Ku-ming" 顧命 chapter (The Testamentary Charge) of the *Book of Documents*, the dying King Ch'eng 成 was wearing his royal cap (*mien* 冕) at the time the important nobles were summoned. Both King K'ang 康, who was about to succeed to the throne, and the officials wore hemp caps as a sign of mourning. The royal guards who attended the ceremony of enthronement wore a variety of conical caps (*pien* 弁), two of brownish leather, four of spotted deerskin, and five others for great officers.[62] Conventionally, classical scholars believed that the royal hat was a square, flat cap decorated with twelve pendants strung with gems, while the cap for great officers was decorated with five pendants embellished with black gems.[63] The differences either represented symbols of rank or particular occasions. No specific archaeological substantiation for these records has been found. Differentiation in burial ritual according to status was indicated by numbers of ritual vessels, however, so similar distinctions in dress according to rank and ceremony could be expected as well.

A common head-cover was called a *kuan* 冠, a cap that every male

61. Pei-ching ta-hsüeh, Department of History, 1979:203.
62. Legge, *She King*, 554–57.
63. Ibid., 556, note to paragraph 21.

adult must have worn. A boy of sixteen years of age was accepted as a full member of society only after a capping ceremony, a ritual of initiation. The *kuan* was worn over the bun and at the back of the head; it was held in place with a long hairpin. The *kuan* was normally black, except on occasions of mourning, when it was white.[64] The *kuan* was supposedly worn by the members of the nobility, the lowest-ranked of whom were the *shih*. The people of lower social status could not wear a *kuan*; instead, they wore a kind of folded scarf (*chin-tse* 巾幘).[65]

During ceremonial occasions, however, they could be dressed in yellow clothes and yellow *kuan*, but this was an exception to the rule. While in the sun or rain, people in the field wore hats of bamboo-leaves over the *kuan* cap.[66] Chou women, of course, had fashions of their own. Ladies of the upper class wore their hair either straight or curled up, and decorated it with long, flowing ribbons.[67] There probably were even more variations in female head dress in the Chou period.

Western Chou clothing must have been similar to that displayed on Shang stone statues and Chan-kuo wooden figurines. A loose jacket, which wrapped the upper body from the left to the right and fastened under the right shoulder, was worn. The lower body was clothed in a seven-gored skirt, three pieces in the front and four in the rear. Underneath the skirt there was a long apron and buskins that covered both knees and legs.[68] In bronze inscriptions, clothing is commonly mentioned as a gift. The colors and the ornamental designs are often specifically described: black clothes with coiled chains and spirals painted on the edge, for instance, or yellow clothes with linked rings embroidered on the edge.[69] Again, these literary passages confirm the Chou concern with symbols of rank and status.

A loose robe *shen-i* 深衣 was popularly worn for casual occasions. With its length reaching the feet and sleeves that covered the elbows, a *shen-i* comfortably wrapped the whole body. A long belt was worn at the waistline.[70] This robe was for daily use, while the above-described jacket-and-skirt combination was for formal occasions. Interestingly, from the Han dynasty on, long robes were regarded as formal dress, while jackets and trousers were regarded as casual.

Two kinds of shoes are described in the literature—double-soled slippers, called *hsi* 舄, and single-soled work shoes, or *lü* 履. *Hsi* were

---

64. *Li-chi*, 29/10.
65. Shang Ping-ho, 1966:29.
66. Legge, *She King*, 307–409.
67. Ibid., 409–11.
68. Ibid., 402.
69. Wong Yin-wai (Huang Jan-wei), 1978:170–72.
70. *Li-chi*, 58/4–5; Jen Ta-ch'un, 1888.

	FOOD						WATER		
	COOKER			CONTAINER			CEREMONIAL ABLUTIONS		
NAME OF CLASS	li	ting	hsien	kuei	tou	tui	p'an	chien	i
FAMILIAR APPEARANCE									
WHETHER SELF-NAMED	yes	yes	yes	yes	no	no	yes	yes	yes
ANCIENT GRAPH AND MODERN EQUIVALENT									
PHASE PRESENT	1 2 3	1 2 3	1 2 3	1 2 3	- 2 3	- - 3	1 2 3	- - 3	- 2 -
NEOLITHIC FORM									

WINE										
CONTAINER					GOBLET				SERVER	
tsun	yu	bu	lei	fang-i	chia	chüeh	chih	ku	bo	kuang
no	no	yes	yes	no	no	no	no	no	yes	no
1 - -	1 - -	1 2 3	1 2 3	1 - -	1 - -	1 - -	1 - 3	1 - -	1 2 3	1 - -

10.4 Bronze ritual vessels (from Willetts, 1965:86–87, courtesy of Thames & Hudson Ltd. and McGraw-Hill.)

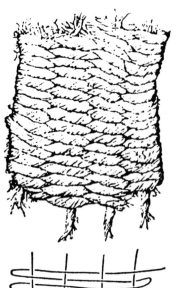

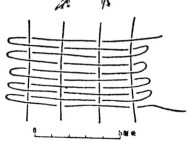

10.5 Woven bark for shoes
(from *KKHP*, 1982 [1]:67)

obviously a part of formal costume. In the *Book of Poetry* are these lines:
"The Duke was humble, and greatly admirable, self-composed in his red slippers."[71] Another passage mentions footgear even more specifically:

> With their four-horse chariot (they came),
> forming a long train,
> In their red knee-covers and gold-adorned slippers
> Princes gathered in accordance.[72]

Another verse mentions red slippers that were given by the king as one of numerous gifts.[73] Their color probably signified use in formal occasion.

Recently from the Shang site at Meng-chuang 孟莊 of Chi-ch'eng 柘城 a sole of a shoe made of tree-bark was discovered. The woven pattern was very similar to that used for straw sandals in north China today (fig. 10.5).[74] Although this was the first archaeological discovery of its kind,

71. Legge, *She King*, 242.
72. Ibid., 289.
73. Ibid., 547.
74. K'ao-ku yen-chiu-so, Ho-nan i-tui, 1982:66.

ordinary Western Chou walking shoes must have had similar bark soles. The red slippers must have been made of silk and been used merely at court and in the palace.

There were many kinds of attached ornaments on the apparel of nobles. Jade pendants named *huang* 璜 perhaps were the most common ones. These consisted of several jade pieces placed in a cluster and hung on the front of the belt on a colorful silk thread.[75] The standard set of accessories carried by a man included a sword, a writing tablet, a writing brush, small knives, a handkerchief, and a flint-stone. A women might have similar items, although a sewing kit replaced the sword.[76]

The fabrics used for dress were mainly wool, hemp, silk, and a linen-like material made from the fiber of an ivy plant. Of course fur and hide were also commonly used. The inscription on the recently discovered Ch'iu-Wei 裘衛 vessels told us that the Wei family were furriers who presented gifts including shoes, clothes, aprons, drapes, chair covers, chariot accessories, belts, and cords—all made from a variety of furs and hides taken from both domestic and game animals. The inscription even classifies the materials into different grades.[77] A kind of coarse felt seems to have been the common cloth for ordinary people to wear on wintry days, while the aristocrats wore fur. These two verses from the *Book of Poetry* demonstrate the contrast:

> His lamb's fur is glossy,
> Truly smooth and beautiful
> That officer
> Rests in his lot and will not change.
> His lamb's fur, with its cuffs of leopard-skin
> That officer
> In the country will ever hold to the right
> How splendid is his lamb's fur
> How bright are its three ornaments!
> That officer
> Is the ornament of the country[78]

and

> In the days of (our) second, the air is cold;
> Without the clothes and garment of hair,
> How could we get to the end of the year?

. . . .

75. Kuo Mo-jo, 1932:180; Huang Jan-wei, 1978:172.
76. *Li-chi.*
77. Chou Yüan, 1976:45–46; Tu Cheng-sheng, 1979A:586.
78. Legge, *She King*, 132–33.

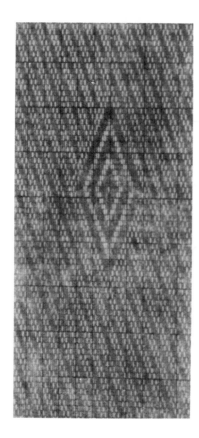

10.6 Reconstruction of woven fabric
(from *WW*, 1976 [4]:62)

In the days of (our) first month, they go after badgers,
And take foxes and wild cats,
to make furs for our young princes.[79]

Sericulture was developed as early as the neolithic, and archaeological
evidence confirms its use during the Western Chou period. Recently,
numerous jade models of silkworms were excavated in the mid-Chou
burial site at Ju-chia-chuang 茹家莊 at Pao-chi 寶雞. Their sizes varied
from four centimeters to less than one centimeter in length. Several
fabric imprints were found at the same site (figs. 10.6–10.8). Some of
them left impressions on bronze vessels; others were found in three or
four layers pressed into the earth. The imprints revealed several different
patterns produced by distinctive fabrication and weaving methods. The
embroidered pieces were dyed with bright red and yellow, and probably

79. Ibid., 226, 229; slightly revised.

10.7 Impressions of fabric (from *WW*, 1976 [4]:61)

10.8 Impressions of embroidery (from *WW*, 1976 [4]:64)

printed after embroidering. The embroidery was worked in single-thread contours by adding multi-thread braids. The field archaeologists reported that the materials were produced with high levels of skill.[80] The level of sericulture reached in the Western Chou period was, of course, a continuation of the high achievements of the Shang period. Much of the skill of weaving, fabrication, and even complicated embroidery was developed by the Shang.[81]

80. Li Yeh-chen, 1976:60.
81. Hsia Nai, 1972:14; Pei-ching ta-hüeh, Department of History, 1979:174–76.

Hemp tissues were next only to the silk as an important material and were discovered in the early Western Chou burial sites at Kao-chia-pao 高家堡 and Chün-hsien 濬縣, where several fragments of hemp-linen were found on the surface of a coffin.[82] Ko-linen (dolichos) was used for summer clothing and was fabricated from the tissue of some kind of ivy plant. The verse "Ko-t'an" 葛覃 reads:

> How the dolichos spread itself out
> Extending to the middle of the valley
> its leaves were luxuriant and dense
> I cut it and boiled it,
> and made both fine cloth and coarse,
> Which I will wear without getting tired of it![83]

The shoes made of ko-fabric were among the gifts that a bride brought for her husband:

> Shoes thinly woven of the dolichos fiber—
> May be used to walk on the hoarfrost
> The delicate fringes of a bride
> May be used in making clothes.
> (His bride) puts the waistband to his lower
> garment and the collar up to his upper
> And he, a beloved man, wears them.[84]

Other tissues from wild plants were used as well to produce fabrics. A poem cited in the Tso-chuan suggests this:

> Though you have silk and hemp,
> Do not throw away your grass and rushes.
> Though your wife be a Chi 姬 or a Chiang 姜,
> Do not slight your son of toil
> All men
> Have their vicissitudes of wants.[85]

The tissues of grass or rushes were not strong enough to produce cloth but were adequate to weave sandals, hats, or even raincoats. In fact, even today such outfits made of grass or rushes are common in China and other Asian countries.

The Chou probably dressed in the same manner as their Shang predecessors had, and as their Ch'un-ch'iu descendants would do until

82. Ko Chin, 1972:7; Kuo Pao-chün, 1964; Pei-ching ta-hsüeh, Department of History, 1979:174.

83. Legge, She King, 6—7.

84. Ibid., 163.

85. Legge, Ch'un Ts'ew, 372.

the change in dress during Chan-kuo period, when the tight narrow-sleeved jacket and trousers from the steppe tradition and a short jacket from the south were introduced. For centuries to come, the Chinese used the same kinds of materials—fur, hair, hide, silk, hemp, and ko-linen—to cover their bodies. Only cotton was missing from the Chou inventory.

FESTIVALS AND THE SEASONAL RHYTHM

From the discussions of food, clothing, and craft industries, it is clear that the Chou secured life resources from both agriculture and the collection of natural materials, including wild plants and the meat and skins of game animals. The importance of seasonal change to their lives is obvious. In the "Ch'i-yüeh" 七月 verses of the Book of Poetry, the effects of the change of seasons are vividly depicted.[86] The significance of seasonal changes was the central theme in Dirk Bodde's studies of the ancient Chinese festivals and songs.[87] He made the three local spring festivals and one harvest festival that he identified the subject of his studies.[88]

Indeed, the ancient Chinese had long paid attention to the movement of time. A monthly almanac called the Hsia-hsiao-cheng 夏小正 (The Regulations of Minor Affairs of Hsia), which was attributed to the Hsia people, listed climate conditions, the behavior of animals, the status of plants, and the positions of stars. It also gave a full ecological description of each month and how it related to human activities in agriculture, sericulture, hunting, administration, and religion. Its literary style is antiquated and its contents are relatively simple, and historians of farming believe that it was of ancient origin and survived unti' the early Ch'un-ch'iu period.[89] In comparison to the "Yüeh-ling" 月令 (The Monthly Ordinance) chapter in the Book of Rites, the Hsia-hsiao-cheng is less sophisticated, a simpler prototype. The "Yüeh-ling" chapter has long been regarded as an interpolation of the third century B.C.[90] and therefore cannot be relied on as an accurate document reflecting Western Chou customs. The Book of Poetry and the bronze inscriptions are principal resources for the identification of festivals. Only the portions of the "Yüeh-ling" that are consistent with the other ancient sources may be taken as survivals of ancient habits.

86. Legge, She King, 226–33.
87. Bodde, 1975.
88. Ibid., 166–79.
89. Hsia Wei-ying, 1981.
90. Li-chi, 14/1.

There were at least two early ceremonies related to agricultural activities. The ceremony of the Chi 籍 (the royal tillage) in the first month of the Hsia calendar symbolized the beginning of farming season. The Chi ceremony is recorded in bronze inscriptions, where mentions of a sacred, reserved field in which ceremonies took place are frequent.[91] The most detailed description of such activities is included in the *Kuo-yü*. Nine days before the date of *li-ch'un* 立春, the beginning of spring (February 4 or 5), the *T'ai-shih* 大史 reported on climate conditions to the king. Five days before *li-ch'un*, the king and participants began a fast, which lasted for three days. On the day of the Chi ceremony a banquet for all the participants, including ministers, officials, and farmers, was held. At the ceremony, the king, escorted by the T'ai-shih, the official in charge of agriculture, tilled the field symbolically by turning up one chunk of soil. Ministers turned up the earth three times; officials nine times; then the farmers worked throughout the entire sacred field. Another banquet for all the participants was held, and other related rituals included archery contests. For good harvest, the king prayed to God Ti. The crops collected from the sacred field were in time offered to the king, who in turn offered them at the temple of ancestors and gods. The grain from the sacred granary could also be distributed to needy farmers.[92] In the verses of the "Ch'i-yüeh," such a ceremony is not specifically described, but the activity of taking implements to the field is discussed. Was this the local counterpart of the Chi ceremony?[93]

The celebration of harvest is described in the "Ch'i-yüeh." Harvest concluded in the tenth month with a happy gathering of farmers at the hall of their lord. A feast was held and the peasants toasted their lord.[94]

A ceremony called Pa-cha 八蜡 was in fact the harvest festival. When the harvest was ready, during the twelfth month, the king would hold a series of rituals of sacrifice to the first farmer, to the first minister of agriculture, to the hundred seeds, to the workers in the fields, to the bounds of the fields (the earth), to the animals, to the water, and to the insects, plants, and trees. It was indeed a thanksgiving for all classes of beings, animate and inanimate, imaginary and real, in groups and individually. Then it was time to rest until the following spring, or for the older ones, it was time to retire.[95]

Hunting games were also regarded as ceremonies in ancient times. In various classics that mention ritual, such ceremonies are included as part

---

91. Shirakawa Shizuka, *KBTS*, 14:811–17, 20:814–16.
92. *Kuo-yü*, 1/6–8; Yang K'uan 1965:219–32.
93. Legge, *She King*, 226.
94. Ibid., 233.
95. Granet, 1975:171–74; *Li-chi*, 26/4–5.

of all four seasons' activities, for they were considered both as a game and as military training.[96] The "Ch'i-yüeh" verses, however, talk of hunting games in the winter months:

> In the day of (our) first month, they go after badgers,
> And take foxes and wild cats
> To make furs for our young princes.
> In the days of (our) second month, they have a general hunt,
> And proceed to keep the exercise of war.
> The boars of one year are for our princes.[97]

The winter, when people had finished their farming and the fields were cleared, was an appropriate time for a general exercise.

In the *Ch'un-ch'iu Chronicles*, the "Great Hunting Game" was not only a military exercise and a reorganizing of the army; it was also an occasion for a general meeting of the nobles who participated in state affairs.[98] The great nobles were required to attend a ceremony where the king erected his flag. The command center was marked by flags. For such an important occasion, it would not be odd for a participating noble to make a great effort to borrow provisions in order to have adequate bounty.[99]

Related to farming activities, yet certainly a reflection of seasonal change, were the spring festivals. Marcel Granet discussed the local spring activities in the eastern vassal states of Ch'en 陳, Cheng 鄭 and Lu 魯. During the spring, warm breezes thawed the ice and released the spell of bitter winter. Boys and girls of the state of Cheng gathered at the riverside to enjoy the river scenery and exchange jokes. At parting, they presented flowers to each other as love tokens. In the neighboring state of Ch'en, dancing was the main expression of love. The children danced to the beat of earthen drums, under the oak and the white elm. At dawn, the girls danced on the way to the market where they were to sell their hemp. At the marketplace, they met the boys again, and flowers were exchanged.[100]

Even the Chou royal couple observed their own spring festival. On the day of the spring equinox, the king and queen offered sacrifices to the spirit of Kao-mei 高禖 (Supreme Intermediary) in a southern suburb. Petitioning for male offspring was supposedly the purpose of such a ceremony. The duty of this deity, the Supreme Intermediary, was

---

96. Yang K'uan 1965:257–79.
97. Legge, *She King*, 229–30.
98. Yang K'uan, 1965:268–74.
99. Shirakawa Shizuka, *KBHS*, 49:257–59.
100. Granet, 1975:147–53; Legge, *She King*, 140–49, 205–07.

allegedly related to that of the swallow, the Shang progenitor. In the ceremony boys and girls were assembled in the second month of the spring equinox.[101] During the next month, the last month of spring, cattle and horses were set free for mating. A ceremony of purification was held by the sorcerers, who wore masks and paraded around in an effort to drive away evil spirits.[102] Finally, a ceremony of communal feast was hosted by dignitaries to honor the elders of the community. Yang K'uan was probably right to point out that the word *hsiang* 饗, used for both feast and the subdivisions within a city, etymologically connected a group of people who shared a common feast. The king, as well as nobles of various ranks, entertained peers with a feast to reinforce their bond. These communal gatherings were also the occasion to confirm or rearrange the hierarchical ranking among those who attended.[103]

Such a gathering, of course, could take place at any time in the year. A verse of "Pin-chih-ch'u-yen" 賓之初筵 in the *Book of Poetry* describes one such feast well:

When the guests first approached the mats,
They take their places on the left and the right in an orderly manner.
The dishes of bamboo and wood are arranged in rows,
With sauces and kernels displayed in them.
The spirits are mild and good,
And they drink, all equally reverent.
The bells and drums are properly arranged;
And they raise their pledge-cups with order and ease.
(Then) the great target is set up;
The bows and arrows are made ready for the shooting,
The archers are matched in classes.
"Show your skill in shooting" (it is said).
"I shall hit the mark" (it is responded),
"And pray you drink the cup."
The dancers move with their flutes to the notes of the organ and drum,
While all the instruments performed in harmony.
All this is done to please the meritorious ancestors,
Along with the observance of all ceremonies,
When all the ceremonies have been performed,

---

101. Granet, 1975:155–56; *Li-chi*, 15/2–3.
102. *Li-chi*, 15/9.
103. Yang K'uan, 1965:280–309.

Grandly and fully,
"We confer on you great blessings"
"And may your descendants also be happy!"
They are happy and delighted,
And each of them exerts his ability.
A guest draws the spirits,
An attendant enters again, with a cup,
And fills it—the cup of rest.
Thus are performed your seasonal ceremonies.[104]

The drinking, the music, the dance—all these indicate that the verse describes a stately affair. Perhaps the feast offered by the king after a Chi ceremony would be of similar luxury and elaboration.

A modest feast in which only roast rabbit, gourd leaves, and wine were served is also mentioned. This was for those in the countryside:

Of the gourd leaves waving about,
Some are taken and boiled;
(Then) the gentleman, from his wine,
Pours out a cup and tastes it.

There is but a single rabbit
Baked or roasted.
(But) the gentleman, from his wine,
Fills the cup and presents it (to his guest).[105]

A communal spirit called the Chou people together, rich or poor, ranked high or low. On such a foundation, perhaps, was the cornerstone of the Chou nation.

LIFE RITUALS

Rituals in the life of individual, from birth to death, and the rituals for deceased ancestors were important markers during the Chou period. Limitations in source materials allow investigation of only a few activities among the male aristocrats.

At the moment of birth, a male received special treatment not extended to the female. One verse relates:

Sons shall be born to him—
They will be put to sleep on couches;
They will be clothed in robes;

104. Legge, *She King*, 395−97.
105. Ibid., 420−21.

they will have scepters to play with;
Their cry will be loud.
They will be (hereafter) resplendent with red knee-covers.
The (fortuitous) king, the prince of the land.

Daughters shall be born to him—
They will be put to sleep on the ground;
they will be clothed with wrappers;
They will have tiles to play with.
It will be theirs neither to do wrong nor to do good.
Only about the spirits and the food will they have to drink,
And to cause no sorrow to their parents.[106]

The real beginning of life, especially for a boy, occurred upon reaching adolescence. Only then was his chance of his growing to adulthood certain, for infant mortality was high. Just as the initiation was to usher the youth into adulthood, the Chou aristocrats had a capping ceremony to usher a boy into full membership in society. Based upon descriptions in various classics, especially the *I-li* 儀禮 (*Ritual Proprieties*) and the *Li-chi* (*Books of Rites*), Yang K'uan summarized the capping. The ceremony was normally held at the age of twenty years. Guests of honor were invited by the father to witness the ceremony. Three times a different cap was placed on the head of the initiate. The first one was of hemp and indicated that the boy had now grown to adulthood and needed to have a cap. The second time, a leather cap was placed on his head. It was part of the military outfit and indicated that every aristocratic male should be a warrior. The third time, a cap for religious occasions was placed on his head, and he was considered a full member of the peerage. Then he was received by his mother, his relatives, the other nobles, and his own lord.

A second name was then given to him, so that he could be properly addressed in the public without using his personal name. The second name often contained a word to indicate birth order, such as *po* 伯 (the eldest), *chung* 仲 (the second eldest), *shu* 叔 (the third eldest), or *chi* 季 (the youngest). Also added to the second name was the title of *fu* 甫 (father) which, of course, signaled that he was recognized as an adult. At the age of fifteen, a girl entered adulthood, which was signified by using hairpins to fix her hairdo. She was also given a name to indicate her birth order and her status as a *mu* 母 (mother). The mention of birth order in names of adults established their appropriate place in the Chou feudal hierarchy. Seniority was important and was closely tied into the *tsung-fa* kinship structure.[107]

The wedding ceremony was also a significant life ritual. A wild goose

106. Ibid., 306–07.
107. Yang K'uan 1965:234–53; *I-li*, 1/1–2/16.

and a deerskin were brought as betrothal gifts to the house of the bride-to-be by the groom. The gifts apparently symbolized that the young man was capable of making adequate provision for his new family. The custom obviously was a survival from an earlier period in which hunting was relied on to provide food.

The wedding was arranged by the two families and witnessed by invited guests. The bride departed from her own home after the parents gave her instructions to be a submissive wife. The newlywed couple was not only received by the parents of the groom but also ushered to the ancestral shrine, where the marriage was reported to the ancestors. The ceremony signified the uniting of two families, not just two individuals. It also confirmed continuity with the past, with one's ancestors, and, extending into the future, with one's descendants.[108]

The funeral ceremony was the last of the series of life rituals. Immediately after someone died, a "caller" ascended to the roof and called the deceased's name three times, so that the soul might return. After this ritual brought no result, arrangements for the funeral proceeded. The name of the deceased was written on a banner erected on the top of a wooden bar, and grain was placed in his mouth to symbolize that he would not starve. The remaining grain was cooked, and the container with the cooked grain was placed next to the body on a wooden bar. The banner and the cooker acted as a temporary name-tablet, to which the spirit could attach itself until a permanent marker was erected. Such a practice seemed to indicate that the spirit of the deceased needed something to "anchor" or "perch" on. The name-tablet was finally placed in the ancestors' shrine, where it joined those of other deceased members of the family. The entire funeral was attended by brothers and kinsmen, each of whom was dressed in a mourning costume determined by his relationship to the deceased. The lord of the deceased person also attended and took this occasion to recognize the status of the successor of the newly deceased. This assured the continuation of the lord-vassal relationship, and reconfirmed the relationship with other peers.[109]

The ancestor shrine was the center of religious activities, where the living could offer sacrifices and entertainment. Serving the ancestors was considered as significant as worshiping the Heavenly God. Each state had an altar for worshiping Heaven in the southern sector of the capital and a complex of ancestral temples where the progenitor and the name-tablets of ancestors from whom the particular branch of agnatic unit was commemorated.[110]

108. *I-li*, 3/1−27.
109. Ibid., 23/2−28/16.
110. *Li-chi*, 34/1−2.

The services at ancestor temples, held several times a year, were not to pay homage to awesome spirits who existed beyond the human world. Rather, they were thought to be communal gatherings for both the deceased and the living. The brethren and the cousins, both close and remote, came there to reassure each other of their kinship bonds. The deceased were impersonated by grandchildren, who wore the clothing of the ancestors and enacted eating and drinking as if they were actually participating in the feast. Singers sang epics to commemorate the group's glorious history. The Chou, for example, remembered the miraculous birth of the founding father, the achievement of the development of farming, the legend of moving to Ch'i-shan 岐山 under the leadership of Kung-liu 公劉, T'ai-wang's 太王 marriage to the Lady Chiang 姜 and the establishment of the Chou state, the conquest of Ch'ung 崇 under King Wen 文 and King Wu 武, and the subsequent expansions.[111]

Some verses in the *Book of Poetry* illustrate well the scene and the atmosphere of such services and feasts offering sacrifices to the ancestor:

> In thick patches are those rushes, shining by the wayside
> Let not the cattle and sheep trample them.
> Anon they will burst open; anon they will be completely formed.
>
> With the leaves soft and glossy.
> Closely related are brethren;
> Let none be absent, let all be near.
> For some there are spread mats;
> For some there are given stools (besides).
>
> The mats are spread and a second one above;
> The stools are given, and there are plenty of servants.
> The (guests) are pledged, they pledged (the host) in return;
> He rinses the cup, and the guests put theirs down.
> Sauces and pickles are brought in
> With roast meat and broiled.
> Excellent provisions there are loads of tripe and cheek;
> With singing of lute, and with drums.
>
> The ornamented bows are strong,
> And the four arrows are balanced.
> They discharge the arrows, and all hit,
> And the guests are arranged according to their skill.
> His distant descendant presides over the feast;

111. Legge, *She King*, 466–72, 448–55, 483–89, 505–10, 569–75; Kao Heng et al., 1980:480–84.

His sweet spirits are strong.
He fills their cup from a measure,
And prays for the hoary old (among his guests)—
That with hoary age and wrinkled back,
They may lean on one another (to virtue), and support one another
  (in it)
That so then age may be blessed,
And then bright happiness (ever) increased.[112]

The first stanza in this verse actually is a description of the birth legend of Hou Chi, the Chou progenitor, while "distant descendant" refers either to his impersonator or to the real host of the service. The feast was also celebrated by holding an archery contest.

In another verse the harvest was gathered and services were offered to the progenitor and the ancestors. Their spirits, who were impersonated by grandchildren of the ceremonial master, were served with trays of food, roasted or broiled by the host, while dishes of grain were prepared by the hostess. Guests and visitors attended in a happy mood and awaited the arrival of the impersonator of the ancestors, who would come to bless all who were present. The priest prayed to the spirits and asked the "filial descendant" to convey the request. "And the spirits have enjoyed your drinks and they confer upon you a hundred blessings; each as it is desired, each as sure as law." Later, the spirits drank their fill. "The great representative of the dead then rises; and the bells and drums escort his withdrawal, on which the Spirits returned tranquilly to their place." The servants and the hostesses then reset the table, and the kinsmen and relatives enjoyed a private feast. Musicians once again played merry tunes, and food was plenty. They feasted until they were filled, then bid each other farewell.[113]

Thus, we see that the Chou kinship group was pulled together not only by the sharing of common interests but also by inclusion of all the past members of the group. Their spirits were visibly present in their costumed impersonators, and they received food, enjoyed entertainment, and bestowed blessings upon the living. The spirit was not a deified and revered being to be feared. The deceased forever remained with the living. Time would extend to posterity; there was no interruption of the family line. The past, the present, and the future were united by ever extending their family lines. The Chou nation, a conglomeration of such lineages, was, therefore, united.

112. Legge, *She King*, 473–75.
113. Ibid., 368–73; also compare 479–81, in which the impersonator was the main character.

SUMMARY

The Chou developed versatile ways to enrich their material life, supplementing agriculture with gathering and hunting in order to supply sufficient provisions. Their food did not compare to the cuisine of Chinese kitchens of today, but they had devised farm implements and cooking utensils that were adapted to cultural and natural conditions. Their clothing was more varied than that of their counterparts in other ancient cultures because they had a fully developed sericulture, a Chinese invention that could be traced to neolithic times.

The social life of the Chou people went on within the framework of seasonal rhythms and life ceremonies. It was the communal and kinship units that bonded the Chou people together. Community festivals probably united members of the Chi (Chou) and local peoples who were descendants of ancient nations. Kinsmen, past and present, formed a permanent community that transcended finite time. The centripetal force of communal sentiment held the Chou together, although the Chou feudal policy could not survive its own centrifugal direction as the Chou vassaldoms inevitably became localized. Nonetheless, the spread of Chou political control forced annexed units into an awareness of Chinese, or Hua-Hsia, cultural unity. With a strong sense of cultural cohesion, Chou tradition expanded and survived constant intrusions by neighboring, alien cultures.

11 Summary and Conclusions

The Chou people rose from a rather obscure neolithic background to become a mighty kingdom, surpassing their predecessors in breadth of territory, size of population, and effectiveness of governance. Such a feat did not come quickly or easily. In the pre-dynastic period, the Chou wandered along the periphery of the Shang cultural sphere. In that transitional zone, between agricultural land and the land of the pastoralists, they learned to absorb elements from different cultures for their own benefit. The great success of the Chou people may in part be attributed to the development of such tolerance and the ability to absorb and compromise.

In their effort to organize a kingdom, the Chou experimented by sending their own children to establish vassal states. There they often had to coexist with hostile indigenous populations. The foundation of the feudal network coincided with the reorganization and blending of populations into vassal states. Thus the Chou nation was finally formed from that collection of vassal states.

Chou culture spread far beyond the Chou royal domain and the vassal states. Throughout the four centuries of the Western Chou rule, the Chou army consolidated its defense lines along the edge of the steppe, east to the Liao 遼 River in Manchuria, and west to the big arch of the Yellow River. The royal forces and the armies of the Chou vassals pushed the non-Chou peoples in the Huai-Han valleys farther into the deep south. Garrison states were installed in the south of the Huai-Han region, with outposts as far south as the banks of the Yangtze River. The areas under direct or indirect political control of the Chou court, therefore, included more than half of present-day China. Chou culture, moreover, influenced the south, in both the Yangtze Valley and the southern coastal regions. For example, southerners copied designs from northern Chou bronzes but cast the vessels locally. In the four centuries that followed, the southerners, under the leadership of the state of Ch'u, challenged the northern political and cultural supremacy that had developed in Western Chou. Chou cultural influence had reached almost all of China proper during the Western Chou period.

To govern a kingdom of such a vast size, the Chou relied heavily upon a feudal network which delegated power to the hands of the vassals. Chou feudalism was reinforced either by kinship bonds or by matrimonial ties between royal house and vassals. The ruling class of the Chou, therefore, was tied into a vast extended household. The kinship network, known as the *tsung-fa* 宗法 system, officially brought the lowest-ranking warrior gentleman and the king together.

In the Chou court, a bureaucracy gradually grew to considerable size. Many of the government offices were filled by household personnel during the early days of the dynasty. Individual aristocrats who were brothers of the king or the leaders of friendly groups shared power with the king and served in posts as high ministers. By the mid-Chou reigns, the bureaucracy was articulated according to principles of divided labor and differentiated roles. The role of the individual personality, however, always remained significant in Chou politics. The exile of King Li testified to the power of the aristocracy, who managed to govern the kingdom collectively for fourteen years. This regency functioned rather well, probably due to the dependability of the bureaucracy.

The last decades of the Western Chou were filled with turmoil. The constant threat of invasion by pastoralists in the north and the northwest brought wars to the Chou home base in the Wei Valley. The center was not only burdened with military defense activities but also with the necessity to maintain a huge standing army. Continuous expansion of the southern frontiers won for the Chou both territory and tribute from the subjugated southern population. Although those victories in the south served the treasury of the eastern capital, the royal domain in the Wei Valley did not benefit. The upper echelon of Chou society in the royal domain probably experienced social changes, for available resources had to be shared by an ever-increasing number of aristocrats. As land was taken by garrison units or by intruding foreign groups, the available land resources were further reduced. The consequence was the impoverishment of the old establishment and the rise of a newly rich class that had direct access to the resources. These social and economic crises were compounded by the occurrence of a massive earthquake that destroyed local agriculture. The Western Chou royal government did not survive the combination of socioeconomic crisis and natural catastrophe.

The life-style of the Chou people was in many aspects developed on a Shang model. Regardless, the Chou developed their own tastes, skills, and technologies. Some of their traditions, such as their official aristocratic architecture, remained the standard in Chinese civilization for centuries.

The most remarkable hallmark of Chou daily life was its lively communal activity. Every stage in the life cycle was actively expressed in the life of the community. Kinship customs were the most commonly performed rituals. By means of this communal spirit the Chou maintained solidarity, and through emphasis on kinship they maintained strong group identity.

But what then was the Chou contribution to China and Chinese history? During the neolithic period several cultures emerged in China. Interactions and mutual exchange between these juxtaposed regional cultures enriched the content of all. Furthermore, local neolithic cultures gradually came to bear general similarities with each other. Although the Lungshanoid culture was the most pervasive in the central plain, there was no single force that, culturally or politically, was dominant until the rise of the Hsia, the Shang, and the Chou. The Shang, indeed, stood far in advance of all their neighboring political entities. Their cultural influence reached well beyond the Shang sphere of political control. Whether the people of the Great City of Shang viewed their neighbors as subordinates, friends, or enemies, they shared a common heritage. Beyond the Shang royal domain, however, there seems not to have developed a common national identity embracing all the peoples in China. The political and military prowess of the Shang helped to stretch their cultural influence, but a pan-Shang cultural unification was not accomplished. For instance, the Shang supreme being generally retained the character of an ancestral or even a tribal deity. The deity was not made universal to extend beyond the Shang culture, their Great City, and their family kingdom. Part of the great success of the Chou was due to their ability to absorb divergent populations and their beliefs into a grand, centralized schema.

The Chou could not claim cultural superiority as had the Shang, but they did not bear the burden of cultural complacency. Throughout the entire process of conquest of the Shang, the Chou leaders repeatedly established alliances with local forces in order to form coalitions. That the Chou kings were welcomed by two-thirds of the known Chinese world was a reflection of their strategy of tolerance and inclusion.

After the Chou overcame the Shang and dominated the central plain, they patiently built up alliances with the Shang people and with local descendants of ancient nations, most of whom were outside the Shang realm. Thus the Chou feudal network was the product of coalescence rather than enslavement of non-Chou peoples. Cultural coexistence between the indigenous Chinese and the Chou ruling classes was manifest in the cultural dualism that was prevalent in practically every vassal state. Thus the Chou organized a political and cultural coalition that eventually served as the foundation of a nation sharing a common Chinese culture.

The most notable change was the emergence of the notion of a universal supreme being. The Chou aristocracy claimed that Heaven was a universal god, concerned with the welfare of all people in the world, beyond the limits of any nation. The Chou kings, like the rulers of previous dynasties, reigned because they received the Mandate of Heaven, and they could lose the throne if their performance did not satisfy Heaven. Thus Chou kingship was founded on the pretense of legitimacy, which in turn depended on accountability to a universal Supreme Being who guided the world of human beings on a moral course.

Karl Jaspers suggested that by the first millennium, or the "axial age" as he calls it, the ancient world experienced a "breakthrough," developing a set of values that transcended the mundane order. In the case of ancient China, Jaspers thought that such a breakthrough coincided with the emergence of Confucianism and other philosophic schools in the sixth century B.C.[1] The prelude to the breakthrough, however, developed at the juncture of the Shang and Chou dynasties with the emergence of the concept of Heaven. Jaspers did not inquire into the causes of such changes, but Eric Weil has suggested that breakthroughs were preceded by a breakdown, one neither normal nor passing.[2] The appearance of a universal moral order in the Shang-Chou juncture coincided with the breakdown of Shang dominance of the ancient Chinese world. The Shang, for all their cultural vigor, failed to survive. The Chou provided a new explanation for their new world order. From then on, the Chinese held that legitimate political authority was the manifestation of high moral principles that served the well-being of the people. They believed society ought to be organized to maintain a secular order that would allow the people to live together under the guidance of a morality ensured by the Mandate of Heaven. Confucius did not claim that he was a founding father; his hero was the Duke of Chou, who had been so instrumental in the early organization of the Chou kingdom. In fact, Confucianism derived from the assumption that a code of universal morality prevailed.

Chou reliance upon kinship ties to reinforce the feudal network was likely the historical context in which Confucius developed his plan for an ideal social order. He assumed that kinship ties were the foundation of society. The Confucian system was essentially one based on family solidarity, in which the state resembled an enlarged household. Thus, an individual would meet his societal obligation by first living as a good member of a good household.

1. Schwartz, 1975; Jaspers, 1953:2–3, 44–48.
2. Weil, 1975.

The emphasis upon kinship and mandated morality survived the Chou dynasty and became the center of Confucianism. These two concepts were the most fundamental tenets of Chinese civilization, and they, inseparable from Confucianism, were legacies of the Chou. Chinese civilization represents a rare instance in which the coincidence of religion and state occurred in accordance with Jasper's theory.[3] Although a united empire was not formed during the Chou period, feudalism served as an essential pattern for political unity. This model may be recognized as a third feature of the Chou legacy.

The Chou guided "the world under Heaven," or *T'ien-hsia* 天下, not a Great City, as had the Shang. They did so by organizing a political coalition, a move meaningful for all dynasties, since the Chou had replaced the Shang in the same manner as the Shang had replaced the Hsia. The conquered group simply had lost the Mandate of Heaven. The fusion of local and regional cultures, coupled with their claim to the Mandate of Heaven, gave the Chou moral and cultural justification for their rule of a universal state.

From then on, the Hua-Hsia, or Chinese, world occupied the central plain and proclaimed a central role as the Middle Kingdom. Chinese history was thereby perpetuated from the past to all posterity, through expansion from the center toward all four directions. The main theme of this epic journey was the preservation and spread of Hua-Hsia civilization and the absorption or incorporation of new, or foreign, features from the periphery of the realm. All peoples were to join the main current, the only "civilized" universal order in East Asia at that time.

The Hua-Hsia order was based on an agricultural economy. After the mid-Chou reigns, however, the Chou had to defend themselves against the pastoralists along the borders of the steppeland. Hua-Hsia ideas simply could not stretch beyond the agricultural zone. By contrast, in the south there was almost continuous expansion because the indigenous peoples there, also agriculturalists, could see the common base they shared with Hua-Hsia farmers. They could cohere to the Hua-Hsia culture and share the advantages of it.

The Hua-Hsia world as a single cultural complex probably embraced more population and area than any other axial age civilization in ancient times. Its cultural coherence outlasted its political institutions. The Western Chou royal house fell for a complex set of reasons in the eighth century B.C., but the Hua-Hsia expression survived the collapse of royal authority. During the Eastern Chou period the former Chou vassals, one after another, led their Hua-Hsia compatriots against intrusions

---

3. Jaspers, 1953:255–57.

by foreigners and continued their cultural expansion into the four quarters. For those four centuries there was no political unification in China, but the momentum of cultural expansion developed in the preceding centuries was impressively strong. Acceptance of the Hua-Hsia order provided solidarity because there was a strong, common identity derived from belief in the importance of cultural coherence.

The durability of the Hua-Hsia attitude is demonstrated by its ability to tolerate a variety of new members from non-Chou cultures. Apparently, it was the universalism of the Hua-Hsia order that made it receptive to foreign elements. Later, Confucius would hold that one should not discriminate against any people in one's mission to teach the civilized way of life. The Hua-Hsia order did not exclude anyone who came to contact with it and aspired to join it. The universalism of the Hua-Hsia order owed much not only to the concept of the Mandate of Heaven but to the rationalism that was derived therefrom.

Solidarity within the Chinese population and the Hua-Hsia tolerance of others were the chief supports of Chinese culture. China survived other axial-age civilizations, in fact, and lasted three thousand years while repeatedly incorporating non-Chinese nations into it. The Western Chou period was the cradle of the beliefs and procedures necessary to preserve this process.

Appendix

Bibliographies

Index

Appendix: The Chou Chronology

Precise dates of neither historical events nor royal reigns have been given in the text, for dating is one of the most perplexing problems in the study of ancient China. Given the present state of historical knowledge, an absolute chronology is nearly impossible to reconstruct. This appendix reviews the nature of the problem and therefore the reasons that have impelled us to discuss Chou history in this fashion.

Difficulties in reconstructing a Chou chronology begin with problems in dating the beginning of the dynasty, in discerning its duration, and in determining individual royal reigns. Since the eighteenth century, when classical Ch'ing studies flourished, several chronological reconstructions have been made. More than a dozen systems have been presented by classical scholars and historians. Confusion abounds, for each reign was assigned a different length in each system. Moreover, the beginning year of the dynasty, at the victory at Mu-yeh 牧野, has been calculated to no less than thirteen different dates, falling anywhere between 1122 B.C. and 1018 B.C.[1] Fortunately, the chronology after the Kung-ho 共和 era (841–828 B.C.) is known in absolute terms, and there are few problems in establishing a year-by-year account by counting backward from the end of the Western Chou period, that is, from 771 B.C. Furthermore, there is no question about the duration of the reigns of Kings Hsüan 宣 (46 years, 828–782 B.C.) and Yu 幽 (11 years, 781–771 B.C.).

The disparities in dating are in part due to what ancient sources different scholars have used as documents and, of course, how they have interpreted those records. The beginning date of the dynasty, for instance, was calculated by the Han scholar Liu Hsin 劉歆 to 1122 B.C., while the T'ang 唐 monk I-hsing 一行 put it in the year equivalent to 1111 B.C.[2] These two scholars combined the available data and tried to accommodate disparities. Both used the most precise calendrical system available: Liu used the San-t'ung 三統 calendar; while I-hsing used the Ta-yen 大衍 system.[3] But the Chou did not make precise calendars, and we do not know exactly what kind of timetable they used to measure and then

---

1. Chou Fa-kao, 1971; Ch'ü Wan-li, 1971: 787; Shirakawa Shizuka, *KBTS*, 44:324; Lao Kan, 1977; Nivision, 1980, 1983.

2. The Chinese did not use the Julian calendar until recent decades. Hereafter, we will simply refer to years B.C. without using the modifier "equivalent."

3. Ch'en Meng-chia, 1977:2–15.

coordinate the lengths of solar and lunar cycles. Furthermore, we do not know how the Chou used the movement of celestial bodies to correct their calendar in case deviation became obvious. The problem then is twofold. Each analyst interprets sources according to his or her sense of appropriateness, and there is a paucity of primary documentation.

The issue became more problematic when modern scholars such as Tung Tso-pin 董作賓 made use of data from, for example, the remnant of a Chou chronicle[4] excavated in the Chin 晉 dynasty and transmitted to our time in fragmentary paragraphs.[5] Supplementary information interpreted in recent times has added to the complexity, rather than to the clarity, of the issue. For instance, the distribution of years of royal reigns included in the ancient version of the ducal house record of the state of Lu 魯 used by Liu Hsin differed from the distribution contained in the currently accepted version of the history of the Lu ducal house in the *Shih-chi* 史記. Simply by working on those disparities in the records of the Lu ducal house, Ch'ü Wan-li 屈萬里 established nine possible combinations that represented the whole duration of the Western Chou period![6]

Modern epigraphic scholars have attempted to reconstruct Chou chronology by using information about dates that appears in Chou bronze inscriptions. At first glance, the possibility of reconstructing a reliable and precise chronology by dating the individual vessels seems likely. The Chou bronze inscriptions often include the date of the ceremony commemorating the event for which the particular vessel was cast. In some cases even the year of the royal reign is mentioned, as "in the *x* year of our King." Commonly a term used to describe the phase of moon is given.

Although ostensibly helpful, these data have not been very useful after all. Often the number of years in the reign of a king is given, but we are not told which king he was. To solve this particular problem the vessels are arranged according to style and morphology, and the historical events and personal names are collated where possible. A relative sequence of the royal reigns, therefore, has been developed. Alas, however, we are not told in which year a particular reign ended and, therefore, a year-by-year chronology of reigns is still not possible.

The actual dates in inscriptions are elusive. They are given as one of the sixty-day cycle of the Kan-chih 干支 (moon-phase) system. This grand cycle of sixty names was produced by combining two cycles. The T'ien-Kan 天干 cycle consisted of ten names (Chia 甲, I 乙, Ping 丙, Ting 丁, Wu 戊, Chi 己, Keng 庚, Hsin 辛, Jen 壬 and Kuei 癸). The Ti-chih 地支 cycle consisted of twelve names (Tzu 子, Ch'ou 丑, Yin 寅, Mao 卯, Ch'en 辰, Ssu 巳, Wu 午, Wei 未, Shen 申, Yu 酉, Hsü 戌, and Hai 亥).[7] As early as in the Shang period, a Kan-chih dating system was in use,[8] but such cycle-names do not indicate which part of the month the date referred to. Since each month

4. *Chu-shu chi-nien.*
5. Tung Tso-pin, 1952.
6. Ch'ü Wan-li, 1971:789–90.
7. Chia-Tzu 甲子, I-Ch'ou 乙丑 . . ., Kuei-Hai 癸亥.
8. Tung Tso-pin, 1952; Keightley, 1978:200.

originally represented a lunar cycle and was about twenty-nine days, it does not correspond to a sixty-day cycle.

The meaning of moon-phase terminology poses another serious problem. There were four terms adopted in the bronze inscriptions. *Ch'u-chi* 初吉 literally meant "the first auspicious date." *Wang* 望 was the full-moon day. The two other terms included a character *pa* 霸 interpreted either as the "white-portion" or the "Soul." *Chi-sheng-pa* 既生霸 , therefore, was "the date *pa* was born"; while *Chi-ssu-pa* 既死霸 was "the date *pa* died." Wang Kuo-wei 王國維 proposed that these four terms represented four quarters of a month, each roughly the length of one week.[9] Tung Tso-pin proposed that two dates were definitely fixed. One marked the beginning of a month, or the darkest night of the lunar cycle, or the turning point from a dark moon to the return of light. That date was called *Fei* 朏 (the beginning of a crescent), or *Chi-ssu-pa* 既死霸 . The other fixed point marked the full-moon day and was designated as *Wang*.[10] Ch'en Meng-chia 陳夢家 followed Tung's suggestion that *Ch'u-chi* meant new crescent, or the second or third day following the beginning of the month. *Chi-sheng-pa*, or the birth of the moon's soul, he argued, should occur a few days preceding the full moon.[11] Shirakawa Shizuka 白川靜 accepted Wang Kuo-wei and insisted that a month was divided into four quarters.[12] At present, scholars are still disputing the merit of these two theories.[13] Neither theory has yet been proven. In fact, one of these four terms, *Ch'u-chi*, may not be a moon-phase date at all. Statistically, appearances of the term *Ch'u-chi* in the bronze inscriptions outnumbered those of other three terms.[14] Possibly bronzes were frequently cast on the beginning date of the month or on the day of the new crescent. It is also possible, perhaps likely, that *Ch'u-chi* was simply a routine term to indicate that the commemorative vessel was cast on the first auspicious day of the month. If this was the case, much of the argument for assigning a Kan-chih date to a certain day or to a certain quarter of the month is lost. And, since *Ch'u-chi* was the most common term in the bronze inscriptions, many of the data that were used as the base of reconstruction of the Chou calendar would be inapplicable.

Because of these problems, and until more materials appear, a precise Chou calendar is not available. Lacking such a calendar as a foundation for the reconstruction of a chronology, we regrettably cannot provide an absolute Chou chronological system. For the sake of practical convenience, however, we present two chronologies here: one developed by Ch'en Meng-chia,[15] and the other by Shirakawa Shizuka.[16]

9. Wang Kuo-wei, 1959:19−26.

10. Tung Tso-pin, 1952.

11. Ch'en Meng-chia, 1955A.

12. Shirakawa Shizuka, *KBTS*, 44:297−98.

13. For instance, Lao Kan criticized Tung's theory while Liu Ch'i-i confirmed the hypothesis of fixed dates. Lao Kan, 1977; Liu Ch'i-i, 1979.

14. Huang Jan-wei, 1978:64; Lao Kan, 1977:50−51.

15. Ch'en Meng-chia, 1977:53.

16. Shirakawa Shizuka, *KTBS*, no. 45 and no. 46.

A.1. Chou Chronology

Reigns	CH'EN MENG-CHIA		SHIRAKAWA SHIZUKA	
	Duration (Years)	Dates (B.C.)	Duration (Years)	Dates (B.C.)
Wu 武	3	1027–1025	3	1087–1085
Ch'eng 成	20	1024–1005	25	1084–1060
K'ang 康	38	1004–967	35	1059–1025
Chao 昭	22	966–948	25	1024–999
Mu 穆	20	947–928	31	998–968
Kung 恭	20	927–908	17	967–951
I	10	907–898	14	950–937
Hsiao 孝·	10	897–888	19	936–918
Yi 夷	30	887–858	39	917–879
Li 厲	16	857–842	37	878–842
Kung-ho	14	841–828	14	841–828
Hsüan 宣	46	827–782	46	827–782
Yu 幽	11	781–771	11	781–771
TOTAL	257	1027–771	317	1087–771

Western Language Bibliography

Backhofer, L. 1946. *A Short History of Chinese Art*. New York: Pantheon.

Barnard, Noel. 1958. "A Recently Excavated, Inscribed Bronze of Western Chou Date." *Monumenta Serica* 17:12–46.

_____. 1961. *Bronze Casting and Bronze Alloys in Ancient China*. Nagoya: Australian National University and *Monumenta Serica*, monograph 14.

Bernstein, B. 1965. *A Socio-Linguistic Approach to Social Learning*. London: Penguin.

Binford, L. R. 1972. *An Archaeological Perspective*. New York: Seminar Press.

Bodde, D. 1975. *Festivals in Classical China*. Princeton: Princeton University Press; Hong Kong: The Chinese University Press.

Boserup, E. 1965. *The Conditions of Agricultural Growth*. Chicago: Aldine Atherson.

Boulding, K. E. 1969. "Zoom, Gloom, Doom and Room." *The New Republic* 6.

Carneiro, R. L. 1970. "A Theory of the Origin of State." *Science* Autumn: 733–38.

Chang, Kwang-chih. 1963. *The Archaeology of Ancient China*. New Haven: Yale University Press.

_____. 1964. "Some Dualistic Phenomena in Shang Society." *Journal of Asian Studies*, 24:45–61.

_____. 1976. "Early Chinese Civilization: Anthropological Perspectives." Cambridge: Harvard University Press.

_____. 1977A. *The Archaeology of Ancient China*. New Haven: Yale University Press. 3rd ed.

_____. 1977B. *Food in Chinese Culture*. New Haven: Yale University Press.

_____. 1980. *Shang Civilization*. New Haven: Yale University Press.

_____. 1983A. *Art, Myth and Ritual: The Path to Political Authority in Ancient China*. Cambridge: Harvard University Press.

_____. 1983B. "Sandai Archaeology and the Formation of States in Ancient China: Processual Aspects of the Origins of Chinese Civilization." In *The Origins of Chinese Civilization*, ed. D. Keightley. Berkeley: University of California Press. 495–522.

_____. 1983C. *7000 Years of Chinese Civilization*. Milan: Silvana Editoriale. 24–44.

Childe, V. G. 1942. *What Happened in History?* Harmondsworth, Middlesex: Penguin Books.

Clark, G. 1977. *World Prehistory*, Cambridge: Cambridge University Press. 3rd ed.

Cohen, R., and E. Service, eds. 1978. *Origins of the State: The Anthropology of Political Evolution*, Philadelphia: Institute for the Study of Human Issues.

Coulbern, R. 1956. *Feudalism in History*. Princeton: Princeton University Press.

Creel, H. G. 1970. *The Origins of Statecraft in China*. Chicago: Unversity of Chicago Press.

Douglas, M. 1982. *Natural Symbols*. New York: Pantheon Books.

Eberhard, W. 1965. "Kultur und Siedling der Randvolker Chinas." Suppl. *Toung Pao*, vol. 36. Leiden: Brill.

———. 1982. *China's Minorities: Yesterday and Today*, Belmont, California: Wadsworth Publishing Co.

Flannery, K. 1972. "The Cultural Evolution of Civilizations." *Annual Review of Ecology and Systematics* 3:399–426.

Fong, Wen, ed. 1980. *The Great Bronze Age of China: An Exhibition from the People's Republic of China*. New York: Alfred A. Knopf, Inc.

Franklyn, U. M. 1983. "The Beginnings of Metallurgy in China: A Comparative Approach." In *The Great Bronze Age of China: A Symposium*, ed. G. Kuwayama. Seattle and London: University of Washington Press. 94–99.

Granet, Marcel. 1975. *Festivals and Songs of Ancient China*, trans. E. D. Edwards. New York: Gordon Press.

Ho, P. T. 1975. *The Cradle of the East*. Chicago: University of Chicago Press.

Hsu, C. Y. 1965. *Ancient China in Transition*. Palo Alto: Stanford University Press. (1968, paper ed.)

———. 1966. "Notes on the Western Chou Government." *Bulletin of the Institute of History and Philology* 36:513–24.

———. 1979. "Early Chinese History: The State of the Field." *Journal of Asian Studies* 38(3):453–75.

———. 1981. "Stepping into Civilization: The Case of Cultural Development in China." *National Palace Museum Quarterly* vol. 16, no. 1:1–20.

Huber, L. 1983. "Some Anyang Royal Bronzes: Remarks on Shang Bronze Decor." In *The Great Bronze Age of China: A Symposium*, ed. Wen Fong. Seattle: University of Washington Press. 16–43.

Jaspers, K. 1953. *The Origin and Goal of History*, trans. Michael Bullock. New Haven: Yale University Press.

Kane, V. 1974/75 "The Independent Bronze Industries in the South of China Contemporary with the Shang and Western Chou Dynasties." *Archives of Asian Art* 28:77–107.

Kao, Chü-hsün. 1960. "The Ching-lu Shen Shrines of Han Sword Worship in Hsiung-nu Religion." *Central Asiatic Journal* 5(3):43–62.

Karlgren, B. 1926. "The Authenticity and Nature of the *Tso Chuan*." *Göteborg Hogskolos Arsskriff*, vol. 32, no. 3.

———. 1931. "The Early History of the *Chou li* and *Tso chuan* Texts." *Bulletin of the Museum of Far Eastern Antiquities* 3:1–59.

Keightley, D. 1978. *Sources of Shang History*. Berkeley: University of California Press.

Keightley, D., ed. 1983. *The Origins of Chinese Civilization*. Berkeley: University of California Press.

Kubler, G. 1962. *The Shape of Time*. New Haven: Yale University Press.

La Plante, J. 1958. *Arts of the Chou Dynasty*. Palo Alto: Stanford University.

Lamberg-Karlovsky, C. C. 1979. *Ancient Civilizations: The Near East and Meso-america*. Menlo Park, California: Benjamin Cummings Pub. Co.

Lattimore, O. 1962. *Studies in Frontier History*. Oxford: Oxford University Press.

Legge, J. 1970. *The Chinese Classics*. 5 vols., orig. pub. 1893–95. Hong Kong: Hong Kong University Press, 1970. vol. 1, *The Confucian Analects;* vol. 2, *The Works of Mencius;* vol. 3, *The Shoo King;* vol. 4, *The She King;* vol. 5, *The Ch'un Ts'ew with the Tso Chuen*.

Li, Chi. 1976. *Anyang*. Seattle: University of Washington Press.

Li, Hui-lin. 1969. "The Vegetables of Ancient China." *Economic Botany* 23:253–60.

———. 1970. "The Origin of Cultivated Plants in Southeast Asia." *Economic Botany* 24:3–19.

Linduff, K. M. 1977. "The Incidence of Lead in Late Shang and Early Chou Ritual Vessels." *Expedition* Spring: 7–16.

———. 1979. *Tradition, Phase and Style of Shang and Chou Ritual Vessels*. New York: Garland Publishing, Inc.

Loehr, M. 1953. "The Bronze Styles of the Anyang Period." *Archives of the Chinese Art Society of America* 7:42–53.

———. 1956. *Chinese Bronze Age Weapons: The Werner Jannings Collection in the National Palace Museum, Peking*. Ann Arbor: University of Michigan Press.

———. 1968. *Ritual Vessels of Bronze Age China*. New York: Asia Society.

Maspero, H. 1950. "Le Régime féodal et la propriété foncière dans la Chine antique." *Mélanges posthumes sur les religions et l'histoire de la Chine*. Vol. 1. Paris: Musée Guimet.

Nivison, D. 1980. "The Ho Tsun Inscription and the Beginning of Chou." Paper presented at the Annual Meeting of the American Oriental Society, San Francisco.

———. 1983. "Datable Western Chou Inscriptions." In *The Great Bronze Age of China: A Symposium*, ed. G. Kuwayama. Seattle and London: University of Washington Press.

Oppenheim, A. L. 1977. *Ancient Mesopotamia: Portrait of a Dead Civilization*. Chicago: University of Chicago Press. Rev. ed.

Poor, R. 1970. "Some Shang and Western Chou Bronzes." *National Palace Museum Quarterly* 3:1–8.

Price, N. 1977. "Note: Once Again on Loehr's Bronze Styles." *Early China* 3:96–97.

Průšek, J. 1971. *Chinese Statelets and the Northern Barbarians in the Period 1400–300 B.C.* New York: Humanities Press.

Pulleyblank, E. J. 1983. "The Chinese and Their Neighbors in Prehistoric and Early Historic Times." *The Origins of Chinese Civilizations*, ed. D. Keightley. Berkeley: University of California Press. 411–66.

Rawson, J. 1980. *Ancient China, Art and Archaeology*. London: Trustees of the British Museum.

Schwartz, B. 1975. "Transcendence in Ancient China." *Daedalus* Spring: 57–68.

Shaughnessy, E. L. 1981. "New Evidence on the Zhou Conquest." *Early China* 6:57–79.

Sherratt, A. 1980. *The Cambridge Encyclopedia of Archaeology.* New York: Crown Publishers and Cambridge University Press.

Steward, J. 1955. *Theory of Cultural Change.* Urbana: University of Illinois Press.

Walker, R. 1953. *The Multi-State System of Ancient China.* Hamden, Connecticut: The Shoe String Press.

Waston, W. 1971. *Cultural Frontiers in Ancient East Asia.* Edinburgh: Edinburgh University Press.

————. 1973. *The Genius of China: The Exhibition of Archaeological Finds of the People's Republic of China.* London: Times Newspaper, Ltd.

Webster, D. L. 1975. "Warfare and the Evolution of State: A Reconsideration." *American Antiquity* 40:464–72.

Weil, E. 1975. "What Is a Breakthrough in History?" *Daedalus* 21–36.

Wheatley, Paul J. 1971. *Pivot of the Four Quarters,* Edinburgh University Press.

White, L. A. 1975. *The Concept of Cultural Systems.* New York: Columbia University Press.

Whitehouse, R. 1977. *The First Cities.* New York: Phaideon.

Wilhelm, R., and C. F. Barnes. 1977. *The I-ching or the Book of Changes.* Princeton: Princeton University Press.

Willetts, W. 1965. *Foundations of Chinese Art.* London: Thames & Hudson.

Wilson, J. 1951. *The Cultures of Ancient Egypt.* Chicago: University of Chicago Press.

Chinese Language Bibliography

An Chih-min 安志敏. 1979A. "P'ei-li-kang, Tz'u-shan ho Yang-shao—shih-lun Chung-yüan hsin-shih-ch'i wen-hua ti yüan-yüan chi fa-chan" 斐李崗磁山和仰韶 — 試論中原新石器文化的淵源及發展. *K'ao-ku* 考古 4:335–46.

⸻. 1979B. "Lüeh-lun san-shih-nien lai wo-kuo ti hsin-shih-ch'i shih-tai k'ao-ku" 畧論三十年來我國的新石器時代考古. *K'ao-ku* 考古 5:393–403.

An-hui sheng po-wu-kuan 安徽省博物館. 1957. "An-hui Hsin-shih-ch'i shih-tai i-chih ti tiao-ch'a" 安徽新石器時代遺址的調查. *K'ao-ku hsüeh-pao* 考古學報 1:21–30.

An-hui sheng wen-hua-chü 安徽省文化局. 1959. "An-hui T'un-hsi Hsi-chou-mu fa-chüeh pao-kao" 安徽屯溪西周墓發掘報告. *K'ao-ku hsüeh-pao* 考古學報 4:59–88.

⸻. 1964. "An-hui Shu-ch'eng ch'u-t'u ti t'ung-ch'i" 安徽舒城出土的銅器. *K'ao-ku* 考古 10:478.

An-hui sheng wen-kuan-hui 安徽省文管會. 1956. *Shou-hsien Ts'ai-hou-mu ch'u-t'u i-wu* 壽縣蔡候墓出土遺物. Peking 北京: K'o-hsüeh Press 科學.

An-yang fa-chüeh-tui 安陽發掘隊. *See* K'ao-ku yen-chiu-so, An-yang fa-chüeh tui 見考古研究所安陽發掘隊, 1961.

Chang Ch'ang-shou 張長壽. 1980. "Lun Pao-chi Ju-chia-chuang fa-hsien ti Hsi-chou t'ung-ch'i" 論寶鷄茹家莊發現的西周銅器. *K'ao-ku* 考古 6:526–29.

Chang Cheng-lang 張政烺. 1973. "Pu-tz'u p'ou-t'ien chi-ch'i hsiang-kuan chu-wen-t'i" 卜辭裒田及其相關諸問題. *K'ao-ku hsüeh-pao* 考古學報 1:93–118.

⸻. 1976. "Ho-tsun ming-wen chieh-shih pu-i" 何尊銘文解釋補遺. *Wen-wu* 文物 1:66–67.

⸻. 1978. "Li-kuei shih-wen" 利簋釋文. *K'ao-ku* 考古 1:58–59.

Chang Chung-p'ei 張忠培. 1980. "K'o-sheng-chuang wen-hua chi ch'i hsiang-kuan chu-wen-t'i" 客省庄文化及其相關諸問題. *K'ao-ku yü wen-wu* 考古與文物 4:78–84.

Chang Hsiao-heng 張筱衡. 1958. "San-p'an k'ao-shih" 散盤考釋. *Jen-wen tsa-chih* 人文雜誌 2:4.

Chang Kwang-chih 張光直. 1963. "Shang-wang miao-hao hsin-k'ao" 商王廟號新考. *Bulletin of Institute of Ethnology* 民族學研究所集刊 15:65–94.

⸻. 1965. "Yin-li chung ti erh-fen hsien-hsiang" 殷禮中的二分現象. In *Ch'ing-chu Li chi-chih hsien-sheng ch'i-shih-sui lun-wen-chi* 慶祝李濟之先生七十歲論文集 Taipei 台北: Ch'ing-hua hsüeh-pao she, 清華學報社. 353–70.

———. 1970. "Shang-Chou ch'ing-t'ung-ch'i-hsing chuang-shih hua-wen yü ming-wen tsung-ho yen-chiu ch'u-pu pao-kao" 商周青銅器形裝飾花紋與銘文綜合研究初步報告. *Bulletin of Institute of Ethnology* 民族學研究所集刊 30:329–315.

———. 1976. "Yin-Shang wen-ming ch'i-yüan yen-chiu shang-ti i-ko kuan-chien wen-t'i" 殷商文明起源研究上的一個關鍵問題. In *Shen Kang-po hsien-sheng pa-chih jung-ch'ing lun-wen-chi* 沈剛伯先生八秩榮慶論文集. Taipei 台北: Lien-ching Press 聯經. 151–79.

———. 1978. "Ts'ung Hsia-Shang-Chou san-tai k'ao-ku lun san-tai kuan-hsi yü Chung-kuo ku-tai kuo-chia ti hsing-ch'eng" 從夏商周三代考古論三化關係與中國古代國家的形成. In *Chü Wan-li hsien-sheng ch'i-chih jung-ch'ing lun-wen-chi.* 屈萬里先生七秩榮慶論文集. Taipei 台北: Lien-ching Press 聯經. 187–306.

———. 1980. "Yin-Chou kuan-hsi ti tsai-chien-t'ao" 殷周關係的再檢討. *Bulletin of Institute of History and Philology* 歷史語言研究所集刊, vol. 51, no. 2:197–216.

Chang P'eng-ch'uan 張朋川. 1979. "Kan-su ch'u-t'u-ti chi-chien Yang-shao wen-hua jen-hsiang t'ao-su" 甘肅出土的幾件仰韶文化人像陶塑. *Wen-wu* 文物 11:52–55.

Chang Ping-ch'üan 張秉權. 1970. "Yin-tai ti nung-yeh yü ch'i-hsiang" 殷代的農業與氣象. *Bulletin of Institute of History and Philology* 歷史語言研究所集刊 42:267–336.

Chang Wan-chung 張萬鐘. 1962. "Hou-ma Tung-chou t'ao-fan ti tsao-hsing kung-i" 候馬東周陶範的造型工藝. *Wen-wu* 文物 4/5:37–42.

Chang Ya-ch'u 張亞初 and Liu Yü 劉雨. 1981. "Ts'ung Shang-Chou pa-kua shu-tzu fu-hao t'an shih-fa ti chi-ke wen-t'i" 從商周八卦數字符号談筮法的幾個問題. *K'ao-ku* 考古 2:155–63.

Ch'ang-hsing hsien po-wu-kuan 長興縣博物館. 1979. "Che-chiang Ch'ang-hsing hsien ch'u-t'u wu-chien Shang-Chou t'ung-chi'i" 浙江長興縣出土五件商周銅器. *Wen-wu* 文物 11:93.

Ch'ang-hsing hsien wen-hua-kuan 長興縣文化館. 1973. "Che-chiang Ch'ang-hsing hsien ti liang-chien ch'ing-t'ung-ch'i" 浙江長興縣的兩件青銅器. *Wen-wu* 文物 1:62.

Che-chiang sheng po-wu-kuan 浙江省博物館. 1978. "Ho-mu-tu i-chih tung-chih-wu-i-ts'un ti chien-ting yen-chiu" 河姆渡遺址動植物遺存的鑒定研究. *K'ao-ku hsüeh-pao* 考古學報 1:95–108.

Che-chiang sheng wen-kuan-hui 浙江省文管會 and Che-chiang sheng po-wu-kuan 浙江省博物館. 1978. "Ho-mu-tu i-chih ti-i-ch'i fa-chüeh pao-kao" 河姆渡遺址第一期發掘報告. *K'ao-ku hsüeh-pao* 考古學報 1:39–94.

Ch'en Ch'üan-fang 陳全方. 1979. "Tsao-Chou tu-ch'eng Ch'i-i ch'u-t'an" 早周都城岐邑初探. *Wen-wu* 文物 10:44–50.

Ch'en Chung-mien 岑仲勉. 1956. "Hsi-Chou she-hui chih-tu wen-t'i" 西周社會制度問題. Shanghai 上海: Hsin-chih-shih Publisher 新知識.

Ch'en Liang-tso 陳良佐. 1971. "Chung-kuo ku-tai nung-yeh shih-fei chih shang-ch'üeh" 中國古代農業施肥之商榷. *Bulletin of Institute of History and Philology* 歷史語言研究所集刊, vol. 42, no. 4:20–47.

Ch'en Meng-chia 陳夢家. 1954. "Hsi-Chou-wen-chung-ti yin-jen shen-fen" 西周文中的殷人身分. *Li-shih-yen-chiu* 歷史研究 6:85–106.

_____. 1955A. "Hsi-Chou t'ung-ch'i tuan-tai" (1) 西周銅器斷代(一). *K'ao-ku hsüeh-pao* 考古學報 9:137–75.

_____. 1955B. "Hsi-Chou t'ung-ch'i tuan-tai" (2) 西周銅器斷代(二). *K'ao-ku hsüeh-pao* 考古學報 10:69–142.

_____. 1955C. "I-hou-tse kuei ho ta-ti i-i" 宜候夨毁和它的意義. *Wen-wu ts'an-k'ao tzu-liao* 文物參考資料 5:63–66.

_____. 1956A. *Yin-hsü pu-tz'u tsung-shu*" 殷墟卜辭綜述. Peking　北京　: K'o-hsüeh 科學.

_____. 1956B. "Hsi-Chou t'ung-ch'i tuan-tai" (3) 西周銅器斷代(三). *K'ao-ku hsüeh-pao* 考古學報 1:56–114.

_____. 1956C. "Hsi-Chou t'ung-ch'i tuan-tai" (4) 西周銅器斷代(四). *K'ao-ku hsüeh-pao* 考古學報, 2:85–94.

_____. 1956D. "Hsi-Chou t'ung-ch'i tuan-tai" (5) 西周銅器斷代(五). *K'ao-ku hsüeh-pao* 考古學報 3:105–27.

_____. 1956E. "Hsi-Chou t'ung-ch'i tuan-tai" (6) 西周銅器斷代(六). *K'ao-ku hsüeh-pao* 考古學報 4:85–122.

_____. 1957. *Shang-shu t'ung-lun* 尚書通論. Shanghai 上海 : Commercial Press 商務·

_____. 1977. *Hsi-Chou nien-tai-k'ao* 西周年代考. Hong Kong 香港 : Hua-hsia 華夏. Reprint.

Ch'en P'an 陳槃. 1969. "Ch'un-ch'iu ta-shih-piao lieh-kuo chüeh-hsing chi ts'un-mieh-piao chuan-i" 春秋大事表列國爵姓及存滅表譔異. Taipei 台北: Academia Sinica 中央研究院.

_____. 1981. "T'ai-shan chu-ssu i chu-sheng shuo" 泰山主死亦主生說. *Bulletin of Institute of History and Philology* 歷史語言研究所集刊 vol. 51, no. 3:407–12.

Ch'en Pang-fu 陳邦福. 1955. "Tse-kuei k'ao-shih" 夨毁考釋. *Wen-wu ts'an-k'ao tzu-liao* 文物參考資料 5:67–69.

Ch'en Shih-hui 陳世輝. 1980. "Ch'iang-p'an ming-wen chieh-shuo" 墙盤銘文解說. *K'ao-ku* 考古 5:433–35.

Chen-chiang shih po-wu-kuan 鎮江市博物館. 1978. "Chiang-su Chin-t'an-hsien Pieh-tun Hsi-Chou-mu" 江蘇金壇縣鱉墩西周墓. *K'ao-ku* 考古 3:151–54.

_____. 1979. "Chiang-su Chü-jung Fu-shan Kuo-yüan t'u-tun-mu" 江蘇句容浮山果園土墩墓. *K'ao-ku* 考古 2:107–18.

_____. 1980. "Chiang-su Tan-yang ch'u-t'u ti Hsi-Chou ch'ing-t'ung ch'i" 江蘇丹陽出土的西周青銅器. *Wen-wu* 文物 3:3–9.

Ch'eng Yao-t'ien 程瑤田. 1829. "Kou-hsü chiang-li hsiao-chi" 溝洫彊理小記. In *Huang-Ch'ing ching-chieh* 皇清經解. Chüan 541:51–53.

Ch'i Ssu-ho 齊思和. 1940. "Yen-Wu fei Chou feng-kuo shuo" 燕吳非周封國說. *Yen-ching hsüeh-pao* 燕京學報 28:175–96.

_____. 1946. "Hsi-Chou ti-li-k'ao" 西周地理考. *Yen-ching hsüeh-pao* 燕京學報 30:63–106.

_____. 1947. "Chou-tai hsi-ming li-k'ao" 周代錫命禮考. *Yen-ching hsüeh-pao* 燕京學報 32:197–226.

_____. 1948A. "Hsi-Chou shih-tai chih cheng-chih ssu-hsiang" 西周時代之政治思想. *Yen-ching she-hui k'o-hsüeh* 燕京社會科學 1:19–40.

_____. 1948B. "Mao-shih ku-ming k'ao" 毛詩穀名考. *Yen-ching hsüeh-pao* 燕京學報 36:276–88.

Ch'i Wen-t'ao 齊文濤. 1972. "Kai-shu chin-nien-lai Shan-tung ch'u-t'u ti Shang-Chou ch'ing-t'ung-ch'i" 概述近年來山東出土的商周青銅器. *Wen-wu* 文物 5:3–16.

Chi-nan po-wu-kuan 濟南博物館. 1974. *Ta-wen-k'ou* 大汶口. Peking 北京: Wen-wu Press 文物.

Ch'i-shan hsien wen-hua-kuan 岐山縣文化館. 1976. "Shan-hsi sheng Ch'i-shan hsien Tung-chia-ts'un Hsi-Chou t'ung-ch'i shih-hsüeh fa-chüeh chien-pao" 陝西省岐山縣董家村西周銅器室穴發掘簡報. *Wen-wu* 文物 5:26–33.

Chiang Hung 江鴻. 1976. "P'an-lung-ch'eng yü Shang-ch'ao ti nan-t'u" 盘龍城與商朝的南土. *Wen-wu* 文物 2:42–46.

Chiang-hsi sheng li-shih po-wu-kuan 江西省歷史博物館. 1980. "Chiang-hsi Ching-an ch'u-t'u Ch'un-ch'iu Hsü-kuo t'ung-ch'i" 江西靖安出土春秋徐國銅器. *Wen-wu* 文物, 8:13–15.

Chiao Hsün 焦循. 1888. "Ch'ün-ching kung-shih-t'u" 群經宮室圖. In *Huang-Ch'ing ching-chieh hsü-pien* 皇清經解續編. Chüan 359–60.

Ch'ien Mu 錢穆. 1931. "Chou-ch'u ti-li-k'ao" 周初地理考. *Yen-ching hsüeh-pao* 燕京學報 10:1955–2008.

———. 1956. "Chung-kuo ku-tai pei-fang nung-tso-wu k'ao" 中國古代北方農作物考. *Hsin-ya hsüeh-pao* 新亞學報 2:1–27.

Chin O 金鶚. 1888. "Ch'iu-ku-lu-li-shuo" 求古錄禮說. In *Huang-Ch'ing ching-chien hsü-pien* 皇清經解續編. Chüan 663–77.

Chin Hsiang-heng 金祥恆. 1959. *Hsü chia-ku-wen pien* 續甲骨文編. Taipei 台北: I-wen Publishing Co 藝文.

———. 1974. "Ts'ung chia-ku pu-tz'u yen-chiu Yin-Shang chün-lü chung chih wang-tsu san-hang san-shih" 從甲骨卜辭研究殷商軍旅中之王族三行三師. *Chung-kuo wen-tzu* 中國文字 52:1–26.

Ch'in-yung k'ao-ku-tui 秦俑考古隊. 1983. "Ch'in-shih-huang-ling erh-hao t'ung-ch'e-ma ch'ing-li chien-pao" 秦始皇陵二號銅車馬清理簡報. *Wen-wu* 文物 7:1–16.

Ch'iu Hsi-kuei 裘錫圭. 1978. "Shih-Ch'ang-p'an-ming chieh-shih" 史墻盘銘解釋. *Wen-wu* 文物 3:25–32.

Chou Fa-kao 周法高. 1951. "K'ang-Hou-kuei k'ao-shih" 康候旣考釋. In *Chin-wen ling-shih* 金文零釋. Taipei 台北: Institute of History and Philology 歷史語言研究所.

———. 1971. "Hsi-Chou nien-tai k'ao" 西周年代考. *Hong Kong* 香港: Chinese University, Wen-hua yen-chiu-so hsüeh-pao 中文大學文化研究所學報 vol. 4, no. 1:178–205.

Chou O-sheng 周萼生. 1957. "Mei-hsien Chou-tai t'ung-ch'i ming-wen ch'u-shih" 郿縣周代銅器銘文初釋. *Wen-wu ts'an-k'ao tze-liao* 文物參考資料 8.

Chou Wen 周文. 1972. "Hsin-ch'u-t'u ti chi-chien Hsi-Chou ch'i" 新出土的幾件西周器. *Wen-wu* 文物 7:9–12.

Chou Yüan 周瑗. 1976. "Chü-po Ch'iu-wei liang-chia-tsu ti hsiao-ch'ang yü Chou-li ti peng-huai" 矩伯裘衞兩家族的消長與周禮的崩壞. *Wen-wu* 文物 6:45–50.

Chou-i cheng-i 周易正義. Ssu-pu-pei-yao 四部備要 edition.

Chou-li cheng-i 周禮正義. Ssu-pu pei-yao 四部備要 edition.

Chou-li chu-shu 周禮注疏. Ssu-pu pei-yao 四部備要 edition.

Chou-yüan k'ao-ku-tui 周原考古隊. 1978. "Shan-hsi Fu-feng chuang-pai i-hao Hsi-Chou ch'ing-t'ung-ch'i chiao-ts'ang fa-chüeh chien-pao" 陝西扶風庄白一號西周青銅器窖藏發掘簡報. *Wen-wu* 文物 3:1–18.

_____. 1979A. "Shan-hsi Ch'i-shan Feng-ch'u-ts'un Hsi-Chou chien-chu fa-chüeh chien-pao" 陝西岐山鳳雛村西周建築發掘簡報. *Wen-wu* 文物 10:27–34.

_____. 1979B. "Shan-hsi Ch'i-shan Feng-ch'u-ts'un fa-hsien Chou-ch'u chia-ku-wen" 陝西岐山鳳雛村發現周初甲骨文. *Wen-wu* 文物 10:38–43.

_____. 1980. "Fu-feng Yün-t'ang Hsi-Chou ku-ch'i chih-tsao tso-fang i-chih shih-chüeh chien-pao" 扶風雲塘西周骨器製造作坊遺址試掘簡報. *Wen-wu* 文物 4:27–35.

_____. 1981A. "Fu-feng Chao-ch'en Hsi-Chou chien-chu-ch'ün chi-chih fa-chüeh chien-pao" 扶風召陳西周建築羣基址發掘簡報. *Wen-wu* 文物 3:10–22.

_____. 1981B. "Fu-feng-hsien Ch'i-chia-ts'un Hsi-Chou chia-ku fa-chüeh chien-pao" 扶風縣齊家村西周甲骨發掘簡報. *Wen-wu* 文物 2:1–6.

_____. 1982. "Ch'i-shan Feng-ch'u-ts'un liang-tz'u fa-hsien Chou-ch'u chia-ku-wen" 岐山鳳雛村兩次發現周初甲骨文. *K'ao-ku yü wen-wu* 考古與文物 3:10–22.

Chu Chün-sheng 朱駿聲. 1968. *Shuo-wen t'ung-hsün ting-sheng* 說文通訓定聲. Taipei 台北: Commercial Press 商務.

Chu K'o-chen 竺可楨. 1979. *Chu K'o-chen wen-chi* 竺可楨文集. Peking 北京: K'o-hsüeh Press 科學.

Chu-shu chi-nien 竹書紀年. Su-pu-pei-yao 四部備要 edition.

Chü Wan-li 屈萬里. 1965. "Tu Chou-shu shih-fu-p'ien" 讀周書世俘篇. In *Ch'ing-chu Li Chi-chih hsien-sheng ch'i-shih sui lun-wen-chi* 慶祝李濟之先生七十歲論文集, vol. 1. Taipei 台北: Ch'ing-hua hsüeh-pao 清華學報. 317–22.

_____. 1971. "Hsi-Chou shih-shih kai-shu" 西周史事概述. *Bulletin of Institute of History and Philology* 歷史語言研究所集刊 vol. 42, no. 4:755–802.

Ch'üan T'ang-wen 全唐文. Taipei 台北: Hui-wen Book Co. 滙文. Reprint.

Chuang-tze 莊子. Ssu-pu pei-yao 四部備要 edition.

Ch'un-ch'iu Tso-chuan cheng-i 春秋左傳正義. Ssu-pu-pei-yao 四部備要 edition.

Chung Feng-nien 鍾鳳年 et al. 1978. "Kuan-yü Li-kuei ming-wen k'ao-shih-ti t'ao-lun" 關於利簋銘文考釋的討論. *Wen-wu* 文物 6:77–87.

Chung Po-sheng 鍾柏生. 1978. *Wu-ting pu-tz'u chung ti fang-kuo ti-wang k'ao* 武丁小辭中的方國地望考. Taipei 台北: Shu-heng Publishing Co. 書恒.

Erh-li-t'ou kung-tso-tui 二里頭工作隊. 1974. "Ho-nan Yen-shih Erh-li-t'ou Tsao-Shang kung-tien i-chih fa-chüeh chien-pao" 河南偃師二里頭早商宮殿遺址發掘簡報. *K'ao-ku* 考古 4:234–56.

Erh-ya chu-shu 爾雅注疏. Ssu-pu-pei-yao 四部備要 edition.

Feng Han-chi 馮漢驥. 1980. "Ssu-ch'uan P'eng-hsien ch'u-t'u ti t'ung-ch'i" 四川彭縣出土的銅器. *Wen-wu* 文物 12:38–47.

Fu Chu-fu 傅筑夫. 1980. *Chung-kuo ching-chi-shih lun-ts'ung* 中國經濟史論叢. Peking 北京: San-lien Book Co. 三聯.

Fu Hsi-nien 傅熹年. 1981A. "Shan-hsi Ch'i-shan Feng-ch'u Hsi-Chou chien-chu i-chih ch'u-t'an" 陝西岐山鳳雛西周建築遺址初探. *Wen-wu* 文物 1:65–74.

_____. 1981B. "Shan-hsi Fu-feng Chao-ch'en Hsi-Chou chien-chu i-chih ch'u-t'an" 陝西扶風召陳西周建築遺址初探. *Wen-wu* 文物 3:34–45.

Fu Ssu-nien 傅斯年. 1935. "I-Hsia tung-hsi shuo" 夷夏東西說. In *Ch'ing-chu Ts'ai*

Yüan-p'ei hsien-sheng liu-shih-wu sui lun-wen-chi 慶祝蔡元培先生六十五歲論文集. Nanking 南京: Institute of History and Philology 歷史語言研究所. 1093–1134.

———. 1952. *Fu Meng-chen hsien-sheng chi* 傅孟眞先生集. Taipei 台北: National Taiwan University 國立台灣大學.

Fu-feng hsien wen-hua kuan 扶風縣文化館 et al. 1976. "Shan-hsi Fu-feng ch'u-t'u Hsi-Chou Po-chung chu-ch'i" 陝西扶風出土西周伯貳諸器. *Wen-wu* 文物 6:51–60.

Han-shu pu-chu 漢書補註. Taipei 台北: I-wen Press 藝文. Reprint.

Hei Kuang 黑光 and Chu Chieh-yüan 朱捷元. 1975. "Shan-hsi Sui-teh Yen-tou-ts'un fa-hsien i-p'i chiao-ts'ang t'ung-ch'i" 陝西綏德墕頭村發現一批窖藏銅器. *Wen-wu* 文物 2:82–87.

Heng-yang shih po-wu-kuan 衡陽市博物館. 1978. "Hu-nan Heng-yang shih-chiao fa-hsien ch'ing-t'ung hsi-tsun" 湖南衡陽市郊發現青銅犧尊. *Wen-wu* 文物 7:88.

Ho-nan sheng po-wu-kuan 河南省博物館 and Cheng-chou shih po-wu-kuan 鄭州市博物館. 1977. "Cheng-chou Shang-tai ch'eng-chih fa-chüeh chien-pao" 鄭州商代城址發掘簡報. *Wen-wu* 文物 1:21–31.

Ho-pei sheng wen-wu kuan-li-ch'u 河北省文物管理處. 1975. "Tz'u-hsien Hsia-p'an-wang i-chih fa-chüeh pao-kao" 磁縣下潘汪遺址發掘報告. *K'ao-ku hsüeh-pao* 考古學報 1:73–116.

Hou-Han-shu chi-chieh 後漢書集解. Taipei 台北: I-wen Press 藝文. Reprint.

Hsia Nai 夏鼐. 1961. "Lin-t'ao ssu-wa-shan fa-chüeh-chi" 臨洮寺洼山發掘記. In *K'ao-ku-hsüeh lun-wen chi* 考古學論文集. Peking 北京: K'o-hsüeh Press 科學.

———. 1964. "Wo-kuo chin-wu-nien-lai ti k'ao-ku shou-huo" 我國近五年來的考古收獲. *K'ao-ku* 考古 10:485–97, 503.

———. 1972. "Wo-kuo ku-tai ts'an-sang ssu-ch'ou ti li-shih" 我國古代蠶桑絲綢的歷史. *K'ao-ku* 考古 2:12–27.

———. 1977. "T'an-shih-ssu (Carbon-14) ts'e-ting-nien-tai ho Chung-kuo shih-ch'ien k'ao-ku-hsüeh" 碳十四測定年代和中國史前考古學. *K'ao-ku* 考古 4:217–32.

Hsia Wei-ying 夏緯瑛. 1981. *Hsia-hsiao-cheng ching-wen chiao-shih* 夏小正經文校釋. Peking 北京: Nung-yeh Press 農業.

Hsiao P'an 蕭璠. 1981. "Ying-hsü chia-ku-wen chung-tzu shih-shih" 殷墟甲骨文众字試釋. *Shih-huo yüeh-k'an* 食貨月刊復刊 (n.s.) 12:521–24.

Hsieh Hsi-kung 解希恭. 1957. "Shan-hsi Hung-chao-hsien Yung-ning Tung-pao ch'u-t'u ti t'ung-ch'i" 山西洪趙縣永凝東堡出土的銅器. *Wen-wu ts'an-k'ao tzu-liao* 文物參考資料 8:42–44.

———. 1962. "Kuang-she i-chih tiao-ch'a shih-chüeh chien-pao" 光社遺址調查試掘簡報. *Wen-wu* 文物 4/5:28–32.

Hsieh Tuan-chü 謝端琚. 1979. "Shih-lun ch'i-chia wen-hua yü Shan-hsi Lung-shan wen-hua ti kuan-hsi" 試論齊家文化與陝西龍山文化的關係. *Wen-wu* 文物 10:60–68.

Hsü Cho-yün 許倬雲. 1968. "Chou-jen ti hsing-ch'i Chou wen-hua ti chi-ch'u" 周人的興起及周文化的基礎. *Bulletin of Institute of History and Philology* 歷史語言研究所集刊 38:435–58.

_____. 1971. "Liang-Chou nung-tso chi-shu" 兩周農作技術. *Bulletin of Institute of History and Philology* 歷史語言研究所集刊 42:803–27.

_____. 1976. "Chou-tai ti i-shih chu-hsing" 周代的衣食住行. *Bulletin of Institute of History and Philology* 歷史語言研究所集刊 43[3]:503–35.

_____. 1982. *Ch'iu-ku-pien* 求古編. Taipei 台北 : Lien-ching Press 聯經.

Hsü Chung-shu 徐中舒. 1930. "Lei-ssu k'ao" 耒耜考. *Bulletin of Institute of History and Philology* 歷史語言研究所集刊 vol. 3, no. 3:11–59.

_____. 1936A. "Pin-feng shuo" 豳風說. *Bulletin of Institute of History and Philology* 歷史語言研究所集刊 vol. 6, no. 4:431–50.

_____. 1936B. "Yin-Chou chih chi shih-chi chih chien-t'ao" 殷周之際史迹之檢討. *Bulletin of Institute of History and Philology* 歷史語言研究所集刊 vol. 7, no. 2:137–64.

_____. 1955. "Shih-lun Chou-tai t'ien-chih chi-ch'i she-hui hsing-chih" 試論周代田制及其社會性質. *Ssu-ch'uan ta-hsüeh hsüeh-pao* 四川大學學報 2:443–508.

_____. 1959. "Yü-ting ti nien-tai chi-ch'i hsiang-kuan wen-t'i" 禹鼎的年代及其相關問題. *K'ao-ku hsüeh-pao* 考古學報 3:53–66.

_____. 1978. "Hsi-Chou Ch'iang-pan ming-wen chien-shih" 西周墻盤銘文箋釋. *K'ao-ku hsüeh-pao* 考古學報 2:139–48.

Hsü Hsi-t'ai 徐錫台. 1979. "Tsao-Chou wen-hua ti t'e-tien chi-ch'i yüan-yüan ti-t'an-so" 早周文化的特點及其淵源的探索. *Wen-wu* 文物 10:50–59.

_____. 1980. "Ch'i-shan Ho-chia-ts'un Chou-mu fa-chüeh chien pao" 岐山賀家村周墓發掘簡報. *K'ao-ku yü wen-wu*, 考古與文物 1:7–11.

_____. 1982. "Chou-yüan ch'u-t'u pu-tz'u hsüan-i" 周原出土卜辭選譯. *K'ao-kü yü wen-wu* 考古與文物 3:59–64.

Hsü Hsü-sheng 徐旭生. 1959. "1959 nien-hsia Yü-hsi tiao-ch'a Hsia-hsü ti ch'u-pu pao-kao" 1959年夏豫西調查夏墟的初步報告. *K'ao-ku* 考古 11:592–600.

_____. 1960. *Chung-kuo ku-shih ti ch'uan-shuo shih-tai* 中國古史的傳說時代. Peking 北京: K'o-hsüeh Press 科學.

Hsü Tsung-yen 許宗彥. 1829. "Chien-chih-sui-chai-chi" 鑑止水齋集. In *Huang-Ch'ing ching-chieh* 皇清經解. Chüan 1255–56.

Hsüeh Yao 薛堯 1963. "Chiang-hsi ch'u-t'u ti chi-chien ch'ing-t'ung-ch'i" 江西出土的幾件青銅器. *K'ao-ku* 考古 3:416.

Hsün-tzu 荀子. Ssu-pu-pei-yao 四部備要 edition.

Hu Ch'eng-kung 胡承珙. 1888. "Mao-shih hou-chien 毛詩後箋. In *Huang-Ch'ing ching-chieh hsü-pien* 皇清經解續編. Chüan 448–94.

Hu Ch'ien-ying 胡謙盈. 1982. "Chi-Chou t'ao-li yen-chiu" 姬周陶鬲研究. *K'ao-ku yü wen-wu* 考古與文物 1:69–73.

Hu Shun-li 胡順利. 1981. "Tui Chin-ning Shih-chai-shan ch'ing-t'ung-ch'i t'u-hsiang so-chien pien-fa-che min-tsu-k'ao ti i-tien i-chien" 對晉寧石寨山青銅器圖象所見辮髮者民族考的一點意見. *K'ao-ku* 考古 3:238.

Hu Tao-ching 胡道靜. 1963. "Shih-shu-p'ien" 釋菽篇. In *Chung-hua wen-shih lun-ts'ung* 中華文史論叢. Shanghai 上海: Chung-hua shu-chü 中華書局. 111–19.

Hu Yü-huan 胡毓寰. 1959. "Ts'ung Shih-ching I-hsi p'ien ti i-hsieh tz'u-i shuo-tao Hsi-Chou she-hui hsing-chih" 從詩經噫嘻篇的一些詞義說到西周社會性質.

In *Shih-ching yen-chiu lun-wen-chi* 詩經研究論文集 , ed. Kao Heng 高亨 et al. Peking 北京 : Jen-min Press 人民 . 225–47.

Hu-nan sheng po-wu-kuan 湖南省博物館 . 1963. "Chieh-shao chi-chien kuan-ts'ang Chou-tai t'ung-ch'i" 介紹幾件館藏周代銅器 . *K'ao-ku* 考古 12:679–82.

――――. 1966. "Hu-nan sheng po-wu-kuan hsin-fa-hsien ti chi-chien t'ung-ch'i" 湖南省博物館新發現的幾件銅器 . *Wen-wu* 文物 4:1–2.

Hu-pei sheng po-wu kuan 湖北省博物館 . 1976. "P'an-lung-ch'eng 1974-nien-tu t'ien-yeh k'ao-ku chi-yao" 盤龍城1974年度田野考古紀要 . *Wen-wu* 文物 2:5–15.

Hua Chung-yen 華鍾彥 . 1959. "Ch'i-yüeh shih-chung ti li-fa wen-t'i" 七月詩中的曆法問題 . In *Shih-ching yen-chiu lun-wen chi* 詩經研究論文集 , ed. Kao Heng 高亨 et al. Peking 北京 : Jen-min Press 人民 . 151–62.

Huang Jan-wei. *See* Wong Yin-wai.

Huang Sheng-chang 黃盛璋 . 1957. "Pao-yü-ming ti shih-tai yü shih-shih" 保卣銘的時代與史實 . *K'ao-ku hsüeh-pao,* 考古學報 3:51–59.

――――. 1981A. "Pan-kuei ti nien-tai ti-li yü li-shih wen-t'i" 班簋的年代地理與歷史問題 . *K'ao-ku yü wen-hua* 考古與文化 1:75–83.

――――. 1981B. "Wei-ho-ting chung chu yü chu-t'ien chi-ch'i ch'ien-she ti Hsi-Chou t'ien-chih wen-t'i" 衞盉鼎中貯與貯田及其牽涉的西周田制問題 . *Wen-wu* 文物 9:79–82.

――――. 1983. "T'ung-ch'i ming-wen I Yü Che ti ti-wang chi-ch'i yü Wu-kuo ti kuan-hsi" 銅器銘文宜，虞，夨的地望及其與吳國的關係 . *K'ao-ku hsüeh-pao* 考古學報 3:295–305.

Huang-Ch'ing ching-chieh 皇清經解 . Kuang-chou 廣州 : Hsüeh-hai Academy 學海書院 .

Huang-Ch'ing ching-chieh hsü-pien 皇清經解續編 . Chiang-yin 江陰 : Nan-ching Academy 南菁書院 .

I-Chou-shu 逸周書 . Ssu-pu-pei-yao 四部備要 edition.

I-li cheng-i 儀禮正義 . Ssu-pu-pei-yao 四部備要 edition.

Jen Ta-ch'un 任大椿 . 1888. "Shen-i shih-li" 深衣釋例 . In *Huang-Ch'ing ching-chieh hsü-pien* 皇清經解續編 . Chüan 191–93.

Juan Yüan 阮元 . 1829. "Ch'e-chih t'u-k'ao" 車制圖考 . In *Huang-Ch'ing ching-chieh* 皇清經解 . Chüan 1055–56.

Kan-su sheng po-wu-kuan 甘肅省博物館 . 1976. "Kan-su Ling-t'ai-hsien Hsi-Chou mu-tsang" 甘肅靈台縣西周墓葬¹. *K'ao-ku* 考古 1:39–48.

――――. 1977. "Kan-su ling-t'ai Pai-ts'ao-p'o Hsi-Chou-mu" 甘肅靈台白草坡西周墓 . *K'ao-ku hsüeh-pao* 考古學報 2:99–130.

Kao Chih-hsi 高至喜 . 1959. "Ch'u-Kung Hui-ko" 楚公豪戈 . *Wen-wu* 文物 12:60.

Kao Chih-hsi 高至喜 and Hsiung Ch'uan-hsin 熊傳新 . 1980. "Ch'u-jen tsai Hu-nan ti huo-tung i-chih kai-shu—chien-lun yu-kuan Ch'u wen-hua ti chi-ko wen-t'i" 楚人在湖南的活動遺跡概述 — 兼論有關楚文化的幾個問題 . *Wen-wu* 文物 10:50–60.

Kao Hung-chin 高鴻縉 . 1962. "Ta-yü-ting k'ao-shih" 大盂鼎考釋 . *Nan-ta Chung-wen hsüeh-pao* 南大中文學報 (Singapore) 1:4–32.

Kao Heng 高亨 et al., eds. 1959. *Shih-ching yen-chiu lun-wen-chi* 詩經研究論文集 . Peking 北京 : Jen-min Press 人民 .

――――. 1980. *Shih-ching chin-chu* 詩經今注 Shanghai 上海 : Ku-chi Press 古籍 .

Kao T'ien-lin 高天麟. 1979. "Kuan-yü Tz'u-hsien Hsia-p'an-wang Yang-shao wen-hua i-ts'un ti t'ao-lun" 關于磁縣下潘汪仰韶文化遺存的討論. *Kao-ku* 考古 1:51–55.

K'ao-ku yen-chiu-so 考古研究所. 1959. *Shang-ts'un-ling Kuo-kuo mu-ti* 上村嶺虢國墓地. Peking 北京: K'o-hsüeh Press 科學.

_____. 1962. *Feng-hsi fa-chüeh pao-kao* 灃西發掘報告. Peking 北京: Wen-wu Press 文物.

_____. 1979. *Wen-wu K'ao-ku kung-tso san-shih nien* 文物考古工作三十年. Peking 北京: Wen-wu Press 文物.

_____. An-yang fa-chüeh-tui 安陽發掘隊. 1961. "1958–1959 nien Yin-hsü fa-chüeh chien-pao" 1958–1959年殷墟發掘簡報. *K'ao-ku* 考古 2:63–76.

_____. Hu-pei fa-chüeh-tui 湖北發掘隊. 1962. "Hu-pei I-ch'un Mao-chia-chü Hsi-Chou mu-kou chien-chu" 湖北沂春毛家咀西周木構建築. *K'ao-ku* 考古 1:1–9.

_____. Hsi-an Pan-p'o po-wu-kuan 西安半坡博物館. 1963. *Hsi-an Pan-p'o Yüan-shih shih-tsu kung-she chü-lo i-chih* 西安半坡原始氏族公社聚落遺址. Peking 北京: Wen-wu Press 文物.

_____. Ho-nan i-tui 河南一隊. 1982. "Ho-nan Chih-ch'eng Meng-chuang Shang-tai i-chih" 河南拓城孟莊商代遺址. *K'ao-ku hsüeh-pao* 考古學報 1:49–70.

K'o-tso hsien wen-hua-kuan 喀左縣文化館. 1982. "Chi Liao-ning K'o-tso-hsien Hou-fen-ts'un fa-hsien ti i-tsu t'ao-ch'i" 記遼寧喀左縣后坟村發現的一組陶器. *K'ao-ku* 考古 1:108–09.

Ko Chin 葛今. 1972. "Ching-yang Kao-chia-pao tsao-Chou mu-tsang fa-chüeh-chi" 涇陽高家堡早周墓葬發掘記. *Wen-wu* 文物 7:7–8.

Ko Chou 葛周. 1982. "T'an Ch'i-hsiang yü Chung-kuo li-shih ti-li-hsüeh" 譚其驤與中國歷史地理學. *Chung-kuo shih yen-chiu* 中國史研究 4:134–44.

Ku Chieh-kang 顧頡剛. 1963. "I-Chou-shu shih-fu-p'ien chiao-chu hsieh-ting yü p'ing-lun" 逸周書世俘篇校注寫定與評論. *Wen-shih* 文史 2:1–42.

Kuang-hsi Chuang-ts'u tzu-chih-ch'ü wen-wu kung-tso-tui 廣西壯族自治區文化工作際. 1978. "Kuang-hsi ch'u-t'u ti ku-t'ung-ch'i" 廣西出土的古銅器. *Wen-wu* 文物 10:93.

Kuo Mo-jo 郭沫若. 1932. *Chin-wen ts'ung-k'ao* 金文叢考. Tokyo 東京: Bunkyūdō 文求堂.

_____. 1954. *Chin-wen ts'ung-k'ao* 金文叢考. Peking 北京: K'o-hsüeh Press 科學.

_____. 1956. "Tse-kuei-ming k'ao-shih" 夨殷銘考釋. *K'ao-ku hsüeh-pao* 考古學報 1:7–9.

_____. 1957. *Liang-Chou chin-wen-tz'u ta-hsi k'ao-shih* 兩周金文辭大系考釋. Peking 北京: K'o-hsüeh Press 科學.

_____. 1961A. *Wen-shih lun-chi* 文史論集. Peking 北京: Jen-min Press 人民.

_____. 1961B. "Ch'ang-an hsien Chang-chia-p'o t'ung-ch'i ming-wen hui-shih" 長安縣張家坡銅器銘文彙釋. *K'ao-ku hsüeh-pao* 考古學報 1:113.

_____. 1972. "Pan-kuei ti tsai-fa-hsien" 班殷的再發現. *Wen-wu* 文物 9:2–10.

Kuo Pao-chün 郭寶鈞. 1959. *Shan-piao-chen yü Liu-li-ko* 山彪鎮與琉璃閣. Peking 北京: K'o-hsüeh Press 科學.

_____. 1964. *Chün-hsien Hsin-ts'un* 浚縣辛村. Peking 北京: K'o-hsüeh Press 科學.

Kuo Pao-chün 郭寶鈞 and Lin Shou-chin 林壽晋. 1955. "1952 nien ch'iu-chi

Lo-yang tung-chiao fa-chüeh pao-kao" 1952年秋季洛陽東郊發掘報告. *K'ao-ku hsüeh-pao* 考古學報 9:91–116.

Kuo Yüan-wei 郭遠謂. 1965. "Chiang-hsi chin-liang-nien ch'u-t'u ti ch'ing-t'ung-ch'i 江西近兩年出土的青銅器. *K'ao-ku* 考古 7:372–73.

Kuo Yung 郭勇. 1962. "Shih-lou Hou-lan-chia-kou fa-hsien Shang-tai ch'ing-t'ung-ch'i chien-pao" 石樓后蘭家溝發現商代青銅器簡報. *Wen-wu* 文物 4,5:33–34.

Kuo-yü 國語. Ssu-pu-pei-yao 四部備要 edition.

Lao Kan 勞榦. 1977. "Chin-wen yüeh-hsiang pien-shih" 金文月相辨釋. In *Chung-yang yen-chiu yüan ch'eng-li wu-shih-chou-nien chi-nien lun-wen-chi* 中央研究院成立五十周年紀念論文集. Taipei 台北: Academia Sinica 中央研究院. 39–74.

Li-chi cheng-i 禮記正義. Ssu-pu-pei-yao 四部備要 edition.

Li-chi chu-shu 禮紀注流. Ssu-pu pei-yao 四部備要 edition.

Li Chien 李健. 1963. "Hu-pei Chiang-ling Wan-ch'eng ch'u-t'u Hsi-Chou t'ung-ch'i" 湖北江陵萬城出土西周銅器. *K'ao-ku* 考古 4:224–25.

Li Chien-nung 李劍農. 1962. *Hsien-Ch'in liang-Han ching-chi shih-kao* 先秦兩漢經濟史稿. Peking 北京: Chung-hua Book Co. 中華.

Li Chih-t'ing 李志庭. 1981. 'Hsi-Chou feng-kuo ti cheng-ch'ü hsing-chih" 西周封國的政區性質. *Hang-chou ta-hsüeh hsüeh-pao* 杭州大學學報 3:48–53.

Li Chung-ts'ao 李仲操. 1978. "Shih-ch'iang-p'an ming-wen shih-shih" 史墻盤銘文試釋. *Wen-wu* 文物 3:33–34.

Li Hsiao-ting 李孝定. 1965. *Chia-ku-wen-tzu chi-shih* 甲骨文字集釋. Taipei 台北: Academia Sinica 中央研究院.

———. 1979. "Tsai-lun shih-ch'ien t'ao-wen ho han-tzu ch'i-yüan" 再論史前陶文和漢字起源. *Bulletin of Institute of History and Philology* 歷史語言研究所集刊 vol. 50, no. 3:431–83.

Li Hsüeh-ch'in 李學勤. 1957. "Mei-hsien Li-chia-ts'un t'ung-ch'i k'ao" 郿縣李家村銅器考. *Wen-wu ts'an-k'ao tzu-liao* 文物參考資料 7:58–59.

———. 1959. *Yin-tai ti-li chien-lun* 殷代地理簡論. Peking 北京: K'o-hsüeh Press 科學.

———. 1978. "Lun Shih-ch'iang-p'an chi-ch'i i-i" 論史墻盤及其意義. *K'ao-ku hsüeh-pao* 考古學報 2:149–58.

———. 1980A. 'Lun Han-Huai chien ti Ch'un-ch'iu ch'ing-t'ung-ch'i" 論漢淮間的春秋青銅器. *Wen-wu* 文物 1:54–58.

———. 1980B. "Ts'ung hsin-ch'u ch'ing-t'ung-ch'i k'an Ch'ang-chiang hsia-yu wen-hua ti fa-chan" 從新出青銅器看長江下游文化的發展. *Wen-wu* 文物 8:35–40, 84.

———. 1981. "Hsi-Chou chia-ku ti chi-tien yen-chiu" 西周甲骨的幾点研究. *Wen-wu* 文物 9:7–12.

Li Hsüeh-ch'in 李學勤 and T'ang Yün-ming 唐雲明. 1979. "Yüan-shih t'ung-ch'i yü Hsi-Chou ti Hsing-kuo" 元氏銅器與西周的邢國. *K'ao-ku* 考古 1:56–59, 88.

Li Min 李民. 1982. "Shih Shang-shu Chou-jen tsun-Hsia shuo" 釋尚書周人尊夏說. *Chung-kuo-shih yen-chiu* 中國史研究, 2:128–34.

Li Tsung-t'ung 李宗侗. 1954. *Chung-kuo ku-tai she-hui-shih* 中國古代社會史. Taipei 台北: Publication Committee of Chinese Culture 中華文化出版事業委員會.

Li Ya-nung 李亞農. 1962. *Hsin-jan-chai shih-lun-chi* 欣然齋史論集. Peking 北京：Jen-min Press 人民.

Li Yeh-chen 李也貞. 1976. "Yu-kuan Hsi-Chou ssu-chih ho tz'u-hsiu ti chung-yao fa-hsien" 有關西周絲織和刺綉的重要發現. *Wen-wu* 文物 4:60−63.

Li Yu-mou 李友謀 et al. 1979. "Shih-lun P'ei-li-kang wen-hua" 試論裴李崗文化. *K'ao-ku* 考古 4:347−52.

Li-shih yen-chiu pien-chi-pu 歷史研究編輯部. 1955. *Chung-kuo ti nu-li chih-tu yü feng-chien-chih fen-ch'i wen-t'i lun-wen hsüan-chi* 中國的奴隸制度與封建制分期問題論文選集. Peking 北京：San-lien Publishing Co. 三聯.

————. 1957. *Chung-kuo ku-tai-shih fen-ch'i wen-t'i t'ao-lun-chi* 中國古代史分期問題討論集. Peking 北京：San-lien Publishing Co. 三聯.

Liang Ssu-yung 梁思永 and Kao Ch'ü-hsin 高去尋. 1962. *Hsi-pei-kang 1001 ta-mu* 西北崗1001大墓. Taipei 台北：Academia Sinica 中央研究院.

Lin Kan-ch'üan 林甘泉. 1976. "Tui Hsi-Chou t'u-ti-kuan-hsi ti chi-tien hsin-jen-shih" 對西周土地關係的幾點新認識. *Wen-wu* 文物 5:45−49.

Lin-t'ung hsien wen-hua-kuan 臨潼縣文化館. 1977. "Shan-hsi Lin-t'ung fa-hsien Wu-wang cheng-Shang-kuei" 陝西臨潼發現武王征商簋. *Wen-wu* 文物 8:1−7.

Liu Ch'i-i 劉啓益. 1979. "Hsi-Chou chin-wen chung yüeh-hsiang ming-tz'u ti chieh-shih" 西周金文中月相名詞的解釋. *Li-shih chiao-hsüeh* 歷史教學 6:21−26.

————. 1980A. "Hsi-Chou chin-wen chung so-chien-ti Chou-wang hou-fei" 西周金文中所見的周王后妃. *K'ao-ku yü wen-wu* 考古與文物 4:85−90.

————. 1980B. "Hsi-Chou Li-wang shih-ch'i t'ung-ch'i yü shih-yüeh-chih-chiao ti shih-tai" 西周厲王時期銅器與十月之交的時代. *K'ao-ku yü wen-wu* 考古與文物 1:80−85.

————. 1982. "Hsi-Chou Tse-kuo t'ung-ch'i ti hsin-fa-hsien yü yu-kuan-ti li-shih ti-li wen-t'i" 西周夨國銅器的新發現與有關的歷史地理問題. *K'ao-ku yü wen-wu* 考古與文物 2:42−46.

Liu Chia-ho 劉家和. 1981. "Shu Tzu-ts'ai jen-yu jen-li shih-shih" 書梓材人宥人鬲試釋. *Chung-kuo-shih yen-chiu* 中國史研究 4:127−34.

Liu Chieh 劉節. 1948. *Chung-kuo ku-tai tsung-tsu i-chih shih-lun* 中國古代宗族移殖史論. Shanghai 上海：Cheng-chung 正中.

Liu Hsien-chou 劉仙洲. 1963. *Chung-kuo ku-tai nung-yeh chi-hsieh fa-ming-shih* 中國古代農業機械發明史. Peking 北京：K'o-hsüeh Press 科學.

Liu Hsing 劉興 and Wu Ta-lin 吳大林. 1976. "Chiang-su Li-shui fa-hsien Hsi-Chou-mu" 江蘇溧水發現西周墓. *K'ao-ku* 考古 4:274.

Liu-li-ho k'ao-ku kung-tso-tui 琉璃河考古工作隊. 1974. "Pei-ching fu-chin fa-hsien ti Hsi-Chou nu-li hsün-tsang-mu" 北京附近發現的西周奴隸殉葬墓. *K'ao-ku* 考古 5:309−21.

Lo Hsi-chang 羅西章. 1980. "Fu-feng Yün-t'ang fa-hsien Hsi-Chou chuan" 扶風雲塘發現西周磚. *K'ao-ku yü wen-wu* 考古與文物, 2:108.

Lo-yang shih wen-wu kung-tso-tui 洛陽市文物工作隊. 1983. "1975−1979 Lo-yang Pei-yao Hsi-Chou chu-t'ung i-chih ti fa-chüeh" 1975-1979洛陽北窰西周鑄銅遺址的發掘. *K'ao-ku* 考古 5:430−41.

Lo-yang fa-chüeh-tui 洛陽發掘隊. 1965. "Ho-nan Yen-shih Erh-li-t'ou i-chih fa-chüeh chien-pao" 河南偃師二里頭遺址發掘簡報. *K'ao-ku* 考古 5:215−24.

Lu Yao-tung 逯耀東. 1979. *Chung-kung shih-hsüeh ti fa-chan yü yen-pien* 中共史學的發展與演變. Taipei 台北: Shih-pao Publishing Co.時報.

Ma Ch'eng-yüan 馬承源. 1976. "Ho-tsun ming-wen ch'u-shih" 何尊銘文初釋. *Wen-wu* 文物 1:64–65.

Ma Shui-ch'en 馬瑞辰. 1888. "Mao-shih chuan-chien t'ung-shih" 毛詩傳箋通釋. In *Huang-Ch'ing ching-chieh hsü-pien* 皇清經解續編. Chüan 416–47.

Mao-shih cheng-i 毛詩正義. Ssu-pu-pei-yao 四部備要 edition.

Mei Fu-ken 梅福根. 1957. "Che-chiang Wu-hsing Ch'iu-ch'eng i-chih fa-chüeh chien-pao" 浙江吳興邱城遺址發掘簡報. *K'ao-ku* 考古 9:479.

Meng Wen-t'ung 蒙文通. 1933. *Ku-shih chen-wei* 古史甄微. Shanghai 上海: Commercial Press 商務.

Mou Yung-k'ang 牟永抗 and Wei Cheng-chin 魏正瑾. 1978. "Ma-chia-pang wen-hua ho Liang-chu wen-hua" 馬家浜文化和良渚文化. *Wen-wu* 文物 4:67–73.

Nan-ching po-wu-kuan 南京博物館. 1977. "Chiang-su Chu-jung hsien Fu-shan Kuo-yüan Hsi-Chou mu" 江蘇句容縣浮山果園西周墓. *K'ao-ku* 考古 5:292–97.

———. 1978. "Ch'ang-chiang hsia-yu hsing-shih-ch'i shih-tai wen-hua jo-kan wen-t'i ti t'an-hsi" 長江下游新石器時代文化若干問題的探析. *Wen-wu* 文物 4:46–57.

Nan-ching shih wen-wu pao-kuan wei-yüan-hui 南京市文物保管委員會. 1980. "Nan-ching Pu-k'ou ch'u-t'u ti i-p'i ch'ing-t'ung-ch'i" 南京浦口出土的一批青銅器. *Wen-wu* 文物 8:10–11, 34.

Ni Chen-ta 倪振達. 1959. "Yen-ch'eng ch'u-t'u ti t'ung-ch'i" 淹城出土的銅器. *Wen-wu* 文物 4:5.

O Ping 鄂兵. 1973. "Hu-pei Sui-hsien fa-hsien Ts'eng-kuo t'ung-ch'i" 湖北隨縣發現曾國銅器. *Wen-wu* 文物 5:21–25.

P'an Ch'i-feng 潘其鳳 and Han K'ang-hsin 韓康信. 1980. "Wo-kuo hsin-shih-ch'i shih-tai chü-min chung-hsi fen-pu yen-chiu 我國新石器時代居民種系分布研究. *K'ao-ku yü wen-wu* 考古與文物 2:84–89.

Pao Ch'üan 保全. 1981. "Hsi-an Lao-niu-p'o ch'u-t'u Shang-tai tsao-ch'i wen-wu" 西安老牛坡出土商代早期文物. *K'ao-ku yü wen-wu* 考古與文物 2:17–18.

Pei-ching shih wen-wu kuan-li-ch'u 北京市文物管理處. 1976. "Pei-ching ti-ch'ü ti yu-i chung-yao k'ao-ku shou-huo—Ch'ang-p'ing Pai-fu Hsi-Chou mu-kuo-mu ti hsin-ch'i-shih" 北京地區的又一重要考古收獲 — 昌平白浮西周木槨墓的新啓示. *K'ao-ku* 考古 4:246–50.

———. 1977. "Pei-ching shih P'ing-ku hsien Liu-chia-ho fa-hsien Shang-tai mu-tsang" 北京市平谷縣劉家河發現商代墓葬. *Wen-wu* 文物 11:1–8.

Pei-ching ta-hsüeh, Department of History 北大歷史系考古研究室. 1979. *Shang-Chou k'ao-ku* 商周考古. Peking 北京: Wen-wu Press 文物.

Pei-tung wen-wu fa-chüeh hsiao-tsu 北洞文物發掘小組. 1974. "Liao-ning K'o-tso hsien Pei-tung-ts'un ch'u-t'u ti Yin-Chou t'ung-ch'i" 遼寧喀左縣北洞村出土的殷周青銅器. *K'ao-ku* 考古 6:364–77.

Shan Chou-yao 單周堯. 1979. "Ch'iang-p'an Ssu-tzu shih-shih" 墻盤黏字試釋. *Wen-wu* 文物 11:70.

Shan-hai-ching chien-chu 山海經箋注. Lang-huan-hsien-kuan edition. 琅環仙館本.

Shan-hsi sheng wen-kuan-hui 山西省文管會. 1955. "Shan-hsi Hung-chao-hsien Fang-tui-ts'un ku-i-chih mu-ch'ün ch'ing-li chien-pao" 山西洪趙縣坊堆村古遺址墓羣清理簡報. *Wen-wu ts'an-k'ao tzu-liao* 文物參考資料 4:46–52.

_____. 1959. "Shan-hsi Ch'ang-tzu ti Yin-Chou wen-hua i-ts'un 山西長子的 殷周文化遺存. *Wen-wu* 文物 2:36.

Shan-tung sheng wen-kuan ch'u 山東省文管處. 1959. "Chi-nan Ta-hsin-chuang i-chih shih-chüeh chien-pao" 濟南大辛莊遺址試掘簡報. *K'ao-ku* 考古 4:185–87.

Shan-tung sheng wen-kuan-chü, Chi-nan po-wu-kuan 山東省文管局, 濟南博物館 1974. *Ta-wen-k'ou* 大汶口. Peking 北京: Wen-wu Press 文物.

Shan-tung ta-hsüeh 山東大學, Department of History. 1979. *Ta-wen-k'ou wen-hua t'ao-lun-wen-chi* 大汶口文化討論文集. Chinan 濟南: Ch'i-lu-shu-she 齊魯書社.

Shang Ping-ho 尚秉和. 1966. *Li-tai she-hui feng-su shih-wu k'ao* 歷代社會風俗 事物考. Taipei 台北: Commercial Press 商務.

Shang-shu cheng-i 尚書正義. Ssu-pu-pei-yao 四部備要 edition.

Shang-shu chin-ku-wen chu-shu 尚書今古文注疏. Ssu-pu-pei-yao 四部備要 edition.

Shen Chen-chung 沈振中. 1972. "Hsin-hsien Lien-ssu-kou ch'u-t'u ti ch'ing-t'ung-ch'i" 忻縣連寺溝出土的青銅器. *Wen-wu* 文物 4:67–68.

Shen Kang-po 沈剛伯. 1974. "Ch'i-kuo chien-li ti shih-ch'i chi-ch'i t'e-shu ti wen-hua" 齊國建立的時期及其特殊的文化. *Chung-hua wen-hua fu-hsing yüeh-k'an* 中華文化復興月刊 vol. 7, no. 9:21–27.

Shih Chang-ju 石璋如. 1948. "Ch'uan-shuo chung Chou-tu ti shih-ti k'ao-ch'a" 傳說中周都的實地考察. *Bulletin of Institute of History and Philology* 歷史語言 研究所集刊 vol. 20, no. 2:21–122.

_____. 1951. "Hsiao-t'un C-ch'ü ti mu-tsang-ch'ün" 小屯C區的墓葬羣. *Bulletin of Institute of History and Philology* 歷史語言研究所集刊 23:447–87

_____. 1954A. "Yin-tai ti-shang chien-chu fu-yüan chih-i-li" 殷代地上 建築復原之一例. *Annual of Academia Sinica* 中央研究院院刊 1:267–80.

_____. 1954B. "Chou-tu i-chih yü ts'ai-t'ao i-ts'un" 周都遺跡與彩陶遺存. *Ta-lu tsa-chih* 大陸雜誌 vol. l, no. 2:357–85.

_____. 1955. "Yin-tai chu-t'ung kung-i 殷代鑄銅工藝. *Bulletin of Institute of History and Philology* 歷史語言研究所集刊 26:95–129.

_____. 1956. "Kuan-chung k'ao-ku tiao-ch'a pao-kao" 關中考古調查 報. *Bulletin of Institute of History and Philology* 歷史語言研究所集刊 27:205–323.

_____. 1959. *Yin-hsü chien-chu i-ts'un* 殷墟建築遺存. Taipei 台北: Academia Sinica 中央研究院.

_____. 1970. "Yin-tai ti-shang chien-chu fu-yüan ti ti-erh-li" 殷代地上建築 復原的第二例. *Bulletin of Institute of Ethnology* 民族學研究所集刊 29:321–41.

_____. 1976. "Yin-tai ti-shang chien-chu fu-yüan ti ti-san-li" 殷代地上建築 復原的第三例. *Bulletin of Department of Archaeology and Anthropology*, National Taiwan University 台灣大學考古人類學系刊39/40:140–57.

Shih Ming 史明. 1974. "Hsi-Chou Ch'un-ch'iu shih-tai li-chih ti yen-pien ho K'ung-ch'iu k'e-chi fu-li ti fan-tung shih-chih" 西周春秋時代禮制的演變和 孔丘克己復禮的反動實質. *K'ao-ku* 考古 2:81–88.

Shih Nien-hai 史念海. 1963. *Chung-kuo shih-ti lun-chi* 中國史地論集 (or *Ho-shan-chi* 又名河山集). Peking 北京: San-lien Book Co. 三聯.

_____. 1981. *Ho-shan-chi* 河三集, vol. 2. Peking 北京: San-lien Book Co. 三聯.

Shih Yen 史言 . 1972. "Fu-feng Chuang-pai ta-tui ch'u-t'u ti i-p'i Hsi-Chou t'ung-ch'i" 扶風庄白大隊出土的一批西周銅器 . *Wen-wu* 文物 6:30–35.

Shih-chi hui-chu k'ao-cheng 史記會注考證 . Taipei 台北 . Reprint.

Shih-ching, see *Mao-shih cheng-i*.

Ssu Wei-chih 斯維至 . 1947. "Hsi-Chou chin-wen so-chien chih-kuan-k'ao" 西周金文所見職官考 . *Chung-kuo wen-hua yen-chiu hui-k'an* 中國文化研究彙刊 7:1–26.

Ssu-ch'uan sheng po-wu-kuan 四川省博物館 , P'eng-hsien wen-hua-kuan 彭縣文化館 . 1981. "Ssu-ch'uan P'eng-hsien Hsi-Chou chiao-tsang t'ung-ch'i" 四川彭縣西周窖藏銅器 . *K'ao-ku* 考古 6:496–99, 555–56.

Su Ping-ch'i 蘇秉琦 . 1954. *Tou-chi-t'ai kou-tung-ch'ü mu-tsang* 鬥鷄台溝東區墓葬 . Peking 北京 : Academia Sinica 中國科學院 .

———. 1978. "Lüeh-t'an wo-kuo tung-nan yen-hai ti-ch'ü ti hsin-shih-ch'i shih-tai k'ao-ku" 略談我國東南沿海地區的新石器時代考古 . *Wen-wu* 文物 3:40–42.

Sui-hsien k'ao-ku fa-chüeh-tui 隨縣考古發掘隊 . "Hu-pei Sui-hsien Tseng-hou-i-mu fa-chüeh chien-pao" 湖北隨縣曾候乙墓發掘簡報 . *Wen-wu* 文物 7:1–24.

Sui-hsien po-wu-kuan 隨縣博物館 . 1980. "Hu-pei Sui-hsien ch'eng-chiao fa-hsien Ch'un-ch'iu mu-tsang ho t'ung-ch'i" 湖北隨縣城郊發現春秋墓葬和銅器 . *Wen-wu* 文物 1:34–38.

Sun-Ch'ang-hsü 孫常敍 . 1964. *Lei-ssu ti ch'i-yüan ch'i-ch'i fa-chan* 耒耜的起源及其發展 . Shanghai 上海 : Jen-min Press 人民 .

Sun Chi 孫機 . 1983. "Shih-huang-ling erh-hao t'ung-ch'e-ma tui ch'e-chih ti hsin-ch'i-shih" 始皇陵二號銅車馬對車制的新啓示 . *Wen-wu* 文物 7:22–29.

Sun Fei 孫飛. 1980. "Lun Nan-Po yü Hsi-Po" 論南亳與西亳 . *Wen-wu* 文物 8:78–84.

Sun Hai-p'o 孫海波 . 1934. *Chia-ku-wen pien* 甲骨文編 . Peking 北平 : Harvard-Yenching Institute: 哈佛燕京學社 .

Sun Hsing-yen 孫星衍 . 1815. *Shang-shu ching-ku-wen chu-shu* 尚書今古文注釋 . Ssu-pu pei-yao 四部備要 edition.

T'an Ch'i-hsiang 譚其驤 . 1981. "Hsi-Han i-ch'ien ti Huang-ho hsia-yu ho-tao" 西漢以前的黃河下游河道 . *Li-shih ti-li* 歷史地理 1:48–64.

T'ang Lan 唐蘭 . 1956. "I-hou tse-kuei k'ao-shih" 宜候夨𣪘考釋 *K'ao-ku hsüeh-pao* 考古學報 2:79–83.

———. 1962. "Hsi-Chou t'ung-ch'i tuan-tai chung ti K'ang-kung wen-t'i" 西周銅器斷代中的康宮問題 . *K'ao-ku hsüeh-pao* 考古學報 1:15–48.

———. 1976A. "Ho-tsun ming-wen chieh-shih" 何尊銘文解釋宮. *Wen-wu* 文物 1:60–63.

———. 1976B. "Yung ch'ing-t'ung-ch'i ming-wen lai yen-chiu Hsi-Chou shih" 用青銅器銘文來研究西周史 . *Wen-wu* 文物 6:31–39.

———. 1976C. "Shan-hsi-sheng Ch'i-shan-hsien Tung-chia-ts'un hsin-ch'u t'u Hsi-Chou chung-yao t'ung-ch'i ming-tz'u ti shih-wen ho chu-shih" 陝西省岐山縣董家村新出土西周重要銅器銘辭的釋文和注釋 . *Wen-wu* 文物 6:31–39.

———. 1977. "Hsi-Chou shih-tai tsui-tsao ti i-chien t'ung-ch'i Li-kuei ming-wen chieh-shih" 西周時代最早的一件銅器利𣪘銘文解釋 . *Wen-wu* 文物 8:8–9.

———. 1978. "Lüeh-lun Hsi-Chou Wei-shih chia-tsu chiao-tsang t'ung-ch'i-ch'un ti chung-yao i-i'' 略論西周微氏家族窖藏銅器羣的重要意義. *Wen-wu* 文物 3:19−24.

———. 1979. "Mieh-li hsin-ku" 蔑曆新詁. *K'ao-ku* 考古 5:36−42.

T'ien I-ch'ao 田宜超. 1980. "Hsü-pai-chai chin-wen k'ao-shih" 虛白齋 金文考釋. *Chung-hua wen-shih lun-ts'ung* 中華文史論叢 4:1−10.

Ting Fu-pao 丁福保. 1928. *Shuo-wen chieh-tzu ku-lin* 說文解字詁林 N.p.

Ting shan 丁山. 1930A. "Chao-mu-kung chuan" 召穆公傳. *Bulletin of Institute of History and Philology* 歷史語言研究所集刊 vol. 2, no. 2:89−100.

———. 1930B. "Chieh-i k'ao" 馘夷考. *Bulletin of Institute of History and Philology* 歷史語言研究所集刊 vol. 2, no. 2:419−22.

———. 1935. "Yu San-tai tu-i lun ch'i min-tsu wen-hua" 由三代都邑 論其民族文化. *Bulletin of Institute of History and Philology* 歷史語言研究所集刊 vol. 5, no. 1:87−130.

———. 1956. *Chia-ku-wen so-chien shih-tsu chi-ch'i chih-tu* 甲骨文所見 氏族及其制度. Peking 北京 : K'o-hsüeh Press 科學.

Ting Ying 丁穎. 1956. "Chiang-Han p'ing-yüan hsin-shih-ch'i shih-tai hung-shao-t'u chung ti tao-ku k'ao-ch'a" 江漢平原新石器時代紅燒土中的稻穀考查. *K'ao-ku hsüeh-pao* 考古學報 4:31−34.

Ts'ai Feng-shu 蔡鳳書. 1973. "Chi-nan Ta-hsin-chuang Shang-tai i-chih t'iao-ch'a" 濟南大辛莊商代遺址調查. *K'ao-ku* 考古 5:272−75.

Tso Chung-ch'eng 左忠誠. 1980. "Wei-nan-hsien Nan-pao-ts'un fa-hsien san-chien Shang-tai t'ung-ch'i" 渭南縣南堡村發現三件商代銅器. *K'ao-ku yü wen-wu* 考古與文物2:16, 4.

Tsou Heng 鄒衡. 1974. "Ts'ung Chou-tai mai-tsang chih-tu-hua p'ou-hsi K'ung-tzu t'i-ch'ang li-chih ti fan-tung pen-chih" 從周代埋葬制度化剖析孔子提倡 禮治的反動本質. *Wen-wu* 文物 1:1−4.

———. 1980. *Hsia-Shang-Chou k'ao-ku-hsüeh lun-wen-chi* 夏商周考古學論文集. Peking 北京 : Wen-wu Press 文物.

Tu Cheng-sheng 杜正勝. 1979A. "Feng-chien yü tsung-fa" 封建與宗法. *Bulletin of Institute of History and Philology* 歷史語言研究所集刊 vol. 50, no. 3:485−613.

———. 1979B. *Chou-tai ch'eng-pang* 周代城邦. Taipei 台北 : Lien-ching Publishing Co. 聯經.

———. 1979C. "Hsi-Chou feng-chien ti te-chih—chien-lun Hsia-cheng Shang-cheng yü Jung-so Chou-so" 西周封建的特質 — 兼論夏政商政與戎索周索. *Shih-huo yüeh-k'an (n.s.)* 食貨月刊復刊 vol. 9, no. 5/6:194−216.

Tu Nai-sung 杜廼松. 1976. "Ts'ung lieh-ting chih-tu k'an k'e-chi fu-li ti fan-tung-hsing" 從列鼎制度看克己復禮的反動性. *K'ao-ku* 考古 1:17−20.

Tung Tso-pin 董作賓. 1929A. "Hsin-huo pu-tz'u hsieh-pen hou-chi" 新獲卜辭寫本後記. *An-yang fa-chüeh pao-kao* 安陽發掘報告 1:182−214.

———. 1929B. "Shang-tai kuei-pu chih t'ui-ts'e" 商代龜卜之推測. *An-yang fa-chüeh pao-kao* 安陽發掘報告 1:59−130.

———. 1952. "Chou-chin-wen chung sheng-pa ssu-pa k'ao" 周金文中生覇 死覇考. In *Fu-ku-hsiao-chang Ssu-nien hsien-sheng chi-nien lun wen-chi* 傅故校長 斯年先生紀念論文集. Taipei 台北 : National Taiwan University 國立台灣大學 1−14.

———. 1964. *Yin-li-p'u* 殷曆譜. Taipei 台北 : Academia Sinica 中央研究院. Reprint.

————. 1965. *Chia-ku-hsüeh liu-shih-nien* 甲骨學六十年 . Taipei 台北 : I-wen Publisher 藝文 .

T'ung Chu-ch'en 佟柱臣 . 1975. "Ts'ung Erh-li-t'ou lei-hsing wen-hua shih-t'an Chung-kuo ti kuo-chia ch'i-yüan wen-t'i" 從二里頭類型文化試談中國的國家起源問題 . *Wen-wu* 文物 6:29–33.

T'ung En-cheng 童恩正 . 1977. "Wo-kuo hsi-nan ti-ch'ü ch'ing-t'ung-chien ti yen-chiu" 我國西南地區青銅劍的研究 . *K'ao-ku hsüeh-pao* 考古學報 2:35–55.

Wan Kuo-ting 萬國鼎 et al. 1959. *Chung-kuo nung-hsüeh-shih ch'u-kao* 中國農學史初稿 . Peking 北京 : K'o-hsüeh Press 科學 .

Wang En-t'ien 王恩田 . 1981. "Ch'i-shan Feng-ch'u-ts'un Hsi-Chou chien-chu-ch'ün chi-chih ti yu-kuan wen-t'i" 岐山鳳雛村西周建築羣基址的有關問題 . *Wen-wu* 文物 2:75–79.

Wang Kuo-wei 王國維 . 1940. "Mao-kung-ting k'ao-shih" 毛公鼎考釋 . In *Haining Wang Ching-an hsien-sheng i-shu* 海寧王靜安先生遺書 . Shanghai 上海 : Commercial Press 商務 .

————. 1959. *Kuan-t'ang chi-lin* 觀堂集林 . Taipei 台北 : Chung-hua Book Co. 中華 . Reprint.

————. 1968. *Wang Kuan-t'ang hsien-sheng ch'üan-ch'i* 王觀堂先生全書 . Taipei 台北 : Wen-hua Publishing Co. 文華 .

Wang Ning-sheng 王寧生 . 1979. "Shih Ch'en" 釋臣 . *K'ao-ku* 考古 3:269–71.

Wang Ssu-chih 王思治 . 1980. "Chung-kuo ku-tai shih fen-ch'i wen-t'i fen-ch'i ti yüan-yin ho-tsai" 中國古代史分期問題分歧的原因何在 . *Li-shih yen-chiu* 歷史研究 5:27–36.

Wang Tsung-su 王宗涑 . 1888. "K'ao-kung-chi k'ao-pien" 考工記考辨 . In *Huang-Ch'ing ching-chieh hsü-pien* 皇清經解續編 . Chüan 1020–27.

Wang Yü-che 王玉哲 . 1950. "Ch'u-tsu ku-ti chi-ch'i ch'ien-i lu-hsien" 楚族故地及其遷移路線 . In *Chou Shu-t'ao hsien-sheng liu-shih sheng-jih chi-nien lun-wen-chi* 周叔弢先生六十生日記念論文集 . Hong Kong 香港 : Longman Book Co. 龍門 .

Wei T'ing-sheng 衛挺生 . 1970. *Chou ch'u Mu-wang tu-Lo k'ao* 周初穆王都洛考 . Taipei 台北 : Chung-hua Academy 中華學術院 .

Wen-wu pien-chi wei-yüan-hui 文物編輯委員會 . 1979. *Wen-wu k'ao-ku kung-tso san-shih-nien* 文物考古工作三十年 . Peking 北京 : Wen-wu Press 文物 .

Wong Yin-wai 黃然偉 . 1978. *Yin-Chou t'ung-ch'i shang-tz'u ming-wen yen-chiu* 殷周銅器賞賜銘文研究 . Hong Kong 香港 : Longman Book Co. 龍門 .

Wu Chen-lu 吳振录 . 1972. "Pao-te-hsien hsin-fa-hsien ti Yin-tai ch'ing-t'ung-ch'i" 保德縣新發現的殷代青銅器 . *Wen-wu* 文物 4:62–64.

Wu Ju-tso 吳汝祚 . 1978. "Kuan-yü Hsia wen-hua chi-ch'i lai-yüan ch'u-t'an" 關於夏文化及其來源初探 . *Wen-wu* 文物 9:70–73.

Wu Shan-ching 吳山菁 . 1973. "Chiang-su sheng wen-hua ta-ke-ming chung fa-hsien ti chung-yao wen-wu" 江蘇省文化大革命中發現的重要文物 . *Wen-wu* 文物 4:2.

Wu Ta-yen 吳大焱 and Lo Ying-chieh 羅英杰 . 1976. "Shan-hsi Wu-kung-hsien ch'u-t'u chü-fu-hsü-kai" 陝西武功縣出土駒父盨盖 . *Wen-wu* 文物 5:94.

Yang Chien-fang 楊建芳 . 1963. "An-hui Tiao-yü-t'ai ch'u-t'u hsiao-mai nien-tai ti shang-chüeh" 安徽釣魚台出土小麥年代的商榷 . *K'ao-ku* 考古 11:630–31.

Yang Ch'ing-shan et al. 楊青山. 1960. "Shan-hsi Lü-liang-hsien Shih-lou-chen yu fa-hsien t'ung-ch'i" 山西呂梁縣石樓鎮又發現銅器. *Wen-wu* 文物 7:51–52.

Yang Hsi-mei 楊希枚. 1952. "Hsing-tzu ku-i hsi-cheng" 姓字古義析證. *Bulletin of Institute of History and Philology* 歷史語言研究所集刊 23:409–42.

_____. 1954A. "Tso-chuan yin-sheng-i-tz'u-hsing-chieh yü Wu-hsieh-tsu ku-shih ti fen-hsi" 左傳因生以賜姓解與無駭卒故事的分析. *Annual of Academia Sinica* 中央研究院院刊 1:91–115.

_____. 1954B. "Hsien-Ch'in tz'u-hsing-chih-tu li-lun ti shang-chüeh" 先秦賜姓制度理論的商榷. *Bulletin of Institute of History and Philology* 歷史語言研究所集刊 26:189–226.

Yang Hung 楊泓. 1977. "Chan-ch'e yü ch'e-chan—Chung-kuo ku-tai chün-shih chuang-pei cha-chi chih-i" 戰車與車戰 — 中國古代軍事裝備札記之一. *Wen-wu* 文物 5:82–90.

Yang Hung-hsün 楊鴻勛. 1981. "Hsi-Chou Ch'i-i chien-chu i-chih ch'u-pu k'ao-ch'a" 西周岐邑建築遺址初步考察. *Wen-wu* 文物 3:23–33.

Yang K'uan 楊寬. 1965. *Ku-shih hsin-t'an* 古史新探. Peking 北京: Chung-hua Book Co. 中華.

Yang Shao-hsüen 楊紹舜. 1981. "Shan-hsi Shih-lou Ch'u-yü Ts'ao-chia-yüan fa-hsien Shang-tai t'ung-ch'i" 山西石樓褚峪曹家垣發現商代銅器. *Wen-wu* 文物 8:49–53.

Yang Shu-ta 楊樹達. 1952. *Chi-wei-chü chin-wen-shuo* 積微居金文說. Peking 北京: Chinese Academy of Sciences 中國科學院.

_____. 1959. *Chi-wei-chü chin-wen-shuo yü-shuo* 積微居金文說餘說. Peking 北京: Chinese Academy of Sciences 中國科學院.

Yao Chung-yüan 姚仲源 and Mei Fu-ken 梅福根. 1961. "Che-chiang Chia-hsing Ma-chia-pang hsin-shih-ch'i shih-tai i-chih ti fa-chüeh" 浙江嘉興馬家浜新石器時代遺址的發掘. *K'ao-ku* 考古 7:345–51.

Yeh Ta-hsiung 葉達雄. 1977. "Hsi-Chou ma-cheng ch'u-t'an" 西周馬政初探. *Journal of Department of History*, National Taiwan University 台灣大學歷史學系學報 4:1–12.

_____. 1979. "Hsi-Chou ping-chih ti t'an-t'ao" 西周兵制的探討. *Journal of Department of History*, National Taiwan University, 台灣大學歷史學系學報 6:1–16.

_____. 1980. "Ho-tsun ti ch'i-shih" 珂尊的啟示. *Bulletin of Department of History*, National Taiwan University, 台灣大學歷史學系學報 7:31–41.

Yen Wan 晏琬. 1975. "Pei-ching Liao-ning ch'u-t'u t'ung-ch'i yü Chou-ch'u ti Yen" 北京遼寧出土銅器與周初的燕. *K'ao-ku* 考古 5:275–79.

Yen Wen-ming 嚴文明. 1979. "Huang-ho liu-yü hsin-shih-ch'i shih-tai tsao-ch'i wen-hua ti hsin-fa-hsien" 黃河流域新石器時代早期文化的新發現. *K'ao-ku* 考古 1:45–50.

Yin Sheng-p'ing 尹盛平. 1981. "Chou-yüan Hsi-Chou kung-shih chih-tu ch'u-t'an" 周原西周宮室制度初探. *Wen-wu* 文物 9:13–17.

Yin Wei-chang 殷瑋璋. 1978. "Erh-li-t'ou wen-hua t'an-t'ao" 二里頭文化探討. *K'ao-ku* 考古 1:1–4.

Yu Hsiu-ling 游修齡. 1976. "Tui Ho-mu-tu i-chih ti-ssu-wen-hua-ts'eng ch'u-t'u tao-ku ho ku-ssu ti chi-tien k'an-fa" 對河姆渡遺址第四文化層出土稻穀和骨耜的幾點看法. *Wen-wu* 文物 8:20–23.

Yü Ching-jang 于景讓. 1957. *Tsai-p'ei chih-wu k'ao* 栽培植物考. Taipei 台北 : National Taiwan University, College of Agriculture 台灣大學農學院.

Yü Sheng-wu 于省吾. 1956. "Shih Mih-li" 釋蓂曆. *Tung-pei jen-min ta-hsüeh, Jen-wen k'o-hsüeh hsüeh-pao* 東北人民大學人文科學學報 2:81–101.

————. 1957. "Shang-tai ti ku-lei tso-wu" 商代的穀類作物. *Tung-pei jen-min ta-hsüeh, Jen-wen k'o-hsüeh hsüeh-pao* 東北人民大學人文科學學報 1:81–107.

————. 1964. "Lüeh-lun Hsi-Chou chin-wen chung liu-shih ho pa-shih chi-ch'i t'un-t'ien-chih" 略論西周金文中六𠂤和八𠂤及其屯田制. *K'ao-ku* 考古 3:152–55.

————. 1977. "Li-kuei ming-wen k'ao-shih" 利𣪘銘文考釋. *Wen-wu* 文物 8:10–12.

Yü Wei-ch'ao 俞偉超 and Kao Ming 高明. 1978–79. "Chou-tai yung-ting chih-tu yen-chiu" 周代用鼎制度研究 (in 3 parts). *Pei-ching ta-hsüeh hsüeh-pao* 北京大學學報 1978 (1) 84–98; 1978 (2) 84–97; 1979 (1) 83–96.

Japanese Language Bibliography

Akatsuka Tadashi 赤塚忠 . 1977. *Chūgoku kodai no shūkyō to bunka* 中國古代の宗教と文化*In ōchō no saishi* 殷王朝の祭祀 Tokyo 東京: Kadokawa Shoten 刀川書店.

Amano Motonosuke 天野元之助 . 1959. "Chūgoku kodai nōgyō no tenkai" 中國古代農業の展開 . *Tōhōgakuhō* 東方學報 30:67–166.

———. 1962. *Chūgoku nōgōshi kenkyū* 中國農業史研究 . Tokyo 東京: Ochanomizu Shobō 御茶の水書房 .

Etō Hiroshi 江頭廣 . 1970. *Shō-kō—Shūdai no kazoku seido* 姓考　周代の家族制度 . Tokyo 東京: Kazama Shobō 國間書房 .

Hayashi Minao 林巳奈夫 . 1959. "Chūgoku Senshin jidai no basha" 中國先秦時代の馬車 . *Tōhōgakuhō* 東方學報 29:155–283.

———. 1968. "In Shū jidai no zushō kigō" 殷周時代の圖象記號 . *Tōhōgakuhō* (Kyoto) 東方學報 (京都)39:1–117.

———. 1970. "In-chūki ni yurai suru kishin" 殷中期に由來する鬼神 . *Tōhōgakuhō* (Kyoto) 東方學報 (京都)41:1–70.

———. 1982. "Chūgoku kodai no ishibōchōgata gyokki to kossan gata gyokki" 中國古代の 石庖丁形玉器と骨鏟形玉器 . *Tōhōgakuhō* (Kyoto)東方學報 (京都)54.

Ikeda Suetoshi 池田末利. 1964. "Chūgoku ni okeru shijōtei girei no seiritsu—shūkyōshiteki kōsatsu" 中國に於る 至上帝儀禮の成立 — 宗教史的考察 . *Nihon Chūgoku gakkaihō* 日本中國學會報 16.

Itō Michiharu 伊藤道治 1975. *Chūgoku kodai ōchō no keisei* 中國古代王朝の形成 . Tokyo 東京: Sōbunsha 創文社 .

———. 1977. "Reii mei kō" 盉彝銘考 . *Kōbe daigaku bungakubu kiyō* 神戸大學文學部紀要 6:47–66.

———. 1978. Shū Buō to Rakuyū—kason mei to Itsushūsho doyū" 周武王と雒邑 — 阿尊銘と逸周書度邑 . In *Uchida Ginpū hakushi shōju kinen Tōyōshi ronshū* 內田吟風博士頌壽記念東洋史論集 . 41–53.

Kaizuka Shigeki 貝塚茂樹 . 1962. "Kinbun ni arawareta reki no mibun ni tsuite" 金文に現われた鬲の身份について. *Tōhōgakuhō* 東方學報 23:1–5.

Kimura Hideumi 木村秀海 . 1981. "Seishū kinbun ni mieru shōshi ni tsuite—Seishū no shihaikikō no ichimen" 西周金文に見える小子について — 西周の支配機構の一面 . *Shirin* 史林 vol. 64, no. 6:62–83.

———. 1982. "Senseishō Bufūken Kyōkason shutsudo no Seishū seidōki meibun shinshaku" 陝西省扶風縣强家村出土の西周靑銅器銘文新釋 . *Jinbun ronkyū* (Kansei gakuin daigaku) 人文論究(關西學院大學) 31–34.

413

Matsuda Toshio 松田壽男 . 1965. "Funsui ryūiki ni okeru genshi nōkō no mondai" 汾水流域における原始農耕の問題 . In *Ishida hakushi shōju kinen Tōyōshi ronsō* 石田博士頌壽紀念東洋史論叢 . Tokyo 東京 : Tōyōbunko 東洋文庫 . 425–43.

Matsumaru Michio 松丸道雄 . 1977. "Seishū seidōki seisaku no haikei—Shū kinbun kenkyū: Joshō" 西周青銅器制作の背景—周金文研究: 序章 . *Tōyōbunka kenkyūjo kiyo* 東洋文化研究所紀要 72:1–128.

Miyazaki Ichisada 宮崎市定 . 1950. "Chūgoku jōdai wa hōkensei ka toshikokka ka" 中國上代は封建制か都市國家か . *Shirin* 史林 vol. 33, no. 2:63–86.

———. 1965. "Tōyō no kodai" 東洋の古代 . *Tōyōgakuhō* 東洋學報 vol. 48, no. 2:153–82.

———. 1970. "Chugoku kodai no toshikokka to sono bochi—Shōyū wa doko ni attaka" 中國古代の都市國家とその墓地 — 商邑は何處にあったか . *Tōyōshi kenkyū* 東洋史研究 28:265–82.

Satō Taketoshi 佐藤武敏 . 1962. *Chūgoku kodai kōgyōshi kenkyū* 中國古代工業史研究 . Tokyo 東京 : Yoshikawa Kōbunkan 吉川弘文館 .

Sekino Takeshi 關野雄 . 1959. "Shin raishi kō" 新耒耜考 . *Tōyō Bunka Kenkyūjo kiyō* 東洋文化研究所紀安 19:1–77.

———. 1960. "Shin raishi kō yoron" 新耒耜考餘論 . *Tōyō Bunka Kenkyūjo kiyō*, 東洋文化研究所紀要 20:1–46.

Shima Kunio 島邦男 . 1958. *Inkyo bokuji kenkyū* 殷虚卜辭研究 . Tokyo 東京 : Kyūko Shoin 汲古書院 .

———. 1971. *Inkyo bokuji sōrui* 殷虚卜辭綜類 . Tokyo 東京 : Kyūko Shoin 汲古書院 .

Shirakawa Shizuka 白川靜 . 1951. "In no kiso shakai" 殷の基礎社會 . In *Ritsumeikan sōritsu gojūshūnen kinen ronbun shū, bungaku hen* 立命館創立五十週年紀念論文集文學篇 . Kyoto 京都 : Ritsumeikan 立命館 . 260–96.

———. 1962–77. *Kinbun tsūshaku* 金文通釋 . Tokyo 東京 : Hakutsuru Bijutsukan-shi, 白鶴美術館誌 vols. 1–46.

———. 1973. *Kōkotsu kinbungaku ronshū* 甲骨金文學論集 . Kyoto 京都 : Hōyū Shoten 朋友書店 .

———. 1978–79. *Kinbun hoshaku* 金文補釋 . Tokyo 東京 : Hakutsuru Bijutsukan-shi 白鶴美術館館誌 , vols. 48–50.

Uehara Tadamichi 上原淳道 . 1965. "Sei no hōken no jijō oyobi Sei to Rai to no kankei" 齊の封建の事情およで齊と萊との關係 . In *Chūgoku kodaishi kenkyū*, vol. 2 中國古代史研究(二)Tokyo 東京 : Yoshikawa Kōbunkan 吉川弘文館 . 85–110.

Utsuki Akira 宇都木章 . 1965. "Seishū shokō keizu shiron" 西周諸侯系圖試論 . In *Chūgoku kodaishi kenkyū* vol. 2 中國古代史研究(二). Tokyo 東京 : Yoshikawa Kōbunkan 吉川弘文館 111–52.

Index

Italicized page numbers indicate figures.

abbreviations, xxiv
agriculture: Chou, 70, 345−55; crops, 28,
   345−46, 355; fallow, 354−55;
   organization, 28−29, 224−35, 238, 241,
   346−50; ritual, 370; slash-and-burn, 5,
   28−29, 355; Shang, 28−30; tools, 5, 17,
   29−30, 70−74, 351−53, *352*; versus
   pastoralism, 192, 225, 262
An-kuo culture, 55, 66−67, 211, 225
ancestor worship, 326, 375−77; Chou
   offerings to Shang, 48−49; shrine, 295
animal motifs, 50−51, 209−10, 318
archaeology, xviii−xix, 37
architecture: in classical texts, 61, 291, 295,
   296, 308; Shang, 21−23; stamped earth,
   8, 289−302; wood, 7−8, 218, 309, *310*
armor, Chou, 81, *82, 83*, 183
artisans: bestowed in lineages, 154, 188

bells, 135, 188, 193, 218, *219*
bird motif, 19, 328−29
bone industry, 338
boundaries, 275
bows, 27, 77, 178, 188
bow-shaped artifact, *42*, 51−52
bricks, 300, 311
bronze art, 19−20; calligraphy, 336−37;
   Chou evolution, 327−36; interpreted,
   318−37; legitimation, 311−12;
   naturalism, 329, 336; social integration,
   312
bronze metallurgy, 9, 11; Chou, 67, 311−
   18; craft specialization, 312; diffusion,
   218; organization, 11, 188; regionalism,
   41, *42*, 57, 207−08, 217, 219, 220, 223,
   318; Shang, 17−20, 41; technology,
   313−17; workshops, 21, 296, 302, 338
bronze ritual vessels, 19−20; reflecting
   rank, 172−77; sacrifices, 218; typology,
   362−63
bureaucratization, 32, 227, 247, 249, 251,
   254−57, 380

burials: commoner, 173; mound, 223;
   Shang royal, 23; Shang customs distinct,
   125, 200; Chou lineage, 166−69; social
   ordering and ritual, 172−77

calamities, natural, 280−84, 380
calendar, 347−50, 385−87; ritual, 369−73
capitals, Chou, 92, 224, 264−65, 289; *wu-i*,
   247. See also Ch'eng-chou, Ch'i-shan
caps: significance of, 360; capping
   ceremony, 360−61, 374
census, 234, 280
Central Kingdom, 326. See also *Chung-kuo*
Chamber of Heaven, 96−99
chariots, 27, 69−70, 77, 81−87, *342*;
   bestowed, 138, 178, 188; burials, *84*, 172,
   211, 341; manufacture, 338, 340;
   organization, 236−37, 341−43
Chinese, 12, 123, 147, 224−25, 268, 381−
   84
circumscription, in Lunghshan, 5−6, in
   state formation, 9
city, 199−200; Ehr-li-t'ou, 10; P'an-lung-
   ch'eng, 218; Shang, 20−21
"city people," 237, 244, 267
civilization, defined, xxi, xxiii, 11−12, 32
climatic change, 65−66
clothing, 350, 360−61, 363−69
cooking, 355−57
commercialization, 317−18, 332, 336
confidence, 286, 318−84
Confucianism, 318−20
contract, feudal, 177−78, 181; renewal,
   250
court, inner, 246−47, 252, 255−57

Chang-chia-p'o, 70, 89, 167, 168, *169*,
   173−76; foundry, 316; houses 303, *304−
   06*, 308
Chao, King, 133−37
Chao (state), 226

415